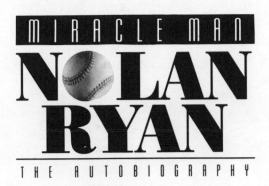

MIRACLE MAN

NOLAN RYAN

THE AUTOBIOGRAPHY

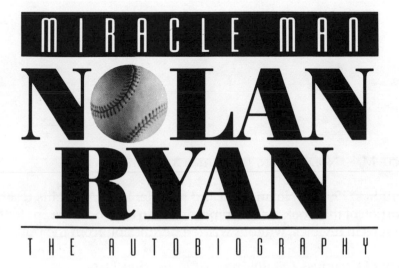

MIRACLE MAN
NOLAN RYAN
THE AUTOBIOGRAPHY

WORD PUBLISHING
Dallas · London · Vancouver · Melbourne

Library of Congress Cataloging-in-Publication Data

Ryan, Nolan, 1947–
    Miracle man : Nolan Ryan, the autobiography / Nolan Ryan
with Jerry Jenkins.
      p. cm.
    ISBN 0–8499–0945–7
    1. Ryan, Nolan, 1947– . 2. Baseball players—United States—
Biography. I. Jenkins, Jerry B. II. Title.
GV865.R9A3 1992
796.357'092—dc20
[B]   92–4973
                                             CIP

Printed in the United States of America

23459 AGF 987654321

To Ruth

You've been more than I could have
ever wished for, and I couldn't have
done anything without you.

Contents

Acknowledgments

Thanks to John Blake and the Texas Rangers public relations department for the latest statistics, and to John D. Miley, Jr., president of The Miley Collection, Inc., for selected career highlights on tape.

The Nolan You Don't Know

*S*eems like everybody who writes about me makes a big deal about how soft-spoken and modest I am. Well, I guess that's true. I never had a goal to be in the spotlight. But what happens when you leave your image to other people is that they make something out of you that may or may not be all true.

My life story's been told and retold so many different times that I want a chance to say some things my own way. I know my image is of a laid-back country guy, and I don't mind that. But just because I believe in traditional, conservative values and try to treat everybody the way I want to be treated doesn't mean I don't have opinions.

We placed all the career statistics in the back if you like that kind of thing, and I'll tell you about a lot of the baseball stuff that hasn't already been hashed over a million times. But if you really want to get to know me better by what I've got to say about things, you picked up the right book.

I like being known as just a regular guy. I'm not perfect. I have my likes and dislikes, my pet peeves, and, like I say, my opinions. You may not like me as much when you read them, but at least you'll have a better idea of who I really am. If you get tired of me or mad at me or disagree with me so much you can't take any more, just pass this book on to somebody else. Maybe they'll appreciate it. I'd rather have you not like me for who I really am than like me for who I'm not.

Nolan Ryan
Alvin, Texas

1

No Lone Ranger

*S*ometimes I think my whole life is made up of numbers. They tell me I even hold a record for records held. I know some of the numbers, but I don't keep track of them the way a lot of folks do. The most important number in my life is *one*. There's one woman in my life, and Ruth has been the only girl I ever wanted to be with since the time I was a teenager. That's never changed. I consider her the best friend I have.

In this day and age it's pretty rare for a marriage to last a lifetime, let alone for the couple to still like and love each other after all those years. I confide in very few people, and I don't confide in anybody the way I confide in Ruth.

People who look at our lives might think Ruth has it made. She's the wife of a famous person, and she can have just about anything she wants. But the one thing she can never have again is her husband all to herself. She'll probably never have the privacy she'd like either. And her identity will almost always be tied to me. Besides what it can do to a family to have your husband and father gone half the time, a woman with any kind of self-worth has to sacrifice and become unselfish to be a so-called star's wife.

Ruth was the prettiest girl at Alvin High School, and I'm proud that she's still great looking and athletic. But the things a young boy looks for in a girl aren't always what makes the best wife. There're a lot of good-looking, in-shape women who have no business being wives. As a young man, you have no idea what you need in a wife, so it's no wonder so many mistakes are made.

Ruth has always been a good listener, and when we started dating, I thought that was just a nice bonus. But that stuff becomes more important over the years. Now I know that it's her looks and all that which are just bonuses. Her character is what really sets her apart.

Like most guys, especially athletes, I had to learn the hard way to treat Ruth right. Before we had kids, she was stuck in New York while I was on the road with the Mets. When I got home, I wanted to stay; she was ready to go out. Traveling and eating out looks glamorous until you do it for a while. It wasn't until we both learned to be sensitive to the other that we started compromising on things like that.

The biggest adjustment comes when you have children. I don't think anybody has any idea of the impact kids have on your marriage and your life in general. Men sure don't. If they're not careful, nothing changes for them. They just keep doing what they've been doing, and their wives end up with all the work. Ballplayers especially push the obligation of the children off on their wives. Everybody has to learn sooner or later how the time and effort that have to be put into raising children restrict a woman's life. I had to understand that I was not the only person in the marriage and that Ruth had desires and dreams and goals too. That's not an easy lesson for someone who's become the center of attention almost everywhere he goes just because he can throw a baseball.

Our kids are growing up; Reid's in college and Reese and Wendy are in high school. But I still have to work at making my marriage and my family a priority. Most men are out of the game at my age, but my career seems to have taken off because of my longevity, because of the records, and because I've become kind of a folk hero to middle-aged people.

re greater than ever, so work-
nt, everyday deal. I've had to
ympathetic and caring. I have
carry my load at home too; it

at so many marriages break up
le don't understand the com-
lly if they get married while
re anything like us grooms,
nking about what they're
vs.
ast year, and I looked
le was saying their
ed at were divorced.
wish and hope and
seem so commit-
ou have to won-
der, How long will this one last?

If you ask me, the divorce rate just shows how screwed up our society is. Those vows before man and God are legal and sacred, but they must have had more meaning when my parents got married and when I got married. There are so many prenuptial agreements now that you just know people are saying, "Hey, if this doesn't work out, no big deal." Ruth and I believed we had made a commitment, and we decided to work together under whatever circumstances came along and work through whatever problems we faced. There were no strings attached to that commitment, no contingency clauses. Part of the commitment was figuring out what had to be done and doing it.

Our marriage has not been perfect. Like any other couple, we've had our ups and downs. I'm sure Ruth's had a lot more frustrations than I have, trying to put up with my schedule and lifestyle and demands on my time. Maybe there've been times when she wondered if it was worth it, but I sure never have. I'd like to think that I get better at this marriage business as I go along because I learn more. Only trouble is, once I think I've got things pretty much under control, more demands complicate my life, and I have to look at my priorities all over again. Ruth and I have worked through that, and the particulars are nobody's business but ours.

People's private lives ought to stay that way, but a lot of professional athletes think they are above any system, that they don't have to conform to the laws of the land, and that they're entitled to do whatever they please without answering to anyone. It's disgusting.

Take Lenny Dykstra's book. He's with the Phillies now, but he was on the Mets when they won the World Series in 1986, and he came out with a book so filthy and full of obscenities that I was appalled. You know that book should have been written for youngsters, teenagers, and young adults, but it was done in such poor taste that it showed the caliber of person Lenny was. I found it very offensive. I understand Lenny has grown up some since he got in a wreck after drinking. I just wish he'd write something about what he learned from that. People seem to want the dirt more though, and that's a sad commentary on our society.

It says something about us too that a superstar athlete with the AIDS virus is made into a hero. Magic Johnson was already a hero, of course, because of his ability and his personality. I've never met him, but like anyone else, I was shocked when I heard the news. I had no reason to think he would ever become a victim, and I'm not one of those who wishes him anything but the best. But I can't say I'm surprised that AIDS is finally starting to spread into all of society. It was just a matter of time before a prominent person who wasn't a homosexual got struck with the disease. We have a major problem here that needs more effort toward a solution. Maybe Magic Johnson's impact will help accomplish that and put things on a higher awareness level.

But I still think Magic is a hero because of what he did athletically, not because he's so courageous and outspoken now. It's good he's doing that, of course, and I'm glad to see he's even starting to say that the only real safe sex is no sex outside of marriage. But I have a problem with making a hero out of him because of AIDS.

I don't often find myself agreeing with someone who defends her bisexuality and has said that this country is so conservative that she might be better off going back to live under communism. But Martina Navratilova made a good point about Magic Johnson. She said that if a woman athlete had announced she had AIDS and that she had slept with a couple hundred men, she would not be considered a hero at all. She would be called a tramp.

Martina's got a point. It could be that she believes that neither a man nor a woman should be criticized and that both should be called heroes. All I know is, you stay married to and sleep only with one person who does the same, and you're not going to get AIDS through sex. It's just sad that it takes someone like Magic Johnson's sacrificing himself before we get around to getting something done about the problem. If Magic had done that on purpose for that reason, then maybe he would be a hero to the cause of AIDS research.

Now we're at a point where if somebody doesn't come up with some kind of miracle vaccine, we're in deep trouble. You can educate people about safe sex and all, but most of them think things like AIDS happen to others. That's just human nature. The morals of our country have fallen to where you're not going to get people to abstain from sex outside of marriage. It's scary. When you look at the numbers and think about your children and what they're exposed to, man . . .

So many innocent people can be affected now. Our attitude used to be that it was a disease of the gay community and that if those people chose to participate in those activities, that risk was part of the price they paid. I think that's the way people viewed it when Rock Hudson died. That's why his tragedy didn't have the impact that Magic Johnson's does, because Magic is looked on through different eyes by the public. But of course, even though Magic was not gay, he wasn't really an innocent victim because of his lifestyle.

Sacrificing someone to get something done is sort of like our country's foreign policy. We give away billions of dollars overseas, but we don't spend much here trying to do some of the things our own people need done. That's what's got President Bush in so much trouble now. And I'm a Bush fan. I've known him since back in my days with the Mets when he was our ambassador to the United Nations. I campaigned for him when he was running for vice-president. I see him a couple, maybe three times a year around Texas, and Ruth and I have been to a state dinner and stayed overnight at the White House. I even went to Honduras with him once.

But I still have to say I'm not real pleased with the way things have gone domestically. I feel that Congress hasn't tried to work with the administration in the best interests of our country. The president's interests have been worldwide, which is good, but we need to address the problems and concerns here. I'm not saying you ignore what goes on in the rest of the world, because it definitely has an impact on us. But we should put the same energy and invest the same monies here in our country. I don't see that happening.

I'm not an advocate of war, but I felt like what we did in the Persian Gulf was justified. We did what we needed to do, but still we bobbled the ball on that deal. We should have gone ahead and finished it off and not have to still be dealing with it. Why we didn't do that, I don't know. What we did accomplish only shows that we could have handled the Vietnam War differently.

People have never quite gotten over the tarnished image we have over the beating we took in Vietnam, and now that we've had time to reflect on it, I think our country is also embarrassed by the way it treated its people who served over there. A lot of people didn't speak out or take stands on what was going on because it wasn't the popular thing to do. They took the position that it's best not to get involved. I'm not saying the war was right, but I know our approach to it was wrong. When we went in there we didn't make a commitment to get a job done. We just sacrificed a lot of money and lives and for what? We still wonder now.

That's where politics comes into play. Politicians will play with lives; they'll play with money. What's really disgusting and hard to understand is what the human race does to itself. Sit down and look through history at what we're capable of doing to each other. It's staggering.

I think we've become too image conscious, too worried about what the rest of the world thinks of us. That's why we didn't finish off Iraq. Other world powers don't worry so much about international opinion, and how has it hurt them? It hasn't. They do what they want, project a bully-on-the-block image, and everybody fears them. We have the mentality that we want to be loved worldwide, but the only people who even pretend to like us are the ones who get handouts from us. They only want our money, and we're gullible enough to think they respect us for it. That's just amazing.

In our own country we don't put enough emphasis on education. That struck home with me one year when I was with the Astros and we were playing the Giants on the road. At Candlestick Park they were honoring the top ten students in the San Francisco Bay area. Seven of them were Asians, one was black, one was Latino, and one was Anglo. Minorities were in the majority when it came to excellence in education. You had to be proud of those families. But what does it say about the rest of us? We Americans who have been here for generations take education for granted. When the Asians and others see the golden opportunity in this country to develop their minds and excel, they take advantage of it. The majority of the population figures education is something they don't have to work for; they're entitled to it. I just hope our society and lifestyle doesn't rub off on our newer citizens. We've brought ourselves down educationally. I may sound pessimistic, but these are things that bother me. These are the kinds of problems I think we need to be addressing.

The next presidential election, in my opinion, is going to be important. I'm going to see who the candidates are and listen to their attitudes and proposals and evaluate them against what George Bush has done. He's done a lot of things right, and I like him as a man. But even though I usually lean toward the Republican side of things, I'm not locked in.

You won't see me running for office, even though I've been approached about being the commissioner of agriculture for Texas. I gave it a lot of thought in 1989 when I thought I might be getting out of baseball. The more people I talked to and the more I investigated it, the more I realized what it means to run for office. Because of the scrutiny of your personal life and the amount of time you spend raising money, it's no wonder we don't have better candidates.

What's most disheartening about our politics is how, unless we're really threatened, we're always fighting each other. Democrats against Republicans, Congress against the president, all that. They can't address an issue without looking at what impact it has on them and their future. They put their individual careers ahead of good common sense unless it's truly a crisis. Then they pull together like they should all the time. That's why I'm not a big political player.

Most people in their right mind wouldn't want anything to do with it. The way the game's played now, they were talking about spending a million and a half dollars or more just to run for commissioner of agriculture of Texas. I could see that much of my time would not be running to get elected but going to fund-raisers. That sounded like a never-ending deal. It's all become dollars, and it looks to me like a guy we need doing agriculture business spends more than half his time running for office and paying for that.

Maybe that's why politics in my state and in the country is in shambles. The last Texas governor's race got to be such a mud-slinging deal that it was embarrassing. I don't know how anybody, winner or loser, could have been proud of that election campaign. And I don't know who I'd have voted for if I'd lived in Louisiana, the racist or the criminal? I guess I would have viewed that as one of those rare occasions when there's justification not to vote. Actually, there are a lot of races I don't vote. I won't vote if I don't know the candidates, and I don't vote if I don't approve of them.

Like I said, I'm basically a Republican, but I voted for Jimmy Carter his first time running for president because I was fed up with the way things were going. My attitude was that Jimmy Carter had to be better than what we had. Now as I look back on it, I honestly don't believe he was. I don't believe he was suited to be president. He tried, but he didn't have the ability. That's my opinion. I didn't vote for him a second time, and I've been real careful ever since if I don't know much about a man.

Ted Kennedy hasn't helped my attitude toward the Democrats either. It killed me to see him sitting up there at the table next to Joe Biden in the Clarence Thomas hearings. That kinda gives you an idea of where we are with our politics in this country. I couldn't believe what I saw on television and what went on in those hearings. If that doesn't wake us up, I don't know what will. The bottom line is you don't know the truth in that situation, but the media sensationalized everything. It came down to people making statements and accusations about each other that couldn't be defended. Once someone says something about you and it's been written, published, or put on the air, it doesn't matter a bit whether it's true or how many people believe it or don't. They never forget it, and you live with it the rest of your life. It casts a shadow on you and your family and on your relationship with everybody. It's a crime.

And in those hearings, that went both ways. Once Anita Hill's private charges were made public, then charges against her were made public. Then people were split right down the middle on who was a liar and who wasn't. It was a nightmare. The moral fiber of this country has to change. Too many people have strayed so far from traditional values that it's become every man for himself. What we need are people who stand by their commitments and return to moral living.

We have to take a different stance in our judicial system, too. We protect criminals while the victims, whose rights have really been violated, have no protection. Someone told me that in Texas the average stay in the penitentiary for a convicted murderer is two and a half years. We're so worried about everybody's rights that we've done a 180-degree turn, and we protect the criminal. Sure, okay, protect the person's rights when he's been accused, but once he's been convicted what would be so wrong with depriving him of his rights?

That might sound extreme, but I think we need to take a hard line on that. Anybody convicted of a violent crime with a weapon, or rape, or murder should lose his rights. He's had his opportunities; why should we continue to protect his rights? We deny him his freedom—for at least two and half years—and he doesn't get to vote. Why don't we go further and put some teeth in the sentencing and keep these people away from the rest of society? They are the ones who have denied law-abiding citizens their right to life, liberty, and the pursuit of happiness.

I'm not talking about denying due process or creating a police state. I'm talking about getting serious about convicted criminals. Something's screwy when murderers are getting out of prison in two and a half years, and a guy who turns himself in on a minor misdemeanor gets hammered for an honest mistake. That actually happened. A hunter accidentally shot a whooping crane he thought was a goose, so he turned himself in to the Texas authorities because cranes are an endangered species in this state. He could have walked away and no one would have ever known. That wouldn't have made it right, but he was being honest, living by his conscience, trying to do the right thing. He was sent to prison for six months and fined $30,000! We do that to him, and we wink at people who have never ever abided by the law! We have so much corruption in our system that it's slanted toward criminals and those who have money.

Well, now that I've offended just about everybody, let me take on the attorneys. We have way too many, and now they're making the laws. I know that's a real unpopular thing to say and attorneys don't like to hear it, but there's a lot of truth to it. What's happened is that there are so many lawyers in our system that they have to find ways to make a living. They're out stimulating business, and that's why we have so many lawsuits. Insurance premiums go up, people settle out of court, and lawyers have nothing involved but their time.

Now let me be clear: I have friends who are attorneys (at least until they see this!), and I'm not saying all attorneys are that way. It's just like the other problems we have in this country: nothing gets done until it becomes financial. Our pollution problem is not going to be solved until it really starts to hurt the income of big business. It would be nice to think we'd clean it up just because it's the right thing to do for us and for our descendants. But it will come down to the dollar just like most everything else.

We had a gas shortage in the 1970s and everybody got serious about conserving because their lifestyles were affected.

Now we're more dependent on foreign oil than we've ever been, but because nobody's suffering, we'll just rock along and pay for it.

Well, I didn't mean to depress you. Would you believe, in spite of all that, I'm basically an optimist? That's because there's one thing about this country: it's resourceful. It finds ways to rise above some of the problems we develop. Sometimes I feel like a dying breed, being part of what has become the minority—people who still believe in old-fashioned hard work and common sense and treating people right. But then I realize that we're probably still in the majority. We just don't make as much noise as the other guys. We're considered out of step or out of date, and we sure aren't as newsworthy as the ones making all the trouble.

You look at all the television shows about crime and about entertainers and about tragedy and you see what the producers think we all want to see. Nobody wants good news and stories about solid values. At least that's what Hollywood and New York think. But the people I live and work with haven't changed. There are still a lot of people all over the country who remember what made it great. You can still be an optimist in spite of all the problems if you know you're not alone. And you're not.

2

Of Images and Reality

*T*here's so much competition in the media nowadays that you can't trust anybody. Nothing's sacred anymore. You can't confide in a reporter because there's so much pressure for those guys to break a story first that they have to figure out some way to get it into print. That's just business. They may promise not to write something you've told them, but they might tell someone else on their staff and then the news gets out from the other writer. I might be talking off the record about something or somebody because I think I've established a friendship with the writer, but once I see that come out in print somehow, I know our personal and professional relationships didn't stay separate. I've learned that lesson enough times that I should know better by now.

In spite of that, I've been fairly well treated by the press. I've had my run-ins and there are people I don't like to talk to, but generally I get along all right. There are always going to be some reporters whose writing I just don't like, or some who get into what I call a negative mode, where they seem to enjoy writing about all the things that are wrong with your team. The doom-and-gloom writers have a tendency to complain more when things are going bad, and they take advantage of players who are doing that too.

Anybody can dig up that kind of stuff if he wants to. Bad news travels fast. They start talking about the shortcomings of a ball team and speculate on what the club needs to do—who they need to trade or fire or whatever, and it creates a lot of discussion and interest. All you have to do is lose a few games in a row and then tune in to one of those postgame radio talk shows. Everybody's got an opinion, a gripe, a complaint, a suggestion. That makes some players say things they maybe wouldn't say otherwise, and of course the writers quote them in the papers and that gets added into the mix. I have a problem with the attitudes of writers like that, and I try to keep from reading their material. I don't want it to affect my attitude and my relationship with them.

It's a lot easier and safer for a writer to predict that a team is going to lose rather than win its division, because there are only four teams who will do that. The writers say that all we players want is for them to be cheerleaders, but their big deal is to be objective journalists. Like this is international politics or something. I don't mind them being honest, but when every writer comes off like an expert or a manager, it gets tiring. I admit most ballplayers don't want anything negative written about them whether it's the truth or not. So, sportswriters aren't in an ideal position. Overall, I feel like they've treated me fairly and I try to give them as much time as I can. All I ask of them is that they do their homework and that they ask reasonable questions.

Sometimes they try to get you to criticize one of your teammates or the management. They ask you a leading question or get you into a situation where you have to start explaining yourself, and you end up talking yourself into a corner. If I feel that I pitched poorly, then I will admit that and so state. If I stunk, I stunk. What really irritates me is when you've won and the team did well, but the first question you get is about something negative. That drives me nuts because I think it shows what track their minds run on.

Maybe I pitched a low-hit game and we won by a run. A sportswriter will ask me if I thought I was lucky to get out of the third inning when a guy hit a line drive right at somebody with a man in scoring position. Or he'll ask how I evaluated the seventh inning when I threw twice as many pitches as any other inning or walked a couple of guys or something. That kind of a question tells you something about a person. When you deal with them on a day-to-day basis as we do, you don't even have to read their articles. They tell you about themselves just by their conversations and by what they ask.

I normally just look at the box scores and read the summaries of the other games. I don't read our game stories. I see our games, and I figure writers have a tough job. They have to come in and ask you questions, and just because you may have had a bad game doesn't entitle you to be ugly to them and make their job harder.

Naturally I've become friends with some writers because of the time we spend together on the road and in the clubhouse. Others, because of their personalities or their interests or the little time they spend with us, I don't get to know as well.

The national media are a little different. They tend to be a little more star struck, and when they're doing their first story about me, they have read all the stuff about my ranches and my banks and my family and my down-home values, so they have a lot of preconceived notions. If they think I'm a country bumpkin, then unless I say something dramatic that changes their mind, that's how their story's going to come out. If they think I'm a soft-spoken gentleman, I probably won't do anything to change their opinion. But sometimes I'm surprised at the difference between the image and who I really am.

Advertising has exposed my face and my voice to more people, so a lot of folks who have only seen me pitch on television now know what I look like and what my accent sounds like. When I said on a commercial that when I take Advil my headache is "long gone," nobody where I'm from gave it a second thought. But I guess because of my Texas accent on the o's, I started getting mimicked all over the country. I don't mind that. I don't hear my accent, but it doesn't surprise me that I sound like where I come from. I'm certainly not ashamed of it.

Because I stay in shape and have done some Wrangler Jeans ads, some people call me a sex symbol for my age group. I don't view myself that way and I never have, and honestly the first time I ever heard anything said like that was when the Wrangler poster came out. That bugs Ruth, and I suppose it would bother any wife to think her husband is being looked at by other women as some sort of an object. I'm proud of the way she looks, but I wouldn't want her to be considered a sex symbol. As for my being one, those kinds of things never cross my mind. It hits me as kind of silly because I don't see myself that way. I think everybody feels like they'd like to improve their looks in certain ways. My kids tease me about losing my hair, and I just tell them that's the way the Lord wanted me so I don't worry about it.

I have teammates who spend a lot of time on their hair and then worry when they see some of it coming off on their comb. I figure whatever hair I've got or not got is all part of the package. I'd never wear a hairpiece, I'll tell you that. You don't fool anybody but yourself if you think people can't tell. I'd rather have people know I'm losing my hair than that I'm wearing a wig and trying to hide it.

I don't spend a lot of time analyzing myself because I think, like most people, that I'm not any more complex than anybody else. I don't want people to have to try to figure me out. If I say anything at all, I just tell you honestly what I think. With me, what you see is pretty much what you get. I'm pretty sure most people don't much care what everybody else's opinion is, so I usually don't offer one unless I'm asked or I'm in a business situation where what I think means something.

Sometimes this image thing makes me think about who I really am, and like I say, I'm no mystery. My parents had the biggest influence on me, and I think it says a lot about how I feel about them and about this part of the country that I still live a few miles from where I was raised. Alvin is no tropical paradise, but its people and their values make it all-American. My parents—like most people around here—were dedicated to raising their kids and doing the best job they possibly could with us. They hardly ever spent any money on themselves. Everything they did hinged on the best interests of the family. That was instilled in me. It wasn't preached to me in any way, but I feel their impact on me every day in the way I see as the proper way of doing things.

My dad worked two jobs to put his four daughters through college, and when I find myself wanting to deal honestly with people, I sense his influence. Besides working all day, he was a distributor for the *Houston Post* to fifteen hundred homes over a fifty-five mile route that took four hours, starting at one o'clock in the morning every day. From the time I was old enough to help, that was my life: waking up at one o'clock and rolling papers, tossing them for four hours, and getting back to bed before dawn.

You learn responsibility that way. You learn hard work. My dad did that to give us kids opportunities he never had, a chance to better our lives. Naturally I have the means to do a lot of things he didn't because of the success I've had in baseball, but everything Ruth and I do is with the same attitude our parents had. Just about everything we do is centered on our family. We hardly ever go off on vacation, especially not for an extended period, without the kids.

My basic philosophy of life came from my parents: Treat people the way you want to be treated, with honesty and integrity. I've never really gotten caught up in doing glamorous things. I'm very conservative. My dad never had to deal with extra money, because there never was any. But no matter what kind of resources I have, I treat them the way he treated what little he had. Baseball is a fleeting thing, which may sound strange coming from a guy who's been in it for so long. But I've never known how long I would be in the game. You don't know from one season to the next, one game to the next, even one pitch to the next. Because of the way I was raised I always believed that no matter how successful you are, it should not change you as a person. It doesn't entitle you to treat people any differently than if you were just another person trying to make a living. I believe I should treat the fan in the bleachers the same way I would treat George Bush—with respect.

Where I come from, treating people that way doesn't make me anything special. That's the way people are raised and, for the most part, that's the way they are. Of course every town has its share of bad apples, but I like a place where trying to be a good person doesn't make you stand out from the crowd. Treating people right has become part of my nature because of my upbringing, and it's nice to have it come naturally. It would be too much work if you had to think about it every time or only did it for your own benefit.

If my baseball career were over next week, I'd be working. I've accumulated a lot of money and a lot of things, and I suppose I could coast for a good while if I chose to. But I'd go crazy not working. I enjoy manual labor. I enjoy working cattle. I get a lot of satisfaction out of doing a good job, whether it's mowing a yard, raking leaves, doing a flower bed, or building a fence. I look out at my property and see the fence I put up, and it makes me feel good that I dug the postholes and did the final paint job. I enjoy building things, and I don't like doing shoddy work. I don't like spending my time on something that isn't what it should have been or isn't going to last. I don't want to have to go back and redo it. Seems like a lot of folks want a shortcut; they don't want to have to do anything.

The bottom line is that even though I sometimes smile about whatever image a writer wants to create for me, I realized early on that I just had to be myself. I can't be worried about what people think of me or what they expect or want me to be. I have to be Nolan Ryan and answer for myself. You don't need such a good memory that way, trying to be somebody different for every person or every situation. That was instilled in me by my parents.

My dad had an inner confidence, and he was a stabilizing force in our family. That was in my mind when I got to New York to play for the Mets. I really wasn't that far out of high school and hadn't had much experience in the world, but all of a sudden, because of my fastball, I was being compared to Bob Feller and Sandy Koufax. I started out thinking I had to go out there and show them what a good arm I had. I might strike out six or seven the first time through the lineup, but the hitters would realize I was wild and didn't have a breaking ball. Then they would get selective, and I wouldn't make it through the lineup a second time.

I realized I was playing right into their hands just because somebody had said something about me and I was trying to live up to it. I wasn't trying to be Nolan Ryan. I was trying to be Feller or Koufax, and nobody can do that.

I used to get upset when people called me a .500 pitcher because I've lost nearly as many games as I've won. That doesn't bother me anymore, because I know that anybody who says that doesn't know much about baseball or about pitching. I know what kind of a pitcher I am. I know what's gone on in my career. I know what I have to do to be effective. They don't. That's why I try to teach my kids to consider the source whenever they're criticized. Don't be influenced by what people say about you. Don't let it bother you to where you're distracted.

That's a hard lesson because everybody likes to be liked. You like to do right and be popular, but you have to look at the big picture and decide whether it's worth it to bend to peer pressure. When our oldest son, Reid, was pitching in high school, one night the guys on the other bench were razzing him pretty good. "Jose Canseco's gonna hit a grand slam off your old man!" they said, and other stuff like that. Ruth was ready to come out of the stands and pop every one of them.

Finally Reid just walked over and said nicely, "I'm proud of my dad. What do y'all's dads do?"

He was serious and interested in them and was trying to take the spotlight off himself and off me. They were speechless. Probably half of them didn't even have dads living at home and the others either weren't proud of their dads or didn't want to say what they did. Whatever, it worked. They quit razzing Reid.

I'm a big believer in listening to people. If you really listen, they'll tell you about themselves without even realizing it. People usually talk about what's on their mind, and what's on their mind is usually themselves. Within just a few minutes of meeting someone new, if you just listen you'll hear something about them that they consider real important. It might be where they work or used to work, or something they've accomplished, or where they graduated from. Most people know enough to just work it into the conversation so it doesn't sound like bragging, but if you listen, you'll hear it. Listen to salesmen too, because the thing they avoid talking about is probably some important negative part of whatever they're trying to sell you. Ask them about it and if they still talk around it, you can be sure.

The more people get to know me, the more frugal they know I am. If they don't know me, all they may've heard is that I make millions or am worth millions or own banks, and they figure I'm an easy mark. That would make the people around Alvin smile. When I go into a store, I don't want some salesperson trying to push something off on me. I want them available if I have questions, but I want to look at the product and make up my own mind. I do very little shopping because of that, and when I do, I usually know what I want and go in and get it. All these one-day specials are just sales gimmicks. They write books on how to do that.

I'm not real popular with the realtors around here either. If anybody thinks money's no object with me, he learns quickly. When I put the ranch together in Gonzales, Texas, I made a lot of land purchases. The realtors get frustrated with someone who doesn't buy on the spur of the moment, and I sure don't. I really think things through and spend a lot of time on it. One thing my dad told me a long time ago and I've tried to instill in my kids is that if something's real important to you and you think you want to do it, sleep on it. If you get up the next morning and you still feel strongly about it, then it might be the right thing. But if your attitude's changed, you need to give it more thought.

I admit I've lost out on some deals that could have been lucrative, but then there have been an awful lot of deals that I passed on—and thank goodness I did. I'm a believer in gut feelings. I pay a lot of attention to how I feel inside, and very few times have I acted on that and been wrong. If I sleep on it and still have that gut feeling in the morning, I'm usually ready to deal. When I miss out on something because of my methodical approach, I just figure it wasn't right and that it's not the last deal that's going to come along. If somebody tries to pressure me into a quick decision, they're going the wrong way with me. It won't work. Anybody making a commission on something I buy is going to earn every dime.

I don't try to buy below market value, but I do try to be realistic and not pay additional fees. If there's a lot of fat in the deal, I can usually find it and cut it out. Otherwise you're just throwing money away. I shop for things, and a lot of times when

I make an offer, I don't lowball just to start the bidding. I'll say, "Look, I'm going to make you an offer of what I can pay and what I feel like the value is, and if you want to accept that, fine. But I don't want you to think I'm going to keep coming up, because I'm not." I want an honest, clean deal without all the games and long, drawn-out motions. If it works, great, and if they can't accept the offer, that's okay too. Let's not waste each other's time. A lot of times people don't believe you when you walk away from a deal, and when it dawns on them that you were serious and they call you, it's too late. If you're going to walk away, be prepared to stay away.

A lot of people with something to sell find out I'm interested and think that since I've got money they can really hook me. My income gets plastered all over the media. It was even on the front page of *USA Today,* so everybody knows that the Rangers paid me $1.4 million in 1990, $3.3 million in 1991, and $4.2 million in 1992. When we started looking into buying a couple of banks, we studied a lot of different deals and talked to a lot of people. Then when it came down to negotiating, I thought, *Wait a minute! Is this the same guy and the same deal?* Once they had attracted our interest by talking price and conditions, they changed their tune. We walked away from a lot of deals that suddenly changed when we got to the bargaining table.

I have my attorney with me—see, I really do like some of them—but I do the negotiating myself. When they start bringing in new contingencies and change the terms, it's time to walk. No matter what my income has ever been, I've tried not to lose sight of the value of the dollar and what it takes to earn a living in the normal world.

That's where most professional athletes fall short, because they don't have these concepts. A lot of them have never worked outside their sport and don't understand what it is to get up and go to work before daylight and work all day and come home after sundown. Some working people don't enjoy the light of day for a week. Too many baseball players are not prepared to work when they leave the game. It's such a shock and rude awakening that a lot of them refuse to make the transition back into the real world. They know there's no money like what they've been making if they try to stay in the game as a coach, so they'd rather go home and live off what little they've saved, and they wind up with lots of personal problems because their pride gets in the way. They don't want to have to really work for a living. I'd rather do business with real working people.

That's why I bought the Express Bank in Danbury, fifteen miles south of Alvin, in 1990 and a new branch in Alvin last year. My goal is that these banks have a down-home feel. All the big banks are going conglomerate and trying to be bigger. We just want to prosper by seeing our customers prosper. When I was growing up, customers knew their banker by name. That's the way it should be. I paid $600,000 for the Danbury bank and it has grown from assets of under $10 million to more than $14 million. The Alvin branch gives us about $20 million more in assets. I've got more tied up in three ranches, so with that and baseball and endorsements, I'm busier than I ever wanted to be.

Sometimes it seems like Nolan Ryan is something besides me. But I know all this is temporary. There are days when doing all this business without the baseball looks pretty attractive. But I know it was the baseball that made it happen in the first place, and as long as the fame is paying off right now, I'll ride this wave.

Once I take the uniform off for good, the commercial requests will taper off. When you're on top it's demanding, but when you become a used-to-be, it has to slow down. I hope. Ruth worries that I'll have an image like Joe DiMaggio, who still can't go out in pubic without being mobbed. That would be prison. It'll sure be good to just do a couple of things well rather than try to do more. I could never be a full-time banker, though. I would get cabin fever being inside all day.

I still get people sending me investment stuff all the time, wanting me to get in on a great deal. But if these are such great deals, why don't these people get a loan and cut the deal themselves? I've got enough deals to worry about with my own banks. I was on the board of an Alvin bank in the 1980s when there were more than nineteen thousand banks in the state of Texas. Almost half of them have closed or been merged since then. There's a lesson there that we've got to learn. We can't risk bad loans. I won't lend money to someone for a store unless I know it's going to be profitable. If we had to foreclose, would anybody buy it? I have to ask that question every time we consider a loan. We have to be better business people when times are bad. The government won't be bailing us out.

I've taken big financial risks, and I've lost money. In the 1980s I lost a million on tax shelters. I've seen land drop 40 percent in value. I invested in oil when it was selling at more than $25 a barrel and saw it drop to under $10. There was a while there when I couldn't believe how many things went bad. I was in a limited partnership on some apartment buildings that were foreclosed when the economy fell. And I sold a ranch to buyers who went bankrupt and I had to repossess it. I learned the hard way that it's not how much money you make that counts. It's how much you keep.

The other part of my nature that doesn't exactly fit with my image is that I can be an emotional person. I try to control that quite a bit, especially when I do something special on the field, like reach a milestone record or pitch a no-hitter. I've never liked showing people up by displaying it, but emotionally I can be moved. What might be emotional for me wouldn't look the same on somebody else. Everyone shows emotion in different ways. Tommy Lasorda and Tug McGraw and those types of guys always make it clear what they're feeling. That's great and entertaining, but it's not me. I feel like I shouldn't get too high when things are going well or too down when things are going bad. I try to stay on an even keel and keep off the emotional roller coaster.

I can still get choked up watching my children accomplish something. It might be a little thing, like just seeing their joy. It also moves me when my teammates share in something I've accomplished. If it's a big deal for them to have been involved in one of the no-hitters, that means a lot to me.

Patriotic stuff moves me too. When the U.S. hockey team beat the Russians in the Olympics in 1980, I was as choked up as anybody who saw that. I take great pride in our country, no matter what I feel about how things are going at the time. When someone loses that love and emotion for his country, he can become a miserable person. I don't want that to happen to me.

Probably the biggest difference between my image and my real nature is how I am on the mound. If you believed everything you read about me, you'd figure I was a slow-talking, slow-walking, soft-spoken guy who just does his job in a detached way and gets on with his life. Part of that is true. I want to give an honest day's work for the enormous dollars they pay athletes these days, but actually I'm a totally different person on the mound than I am on the street.

The casual country gentleman, if that's what I could be called, wouldn't get anybody out in the big leagues. At that level you have to be single-minded, focused, and tough. I mean really tough. You've got to go after the hitters, take every advantage you can, work on their weak spots, and want to beat them. There's no playing around out there, no experimenting just because you've got a few effective pitches. Anybody who's ever been on a big league mound knows that you're always one pitch from failure.

When I'm on that mound, I don't even look the same. I don't feel or act the same. I'm there to do a job and to get people out, and if that means pitching inside, I pitch inside. If that means setting up a guy outside and then busting one in close, that's what I do. I spend a good bit of my life staying in shape and preparing for every start, and nobody's going to distract me or get my focus off my job. There's plenty of time after the game to be the other Nolan Ryan.

3

The Other
Nolan Ryan

*T*he baseball field is the only place I'm so fiercely competitive. I mean I can be stubborn and single-minded, and I'm kind of wary of people I don't know. I'll look at a deal every which way and can get pretty cold if I think you're trying to take me. But that focus on the task, that almost meanness about challenging the hitter, that's only on the mound.

If I go out to play tennis or basketball or any of that, I'm not that way. I was when I was in high school and competing, but now when I go out to enjoy a sport, sure I play to win, but I find it offensive if people get too excited about it. I'm out there for the enjoyment and the exercise and the socializing. We all do our best and we usually keep score, but the outcome doesn't mean a thing to me. If you make it obvious it means a lot to you, I might be busy next time you want to play.

Off the field I don't mind trying to live up to the image most people have of me. I get amused when people think I could succeed at pitching as a nice guy. There's nothing nice guy about it. I would never intentionally hit somebody, but boy I'll go after you and make you earn your hits. If anybody thinks I'm gonna shrug and say "Aw, shucks" if I start getting hit, they're crazy. My whole life's been fixed on power pitching. That's what got me in the game and that's what's kept me there.

Nobody would want to be that way off the field, and nobody could stand me if I was. Every once in a while you get a guy who thinks he needs to have his game face on and his attitude focused all the time. He's mean on the field and off the field. People usually just roll their eyes at a guy like that. It's not necessary. To me there's nothing inconsistent about being one way in the game and another way in real life. Imagine what kind of a dad I'd be if I was the same with my kids as I was with big league hitters. I want my kids to have memories of their growing up years as good as I have of mine, and that means my being easy to get along with.

I can be strict and firm, and I expect the kids to do their part. But I think they also can tell how much I love them and want them to enjoy life. They've grown up with a dad who's a big leaguer, so it's been a way of life for them. It's been exciting for them, I know, but I'm sure at times they wished I was more available. During the season I'm gone half the time, and during the off-season I'm sometimes busier than ever, depending upon my schedule. They understand some of the benefits that come with my being in demand, and they've gotten to do a lot of traveling because I always take them with me during the summer.

I've made a point of carrying them with me ever since they were big enough to go. Truth is, they're one of the reasons I'm still playing. Every year for the past several years I've thought about whether it's time to retire. You keep thinking you'll know because you've lost something on your fastball or your aches and pains are worse than ever, but with me it's mostly just been wondering if I've had enough. But the family wanted me to continue. They weren't ready for me to retire. So since I didn't have to, I kept on.

Kids of sports stars can have problems. They are either real proud of their dad or they're a little embarrassed about it and get teased. Sometimes they live and die with how their dad does on the field. If the team is losing or I'm losing, they'll hear about it at school. But mostly I know they're proud and they like having a dad who does something that most people don't do.

We've tried to stress with our kids that they should develop their own interests and their own personalities and their own identities. That's a tough battle at times, because no matter what they do athletically, they're going to get compared to their dad. Reid is a pitcher who was good enough in high school to go on and pitch in college. He may or may not play pro ball, but you gotta know everybody who watches him and knows who he is asks the same big question and compares him to me. I mean, do they really expect a kid to throw like I do? Experts tell me only 7 percent of all the pitchers in the majors throw as hard as I do. It's not fair to say Reid doesn't have my fastball. It'd be an amazing coincidence if he did. I wish they'd just let him pitch and play and enjoy the game. He was good enough that he could have played college basketball if he'd wanted to, but even then people would compare how he was as a basketball player to how I am as a baseball player. Silliness, really. Let him be himself.

The only time it really bothered him though was when some guys razzed him. He'd come home and say, "Why do people have to be that way? Why do they have to be mean and ugly like that?" But that comes with the territory, and you have to take the bad with the good. If nothing else, that teaches him a lot about human nature and people in general. You can't let it affect how you treat people. I figure, if nothing else, it'll show him the value of being a basically quiet and well-mannered person.

Reese, our younger boy, is a real responsible kid too. While Reid's mind was always on sports and he didn't like working around the ranch, Reese enjoys making spending money by doing chores. He'll always check to see what needs to be done first and how I want it done. I'd like all the kids to just do chores for the fun and accomplishment of it, but I guess that's too much to ask in this day and age.

One day last summer Reese was working at home alone and accidentally let one of the dogs in and didn't know it. When he came in later, he discovered the dog had torn up the drapes and gnawed on the door trying to get out. On his own, Reese called the interior decorator and got her out there to tell him what needed to be done, and he paid for it out of his own money. Ruth was pretty upset with him at first, but we were both impressed when he took that responsibility and wanted to make it right.

One of the toughest things about raising modern kids, especially when you really don't have to worry about money, is teaching them the value of a dollar. That came sort of naturally to me because we never had much extra when I was growing up, but it would be hard for me to convince my kids I can't afford something. One thing I can't afford, though, is to give them whatever they want. I know what that can do to a person, and it's not good. They'd start thinking that's how life is. What kind of adults would I be turning out if they get the idea that someone's going to be financing them all the way? I want my sons and my daughter to make their own ways.

There were things we were glad to see Reid discover when he went off to college. He played ball in Alaska for a season and then he went to school. For the first couple of years he wrote Ruth pretty regularly telling her how much he appreciated all she had done for him and how much he learned from the things I used to tell him. He thought I was crazy when I said them because a lot of what I say goes against current trends. You sit your kids down and try to tell them things and they look at you like you're from another planet. Then they get out in the real world and find out how things are, and they're amazed at what you know.

Our house is always open, and we want our kids' friends to feel welcome. Most of all that made Reid appreciate us as parents and the home life and stability he had. I know that'll happen to Reese and Wendy too, but they'll probably have to leave home to discover it. That's sure the way it happened with me. Nobody ever seems to learn lessons the easy way. At least not kids.

Like any other child of my generation, I didn't know how great my life was because I didn't know there was anything special about it. There are probably nicer places to grow up than hot and humid and mosquito-infested Alvin, Texas, but for some reason I came back here and will likely die here. A lot of it has to do with the memories from my childhood that, like I say, got better as I traveled and found out what I had.

Every spring we used to build a baseball diamond in a vacant lot not far from where I lived. The neighborhood kids would get their lawn mowers and trim up an infield, lay out the bases, and build a backstop. In the summertime there was always a baseball game, and all we'd do is play ball. It was horribly hot and humid, but we didn't care until sometimes in the middle of the day when it was so hot you couldn't stand it out in the sun. Then we'd lie around in the shade until it cooled down a few degrees and we could get back at it.

That's one thing you hardly see anymore, kids playing ball basically from sunup until sundown. You know, even if you didn't have good mechanics or any coaching, playing hour after hour after hour in the sun for the enjoyment was also good for your game. You got used to the ball. Your brain recorded angles and bounces and hops and even sounds. There's something about hitting a hundred different times in a day-long game, about throwing and fielding and running. You've got to wonder if today's kid could play that much.

There was no air conditioning in our houses back then and there was sure nothing on television. Our mothers wanted us out of the house, and we were glad to get out. We had gloves and bats and baseballs and that field we'd made ourselves. We didn't need anything else.

When I first broke into big league baseball most of the guys were my age or older of course, so they had all played ball like that. You'd start as soon as you had enough guys, while it was cool and there might even be dew on the grass. By mid-morning everybody was there. You'd break for lunch and to get out of the sun for awhile, but pretty soon everybody would be back at it. We never quit on our own. It was almost like that was against the rules. One by one we'd hear our moms or dads holler. You couldn't pretend not to hear them for long. The last several at bats were dangerous because we tried to squeeze in just one more time before it was too dark to see the ball.

It wasn't unusual to play ball seven or eight hours every day. You learn an awful lot that way. And when you got old enough for Little League and had your eye on those uniforms and especially the caps—which we all wore proudly to school to show that we were part of a team—you still played all day and then went to practice at four in the afternoon.

We couldn't get enough baseball. Sometimes I still feel that way. Maybe that's why I'm still in the game at forty-five. Somebody's hollering my name and telling me it's time for supper or that it's too dark and I've been playing too long. But c'mon. There's time for one more pitch. Just one more. Please?

4

From Little League to the Bigs

*T*he attraction of Little League for me was that it was the first opportunity I had to play organized team sports. It was a big deal to get a uniform and take pride in your team, win or lose, and know that adults even took an interest in the games. Kids didn't have all the t-shirts with sports logos on them you see everywhere today, and you didn't see kids walking around in big league replica uniforms. So Little League was the only place you could pretend to be a big leaguer and really look the part.

Now baseball wasn't just a pick-up game in a vacant lot anymore. We had real bases and chalk lines and batter's boxes, a pitching rubber and a plate, coaches, the whole thing. The best part about our Little League was that, because of everybody's schedule and the climate, they put up lights and we played all our games at night. All of us kids fantasized about making the All-Star team and going to Williamsport, Pennsylvania for the Little League World Series. Of course only a few teams in the whole country ever made it that far each year, but that was our dream. They didn't televise it in those days, but you read about it in the paper, and it was what everybody talked about.

I made the All-Star team, but I wasn't the best player and we didn't get far in the postseason tournaments. Still I have to say that those were some of the best days of my life. I loved the excitement and the drama of it. It was great to be part of something with your friends and to learn and have fun. There's something about baseball that reached a certain part of my nature. You could be yourself and you could be competitive, but everything was structured and measured and controlled. It was fair. We were all pretty much the same age, and when we walked out between those foul lines, everybody was playing by the same rules and within the same boundaries.

I couldn't get enough of it, and I'm still proving that. Some people would call me the Peter Pan of baseball, never wanting to grow up. I sometimes see a picture of myself on the mound, maybe tipping my cap, and see a face that belongs on a coach and a hairline that belongs on somebody long out of the game, and it even surprises me. When I'm out there doing what I do best, I know it will take me longer to recover physically and it means more and harder workouts to stay in shape. But when I check my defense, stare in for that sign, consider the situation, and make a decision on a pitch, I'm thinking of nothing but that moment. I might as well be twelve years old, big ol' floppy glove on one hand and a ball too big for my hand in the other. I keep my eyes on that target and go into my own unique windup, and when I let fly the pitch, my age doesn't mean a thing.

If I have to come charging in to cover the plate or get behind third to backup a throw or angle over and beat a runner to the bag and take a toss from the first baseman, I'm ready. My uniform shirt has said New York, California, Houston, and Texas. Mets, Angels, Astros, and Rangers. But when I'm in the middle of a game it might as well say Alvin All-Stars, and those form-fitting uniform pants might as well be the billowy flannels, tucked just so under the knees, that I wore as a kid.

Big league baseball is a business, a serious, tough, competitive, and even dangerous thing that can't be done lightly. But the professional who really loves the game never loses sight of the fun and the challenge and the joy of it. The travel gets old, the season gets long, and the body suffers. But once the game starts you never want it to end.

In Little League I wasn't the kid who dominated the league or anything like that. I pitched and played the infield, but there were a lot of other good players. Once I got into high school and people saw how hard I could throw a ball, I became better known. I always hit third or fourth in the lineup, and I hit .700 in the 1965 state tournament, but it was my pitching that set me apart. I was 20–4 as a senior and was All-State. Since I was also a basketball player, I won the Outstanding Athlete Award at Alvin High. What was even more important, though I didn't realize it at the time, I had been discovered by a big league scout.

At first I had no idea what that might mean. Anybody likes to be thought of as a major league prospect, but I was just trying to grow up. I thought maybe if I could make the pros somehow I might be able to afford college without being such a burden on my dad. Otherwise, I had been a pretty typical high school kid, trying to take shortcuts and get out of what my parents wanted me to do. I wanted to satisfy them, but I wanted to get my job done and get out of it as quickly as possible. I hardly ever got away with that. It always came back to haunt me.

In Texas back then, because kids worked on the farms and ranches, you could get your driver's license at age fourteen, which I did. Because we had that *Houston Post* distributorship, I was often out in the middle of the night driving around, and I had to learn to deal with the responsibility of that freedom.

A lot of my friends found it exciting to be able to go down and help me roll papers on the weekend and be able to run around town after midnight. We weren't above stealing hubcaps and doing other mischief like that, even though we knew better. We justified it by not trying to profit from it by reselling them or anything. Some of the guys put the fancy ones on their own cars because they couldn't afford them otherwise, but I never could have placed unexplained "new" hubcaps on my car without my dad's knowing. A few close calls just added to the excitement. Mostly we were bored country kids who got a rush by trying to get away with something.

We never got caught, and it's a good thing. I would have been punished severely. I'd have been spanked, yes, even at that age, and grounded a good long time. I'm so glad my dad never knew about the time my friends and I stole some donuts at 4:00 in the morning. I felt more fear of getting caught than guilt, which is normal for a kid I guess. I knew I'd get punished and have to apologize and make it right—which kept me from doing it again even after the fear wore off. That was the end of my life of crime.

By the time I got close to the end of my high school years, all I could think about was getting away from home. Thinking I knew everything and having no clue to what the world was really all about, I thought my parents held tight rein on me and wouldn't let me do a lot of things. It would only be later, when I was off on my own, that I would realize how much they meant to me and how thankful I was for what they did for me and the opportunities they gave me.

What they gave me was sure not material things. When school started each year we'd go to the store and I'd get two pairs of jeans, three or four shirts, and a pair of shoes. That was my wardrobe until Christmas, when I'd get a few more things. My mother would wash and iron my dirty jeans so I'd have a clean pair every day. I don't ever remember feeling deprived just because some of the other kids' dads owned car dealerships or big businesses and gave them cars and motor scooters and stuff.

I didn't feel the peer pressure kids do nowadays. When I take Wendy to school these days I'm amazed to see how kids are dressed. They have the latest styles and fashions, and I'm thinking, How do these people afford those clothes? Both parents work because they don't want their kids to feel deprived of anything.

My parents did the same thing, but not for the same reasons. With four girls and two boys, my dad and mother believed she couldn't afford to be away from home to work. That's why dad had two jobs. That's just the way things were done in those days. As long as the father could bring in enough income to make that work, that's how it was. It wound up basically killing my dad, but that was his commitment to his family.

My mother's job was thankless, but she found personal rewards in doing for her kids. I always tell our kids that if there's one person they should respect in this world, it's their mother, because she makes the biggest sacrifice of anybody. There's nothing more tender or selfless than a mother's love, and that's why I take my hat off to all of them. I feel sorry for single mothers that have to work to support their families. They are really under a burden. They are dedicated to doing what they have to do, and because there are so many of them in the work force, we have come to depend on them as part of the backbone of our country. I just hope their kids become healthy adults in spite of having only one parent, and that one working most of the day.

My parents came to as many of my ball games as they could when I was in high school. They were there the day in the spring of my senior year when we were playing Deer Park for the district championship to see who would go to the state playoffs. By then I was pretty well known for my fastball, but I was wild. It worked to my advantage that day. I hit the first kid up squarely in the helmet and split it. I hit the next guy in the arm and broke it. The third kid went and begged his coach not to make him hit. That coach assaulted him verbally in front of everybody and shamed him into standing in there.

I had them after that. If I didn't walk them, I struck them out because they were up there at the edge of the batter's box on their toes, ready to bail out. They were so far from the plate that the inside corner was outside to them. I had no strategy and no finesse. I just kept winging them in there, trying to get as close to the plate as possible. They'd forgotten about trying to win the district. They just wanted to go home without any more injuries.

I'd been scouted for quite a while, but believe it or not, I didn't give the majors much thought. I saw the Astros play in Houston a few times, and the big leaguers looked so strong and polished that I knew I wasn't anywhere near their class. I was tall and skinny and wild, and even though everybody always talked about how hard I threw, I had no idea I could make a career out of that. I might have been impressed if I had been picked high in the draft that summer, but 294 high school and college players were picked before I was taken in the tenth round. I'd had a bad game when Red Murff, a scout for the Mets, had brought his boss, Bing Devine, especially to watch me. Getting to the majors hadn't been that big a deal to me anyway, but I figured my chance was gone after that.

I had no idea that of all the hundreds of kids drafted out of high school every summer, only one in a hundred winds up making a living in the majors. All I knew was that they thought almost three hundred kids had a better chance than I did to start with. I didn't really understand the draft and all that went with it, but I was pretty sure I didn't have what it took to make it. The worst part was I really didn't know if I had the desire. I know that sounds crazy, and maybe it was just a way of protecting myself from disappointment, but you have to understand, I wasn't one of those kids with a dream, imagining myself in the pros. I was so far removed from the big leagues that I had no clue.

When the Mets finally came to try to sign me I honestly didn't know what I should do. I didn't want to waste my time in a profession where so many people were already considered better. I had been thinking about college for years and didn't know if I should do that, get a job, or try baseball. The Mets probably thought I was playing hard to get, but I was just thinking it through. Somehow, even at that age, I was determined to make a careful choice. By the third meeting the Mets were offering a $20,000 signing bonus and $500 a month. My dad wasn't making much more than that every month as a longtime employee of American Oil. And the bonus alone would set me up for college if things didn't work out in baseball. Dad felt like it was an offer I couldn't turn down. A lot has been made of the pressure put on me by other people, but my dad's opinion and my own were the only ones I really cared about. And that's why I signed with the Mets on June 26, 1965.

That summer, seventy players came through in waves to play at one time or another for the Mets' rookie league team in Marion, Virginia. I was one lonely eighteen-year-old. Everybody I knew and loved was left at home when I took my first plane ride to get to Marion. By the time I got there, they had already started their season, and I had to wait until they cut someone before they had a uniform for me. Problem was, the guy they cut was a little second baseman who'd had his pants shortened to fit him just right. Here I was, six-foot-two and skinny, walking around in pants way too short. It was all I could do to keep from showing bare leg between the bottoms of my pants and the tops of my socks.

I was so homesick, especially for Ruth, that the only thing that saved me was her dad's agreeing to bring her to visit me. That gave me something to look forward to. Maybe everybody else was looking forward to the big leagues, but I was only there because I had signed a contract, and I had only signed the contract because my dad recommended I sign it. The only real ambition I had was to see my girlfriend.

5

Growing Up in
the Majors

Seeing Ruth was the highlight of that summer for me, but I also struck out 115 hitters in 78 innings. The Mets saw something they liked in my fastball and had me come to the winter instructional league in Florida. Only the top twenty prospects in the organization were invited, so I knew something was happening.

At minor league spring training the next spring I met Tom Seaver for the first time. Now there was a guy who had a goal and was focused on it. I was just there trying to have fun and make a living with a gigantic fastball. He wanted to be an excellent, thinking pitcher. I was amazed just to hear him talk about it. I was thrilled for him when he made the Hall of Fame this year by the biggest vote ever. He and I have been friends since those early days with the Mets.

Pitching in the instructional league and in spring training put me in contact with big league pitching coaches and more help and advice than I knew existed. I know it helped, but at first all it did was show me how much I didn't know. I had no idea there was so much to the game, let alone to pitching. I had a long, long way to go.

Whatever I learned paid off quick. While Tom Seaver was sent right into triple A, I was shipped to Greenville, South Carolina to play class A ball. Though I was just nineteen years old and still wild, the hitters in that league were overmatched by my speed, and I had the best statistical year of my career. I was 17–2, with nine complete games, five shutouts, and 272 strikeouts in 183 innings. I also walked 127 batters, but the night my parents and youngest sister and Ruth came to see me pitch against Gastonia, I was on. In a seven-inning game I got nineteen of the twenty-one outs on strikes.

Late in the year I was sent to Williamsport, Pennsylvania, for about ten days in AA ball. I had never made Williamsport as a Little Leaguer, but here I was passing through as a pro. I knew I still had a lot to learn as a pitcher, but my success in Greenville had made me feel better about myself. I wasn't so homesick, and I was maturing and learning to be a little more independent. Though I was 0–2 in Williamsport in three games, I struck out thirty-five in nineteen innings (walking twelve), and had an 0.95 ERA.

I was set to pitch four innings in my last start and then catch a plane to join the Mets in the big leagues. At the end of those four innings I had a no-hitter going and my manager, Bill Virdon, asked if I wanted to stay and go for it. I couldn't see how a no-hitter in the minors could compare with making the majors, so I told him I'd just as soon get going. He wished me the best. In just over a year I had pitched in three leagues and was heading to the majors before I was twenty years old.

I got into a couple of games with the Mets, started one, and got hit around pretty good. I found out it was no picnic pitching to the best hitters in the world. The next year I served in the military for six months, then injured my arm in the minors and wondered if I'd ever pitch again. In four games for two minor league teams I didn't do much of anything. But Ruth and I got married in June, which was more important than whatever happened to me in baseball.

In the winter instructional league my arm came back around and I did well in spring training. Tom Seaver had been

Rookie of the Year in the National League for the Mets in 1967, and the press made a big deal about the other fastballing righthander in the organization: me. It was flattering to be compared to Bob Feller and Sandy Koufax, but it was also pressure. I wasn't really a pitcher. I was just a hard thrower. Whitey Herzog told somebody that he just knew I'd be brought along before I was ready because I had such a good arm. At twenty-one years of age I was a big leaguer, and though the next four years in New York were rocky and I'd lose more games than I won, I never looked back.

I was frustrated as a Met. Because of my military duty I kept missing opportunities to pitch, and the Mets didn't seem to care about making up for it. I was wild and getting wilder, had a lot to learn, and wasn't learning it. I needed to be on a team that needed me. The Mets had great pitching and would win that amazing 1969 World Series while I was there, but I was hardly part of it. I wanted out and let it be known. Ruth wasn't happy in New York either. After four years I knew I hadn't progressed much, and I didn't see much of a future in baseball if I stayed with the Mets. I had the feeling that my manager, Gil Hodges, didn't like me, but as I look back on it I was probably wrong. I was just thinking like a kid. His style and personality were such that he was quiet and stern and not much of a communicator, and anyway, I was not one of the mainstays of his staff.

It wasn't the Mets' fault. I was in the bullpen most of the time, but they didn't use me in relief much because of my lack of control. And I had control problems because I wasn't pitching often enough to be effective. So it was one of those no-win situations that was only going to be solved if I went where I was needed. The Mets were trying to win championships, and they couldn't afford the luxury of bringing along this kid with the big gun.

It didn't help my state of mind that my dad died during that time. He'd always been a heavy smoker, but he even smoked in the night because of that newspaper distributorship of his. I hardly ever remember him not smoking. Because of all the health problems cigarettes brought him, I never had the desire to smoke. Seeing what he went through and what a horrible way that is to die squelched any temptation to think there was anything good about smoking. Because of how young I was and how much my father meant to me, it was traumatic to watch him go through that and to lose him. Being the last of his six kids, I felt the loss in a bad way and it was a real hard period for me.

I'd been home to see him when we were in Houston to play the Astros. I visited him in the hospital for three days, and when I left I felt he'd deteriorated to where it wouldn't be long before he died. One of my sisters called me in New York a few nights later to tell me he'd passed away. I headed straight home.

It wasn't a surprise, but you're never really prepared for that. I kind of crawled into a shell and wanted to be left to my own thoughts. I was relieved that he was not suffering anymore, but other than his smoking I had respected his judgment and counted on it a lot. I enjoyed being around him because he was more than my father; I also considered him a friend.

I had Ruth and I had baseball, but a lot of times I felt like I should pick up the phone and call my dad about something before I remembered he was gone. There was a void in my life and I had to learn to deal with that. To this day I've never heard anybody speak poorly of him. He understood that the paper route was a service-oriented business, and he expected us to deliver those papers where people wanted them and when they wanted them. If anybody called and said that they didn't receive their paper or that their paper was wet, we had to take them one right then. He didn't take any shortcuts, and he darn sure didn't expect us to. I came to respect that constant attention to basic values.

The next year I got to pitch more, but I completed only three of twenty-six starts and wound up 10–14. I had 137 strikeouts in 152 innings, but I also walked 116. Everybody knew I had the ability, but I was still a long way from being a consistently effective pitcher. I could blow the ball past just about anybody, but nobody knew if I could really pitch.

When Ruth and I left New York at the end of the season, I told her I was sure we wouldn't be back. She was pregnant with our first child, and Reid was born that November, two weeks before the baseball winter meetings. That's when a lot of deals are made, and I told Ruth that if the Mets were going to trade me, it would happen then. We were thrilled with the new life in our home, and I was excited that I might be getting a whole new opportunity the next season.

When the Mets called and told me I was on my way to sunny California, I immediately thought of the Dodgers. I was a National Leaguer and had hoped to maybe go to the Astros so I'd be a half-hour away from Alvin. But I wasn't going to Houston or Los Angeles. I had been traded to the California Angels in Anaheim. I went there along with three other players for veteran Jim Fregosi, who was to be the answer to the Mets' third base problem. It hurt me to read that Gil Hodges approved the deal not only because he wanted Fregosi—which made sense—but also because he thought I was the starting pitcher he would miss the least.

I may not have been an effective big league pitcher yet, but I sure wanted to make him regret that trade—or at least that comment. Though I still had a lot to learn about pitching, I was a willing student and was eager to do my best for my new team in 1972, even if it was in the American League.

In those days a lot of us players had to work during the off-season to make ends meet. It's hard to believe now, in light of today's salaries, but I was raised from $24,000 a year with the Mets to $27,000 for the Angels. I began an eight-year career with California that was really something. I would be in double figures in wins and losses every year, having only two losing seasons. Five out of the next six years I would strike out more than three hundred hitters each season, leading the American League seven out of eight years.

In my first year alone I was 19–16 starting thirty-nine games and finishing twenty with an ERA of 2.28, nine shutouts, and 329 strikeouts in 284 innings. I had seventeen games in which I struck out ten or more hitters, including two fourteens, a fifteen, two sixteens, and a seventeen. On July 9, pitching against Boston, I struck out sixteen, including eight in a row for an American League record. The next season my salary would be doubled to $54,000. It seemed like a lot of money back then.

Something much more important happened in 1972 than that: I finally turned around and had one of my best years as a pitcher. I discovered the weight room at Anaheim Stadium. It hadn't been installed for the baseball players, because back then it was believed that weight training made you musclebound. It must have been there for a soccer team or something. Anyway I started slipping in there and working out, being careful not to overdo it and letting my body tell me how it was responding. In my own way I learned how to work different areas of my body for balance and flexibility, taking a day off now and then to recover.

I've since worked with a lot of strength and conditioning coaches, and Tom House (strength coach for the Rangers) and I even wrote a book called *Nolan Ryan's Pitcher's Bible.* In it I talk about everything from mechanics to conditioning to diet. It's really everything I've learned in my own conditioning program and in working with such good coaches and trainers over the years.

Things have changed for me as I have gotten older. I've had to vary my workouts to make up for longer recovery times. And as I've worked through injuries or pain, I've worked around some muscles and concentrated on others. Thanks may be due to some genetics that have allowed me to age more slowly than most, but there's no secret to what it takes to stay in shape at this age. And that's hours and hours of workouts, usually every day.

If that sounds boring or not worth the effort, you feel the same way that most big leaguers feel. I can't swear to it, but it may be one of the reasons most of them leave the game in their thirties. I feel many effects of age. My back bothers me at times. I get stiffer quicker and need to loosen up and stretch longer. I can run only so much and so hard and so long. But I still put myself through the paces of a long, hard workout nearly every day, because it's worth it to me.

I enjoy feeling good and strong and hard, especially at my age. I can't guarantee that a pitcher's fastball will still be with him twenty-five years in the big leagues if he does my workout, but something's working for me. I have to work harder and smarter every year, but the key is deciding to keep with it. Sure it would be easier to skip it. But at my age I would probably get soft or fat and, for sure, I would be out of shape.

A lot of people are amazed to see me on an exercise bicycle immediately after a game while my arm is being iced. Do I need exercise after I've thrown a complete game? No. I need to get started on my preparation for the next start. I'm cleansing my muscles of lactic acid, getting an aerobic benefit that pitching can't give me, and staying on course with my training.

I can't run three days in a row like I used to because I get too sore or too stiff, but I still have to run two or three times a week. Nothing takes the place of running. During the off-season I get a lot of road work in, just logging the miles. During the season I do sprint work if I'm healthy and my Achilles tendon isn't bothering me.

On days when I work out for four or five hours, I try to break it up and not do it all at once. I get more out of it that way. I do it in two- to two-and-a-half-hour increments and feel like I'm making progress. The morning after a start I get into my weight room by nine or ten o'clock and start an hour and a half of weight lifting in a complete program for upper and lower body. The first day I'll do four and a half to five hours, then the next day maybe two and a half to three. The third day I'll repeat the first day's workout and throw three-quarter speed off the mound for twenty minutes, just working on mechanics. The day before a start I'll back off the work schedule and give my body a recovery day.

There's no doubt in my mind that if it hadn't been for that weight room, I would have been out of the game many years ago. Not only has it helped me prevent injury, but it's also kept me strong so I could continue to hold up over the long grind. I'm a firm believer that you're only as strong as your weakest link, so I'm careful not to do just upper body and leg work, but also abdominal training. I don't want to break down in any area.

The first three years after discovering that weight room, I pitched a thousand innings, but I always felt there was more I could do to stay strong. I didn't want to be like a lot of the guys I saw in the Met clubhouse the first time I walked in there. They were in their thirties, but some looked like old guys, paunchy and out of shape. Many of the pitchers were all fifteen to twenty pounds overweight and it affected their effectiveness. I decided that if there was any way to keep that from happening, I was going to do it. The universal gym I found in Anaheim was a trial-and-error tool that really paid off.

It may have been only coincidental, but the next two seasons would be the best of my career. If you look at my stats in the Appendix, you'll see that my records in 1973 and 1974 were almost identical. I pitched nearly the same number of games and innings, and most of my other numbers were close too. I was a power pitcher with a lot of wins, a record number of strikeouts, and an ERA of under three. In both seasons, the only times I did it in twenty-four full big league seasons, I pitched more than three hundred innings.

On May 15, 1973, I pitched my first no-hitter, shutting out Kansas City on the road, 3–0. Exactly two months later I pitched another no-hitter, beating Detroit 6–0 and striking out seventeen. I had struck out sixteen in the first seven innings and probably should have gotten the single game strikeout record, but we batted around in the top of the eighth and I stiffened while sitting on the bench.

Having pitched two no-hitters in two months and having such overpowering stuff made people wonder if I could pitch two no-hitters in a row. It had been done only once in big league history, in 1938 by Johnny Vander Meer. I thought I had a better shot at striking out twenty in a game than pulling off something like that. But I almost did it. In my next start against Baltimore I took a no-hitter into the eighth before Mark Belanger, a .200 hitter, blooped a single. Not only did I lose the no-hitter, but in extra innings I also lost the game, 3–1.

In 1973 I struck out ten or more hitters in a game twenty-three different times, breaking Sandy Koufax's record of twenty-one in 1965. Besides the seventeen-strikeout no-hitter, I struck out sixteen in the last game of the season to break Sandy Koufax's single season record of 382 by one K. I had become only the third pitcher in history to strike out three hundred hitters in two straight seasons.

All I had needed was a chance to pitch regularly. I could hardly wait for the 1974 season.

6

Wearing Out
a Welcome

*R*uth and I came back to Alvin after each season, but we enjoyed our lives in California. It was fun to play for an owner like Gene Autry who was personable and friendly and loved the game. The Angels increased my salary to $100,000, which was big money in those days, and some people thought I was the best pitcher in baseball. At age twenty-seven, I felt like I was on top of the world.

The 1974 season was almost identical to the one before. In fact, I almost pitched two no-hitters again. I struck out ten or more hitters in a game thirteen times, three times striking out fifteen and three times nineteen. Only five pitchers in this century have struck out nineteen hitters in a game, and I'm the only one who's done it more than once. Three of my four times came in that one season.

In early August I took a no-hitter into the ninth inning in Chicago against the White Sox, but Dick Allen beat out an infield roller to break it up. In my last start of the year, September 28, 1974, I no-hit Minnesota, putting me one behind Sandy Koufax's career record of four no-hitters.

After the game my manager, Dick Williams, was interviewed, and he said something amazingly prophetic. "He's twenty-eight now," he said, which wouldn't be true until January. "If he wants to, conceivably he could pitch for seven more years." Well, that wasn't the prophetic part, because in 1992 I started my eighteenth season since then. But get what he says next. The announcer asked him, "So, more no-hitters?" And Williams said, "Every time he goes out I can see a potential no-hitter. I can see Nolan Ryan spinning three, four, or five more no-hitters, and that is unheard of in the history of professional baseball."

The announcer asked him, "So, do we put him up there with Walter Johnson and Cy Young?"

Dick said, "If he can conquer the habit of walking a man in a ball game, there's no telling how great a pitcher he can be."

That win was the twenty-second of the season for my highest total ever. I had no way of knowing it would be my last twenty-win season, and if you had told me I would still be pitching today and have more than three hundred wins, I'd have thought you were crazy.

I also remember the 1974 season for two other reasons: I recorded the fastest pitch ever scientifically timed, 100.9 miles per hour, and I accidentally hit a batter in the head with a fastball. Doug Griffin of Boston was knocked out, and I was afraid I had killed him. When I called his home to check on him later, his little girl told me her Mommy was at the hospital with her Daddy. That got to me, and it was quite a while before I felt confident pitching inside again. Griffin missed fifty-one games. I don't know what I would have done if he had been permanently injured.

In three seasons I had pitched over a thousand innings, struck out more than a thousand, and won sixty-two games. In 1975 I suffered several minor but nagging injuries and my production was down in almost every category, but I was still a power pitcher, striking out almost one hitter per inning. Though I won six of my first seven decisions, I'd had two groin pulls and bone chips in my pitching elbow. The highlight came in my twelfth start, pitching a no-hitter against Baltimore at home, even with throbbing pain. I'm glad it was in Anaheim, because Ruth was there. She had never seen me pitch a no-hitter live. In a *Time* magazine article on me that week, Oriole manager Earl Weaver had been quoted, "Ryan could pitch a no-hitter every time he goes to the mound."

Besides my three no-hitters up to that point, ten times as an Angel alone I had not allowed a hit before the seventh inning. You never set out to throw no-hitters, but you sure start thinking about them late in the game. And when one slips away you rehash every pitch, thinking about the might-have-beens. I've had nineteen games in my career where I allowed one hit or less, and when I think how close I came to no-hitters in all those one-hitters, it makes me wonder where the no-hit record might be but for one pitch or one bad break.

Anyway, in that June 1, 1975 game against the Orioles, I struck out Bobby Grich on a changeup to end the game and tie Sandy Koufax's career no-hitters record. So much was made about the record that most people lost sight of the progress I'd made, not as a fireballer but as a thinking pitcher. My temptation a few seasons before would have been to challenge Grich with my best fastball. But of course that was what he and everybody else in the ballpark was expecting. Maybe I would have gotten him, maybe I wouldn't have. But if I get that changeup over the plate, he doesn't have a chance. He told the press later that I had fooled him good. So much for being a one-pitch pitcher.

A huge crowd turned out for my next start, hoping for back-to-back no-hitters and a record-breaking career fifth. I took a no-hitter into the sixth with two outs before Hank Aaron broke it up with a single. I still won a two-hit shutout, giving me five shutouts with a record of 10–3. Then the bone chips in the elbow caught up with me and my season fell apart. By the time I finally agreed to have the chips surgically removed in August, I had pitched less than two hundred innings and my record was 14–12. At one point I lost eight straight games. I had gone from being a dominating power pitcher to one the hitters couldn't wait to face.

I was amazed at how quickly the writers started speculating on what was wrong. I was accused of everything from laziness to giving up. Instead of defending myself I quit talking to the press, and that only made them come after me harder. By now I was in the middle of a two-year deal at $125,000 a year, and people expected nothing less than perfection. That's all I wanted too, but when your body's not cooperating, there's not much you can do.

Reese's birth in January 1976 was the highlight of that off-season. My arm felt good, after having been immobilized through the end of the season, so I hoped to come back strong. I wound up leading the league in shutouts and struck out 327 hitters in 284 innings. I pitched four three-hitters in the second half of the season.

Our daughter Wendy was born the following spring (1977), and I celebrated by signing a three-year deal with the Angels (at $300,000 a year). I then had a year similar to '73 and '74. I won nineteen, led the American League in strikeouts for the fifth time in six years, and was named American League Pitcher of the Year by the *Sporting News*.

The following season, 1978, was disappointing for me. I turned thirty-one and felt the effects of my body adjusting to getting older. I missed several starts and wound up 10–13, my worst year since my last one with the Mets. Still, I led the American League in strikeouts and pitched three shutouts and fourteen complete games. No one knew that I wasn't even halfway through my career yet, because already I was one of the old men in baseball and the ranking veteran on the Angels. No one else was still around from the 1972 team. In seven years I had pitched forty-one games in which I had allowed three hits or less, and I was already eighth on the all-time list for career strikeouts.

Just before my thirty-second birthday I let Angels general manager Buzzie Bavasi know that I wanted a contract extension. I asked for a three-year deal at $400,000 a year, plus $200,000 for signing—a total of $1.4 million for three years. I heard back that he would not discuss my request till the end of the '79 season.

That would be another good season for me. I was 16–14 with seventeen complete games, five shutouts, and an average of a strikeout an inning for 223 innings to lead the league again. I also took the Yankees into the ninth inning on no hits before Reggie Jackson singled on July 13. He ruined my chance to break Koufax's no-hit record, but there would be more opportunities.

It was amazing that I could concentrate on pitching at all that season. Early in the year Reid, then seven, had been hit by a car and suffered severe internal injuries, including losing a kidney and his spleen. With two younger children at home, Ruth needed me. I went on road trips only the day before I was scheduled to pitch. It was a disrupted time when the things that really matter come into focus. That was one long season, much of the summer spent in the hospital with Reid.

I sensed that my time with the Angels was coming to an end. I had felt like Bavasi didn't care as much for me as Gene Autry did, but I sure wasn't going to run to the owner about my problems with management. I had always done my own negotiating, but now I hired Dick Moss, who had been legal counsel for the players' association, because I knew I might be getting into free agency if the Angels didn't get serious about re-signing me. I didn't want to disrupt my family and my life by moving on, but it seemed to me the Angels were dragging their feet. At one point during the season, Bavasi asked Moss what it would take to sign me. Dick told him $500,000 a year for two years and $700,000 for a third year. Later Buzzie was quoted as saying that I had demanded a million dollars a year and that all he would have had to do to replace me was to pick up two pitchers with 7–6 records.

That really hurt. I thought I deserved more than comments like that. I had given everything I had to the organization, and I felt good about my relationship with the fans. The only person I was upset with was Buzzie. Some people think everything can be forgiven with a big pile of money, but I couldn't imagine the Angels coming up with any amount that would have made up for his making me feel so unwelcome. At the end of the season we sold our house and moved back to Alvin. It had been a long, hard, bitter year with a lot of hurtful things said, and it felt good for Ruth and me and the kids to be back home.

I was hoping to find a team willing to pay me around $600,000–$650,000 a year, but Dick Moss thought I could get more. When more than twelve teams drafted me I thought he might be right. Yankees owner George Steinbrenner contacted Dick about my signing with the Yankees. Dick said that it would take a million a year, and George said that that would not be a problem. But I didn't even want to consider moving back to New York. Still, we had that offer to fall back on.

At one point I was called by an old friend from the Angels who wanted to know what it would take to get me to stay. I basically told him it would take Buzzie Bavasi's leaving. I didn't want to play for the man or be associated with him. In all fairness I have to say that later Buzzie admitted that letting me go was a big mistake.

When I found out that Houston had drafted me and wanted to talk to Dick about signing me, I told him to try hard to get it done. What could be better than playing for a team a half-hour away? I didn't want to get into a bidding war, as fun and exciting and ego-inflating as that might have been. Who knows what the numbers might have gotten up to? Dick told the Astros that if they could match the Yankees' offer, he was sure I would play for them. They did and I did. At a million a year for three years, I figured I would have financial security and be ready to settle in and finish out my career at home.

7

Astro-nomical Problems

I moved into a new decade with a new team, the one I had dreamed of playing for since I was a kid. Now my friends and relatives could see me pitch in person if they wanted to.

The Astros had been bought by a man named John McMullen in 1979, and when he made me the highest paid player in team sports up to that point, he bought himself some trouble. Many executives in the game criticized McMullen for reaching the million-dollar plateau. McMullen wasn't stingy, I'll give him that. He paid a lot for several players. Nowadays a million dollars a year doesn't sound like much, when you think of the guys making five times that and more. But you can imagine the heat I took for being the first to break the million-dollar barrier.

Even in Alvin people were concerned about it. They'd been awful proud of their local boy going off and becoming a big league pitching star. They were thrilled when I came back home and would be pitching just up the road. But a million dollars? For throwing a baseball? Something wasn't right. How could anybody be worth that? You've heard all the arguments, how little we pay teachers and how little we pay the president of the United States, how anybody making that kind of money will lose his incentive and won't ever work hard again.

The biggest problem for me was that people expected a guy being paid like that to be a better pitcher than he was. I had always done the best I could and felt I worked as hard as anybody in the game. I took care of my body, lived a clean life, had good habits, and worked out constantly. I didn't let myself go over the winter and then have to overdo it to get in shape during spring training. I did my part, pitched my innings, and stayed out of trouble. I was a strikeout pitcher, a low-hit pitcher, a workhorse with a lot of innings. I was a dependable starter who was a threat to throw a no-hitter. I was an all-star-caliber player, and I could usually win you a bunch of games a year. But if people thought that now that I was making a million dollars I ought to all of a sudden be perfect and unbeatable and win twenty-five games a year, I had a problem.

I felt conspicuous in Alvin where everybody seemed ill at ease around me. I guess they kept expecting me to splurge and buy a yacht or a mansion or a foreign sports car. It took a long time for them to see that my income was a private matter with me. The only reason I ever talked about it was because it was plastered all over the newspapers and people asked me about it. I was embarrassed over it, but I wasn't about to turn it down, and I doubt anybody I knew would have either.

I wanted to get the season started and see other players pass me up in salary. I knew that in a few years that million dollars would not loom so large, but it was hard to convince anybody of that back then. The people in Alvin would soon realize that I was still Nolan Ryan, local guy. The money wouldn't change me. The people in Houston who expected me to be a better pitcher than I was, well, I didn't know what to do about that. All I could say was that they should look at my record, see that I'd been averaging fifteen wins the last five years, despite lots of injuries and playing for a team that was not usually a big offensive threat. I didn't want to blame my record on anybody or put down my teammates; I just wanted people to be realistic about their expectations. I mean, when did it become a terrible thing for a guy to pitch more than two hundred innings in a season and win in double figures? That's what I felt capable of doing, and if John McMullen thought that was worth $3 million over three years, that's what I had to offer.

I know part of the money had to do with the market. He knew other teams were prepared to come to the table with offers like that and maybe more. But they all knew what they'd be getting too. Most pitchers in my category, fastballers with lots of innings behind them, were looking at the twilights of their careers at my age. I'm sure the Astros thought it would be great if I could go out with three decent years and maybe one or two more if I was healthy. That's even the way I was thinking.

I tried to stay quiet about the money because of how uncomfortable it seemed to make everybody, but down deep I was overwhelmed myself with how much I was making. From one season to the next I more than tripled my salary. I wanted to buy a ranch and acquire a few things I'd always dreamed of having, but none of it was going to be showy. That wouldn't have looked good and it wasn't me anyway. I didn't want to be any less frugal with a million dollars than I had been with $7,000 when I joined the Mets as a teenager.

My new tax bracket was 50 percent, so I started looking hard at how I could protect myself from handing that much over to the government. I was very conservative and felt like I had a reasonable investment game plan until we had a player strike in 1981. Then I would be in trouble.

Meanwhile there were some immediate benefits to coming to the Astros, besides the money. Dr. A. Eugene Coleman, a professor of human performance at the University of Houston, was the Astros' instructor of strength and conditioning. He had done a lot of research and worked with NASA's astronauts. I have to say that meeting up with him was a turning point in my career. Up to then I had been pretty much self-taught and self-motivated. I had done okay, but now here was a man who really knew what he was talking about. He was like an oasis in the desert. The Astros had more sophisticated Nautilus machines and plenty of them, and Gene walked me through how to use them for my entire body. He showed me what part of my workout was a waste of time and what I could add to enhance my routine. I was off and running, and some would say I have been obsessed with conditioning ever since. I was really into it before, but now with the confidence that everything I was doing had a purpose and would show a benefit, I immersed myself in it.

It took me a while to get used to the National League. The strike zone was different, and back spasms didn't help my conditioning. I got a rocky start and wound up 11–10, but we won the National League West in a one-game playoff over the Dodgers. They had swept us in the final three-game series to tie. We wound up losing in the playoffs to Philadelphia. Despite my mediocre start, I did pitch 234 innings, strike out 200, and pitch a couple of shutouts.

I started out much better in 1981, but that was the year of the players' strike that lasted fifty-two days. It was a depressing, frustrating time that nearly turned the fans off to the game. The league and the players had lost something like $100 million. I might as well have. If a person with my kind of income can have a cash-flow problem, I had one. I listened to some advisers about getting into some very speculative tax shelters. I was uncomfortable with them from the day I bought in until the day I paid heavily to get out.

What had happened was that I had made a large land purchase and—not anticipating being on strike for six weeks—planned to pay my taxes at the end of the year. Those six strike weeks meant no income out of what was normally a six-month pay-out period, so a huge chunk of income was gone. At the end of the year I didn't have the cash to cover my tax obligation, so instead of just going down to the bank and borrowing the money to pay the taxes and then paying off the note the next year, I listened to people who thought I could get out of the taxes through sheltered investments.

Some were oil investments. Some were cargo containers for ships. One was a thoroughbred breeding program. They solved my tax problem temporarily, and when the investments matured I was supposed to have enough cash to do everything I needed to do.

The oil investments soured when they struck only gas.

The cargo deal was eventually disallowed by the IRS.

And the horse market fell to where my thoroughbreds were worth forty cents on the dollar.

It was a good thing I knew how to pitch and was still healthy. I had nothing to show for the investments and still had the tax obligation. It was a tough pill, but I was fortunate to be able to play long enough to overcome those mistakes. A lot of baseball players who got into that situation were soon out of baseball and wound up having to declare bankruptcy.

I was never keen on investments just for their tax consequences. An investment should stand on its own two feet (or four in the case of the horses), and if it didn't make sense from an investment standpoint without the tax angle, I never should have made the moves. I have since paid off my land purchases and our home, and now I have assets free and clear that are important to me regardless of their value in a fluctuating economy. We enjoy what we have, and we can keep it in the family. But that was a hard lesson.

Now as a banker I hate the bankruptcy laws even more than I used to. All they provide is a giant loophole allowing people to run up a lot of debt and then throw up their hands and say, "Time out. King's X. I'm sorry, but I can't pay you and the law's going to protect me." That's not right. It's not fair to the creditors. The laws today are so slanted toward thieves that honest people aren't protected. They're designed to reward failure. It's like we want to do everything for the people that aren't successful. We pity them, but they brought it on themselves.

It's just like the savings and loan fiasco. I'm not sure most taxpayers understand that we're having to pay to let the same people who were the stewards of the S&Ls steal and run rampant. I mean, no one's even being prosecuted or forced to return money in any substantial amount. And then the Resolution Trust Corporation, which took all the properties that were foreclosed, began discounting them all and trying to move them, but there's something crazy going on. They're letting the same people who were in the S&L business come back and buy the loans they originally made on these properties and go out and resell them to other investors. They may double the loan and double their money. The whole thing is complex, and it's run by bureaucrats and is a total mess.

Some say we're not in a recession, but I don't believe that. I go out and talk to people about their businesses and try to stay in touch with the working person through my banks. I don't want to be just a figurehead banker. The people I work with are people I grew up with, and we care about the economy and the people it affects in our area. People who take advantage of all the loopholes are not honest. I look at it from a moral viewpoint. I don't care how much money there is to make, if it's not morally right, I'm not going to do it.

A lot of people say, "Hey, that's just business, and business is business." I've had people say that to me. That's one of the problems with our country. Our moral attitude has deteriorated to the point that it is affecting everything. People say that there are no absolutes and that everything's relative. I say it's wrong; they say it's business. That's a shaky foundation for the future.

Well, back to baseball. The Dodgers had been leading our division before the strike, and it was decided that a new short-ened season would begin right after the strike and the winners of the two halves would play for the pennants. That gave us new life, and we went after that second half in a big way.

On Saturday, September 26, 1981, I pitched against the Dodgers in Houston in a big game against their superstar rookie Fernando Valenzuela. We were fighting it out for first place in the second half, so the game was televised nationally. Ruth, my mother, and a lot of our friends were there. I started a little slow, walking three batters in the first three innings, but not giving up any hits. Twice during that season I had lost no-hitters in the seventh, and I was starting to think I no longer had the stamina to get that fifth no-hitter. I hadn't had one since I was twenty-eight years old, and now I was thirty-four. People may think that once you've pitched four, it's only a matter of time before another one comes along. Only thing is, they don't just come along. Everything has to be right. You have to be on. You have to get some breaks. There are usually a couple of key defensive plays. And there's always a little luck too.

What I began to notice, especially in long, tough games, was how difficult those last three innings were. It wasn't about just hanging on. To stay on top of hitters who've had a couple or three plate appearances to study you, you have to have some extra pop, something special. You have to get stronger as the game goes on, and that goes against logic.

Against the Dodgers I went into the ninth inning with a 5–0 lead and had retired sixteen hitters in a row. I added Reggie Smith, Ken Landreaux, and Dusty Baker in the ninth, and I had set the career no-hit record. I was glad my teammates were so excited about it. They carried me off the field and really seemed thrilled to have been part of history. One of the first phone calls I took after the game was from Gene Autry. I always appreciated that he had no hard feelings for my leaving California. We remained friends and he was always gracious about my achievements.

Best of all, we were still in the pennant race. We wanted another shot at the Dodgers to see if we could get into the play-offs and the World Series.

8

No Longer at Home in the Dome

We wound up winning the second half of the strike-shortened 1981 season and facing the Dodgers in a five-game playoff for the Western Division championship. I was the winning pitcher, 3–1, in the first game, again against Fernando, and we won the second too. But we were snake bit by the Dodgers. I guess we couldn't forget that they had won three straight at the end of the 1980 season to force us into that one-game playoff, and somehow we let them do that again. Only this time, it was three straight losses and we were out. We had come so close.

What a season that had been. There was a lot of dissension and uncertainty because of the strike, and worst of all it seemed we had offended the people who made the game possible—the fans. Some of us wondered if they would ever support us like they used to. But people are forgiving, even when they don't understand you. The truth is, they love the game more than any individual player.

I had had a good season, short as it was. I led the National League in earned run average with a 1.69, and I had gone 11–5. The next year, 1982, even though the Astros were out of the pennant race early, I went 16–12, started thirty-five games, completed ten, had three shutouts, pitched a one-hitter and a two-hitter, and struck out 245 in 250 innings. I wound up the year fifteen short of Walter Johnson's career strikeout record.

Because of minor injuries and illness, I pitched only eighteen innings in spring training in 1983 and didn't break Johnson's record until my fourth start of the year, in Montreal. For some reason that record meant as much to me as my five no-hitters. I had accomplished it in twenty-five hundred fewer innings than Johnson. I had no idea if I would keep the record, because two or three others were within striking distance (pardon the pun). Of course by now I've outlasted them all and most people think I've put the record far out of reach at more than five thousand.

Something that really disappointed me was that our owner, Mr. McMullen, was neither at the game nor called to congratulate me. By the time I got to that game, I only needed five strikeouts. The record came in the eighth inning, and I got a huge ovation from the crowd, but neither my owner nor the commissioner of baseball was there, and I never did hear from McMullen. I even heard from Gene Autry, but not from my own team's owner. The press sure made a big deal out of the record, but I never did figure out why it didn't seem that important to the man who was paying me all that money to do just what I had done.

I had been in Houston for three seasons, and that was long enough to see that things weren't quite right. I sure couldn't complain about my salary, but most people realize that big leaguers would play ball for nothing if they had to. They need to be treated with respect and dignity, and it's the little things that count the most. I'm sure it sounds petty and maybe amazing when you hear that multimillion-dollar athletes complain about not enough soap in the shower room or not enough food on the snack table. Maybe we get upset about our wives not getting invited on certain trips or that some other little thing has gone wrong. But those things are signals to players of whether they're appreciated as people. Sure, the money is great, but we all know the owners hate to pay the way they do and that that's all part of the business. The little personal things make a man feel as if someone cares about him. They cost so little and mean so much that you wonder why someone doesn't pay attention to them.

I won't apologize for how much of myself I gave to Houston during my nine years there. I worked hard and produced, and I was willing to give whatever it took to be as effective as possible. But it didn't seem to me the ball club was promoted the right way to the community. The owner didn't do what he really needed to do to make people feel welcome at the ballpark, to get all the employees happy and cheerful and greeting the paying customers. Basically I guess he was not a happy man, and that filtered down through the organization. It seemed he resented one of the limited partners, a man named Don Sanders, who was a local guy and very popular with us players. Don spent a lot of time in the clubhouse and had us over to his place, and I think John McMullen was jealous of his popularity. Don was a baseball fan and brought his kids around. He was one of the big sponsors of my golf tournament, and we became friends and often went out together. He even came on some road trips. Eventually McMullen barred outsiders from the clubhouse, including, if you can believe this, Sanders and the other limited partners. I think McMullen envied Sanders' friendships with the players, but John couldn't become friends with us when we only saw him two or three times a year. He was an absentee owner and still is, as far as I know.

McMullen didn't promote me the way he might have either, and I don't say that because I wanted the ego strokes of being played up as a star. We had plenty of stars. But when a guy is setting records or achieving outstanding numbers, it seems you'd just naturally start publicizing that to build interest so that more people would come out the next time the guy pitches. That's just good business.

But I didn't jump when McMullen said jump. I never attended his golf outings after the season, mostly because of time pressures and because, even though I host my own tournament for charity every year, I'm not really an avid golfer. John's deal was up at Pine Valley and involved four or five days in October. That's not my idea of a good time or the right use of family time. I'm sure he saw my absence as an independent attitude. He never told me that, but it filtered down.

Another thing I could never figure out about McMullen was that after Enos Cabell was traded away from Houston, John started talking about him as if he and John had been close friends. I knew Enos was about as opposite from John as a guy could be, and I felt that Enos used John's friendship to benefit Enos. John had gone to the Naval Academy, was educated in Europe, earned a doctorate, retired from the Navy, and owned a ship-building business. Enos was from Los Angeles and had a drug problem when he was in Pittsburgh, but somehow he and John had become buddies?

McMullen even told me that after Enos was traded to the Dodgers he would invite John out for dinner when he came to town. "None of you guys ever did that," he said. I didn't know a player was supposed to call the owner and invite him out to eat. I'm sure he felt I didn't appreciate him bringing me to Houston, but I did. I'd be crazy not to be glad about getting back home and making that kind of money. But maybe he took as much heat as I did over the size of the deal and eventually regretted it, I don't know.

I was my own person, and I had to decide if something was worthwhile or not. I felt like his attitude was that we were employees, he owned us and expected us to exhibit the attitudes and traits of employees. I'm a loyal person to the organization, but I also felt there was another principle involved. There's a limit to a man's obligation. I was paid to win ball games, and I didn't shirk at all when it came to things that contributed to that.

I know I have to be loyal and make a commitment because I'm accepting a salary. I always want to give an honest and fair effort, but it's also important that the ball club take that same attitude toward the players. Do they respect us and appreciate us, or are we supposed to act like servants? A lot of times ballplayers don't hold up their end of the obligation. They don't consistently work out or stay in shape or take care of themselves with proper diet and rest and conditioning. But a lot of times the ball clubs take an approach that's detrimental too, even to those of us who do give our all to the team.

When it feels like it's front office against the clubhouse and clubhouse against the front office, there's always friction. And those clubs don't win. The only time I ever saw a team win in spite of disagreements between the players and the owner was in the early '70s when the Oakland A's won three World Series in a row, even though it seemed they couldn't stand Charlie Finley, their owner. Those guys didn't seem to care for each other either, but they sure put all that behind them when they went onto the field.

The Astros were going south. We fell in the standings, and our attendance dropped off. The team had mediocre years and sometimes drew crowds that rattled around in that big dome. We had a couple of games where we drew less than four thousand. That's demoralizing, and it's ridiculous. You can't tell me there isn't a way to drum up more interest than that, even in a team that's going badly. Look what the Mets did when they started out. That was one bad team, but they were beloved and drew huge crowds. And look how the Cubs have done over the years. They've had some good teams in the last couple of decades, but they haven't won a pennant in nearly fifty years, yet they keep drawing the fans. They're doing something right in their community, and they know how to promote.

In 1985, just before the All-Star break, I was closing in on four thousand strikeouts. You would think a team would know how to build support for something like that. I was nearly five hundred past the old record and would be the first in history to reach four thousand, but the Astros didn't even have a team photographer in the dome that night. Danny Heep of the Mets, a former teammate on the Astros, became my four thousandth K, and the only picture taken of it was by a friend of some of the players. He sold many a copy of that picture.

At the All-Star game Pete Rose and I were chosen to throw out the first pitches because he had reached four thousand hits and I had reached four thousand strikeouts. That was a real honor, but I have to say it felt strange to be recognized nationally by baseball itself when in Houston the event sort of came and went unnoticed. It wasn't like the record was something that crept up on the team. Everybody else seemed to know it was on the horizon.

Experts predicted the struggling Astros would lose a hundred games in 1986, but they didn't know Mike Scott would win the Cy Young Award for us. They didn't know power-hitting first baseman Glenn Davis would have an All-Star year and hit thirty-one homers. They didn't know Kevin Bass would be outstanding at the plate. And they sure didn't expect an aging pitcher like me to return to form, go 12–8, start thirty games, and strike out 194 in 178 innings. We won the division going away but lost a heartbreaking championship series to the hated Mets. I had been on the disabled list twice, but I came back strong both times.

I was not happy with our new general manager, Dick Wagner, who once put me on the DL without even consulting me. I was in my twentieth big league season and was closing in on my fortieth birthday, and he thought he knew what was best for me. Even though I was 5–1 in my last ten starts with a 2.31 ERA, winning my last four decisions to reach 253 career wins (sixth among active pitchers at the time), I was in for a shock in 1987.

I started the season without pain and threw about 135 pitches per game for a couple of games. Then I got the news that Wagner had told my manager, Hal Lanier, that I was to come out of a game after 115 pitches, no questions asked. I was mad and fought the decision, but nothing changed. It didn't make any difference that I was no longer pitching with pain, and it wouldn't have made any difference if I had had a no-hitter going, I guess. Once I pitched my limit, I was gone. I lost a lot of decisions when the club lost the lead. Ironically, my strikeouts were up, my walks were down, and I had Cy Young-type statistics except for my horrible won-lost record. The limit was expanded to 125 pitches late in the season, but I wound up 8–16. I had led the league in ERA (2.76) and strikeouts (270).

It was almost funny to be under a pitch limit and still lead the league in K's for the first time in eight years and ring up my highest total in ten seasons. I had walked only eighty-seven hitters and suddenly I was known as a control pitcher. Maybe Dick Wagner would like to take credit for extending my career, but somehow I think I could have completed a lot of games without hurting myself. I mean, I was a forty-year-old strikeout king with a fastball that could still get into the high nineties. I had broken a big league record by averaging 11.48 strikeouts per nine innings.

I was still making the same money I had signed for going into the 1980 season, and that was fine with me. Many players had passed me up salarywise, but I felt there were a lot of benefits to pitching close to home and seeing my family grow up. Maybe I was worth twice as much or more on the free-agent market, but it wouldn't have been worth it to me to uproot. I knew I had to kiss the hope of another no-hitter good-bye because of that crazy pitch limit, but I figured another no-hitter at my age was an impossible dream anyway. It had been six years between numbers four and five, and I was about to go into my seventh season since *then*. It was miraculous enough that I could still throw hard.

Dick Wagner was fired after the season, to be replaced as general manager by Bill Wood. I knew there would be little change in how the club was run because McMullen was still the owner. There were a lot of advantages to playing in Houston. My million-dollar-a-year contract had been renewed every season, and I looked forward to 1988 as maybe my last year in baseball. It wasn't, but it would be my last in Houston.

9

Moving On

*I*n 1988 I got out from under the pitch limit and led the National League in strikeouts. I also pitched two complete games in a row without a walk, the first time I had ever done that. I only allowed four earned runs over my last forty-one innings and felt as strong as I had in years. Early in the season, April 27, I took Philadelphia into the ninth with a no-hitter before Mike Schmidt broke it up with a one-out single. It was the third straight time I had a ninth inning no-hitter broken up with one out.

Frankly I couldn't believe I had flirted with a no-hitter for that long. I'd gone a lot of innings without allowing hits before, but to go into the ninth again was like going back in time. That was the first time I had gone into the ninth with a no-hitter since my fifth in September 1981.

I also finished 1988 with 4,775 strikeouts, so unless I had a serious injury I had a decent shot at hitting five thousand in 1989. All I needed to do was to get close to 1988's K production. I would have thought that alone would have been enough reason for the Astros to want to keep me happy and keep me around. But my contract had expired and I waited to see what they wanted to do about extending it. I would have been perfectly content to go another year at slightly more than a million dollars. Again, no raise for nine years was not an issue with me because of the benefits that outweighed everything else.

I had never been a free agent or taken a hard stand because it was so convenient for me to be able to maintain one household the whole year round. Now I was at a point where I figured I had one more season in me, and I assumed that was what the Astros thought too.

It had been a long time since I had been the highest paid player in the game, but I didn't get wrapped up in those kinds of numbers. My situation was unique, but there were storm clouds. I still wasn't jumping when McMullen said jump, and I sensed the attitude of management toward the players had gotten worse.

It seemed like the club didn't want kids around. For several years, when Al Rosen was the GM, the players' kids had a lot of freedom, but now they were not allowed in the clubhouse before or after the game. They weren't ever allowed on the field, and most of them had gotten to the age where they didn't want to go to the Astrodome and sit around in the stands waiting for the game to start. There were few benefits to being a player's kid anymore. There had never been favoritism to my kids versus anybody else's. They were all in it together and everybody suffered. I always said it was kinda like prison. We were allowed family visits for an hour on Sundays and that was it. I don't care how much you're paying a ballplayer, when you treat him and his family like that, you're sending a loud message.

My kids didn't even want to come around on Sundays because they felt they weren't wanted, and they were right. The rest of the staff at the Astrodome felt the same way. You could tell that people just weren't having any fun at their jobs, and that always shows. Everybody from the ushers to the concessions people to the front office staff seemed to be looking over their shoulders, trying to stay out of trouble. That's no way to build a family or have team spirit.

A few days after the end of the season Bill Wood asked me to come in and talk about my contract for the next year. They didn't have an option, so I had wondered what was going to happen. I told my agent, Dick Moss, that I would just go in alone and see what was up. Dick and I talked about what I should try to accomplish and my attitude was I would see what the club position was and bring him in when it got down to details.

"Nolan," Bill said in his office, "we want to offer you a contract for '89, and we'd like you to consider taking a 20 percent cut from your present level." I stared at him, expressionless and speechless. He couldn't be serious. "You've had a remarkable career and accomplished a lot, but at 12–11 and with your performance not quite what it's been, well, we can maybe put in a few incentives so that if you return to form you can make about what you're making now."

"Bill," I said, "I finished strong and everybody knows it. There's no doubt I can still pitch effectively. I've always been honest and fair with this club, and if I get into a position where I don't think I'm worth what I'm making, I'll let you know."

I could tell from the look on Bill's face that *he* was letting *me* know. I quickly realized what was going on. I had been so grateful for the situation for the last several years and had said how pleased I was that I had such a good setup, that they thought I would never leave. Here's a middle-aged man finishing out a lucrative career, pitching virtually in his own backyard, so he'll take a cut in pay without a word. What they hadn't thought of was that I wasn't just hanging on. I was pitching as well as I ever had. I may have lost a couple of miles an hour off my fastball, but Gene Coleman had told me himself that only 7 percent of the pitchers in the big leagues could throw a ball ninety miles an hour. I was still throwing a lot harder than that.

If I had felt like my body was falling apart and that I would be lucky to last another season, I wouldn't have stayed just to milk another year out of them. That would have been dishonest and unfair. I would have retired and not taken their money under false pretenses. To think I would agree to a cut was an insult. The more I sat there, the worse I felt. Here was an organization, crying about keeping costs down and insulting their players to do it. They figured if they could get me to take a cut that would take the wind out of the sails of anyone else who came in with demands. I hadn't even made a demand. I figured they'd offer me the same deal I'd had, and I would have been inclined to take it.

I tried to stress to Bill that the Angels had made the same mistake. Buzzie Bavasi thought I would stay because of my friendship with Gene Autry, but there comes a time when a man can't be party to someone else's trying to prove a point. If the Astros were trying to keep salaries down by starting with me, well, that only fit in with all the other ways they were treating employees. I could see the direction things were going, and I knew nothing was going to get better. The club had developed a petty, negative attitude about everything. Maybe a $200,000 cut in pay shouldn't be considered petty, but it was indicative of their attitude about everything. Insulting one of your starting pitchers is no way to go about making yourself a contender and a winner.

I knew it wasn't Bill Wood's fault. It was McMullen's move, and Bill was only doing what he was told. Still I told Bill, "I won't accept that. There's no way I could agree. You know I'm going to have to test the market and see what's out there." Leaving Bill's office that day, I knew that Houston was no longer the type of an organization I wanted to be associated with. I'm sure he and even McMullen were thinking, *Sure, go ahead and go through the motions of free agency. Play the game and see what happens.*

Baseball had a system then where all the clubs could call in and find out what the current offers were to free agents, so there would be no secrets. The Astros had to be thinking there wouldn't be much interest in what they thought was an overpriced, overage pitcher. I was convinced they were certain I'd be back to accept their deal. If nothing else had materialized, I really don't know what I would have done. I like to think I'd have had too much pride to take a cut at that stage of my career. It came down to principle. What would that have said about my self-image, especially after I had stayed at the same salary for almost a decade?

I had come to Houston to finish my career. I had even had an interest in staying involved with the organization after my career was over. Now I could see it all sliding away. Nobody takes a 20 percent cut. Who was the last guy you ever heard of who stood still for that? It was absurd, but the Astros took that position and sat on it for quite a while.

I called Dick Moss at his office in Los Angeles and told him what Wood had said. He was more incensed than I was. I have a tendency to low-key those kinds of things. My attitude was that now that we knew where they stood, we could go about our business. Dick was insulted for me and quickly prepared to file for free agency. "You're going to be amazed what we can do," he said.

As soon as word got around that I was testing the market, we heard from the Angels. Gene Autry had wanted me back for years, and now he saw his chance. He made it clear that money would be no object. He would pay what he had to and beat any other offer. Meanwhile the Astros were still trying to get together with me, but they weren't budging from their insulting offer. They just wanted to get it done and announce it so they could move on. They didn't imagine that I would be the one moving on.

I knew something would break at the winter baseball meetings in Atlanta, and, frankly, Ruth and I thought we would be going back to California. That wouldn't have been all that bad, because it's nice to feel wanted, and Gene Autry was a good person to work for. Though they had never won a

World Series, the Angels organization had a winning attitude. I didn't like the idea of moving my family halfway across the country for the better part of a year, but I didn't see any other choice. If I'd done what I wanted to, I'd have stayed with the Astros. But with the Angels' offer on the table, the Astros would have had to more than double theirs to match the Angels. It would have taken an awfully huge number to get me to say that bygones would be bygones after the way I felt I had been treated.

The kids got excited about the possibility of living in southern California, but to tell you the truth, if they had said they'd rather I retire and spend more time with them, I would have. I knew I had at least another year in me, but I'd had a lot of great years and would have been happy to quit. It wouldn't have been easy and I would have missed baseball, but what my family wants is more important to me than any personal goals. The kids loved the life baseball offered us, though, and they didn't want me to give it up. I wasn't wild about moving, but I became willing.

It was no easy decision, because my mother, who lived alone nearby, was getting up in age and I felt responsible for her. I took it upon myself to make sure everything was right with her and I took care of any needs she had. Though she was not as mobile as she used to be, she did make it to a lot of my home games because we were so close. She had trouble with her feet, but Ruth could drive her right up to one of the entrances to the Astrodome. Being indoors at a constant temperature was a big help to her. She didn't have to do a lot of walking and was in comfortable surroundings. I knew this move of mine would mean the end of that too.

She was proud of me, but whenever reporters asked her about that she was quick to say she had six kids and was proud of every one of them. She was a special lady. I would see her at least once and usually twice a week when I was home, just to sit and spend an hour or so with her. We'd often take her to lunch and get caught up on things. Our kids had a special relationship with her because when they were sick she wanted them at her place where she would wait on them hand and foot. If they ever got sick at school, they'd call her first and wind up over there. We had planned a big Thanksgiving 1988 bash at the ranch with my sisters, my brother, my mother, and about thirty other relatives.

The Astros heard that other teams might be interested in me, so Bill Wood called and said McMullen wanted a meeting on Wednesday before Thanksgiving. John was going to be in Houston. I told him the timing was bad and that I just couldn't come to Houston with our plans to be at the ranch. Later Bill called back and insisted that we all get together. I told him I didn't think it was that urgent and that the only reason John wanted it then was for his own convenience. Bill called me again and said McMullen would come to the ranch to make it easier for me. We figured out where he could fly into and where we could meet and all that, but the more I thought about it the more irritated I was. I called Bill about a week before Thanksgiving and told him I just didn't want to have them coming to the ranch with all my relatives there because it was a family and a social thing and I didn't want to have to contend with business at that time.

Later Bill would say that I had missed meetings and lied to him, but it just wasn't true. The only thing I had done wrong was to temporarily agree to the meeting in the first place. Finally deciding to refuse to have it at that time and at that place was the right thing to do. I wasn't bargaining, negotiating, or playing hard to get. I wasn't even making them pay for their insulting offer, which they still weren't budging from. It was just bad timing, and I should never have even considered it to begin with.

As the winter meetings approached (they would be the first week of December), I realized that this was a time I should be enjoying. But agonizing over leaving the Astros, maybe moving, not knowing what to do or how to sort it out really got to me. It was a pressure-filled time for me and Ruth and the family, and I just wanted to make a decision and get it over with. It should be a real emotional high to be pursued by four major league teams (San Francisco and Texas had indicated some interest in addition to California and Houston), but I was much too realistic to think I should get too excited.

We had a good time at Thanksgiving until my sister and my mother were pulling out of the ranch and had a bad auto accident. My mother was buckled in, but the impact bruised her chest and ribs and even her heart. She was admitted into the hospital in Alvin, but for about a week she didn't seem to be getting any better. I called the doctor and said, "Look, I want you to meet me at the hospital, because I've been here every day and I can see that something's wrong. Her condition is getting worse, and we've got to do something about it."

He came right out, and when I repeated that I wasn't happy with what I was seeing, he examined her and said, "I think you're right." He transferred her to Methodist Hospital in Houston where specialists took over. I had just returned home about eleven o'clock that night when the heart specialist called to tell me he had found an accumulation of fluid around her heart. He wanted permission to do an MRI and then immediate surgery if necessary. I told him to go ahead. The doctor had told me the procedure wasn't painful, but it would take about forty-five minutes. I've had an MRI, and I knew if Mother was not claustrophobic going in, she sure would be coming out.

By the time I got there, Mother was in what I call the torture chamber, where the image reader is close to your face, and she was giving the staff fits. Fortunately they didn't find what they thought they were going to find, and she didn't need surgery. She came out of the hospital after several weeks, having had just about every test you can have. She got a clean bill of health, though she had been slowed down a good bit and took a while recovering completely.

She had always feared cancer, because my dad had died of that, so all the tests put her mind at ease. She was still a very independent person and insisted on going back to live in the house she raised me in, driving her own car, and taking care of herself.

One day while I was in Houston visiting with her doctor about some tests, Bill Wood called and asked for a one o'clock meeting at the dome. I figured I could do that, but then I got hung up at the hospital. I called him to apologize and say that I was just not going to be able to make it. He sounded as if he understood and said it was fine, but I found out later that he had already scheduled a press conference for 1:30. He had planned to tell me that the Astros were not going to offer me arbitration, so I could either take their offer or leave it. If I left it and if I didn't sign with them by January 22, the rules wouldn't allow me to come back to them until the middle of May. They were so sure I would buckle under that pressure that they were ready to announce my signing, or my losing out on arbitration, that same day.

It was a power play I had foiled without even knowing it.

Right about that time the Texas Rangers' general manager, Tom Grieve, contacted Dick Moss. Tom told me later that he was just testing the waters because he believed, like everyone else in baseball, that Houston was just doing some creative negotiating and would never let me get away. "There are no guarantees," Dick told him.

When I heard the Rangers had asked about me, it changed the picture completely. Ruth and I had been sure we were headed back to the Angels and a nice offer from Gene Autry. But that big league data bank everybody had access to was going to keep even Gene's offer as low as possible, because all he had to do was beat the next best offer by a hundred thousand dollars. That was just like collusion and doesn't exist anymore, but everybody was checking the data bank back then.

Ruth and I decided that if Texas was really interested, we had to be too. It wasn't as close and convenient as Houston, but we wouldn't have to move, we wouldn't have to buy or rent in California, and we wouldn't have to switch the kids' schools. I told Dick to keep Texas warm. He was to simply tell Grieve, "Nolan has a great deal of interest in Texas."

The Rangers were an up-and-coming club with a lot of potential, but their attendance was declining and they had had some rough years. Grieve said he knew that if they could actually sign someone like me, people would know they were serious about winning. He thought it was a long shot, but he and manager Bobby Valentine got excited about the possibilities.

The Giants, the Rangers, and the Angels were talking salary figures in the $1.5–1.8 million range. I was looking for one year, but some were offering two, which was even better. The Angels would have gone $1.8 million for one year, plus incentives. The Astros finally saw the handwriting on the wall and backed away from insisting on my taking a cut. Now they were back up to my original million-a-year base with another $300,000 or so in incentives. I could have told them right then that they weren't even close, but I didn't. They would have to be at least in the same range as the other offers, and then we'd see how much difference their location and its convenience meant to me.

Dick Moss had also heard from the Japanese, and that started me thinking. I only wanted a one-year deal, and for the right price—as long as I was likely going to have to uproot my family anyway—I might be tempted to pitch overseas. I would take the whole family. It would be for only about seven months, and it would be a good educational experience for them. I told Dick to tell the Japanese that for the right offer, I'd make the commitment.

10

Another New Start

*S*everal representatives from Japanese teams were in the United States to go to the winter meetings in Atlanta, so Dick arranged for the team that showed interest in me—the Tokyo Swallows—to come to Alvin and meet the family and talk details. Dick and I picked them up at the airport, and we had quite a meeting over a Texas-style meal Ruth prepared at our home. The Swallows' general manager spoke no English, so their U.S. representative interpreted.

The kids were real uptight about this, because Japan sounded like another planet to them, and they didn't want to have anything to do with it. The Swallows' U.S. representative seemed to be able to tell the kids were skeptical, so he tried to sell them.

"You know you'd be going to an international school with kids from other countries," he said. "I went to that school and there are lots of students whose parents work in the embassies. You might be sitting next to an American on one side and a Russian on the other."

Reese said, "Russians! I'm not going to school with any Russians!"

The kids asked him about Sumo wrestlers and Ninjas and stuff like that. Meanwhile, Dick and I told the Swallows that their offer of $2 million for one season was half where it needed to be. We told the GM that if he could see his way clear to offer $4 million, I would make the commitment right then and we wouldn't negotiate with the U.S. teams.

While their representative translated very seriously to the GM, we watched their faces for clues. It didn't appear to be a major problem, though they both looked thoughtful. Finally the GM spoke quickly and the rep translated.

"In all honesty, the money is not an issue." For a split second, I thought I was going to Japan. "We'd be willing to pay that, but we do have a problem. We have an understanding with the commissioner of baseball that if a U.S. major league club is interested in a free agent, we're not allowed to offer more than the U.S. club."

Dick and I looked at each other. That was collusion pure and simple and on an international scale. We knew then we were dead in the water. No U.S. club was going to give me $4 million, and if they did, I would have taken it. There was no sense going halfway around the world for the same money I could make here.

We thanked them for coming and making the effort, but they didn't give up. They told me they could match the top offer and virtually guarantee that I would make up the difference in endorsements in Japan.

"Guaranteed?" Dick said.

"Well, if he does well. If he gets hurt or gets off to a bad start, no."

That was no guarantee, and I wouldn't have expected one. Still, I had found the meeting interesting and appreciated their regard for me.

When Dick and I flew to Atlanta a few days later, I was still in agony. I was leaning toward the Texas Rangers, but I worried about pitching outdoors in the heat and humidity at my age. The dome had been perfect for me. Pitching half my games in perfect weather with a big outfield is a pitcher's dream. The other difficult part was that I had personal friendships on every team that was interested. On the one hand, there's a wonderful feeling in knowing that big league baseball franchises are bidding for your services. But, on the other, I couldn't imagine turning any of them down. Mr. Autry had already gone on record that he would top any offer, so if I didn't go with the Angels, I would be settling for less than I could have made. And how do you tell someone you don't want the highest figure?

No matter where I went, unless the Astros surprised us with a huge new deal, I was going to be uprooted from the ball club I had been on for so many years, have to get used to a new bunch of guys and coaches and fans, and get comfortable in a new clubhouse and on a new mound. I'd been treated so well by the fans in Houston that I was distraught over leaving them, and I knew they wouldn't understand. It was going to look like I was just leaving for the money. In a way I was, of course, but it was only because the money represented something. It represented how the Astro ownership felt about me. They hadn't tried to cut my pay just as a bargaining ploy. They were serious. They meant it, and they expected me to take it. But if I was going only for the money, I would have gone to the Angels. Then the fans could have criticized me all they wanted, and they would have been justified.

The decision dominated Ruth's and my thoughts day and night for weeks, especially the two weeks before going to Atlanta. Between us we had pretty much decided that all things being equal, we would lean toward the Rangers for the sake of the family. The Astros could still surprise us and turn our heads, but we just didn't see that happening. Too much had transpired. You never know what's going to happen, though, in the heat of battle, so though Ruth thought she knew what I'd do, she wouldn't have been surprised if I'd called with some other deal out of the blue. People who haven't been through it don't realize that this type of a decision is as unsettling for a big leaguer as it is for any man making a major career move.

Dick and I checked into a room in Atlanta and contacted the four interested clubs. I felt I owed it to all of them to make my decision there so they could know what to do about their other trading needs. Lots of dominoes are in place when you sign an expensive player, and if that money is freed up, there are a lot of other things you can do. The Rangers, for instance, had a lot of pitching needs, so what I did would determine what else they had to do at the meetings.

I asked Dick to start with the Astros, because this was going to be a process of elimination. In my mind they were basically already out of the picture, but officially I was still with them and willing to stay if things could be worked out. From strictly a convenience standpoint, that would have been even better than going with the Rangers. But first they were going to have to substantially increase their offer. If we could have worked something out, I would have immediately told the other clubs so they wouldn't have been misled. I made it clear to everyone from the beginning that it wasn't just about running up the numbers and that I wasn't trying to play games. I wanted square dealings, and while both Dick and I were rightly upset about the fact that each knew what the others were offering, we wanted to be aboveboard anyway.

Bill Wood and John McMullen came to our room, and I told them that even though I wasn't happy with how they'd treated me recently, I wasn't one to hold a grudge and was willing to listen to a serious offer. Then and only then did they significantly raise their offer, but it was still a long way from where the other clubs were. I could tell they thought I'd still want to stay. They were banking on it.

I told them they were too far from what I could get somewhere else. John McMullen said, "Nolan, the Houston Astro organization has an obligation to Mike Scott. We can't pay you more than we're paying him, and he's already under contract. We're not willing to go back and renegotiate with him because of what we do with you."

It sounded to me like they had guaranteed Mike he'd be the highest paid player on the team, which was fine. What another guy can get for himself is none of my concern, unless it keeps me from being where I feel I need to be. If Mike Scott made twice as much as me, that would have been all right, as long as I felt I got what I was deserving. I said, "John, if that's your offer, I'm going to tell you now that we're not going to sign with you and that we will sign within the next day or two with another organization."

I also told him I appreciated him bringing me to Houston and that I'd had a great time there. There were no hard feelings on my part, and though the Astros later started answering the criticism for letting me get away by saying that I had misled them and missed meetings, that day in Atlanta I thought we were okay on a personal basis. I only wish that when a guy makes a mistake he would admit it and not try to cover himself by spreading stories about the other person.

We followed with a meeting with the Giants. Al Rosen and his assistant offered pretty much the same deal as the Angels and the Rangers had talked about, but they made it two years guaranteed. That was a good effort and a generous approach, and I appreciated it. Dick and I asked a lot of questions, and we felt good about their interest, but I think they left knowing I was leaning toward either staying closer to home or taking the Angels up on their offer to top any other deal. I didn't tell them no on the spot, but I felt sure they knew.

Then we asked the Rangers to come over. General Manager Tom Grieve, Manager Bobby Valentine (who had been a younger teammate of mine with the Angels), and Mike Stone (the president of the club at the time) visited us and formalized their best offer. It was right in there with the Giants offer, but rather than two years guaranteed, it called for one year and an option on a second. I told them that if I signed I wouldn't have a problem with the option clause, although privately I doubted I would pitch more than one more year. In a way I liked the option idea better than a guarantee, because then I wouldn't feel obligated. This way, if I was going well and felt good, they would want me back and I wouldn't feel like I was holding a gun to their heads.

We talked quite a while, and I raised all my questions about climatizing and changing clubs and all that. They were sympathetic and encouraging, but they didn't try to fool me. I also appreciated that they didn't glad-hand me and try to hard-sell me. They had enough respect for me to know that I would make up my own mind and make as rational a decision as I could. I don't think I hid my discomfort. This was not as enjoyable a process as it might have been for a young man with no clue as to the complications.

I don't know how those guys felt when they left our room. I had made it pretty clear that I wanted to stay in Texas, and I think they knew Houston wasn't knocking the door down. But I'm also sure they still thought it was a long shot because of my doubts about the weather. They also knew, of course, like everybody else did, that Gene Autry did not want to be denied. If it was about money, they knew nobody had a chance against the Angels.

As the Rangers left us, we told them we'd get back to them. I didn't tell them my mind was pretty much made up.

Since the Angels were the first club to show an interest in me that fall and Gene Autry had always been a great owner and a good friend, I felt I owed it to him and to protocol to meet with him and his people in his suite. He was there with his man Mike Port, and we sat around talking about his club for the longest time. They said nothing about their offer, but unless they doubled it or something, it wasn't going to be a surprise to us. I was thinking how hard it was going to be to tell him that I was leaning toward Texas.

Gene's wife Jackie came in and greeted me warmly, then said something that made my decision as final as it could be. She said, "Nolan you just have to sign with the Angels and win us a World Series."

I know she meant well, and that's the kind of confidence that makes a lot of athletes feel wanted and needed. But I also knew the Angel organization. They were farther from a World Series than one strikeout pitcher who might win them a dozen or fifteen games. I mean, in one way I was flattered to know that she thought I could make the difference, but I also knew she was wrong. If they'd had the hitting and the other starters and the bullpen, she might have been right. They weren't bad, but they weren't in a position where I was the one missing ingredient. I knew then that even if they could have turned my head with a great offer, I would be a disappointment to them if we did anything but win the World Series.

They didn't finalize their offer during the time we spoke. Mike asked if he could speak with the Autrys alone and then come and make a final proposal in our room. We agreed and went to wait for him. The offer was a good one, clearly the best of the bunch, but by then I felt more confident of my decision. I didn't have much more peace about it, and there were still a lot of unknowns, but I had decided. When he finally left our room, without our answer, it was about one o'clock in the morning.

Dick wanted me to go to California. He thought it would be great to return there, to take the great offer, and to finish my career with a bang. He pushed as hard as was appropriate, but I explained that Ruth and I really wanted to stay in Texas. "Neither of the California deals would be right, 'cause it's not gonna work for the family."

He said, "You've got to do what you've got to do."

The next morning, after a final talk with Ruth on the phone, I told Dick I'd decided on Texas and we invited them over.

"Money was not the determining factor," I told Stone, Grieve, and Valentine. "I'm a die-hard Texan, so if we can hammer out a few details, I want to stay in Texas." I told them some of my conditions, and they met alone in the other room. When they came out we shook hands and we had a deal. They acted happy, but I only found out later that when they left, Bobby jumped and clicked his heels.

We had already made clear to the Astros that they were out of the picture. I called Al Rosen and told him I appreciated the Giants' interest in me but that I had just signed with the Rangers. He was great. He said he understood and wished me the best.

I tried to get hold of Gene, but he was in a meeting. The Rangers wanted to announce the signing. I didn't want Gene to find out that way, but I had a plane to catch. We told Mike Port what the deal was, and he agreed to pass it on. Dick said he would also get to Gene and explain, and I talked to Gene later on the phone too. He was fine. In fact, he was not as disappointed as I thought he might me. I'm sure in his mind he had made an honest effort, and it didn't work out. He understood my reasoning and accepted it. I'd really like to see Gene get his World Series. Lord knows nobody has pumped more money and effort into a situation and gotten less out of it.

I was glad the decision had been made, but I still had a lot of apprehension about going up to play in Arlington. I was switching leagues again and would have to learn the new strike zone and all the hitters, not to mention my teammates and the fans. Would they accept me or resent me? Would they expect too much? Would they think, like Mrs. Autry did, that I was going to win them a World Series?

I wanted to tell people not to expect miracles. They might look forward to my five-thousand-strikeout milestone and maybe fifteen or so wins, but I didn't want them to expect me to be an even better pitcher than I was. I figured I had a good year left in me. I would be forty-two years old by the time the season started, and I would give it all I had, just like I always do. I couldn't give them more than that, and I hoped I wouldn't disappoint them.

Lynn Nolan Ryan, Jr., eight years old.

Lynn Nolan Ryan, Jr.,
16 years old.

Nolan and Ruth dating in 1966.

Nolan and Ruth on first Nolan Ryan Day in Alvin, Texas, 1969.

The Ryan Family: seated, Mr. and Mrs. Lynn Nolan Ryan, Sr. Standing from left: Judy, Bob, Nolan, Lynda, Jean, and Mary Lou.

Nolan and Ruth,
Alvin, Texas, 1973.

Nolan Ryan,
California Angels, 1977.

*Nolan and Ruth with first
baby, Reid, in 1972.*

Ruth, Reid, Reese and Wendy Ryan, June 1991.

Nolan Ryan, rancher.

Nolan on his south Texas ranch.

Nolan with Angels coach, Jimmie Reese,
for whom their second son was named.

Nolan Ryan,
Houston Astros.

Nolan Ryan,
Texas Rangers, after 7th
no-hitter, May 1, 1991
against Toronto.

Nolan Ryan, Texas Rangers.

Nolan Ryan,
Texas Rangers.

Nolan Ryan,
Texas Rangers,
300th victory,
July 31, 1990
at Milwaukee.

*Then-Vice President Bush
throwing out the opening
pitch in the Astrodome,
August 28, 1988.*

Nolan with President George Bush, a friendship that began during Nolan's career with the Houston Astros.

Nolan and Ruth Ryan with President George Bush and First Lady Barbara Bush at the White House, January 1991.

From left: Nolan, Ruth, Reese, Wendy, and Reid Ryan, New Year's Eve, 1991.

Nolan and Muhammad Ali.

11

Texas Heat

*T*he previous season, 1988, the Rangers had finished sixth in their division and lost ninety-one games. Their attendance had dropped by nearly two hundred thousand. I knew nothing would be more exciting than if I had a good year and the club started to win. If we could set attendance records, people would talk about 1989 for years. Flirting with a couple of no-hitters the year before had me wondering if I might be able to do something really special, but I started slowly, injuring a hamstring in spring training and being able to go only one inning before a record crowd. I was able to throw about ten minutes just warming up on the sidelines a couple of weeks later, but then I went seven innings against the Astros. I knew then I was ready.

I started the regular season with a no-decision at home, then pitched against the Brewers on a cold April night in Milwaukee. My fastball was alive, so I stayed with it and I shut down the first twenty batters. I didn't allow a hit until Terry Francona hit an opposite field single in the eighth. I wound up striking out fifteen.

April 23, on another cold night in Toronto, I went into the ninth inning without allowing a hit for the ninth time in my career. Nelson Liriano broke it up with a one-out triple. It was the fourth time I'd lost a no-hitter with one out in the last inning.

That was my fifteenth game allowing fewer than two hits, breaking Bob Feller's record.

People were amazed all over baseball and all over the country. What was this old man doing teasing them with almost-no-hitters as he had done years and years ago? People who didn't know better probably thought old Nolan Ryan had discovered a knuckle ball or some junk to hang on for so long. Nobody expected me to still be blowing away hitters.

In June I pitched a one-hitter in Seattle against the Mariners. Later that month I had a no-hitter until two were out in the eighth and Brook Jacoby of Cleveland doubled. That was the longest any Ranger had gone without giving up a hit at Arlington Stadium. I was 9–3 and cooking.

Every time I just missed another no-hitter it disappointed me more. I knew enough not to get excited about them until one actually happened, because so much can go wrong in those last three innings. But to come so close . . . Everybody thought it was just a matter of time, but I felt that every no-hitter that slipped away might be my last chance.

I went back to pitch against the Angels in Anaheim in July, my first time there in ten years. I was really moved by a long standing ovation that was one of the highlights of my career. I pitched a three-hit shutout, then pitched in the All-Star game there five days later and became the oldest pitcher to win that classic.

On August 10, at Arlington, I took Detroit into the ninth without a hit. Dave Bergman got a single off me with, you guessed it, one out, and I had my fifth ninth-inning no-hitter broken up.

On August 22, with a pitch clocked at ninety-six miles an hour, I struck out Rickey Henderson for the five thousandth K of my career. People had come from all over to see the milestone, and I had ignored the 101-degree heat. What made it so special was that when I got to within one strikeout, it seemed everybody in the sellout crowd flashed their cameras on every pitch. The tension rose and fell with each call. I was also impressed that George W. Bush, our managing general partner, was there for the occasion, along with A. Bart Giamatti, then commissioner of baseball.

A month later, in my last start of the year, I took a no-hitter into the eighth before giving up a single to Brian Downing. That made five times in one year, at forty-two years old, that I had taken a legitimate shot at a no-hitter. Earlier in my career I would have told myself I'd have a lot more opportunities, but now every time I missed one I knew it could easily be my last chance. I tried not to let myself dream about how exciting it would be to add one more no-hitter to my record, especially at my age.

I had had a fantasy year, far surpassing all my expectations. My sixteen wins were the most I'd had since 1982, and I became the oldest pitcher to ever strike out more than three hundred in a season, leading the league for the third year in a row. Striking out 301 in just 239 innings was also a record, and that was the most strikeouts in the American League since I had struck out 310 in 1977. Hitters batted .187 against me for the season.

Every game seemed like a bonus to me, but I felt so good that I accepted the Rangers' option and signed on for 1990. I signed that deal pretty certain it would be my last, but I've learned to just take them one at a time now. That would be the only season I would go into actually shooting for a statistic. I was eleven games short of three hundred career wins. A lot of the records I didn't really care about, but I did want to win three hundred. Only nineteen pitchers in the history of baseball had ever won that many.

The 1989 season had been one of the most enjoyable of my career. I was as surprised as anybody with my popularity and the attention I received, but the Rangers were the first organization to put me out front and promote me like that. They acted like they truly appreciated my being there, and so I've tried to accommodate them in every way possible. I somehow became more of a phenomenon in Arlington than I had been in Houston, because the Astro organization never would have pushed me or appreciated me the way the Rangers have.

I like the attitude at Arlington from the owners to the people who work the stadium. The whole organization is relaxed and having fun. Just like John McMullen's tension filtered down to everybody on the staff, the looseness in Arlington infects everybody too. The pride in the organization shows, and our whole family has enjoyed the situation.

My teammates have accepted me warmly, and I try to treat them right. I care about what goes on with them, and even though I'm old enough to be a father to some of them and certainly old enough to be their coach, I try to be just a teammate. I don't expect preferential treatment from management, even though a certain amount of it comes naturally because of my years. But players notice whether you demand that and how you react to it, and I think they know by now that the team comes first with me.

In January 1990, just before my forty-third birthday, I had to go to Dallas on a deal affecting my ranch. On the way that morning, I called to check on my mother as I often did, but I got no answer. During the winter I called her every day, and during the season at least twice a week. When I got back to the Houston airport that night, Ruth called me in the truck.

"I have some bad news, Nolan," she said. "Your mother passed away this morning."

I was stunned. My sister, a counselor at the high school in Alvin, had also called Mother in the morning without getting an answer, so she went over to check on her. The car was there, the dog had been let out into the yard, and the coffee had been made. But when my sister got back to the bedroom she discovered our mother on the bed. The bed was made, and

Mother was dressed, so all we can guess is that she had gotten up and had done some of her chores, then laid back down when she didn't feel good.

I had worried ever since her accident whether she was okay there by herself, and I had thought about when she should move in with us or what other arrangements we might be able to make. She was such a big part of our lives that her death was really a shock, and dealing with the loss was a long process. All of a sudden I realized I had no living parent. I missed my dad a tremendous amount when he passed away. Now there are times when I still catch myself thinking about calling to check on my mother.

Just like when my dad died, I didn't want someone to talk to or someone to console me. I just wanted to be left alone to my thoughts. I like to deal with things on my own terms. I had to resolve in my mind to put the experience in its place and learn from it. I went through some regrets about having been busy and seeing so little of her, which is natural. But you can never do as much as you'd like for your loved ones. I always felt I could have done more. I just had to come to grips with it and know I did the best I could. Time is a healer, but we all sure miss her. The kids really felt it after having been so close to her. I didn't think I could do any more growing up and maturing at my age, but that was a sobering, learning experience.

That made me feel a little older when the season started, but I didn't have any less enthusiasm for what I was doing. In the opener against Toronto I had a no-hitter for five innings when Bobby Valentine took me out. He was criticized for it, but not by me. He said, "We're playing a season, not the Super Bowl." In my fourth start, I struck out sixteen White Sox in a one-hitter, giving up a second-inning single to Ron Kittle.

My back started bothering me after that. Here I was 4–0 but having muscle spasms. I had to leave my next two starts early and then went on the disabled list. Everybody was sure it was the beginning of the end for me, and I wasn't so sure myself.

On June 11, for my second start after coming off the disabled list, I was in Oakland on a chilly Monday night to face the Athletics, the defending World Series champions. It's tough enough facing a lineup like that without having to do it on the road. My back was still sore, but I knew early in the game that I had good stuff. I didn't allow a base runner until the third, when I walked Walt Weiss. We had already scored three runs by then, two on a homer by Julio Franco in the first and one on a solo homer by my catcher, John Russell, in the second. Ironically, John had never caught for me before. In fact, he had been cut by the Braves in spring training and had just joined the Rangers less than a month before.

Franco hit another two-run homer in the fifth to give us a 5–0 lead, and I didn't allow another base runner until the bottom of the sixth, when I walked Mike Gallego with one out. Between pitches I had to bend and stretch on the mound to keep my back loose. And between innings, Reese (then fourteen years old), who had come along as one of our bat boys, massaged my back.

In the ninth, with one out, I went to a 2–2 count on Rickey Henderson, who was batting .342 at the time. He hit a slow roller to Jeff Huson at short, but Jeff charged the ball and threw him out. Jeff shook a fist at me, and I said, "Nice play." You could see how excited he was. It was written all over him. Then I got Willie Randolph on a fly to Ruben Sierra and, believe it or not, I had been perfect since the second walk in the sixth. I had struck out fourteen and walked only those two for my sixth no-hitter. I was mobbed, but John Russell was the first to get to me. He told me later he had never seen a look in a pitcher's eyes like he had seen in mine that night.

I was as shocked as anybody, and the news sure swept the country. The best part about it for me was how excited my teammates had been to be a part of it. I don't show much emotion, but that moved me. I became the oldest pitcher in history to throw a no-hitter. Obviously I wasn't counting, but they tell me I was forty-three years, four months, and twelve days old. I was also the only pitcher to throw no-hitters in three different decades. To me it wouldn't have been half as amazing if I wasn't basically the same kind of pitcher I had always been. Someday somebody might match my no-hit record and even pitch no-hitters decades apart, but it is hard to imagine someone throwing fastballs and striking people out in what should be the twilight of his career.

It was my first no-hitter since September 26, 1981, the longest time between no-hitters ever. More amazing to me, it was seventeen years after my first one. The only drawback was that I wished it had happened in Arlington where those fans had been so wonderful to me.

On July 20, still hurting, I won my 299th game, my tenth win that season in fifteen starts. My next start was against the Yankees in Arlington, and I wanted more than anything to reach a milestone there for those fans. They came from all over, the way the media did. I just wanted it to be over so I could get back to a little more sane routine. There's nothing like being hounded everywhere you go by people asking any question they can think of.

The ballpark was sold out and it had the atmosphere of a playoff game. I thought I was ready for win number three hundred. Deon Sanders led off the game with a triple off me. I was wild in the strike zone and couldn't get untracked. The Yankees scored seven runs, but Bobby kept me in the game because we were scoring too, and he thought maybe I could hang on and win it. But I never got into a groove where I had any consistency, and it just kept getting worse and worse. I wound up with a no-decision, but it was one of my poorer outings of the year. I was really disappointed, feeling I had let down all those people.

I finally got my three hundredth win eleven days after number 299. It was a thrill, but it came on the road, in Milwaukee. I went seven and two-thirds innings in an 11–3 win, only wishing again that I could do something meaningful at Arlington Stadium. Those fans had made my last two years so special that I felt I owed it to them.

12

Never Enough

*I*f I had ever felt unappreciated in my life, the attention I got after that sixth no-hitter made up for all of it. Everybody knows I'm pretty much a quiet guy, not looking for the spotlight, but I also get satisfaction out of what I've accomplished. Some folks are surprised to learn that with my daily workouts and what I have to do in the clubhouse and the training room and for the media, I spend seven or eight hours a day at the ballpark. It's amazing, but people who don't follow the game closely think there's something fluky that lets me keep pitching at my age. Fact is, and Tom House has been preaching this for years, anybody can be effective into his forties if he trains his body the right way. I'm not saying the fastball will stay with a man for twenty-five years, but I'd be the wrong one to say it wouldn't, too.

I'd been getting a lot of press coverage for being the oldest man in the game, showing up for spring training again, leading a much-improved Rangers team, and all that. Every time I flirted with a no-hitter, people in the press wrote glowing stories and shook their heads, wondering if I could actually pitch another one at my age. I can't speak for them, but I'd guess none of them would have put any money on it. I wouldn't either. As I've said, it gets harder and harder as the game gets longer, and of course I had everything working against me. But when that sixth no-hitter was over, the attention from the fans multiplied.

People would be amazed to see how much stuff I have to sign every day. First of all, I get between three hundred and four hundred letters a day, almost every one of them requesting an autograph, a card, or a picture. A lot of them come with those items ready to be signed. You can see what happens if I'm on the road and fall behind by a week or two. I'm not the kind of a person who would have other people fake my autograph or use one of those signing machines. I'm also not the type of a person who just gets in a scribbling mode and dashes off a scrawl on everything that passes under my nose. I admit it only takes a few seconds for each autograph, but I do each carefully and as legibly as possible. Some of these are on baseballs that will be sold as authentically autographed, and as I get paid for doing that and people pay their own money for them, I want them to look nice.

Every spare minute I've had for the last couple of years has been spent sitting somewhere with box after box of dozens of baseballs, stacks of color photos, and other memorabilia I have to sign. Whether I'm being interviewed, chatting with friends, or even talking on the phone, I've usually got a pen in one hand and a ball or something in the other. I sign hundreds and hundreds and hundreds of items every single day, and I'm still so far behind that I hate to even think about it.

It sounds terrible, because I do appreciate all the love and interest from the fans, but it's a never-ending deal. If you asked Ruth and me what we hate about our career in baseball, it would be the volume of mail and demands for autographs. There are good things and bad things, pluses and minuses, and this is the big minus that nobody understands.

I guess the reason they don't understand is that unless you've had to deal with it, it looks pretty glamorous. I mean, who wouldn't want to be known and loved and recognized by everybody? You're worshiped and people just want to be able to say that you took a second to sign your name on their baseball or card. Before you have that kind of recognition, you're jealous of anybody who has it. It's a sign that you've achieved something, that you've arrived, that you're somebody.

But then, when it happens, you realize what a monster it can be. I know how that sounds, and I know people are thinking, *Man, you make millions of dollars playing a game and you can't sign a few autographs for the people who made you what you are? If it weren't for the fans, there'd be no money in baseball.*

Well, that's true. But the autograph game has changed. I can usually tell when a kid just wants his moment with a big leaguer, and I try to give it to him. He's in awe, he's thrilled, and he wants to say he talked with Nolan Ryan. Great. I'll do it and give him a smile and shake his hand and even sign whatever he wants. But I can also tell these guys, and some of them are kids, who are only buying and selling autographs. That's why I don't criticize some of the ballplayers who charge for their autographs at card shows, and that's why I don't feel bad about taking money to sign stuff that will be retailed. If I knew nobody was making money off my signature, I wouldn't mind signing all this stuff if time allowed me to. But when I know what it does to my schedule and my family life, I wish I could tell for sure how many of the requests come from legitimate fans and how many come from autograph brokers.

A lot of the people I play with get a box or two of letters in a whole season, and they just let them sit. At the end of the year they take them over to the garbage can and dump them. There are days when I wish those were all I had to deal with. I guarantee I wouldn't throw away even one. I've had to hire a fulltime secretary just to handle the mail and the requests for appearances. I know. You might think, *Nice problem.* The day may come when all this is gone and I'll miss it and wonder if anybody remembers ol' Nolan Ryan. I may walk down the street and feel neglected and unappreciated. I don't know. Right now that sounds pretty good.

When I was in high school I saw a couple of Houston Colt .45s at the ballpark. One was a backup catcher and the other was a pinch hitter. My buddies and I hardly recognized their names, but we were saying, "Man, if I could make fifteen thousand a year for just sittin' on the bench, I'd be happy as a lark." But when you get in the game, your competitive spirit won't let that be true. You don't want to take money for doing nothing. You want to excel, to achieve. That's the same attitude that got you to the big leagues in the first place. Like anything else, it looks different when you're on the outside looking in. Today kids look at us and say, "I'd sign autographs twenty-four hours a day for that kind of money." Maybe you would. Maybe you'd toss them all at the end of the season. I can't bring myself to do that, but sometimes it seems like I'm signing my name twenty-four hours a day.

People think the traveling life of a big leaguer is glamorous too. Once you've experienced it for a while, believe me your attitude changes. I don't know of anything in life that you have to do on regular basis as part of your job that isn't a lot different from how you once imagined it would be. For me, every new town I arrive in means another crush of media and fans. Again, I know, I sound ungrateful. And people who spend their whole lives in anonymity are thinking, *Send me some of that attention.* Believe me, if I could I would. It doesn't make me mad or bitter; it just wears me down.

See, I know I'm not worthy of being worshiped. Yeah, it's great to be appreciated. But somehow being able to still do with a baseball what I did twenty years ago has turned me into something else—an industry. I know who I am. I'm a country kid from Texas with the ability to throw a ball and the dedication to keep myself in shape. I love the cheers and the applause and I'm grateful people come out to watch me pitch. I even appreciate that people like to see me in person and talk to me and get an autograph. But I'm just a man. I'm no better than anybody else, even if I have an unusual and marketable talent. I'd rather sit and chat with you and hear about you and your family and your work than to pretend that I'm some royal being who can thrill you with a handshake or a signature.

I know I should be flattered and thrilled with all the attention, but if you think about it you can understand that too much adulation can make a man feel guilty. He knows he doesn't deserve all that, and if he starts thinking he does, he's going to be impossible to live with.

I have to say that, by and large, most of the people who ask for my autograph are wonderful, considerate fans. But it only takes a few of the rude ones to ruin your day. Some people are so self-centered that all they're concerned about is what they want and not whether they're imposing on me or the rest of the fans who are being patient. When people are rude and pushy it's an irritant, but I feel better about myself if I don't display my true feelings. When I do that I feel guilty and know I could have done a better job in that situation. I should never let people cause me to behave in a manner I don't consider acceptable. Just because somebody else is rude doesn't entitle me to be abrupt or discourteous in return. I try not to let myself be brought down to their level. That's not easy, because I'm not the best at disguising my feelings.

Some days it's easier than others, depending on what's been going on. I try not to get into positions where I'm going to be tied up for long periods. That can really ruin my day. There are appropriate ways to approach someone for an autograph. For instance, if Ruth and I are out for lunch, people should wait until we're through eating. I've had people butt right into a conversation. I've had someone interrupt me right when I'm putting a bite of food in my mouth. Some will just toss something in front of you to sign, right onto your plate.

On the other hand, some people will wait outside for us, sometimes as long as thirty minutes, and then politely ask for an autograph. I'm always happy to comply. If it means that much to them, it means a lot to me too. It's very important to me also that they acknowledge Ruth. She doesn't want star treatment, but it can wear on you when people walk over you or look through you to get to someone else. She's my wife. She's not an obstacle.

When I'm in a hurry, I just tell people, but I still try to sign unless they have a whole bunch of items. That can be the most irritating, when you sign a card or something and then they start producing every other thing that can fit an autograph.

One of the worst experiences I had was at the Astrodome in the late 1980s when I was leaving a game. I pulled out of the players' protected parking area past some barriers where the fans waited for autographs. I rolled down my window to sign for a few people as I rolled by, and there were maybe twenty people there. On some nights, when there were hundreds, security wouldn't be able to control them, so I couldn't stop. I never would have gotten out of there, and people would have been mashed up around my truck. But with just those twenty or so, I stopped.

A couple of young men in the crowd, both very drunk, shoved their programs in my face and demanded I sign them. It was all I could do to remain calm, they were so rude, but I gritted my teeth and signed. While I was signing for one, the other guy reached into the cab of my truck, right across my body, and grabbed for one of the baseball caps on the seat. "Hey, lemme have one of them caps," he said.

I was about to explode, and I don't know what would have happened if I'd broken his arm. Luckily a Houston police officer was standing there and saw what happened. He wrapped a forearm around that guy's neck and liked to tear him out of his shoes dragging him away from my truck. I was really grateful, because that could have gotten ugly.

Sometimes the worst offenders are kids around junior high age. If a crowd has a bunch of them in it, I know I'll get some obnoxious comments or actions. Usually I figure if I'm out of sight, I'm out of mind, so I try to avoid big crowds. I don't try to walk past and ignore them, because that looks terrible. They know you can see and hear them, and you look rude. So I go out different exits and slip away. That way they might go home and complain that they didn't see me, but they won't tell everybody that I ignored them. I could go out there and sign a couple of hundred autographs a night, and there would be another two hundred who would complain that I didn't sign theirs.

The Rangers ball club got a letter last summer from a woman in Colorado who complained that she and her husband drove all the way to Arlington Stadium and yelled at me on the field and I wouldn't even look up so their son could take a picture. Well, I had no clue. When I go out before a ball game and do my running, first of all I try to do it early so there aren't a lot of fans. But at Arlington they have a policy of having the gates open for all but thirty minutes, so there are always lots of people in the stands. Well, I have my own policy that once I start my running I don't stop and do autographs, because if I stop and sign for one, then I have to sign for others. Before I know it, I don't get my workout done.

Part of my workout is sprinting out and walking back several times, and if I hear someone yelling for a picture I might look and wave. But I cannot go to the stands and start signing. If someone catches my eye and asks me point blank, I tell them nicely, "I'm sorry, I've got to get my work in." Most people accept that, but some will say, "Oh, come on, you can do one for this kid. He's your biggest fan." Then I try to explain that if I sign his, what will the kid next to him say? I can't discriminate. But for a woman to say I ignored her son who wanted to take a picture, that was too much. My name is shouted hundreds of times a night at the stadium. I'd sure never ignore an individual on purpose.

The more popular I have become, the more creative I need to be to avoid people without offending them. The last thing I want to be is rude, but there's only so much you can do for people and still do what you have to do for the ball club. I try to figure when is the best time to work out, where's the best place to park, all that. But people learn your routines and they know my vehicles. They know that if I pitch one night I'll get to the ballpark at nine the next morning to work out, so many will be waiting.

With them standing there expecting me to sign, out of guilt, I stop and do it. I tell them that I will sign for everybody, but only one item each. The only problem is, two and a half hours later when I come out, there are many of the original thirty people and maybe twenty more. One day I told them, "Look, I don't have time. I'm going to stop and sign one time, one item for each, so you might as well tell people that if I sign on the way in, I'm not signing on the way out."

But then that made them mad. I looked like a difficult guy. So I started driving in a different way and parking way out by the center field entrance instead of the players' parking area. I had to walk all the way across the field to the clubhouse, but I avoided upsetting the fans.

Well, one guy caught on to what I was doing. He said he was a schoolteacher and that he always had me sign something so he could reward his students for excelling in reading and stuff. Frankly I didn't believe him. Maybe that wasn't fair, but he sure had a lot of stuff, and he was always there. The day I parked in the parking lot he still found me. I got in the car and he flagged me down. I rolled down the window and told him I had an appointment and I only had time to sign one thing.

"You seem irritated with me," he said.

"Well, why do you think I parked all the way out here?"

"I don't know."

"Because I don't have time to stop and sign for everybody, and you're here every day expecting me to sign. I think that's enough."

He was offended and I never saw him again. I don't know. I felt bad about doing it, but he was really being presumptuous and infringing on my time. I knew it needed to be said, but it's so against my nature to be confrontive that I felt guilty about it for a couple of days.

I'm a real believer that you can't make everybody happy and not everybody is going to like you. I don't have problems with the fact that there are media and baseball people who like me and those who don't—I understand that. But there's something about the relationship with the fans, trying to accommodate them and keep them happy, that has given me a lot of trouble personally, inside.

If I knew they were getting my autograph because they respected me and it was a keepsake, that would be one thing. But for many it's not a hobby; it's a business. Still, I try to give twenty to thirty minutes every day during the season to sign autographs for the fans, and I carve out at least another thirty minutes a day for the media, and some days it may be as much as an hour and a half. That adds up to a lot of time, but it's never enough to satisfy everybody.

When I was a young player I didn't even dream about these kinds of demands. I never had any idea there would be days like this. Still, what I wanted to give the fans was not myself, my whole schedule, my family, my life. I wanted to give them something to really remember, something special they could talk about the rest of their lives. I wanted it to be more than an autograph, more than a picture, more than a glimpse of me in person.

I wanted to do something at Arlington Stadium for the people who had treated me so nice. It should be something that came from all the work and dedication I'd given to the sport. The five thousandth strikeout had been at home before a sell-out crowd in 1989, but my sixth no-hitter and my three hundredth win had been on the road in 1990. With the back problems I'd had, I couldn't guarantee I'd be the same pitcher in '91, but it wouldn't be for lack of trying.

Two days after the sixth no-hitter I had been examined in Los Angeles by Dr. Lewis Yocum, the Angels' orthopedist and an old friend. He said I had a stress fracture and prescribed medication and exercises. It was still tight the rest of the season, but I didn't miss another start. It was a big help to understand what I was dealing with. I could pitch with the pain without injuring my back any worse. The last six weeks of the season I quit throwing off the mound on my off days and that seemed to give my back enough time to quiet down between starts. I could only hope that 1991 would be another great year. I was through predicting whether or not it would be my last.

13

Something Special

*T*hings looked great for the Rangers for the 1991 season. We looked to have good hitting and a lot of pitching—at least until the first four games. I lost the opener to Milwaukee and then we lost three more straight. It was a good thing we won six of our next seven or we would have been in a real tailspin. By the time I started my fourth game, we were 6–6 and I was 2–1. I lost 5–2 to Cleveland on a Friday the thirteenth at Arlington, and I had thrown 133 pitches.

I was scheduled to pitch again the following Wednesday, May 1, with only four days' rest. I hadn't been that successful in '90 with less than five days' rest, but I was ready to give it a try. By game time we were 8–8 and needed to get on a winning track. We would be at home against the Toronto Blue Jays, one of the best hitting teams in the majors.

Ruth almost always comes to my home games, but if she can't she watches them on television. The only one she missed when I was with the Angels was when she was moving us back to Texas and I was making my last start in 1974. She still hasn't forgiven herself for missing that no-hitter.

So, when she found out, late in the afternoon, that the Toronto game wasn't going to be televised, she called one of my ranching partners, Jim Stinson, and asked if she could watch it at his place, because he has a satellite dish. "He's not pitchin' tonight," Jim told her. "He's pitchin' Friday in Detroit, right?"

"No," she said. "He's pitching tonight."

"Well, if I'd known that I'd have flown to the game. In fact, there's still time, Ruth. You wanna go?"

So Ruth flew into Arlington with Jim in his private plane. I was glad she was there. Harry Spilman, my old Astros teammate and now a neighbor who catches for me in January before spring training and whose wife Kim is my secretary, listened to the game on his car radio by driving all over the place. He thought it was going to be on television too. When I took a no-hitter into the seventh he called my kids, and they watched the end of it when ESPN cut away from the Detroit-Kansas City game to follow my progress.

I didn't expect to pitch well at all that night. I woke up with a sore back and took painkillers all day before leaving for the park. I went through extra stretching and exercises and even wore a heating pad during the scouting meeting where we go over the hitters. That wasn't the only thing wrong with me. While I was warming up I told Tom House, who was also forty-four years old at the time, "I don't know about you, but I feel old today. My back hurts, my finger hurts, my ankle hurts, everything hurts." Scar tissue tore open on the middle finger of my pitching hand in the bullpen, and I had one of my worst warmups ever. I didn't know it till later, but House told Bobby Valentine to keep an eye on me and not leave me in too long.

Before the game Bobby asked me how my back was. I told him that it was stiff. He said, "How will it be once you start pitching?" I said, "It'll be history." Adrenaline always takes over when I'm on the mound, and it did again, in the first inning.

With two out in the first, I lost Kelly Gruber on a full count and walked him. I was mad at myself, but settled down and got out of the inning by retiring Joe Carter. In the second I struck out the side on three curveballs. Steve Buechele, our third baseman, and shortstop Jeff Huson told each other as they came off the field that all we needed was one run that night if I had stuff like that. I had to admit my curve was really working, and I didn't have any trouble hitting my spots. The fastball was hopping too.

We scored our only three runs in the bottom of the third, two on a Ruben Sierra homer. After the Gruber walk in the first, I got eighteen straight hitters out before giving up another two-out, full-count walk in the seventh, this time to Joe Carter. Manny Lee had hit a blooper to center in the fifth, but Gary Pettis raced out from under his hat to catch it at his knees. He's one of the best. I'd thought that ball had a chance to drop in before Gary chased it down.

After the walk to Carter in the seventh, I retired the next seven hitters and the place went crazy. I had struck out sixteen, allowed only two base runners who never got past first, and had pitched my seventh no-hitter. Even I couldn't keep from grinning as the team raced out to the mound to congratulate me. I had been the oldest no-hit pitcher when my sixth came the year before. Who would have ever thought there'd be another one, especially in the condition I was in that day?

Ironically, my last out was a swinging strikeout of Blue Jay second baseman Roberto Alomar. His father, Sandy, had been my second baseman for the Angels in my first two no-hitters eighteen years before. In fact I remember little Roberto asking me to help him become a pitcher someday.

They tell me I threw 122 pitches, 83 for strikes, 62 of those fastballs. Of the sixteen strikeouts, all but the three in the second inning were swinging. The radar gun showed my fastest pitch at ninety-six miles per hour against Carter in the fourth, with an average of ninety-three miles per hour for the game. My last pitch, the one that got Alomar, was also at ninety-three miles per hour.

There's a lot of debate about which of my seven no-hitters was the best and in which one I had my best stuff. I'm not sure myself, but I know that the seventh was especially gratifying because it was at home before that Arlington crowd. My stuff was surprisingly good, considering all that was wrong with me that day. Somebody said my teammates were like spectators because I was that dominant, but I know better than that.

I had several other good outings before 1991 was over. On June 11, I shut out the White Sox on six hits, then I had a scare. I suffered such severe chest pains one morning early in July that I got myself to the hospital, worried about a heart attack. I was relieved to find it was only a pulled muscle near the sternum. A few days later, on July 7, just before the All-Star break, I retired the first eighteen hitters and took a no-hitter into the eighth inning against the Angels before Dave Winfield singled. Fifteen times during the season I allowed less than two runs and eleven times two or less hits.

I missed a lot of starts by being on the disabled list two different times, so my twenty-three starts and 173 innings were my fewest in twenty years in the majors. Still, fourteen different times I worked at least seven innings. I was frustrated with the down time, but starting June 6, I went 9–2 the rest of the way to finish at 12–6 with a 2.91 ERA. I was 5–1 in my last nine starts and 4–0 in my last seven, winning my last six decisions at home. I was pleased that I didn't allow a homer in my last nine games.

When the season was over I had 314 career victories and 5,511 strikeouts. I ranked third on the list of all-time leaders in starts with 733. On July 23 I set a record by making my 545th straight start since my last relief appearance. That record stood at 554 by the end of the season.

If my season had ended with the injuries instead of coming back with good closing appearances, I might have seriously considered hanging it up. But I seemed to return to form at the end, and I'm excited about the Rangers' future. They signed me for one more year, with an option on 1993. I also signed a ten-year personal services contract. That means that when my career is over I will give them one to two months a year for either promotional appearances or evaluating talent or whatever they need. I hope it won't involve much travel. I'm about all traveled out.

All that commercial stuff and the demands on my time that I complained about after my sixth no-hitter just multiplied with number seven. I've become as well known for Bic shavers and Advil as for my pitching, I think, but eventually that stuff will all come to an end. I've done enough of it by now that I'm starting to get more comfortable with it. I have a better idea what they want, and I'm learning to deliver with every take. No way I'm going to become an actor or anything like that, but I think I'm less stiff and self-conscious in front of the camera now than I used to be.

Like I've said, I know these opportunities won't always be here. It's the baseball that has made them possible, and since the extra income allows me to do things for my family I wouldn't have been able to otherwise, I carefully select the right ones and accept them. Some guys get on camera and think they've found a whole new career, but you don't see too many guys who are as good on the screen as they were on the field. I have no illusions about that. Even if somebody thought I was the hottest thing on television and could make a lucrative living off it, I wouldn't be interested. I'm on television because of baseball, and baseball is what I love.

There's something about the game that makes it the biggest challenge of my life. Of course it has dominated my life for so many years and naturally I've played it for so long that I understand the game now in ways I never did as a young player. Understanding the game and seeing its challenges are what made me come to love it.

At first I didn't have that burning desire to play and accomplish things. The pressure to do that was thrust on me because of my natural ability, and without much of a mind of my own at the time, I just followed. People thought I could pitch, so I pitched. They thought I should be a pro, so I went pro. They saw me as a power pitcher, so I threw as hard as I could.

I said earlier that Tom Seaver opened my eyes when I first met him, because he had a plan, a goal. He wanted to be great, to be one of the best. Before he ever pitched a big league inning he knew the history of the game and who held the records he would be shooting for. I didn't know who Walter Johnson was until Tom told me about his strikeout record. I was only in baseball because I had talent, and until I got focused I was really never an effective pitcher.

Now I've learned what to look for in a pitcher's record to be able to sense his effectiveness and his potential, and I'll tell you, it has little to do with his won-lost record. I've proved that more than once. The year I lost twice as many games as I won, I led the league in strikeouts and earned run average, so that ought to tell you something.

They show the stats of local minor league players in the Sunday paper. With a quick glance at their numbers, I can tell what kind of futures they have before them. Are they striking people out? Are they keeping runners off base? Are they staying away from walks and high earned run averages? How many hits are they giving up? What kind of innings are they pitching? Their hits, walks, and strikeout ratios give you a pretty good idea, especially if they have a good ERA.

Pitching has changed some since I broke into baseball. The split-finger fastball is the most dramatic new pitch. I've never thrown it in a game. With my curve I don't really need the splitter. It has changed some guys' careers though. Mike Scott won the Cy Young with it for Houston. Bruce Sutter became a dominant reliever with the Cubs and the Cardinals with that pitch. It seems to explode down in the strike zone after making the hitter think it's up where he can reach it. Few pitches make good hitters look worse.

The splitter has had more of an impact on baseball even than the spitter. Of course the spitter is illegal, but there are some guys who throw it. The thing is, not many can really control it, and if you can't control it, it doesn't help you a bit. It's the same thing with scuffing a ball. It makes it so hard to control that you don't see a lot of it going on. The benefits are exaggerated and the number of guys who know what to do with a scuffed or lubricated ball is getting smaller all the time.

When Mike Scott first learned the split-finger fastball from Roger Craig, a former pitcher and then manager, it gave Mike confidence. The more people became aware of his splitter and were afraid of it, the more effective his fastball was. You fool a guy with a bottoming-out splitter a couple of times and then bust a live fastball in there, he won't know whether to swing or sit down. That gives a pitcher just enough of a mental edge to make him more aggressive and confident.

I never felt I needed a split-finger with my repertoire. It can be a tough pitch to master, and it can be hard on your arm and hand if you don't do it just right. I did develop what's called a circle change, where you use your forefinger and thumb to form a circle and hold the ball in your palm. As you release the ball, you keep the thumb and forefinger touching (in fact, I curl the index finger almost down to the first bend in the thumb), causing the ball to slide out of your hand and off your remaining three fingers. Depending on the trajectory and the arm speed, the ball does all kinds of interesting things. Mostly, you can bring your arm down with the same speed as you would a fastball, but the pitch has less power behind it and becomes a wicked, moving changeup. I could never get consistent with any other kind of a changeup, but that has worked for me and made my fastball and my curve more effective. Still, the circle change is a tough pitch. I need to take enough velocity off it to fool a hitter, but if I get it up, it's my most hittable pitch and I can get hurt with it.

I've stayed away from sliders because I've never known of a pitcher who had both an outstanding curve and an outstanding slider. They tell me my curve is one of the better ones in the game, so people who say that I've succeeded for so long only because of my speed are wrong. Sandy Koufax had a great curve to offset his fastball. Walter Johnson and Bob Feller had the good curves. Tom Seaver, Steve Carlton, and Bob Gibson had excellent sliders. Most dominant-type pitchers do have a good breaking pitch too. But I didn't want to take away from my curve by throwing a slider. It seems to me a slider is harder on the arm.

I also believe—though this is just my opinion—that the slider shortens your career from a velocity standpoint. In other words, people who are successful with a slider seem to lose something off their fastball earlier in their career than they should. I don't know if the two go together or if pitchers just start relying on the slider more or what, but that's something I've noticed. And I've studied more than a few pitchers.

Back in my California Angel days I pitched in the ninety-seven- and ninety-eight-mile-per-hour range for a game. Now I'm at ninety-two/ninety-three, so I figure I've lost a couple of miles per hour off my fastball every ten years. That doesn't mean I still don't throw a good fastball, but it's not too often I throw one ninety-six or so. Early on I had an exceptional fastball. You get ahead of a guy with a pitch like that, he has to be ready to be quick or he'll strike out. Fool him with a curve, and there's no way he can hold up. If he does hold up and you get the pitch over, you've got him anyway.

I had such a live arm back then that people swore my curveball was coming in as fast as my fastball, but it wasn't. It was in the low eighties and now it's often in the seventies. The key to the breaking pitch is not how fast it is, but how much difference there is between it and the fastball. If a guy is throwing only eighty-five-mile-per-hour fastballs, his offspeed pitch can be pretty effective if it's a lot slower. And a guy throwing in the high nineties can surprise you with an offspeed pitch that's in the high eighties but is still faster than a lot of guys' fastballs.

The difference in the speed of my two primary pitches is eight to ten miles per hour. To get away with that, I have to keep the ball down. When you see me getting hit all over the yard or leaving a game early, it's because I've been unable to keep the ball low. That will be true with just about any pitcher, especially a power pitcher.

I'm not saying they were bad pitches, but I made a mistake as far as location. One thing I try to stress to young pitchers is that they shouldn't be upset when guys do hit their best stuff, because the advantage goes to the hitter when you fall behind him in the count. You've left yourself with fewer options. The guy pretty much knows what's coming, and if he can catch up to it, knowing you have to get it into the strike zone, he's got the edge.

He's seen your pitches, knows your location, and you have to take all that into consideration. When I give up home runs it's usually because I'm behind in the count 3–1 and can't get away with a breaking ball. Still, a pitcher has no one to blame but himself, because he's the one who got behind in the first place.

I'm not one of those pitchers who gets into a groove and feels like he can't be touched. I know when I've got good stuff, but I've also been successful when nothing seems to be working. And I've been hit well when I thought I was overpowering. Plus, even when I'm in the middle of a no-hitter late in the game and seem to be mowing people down, I know how quickly things can change. I never go for a strikeout unless I've got two strikes on a guy and we need to get him that way. I try to stay within my game and keep us out of trouble, worrying more about the win than the no-hitter. Yeah, if we're leading by several runs and I still haven't allowed a hit by the seventh or eighth, I think about the no-hitter. But I don't start overthrowing. I stick with what got me there and try not to make mistakes.

One thing I never do is get too careful. If there's one thing I wouldn't mind being remembered for it's that when I throw my fastball, no matter where in the game it is, I give the hitter my best stuff and go right at him. That takes a lot of work and concentration and confidence, but to me that's the only way a pitcher like me should pitch.

Because of adrenaline, my last pitch in a no-hitter might be close to my fastest pitch of the night, but I don't plan it that way. I'm careful not to overthrow, because if I hurt myself I'm out of the game anyway, maybe forever.

I was disappointed when I came so close to so many no-hitters in '89, but I had learned not to worry about them. You can't make them happen. Sometimes the flukiest things break them up, and then you have to keep yourself together so you don't lose the game besides. If you get all rattled because some guy beats out an infield roller, you might let him steal second and see him score on a routine single. You've still pitched a great game, but not a smart one. If a no-hitter is going to happen, it'll happen. It's not automatic and you have to stay focused, but that's all you can do. A man can't control more than he can control, so I figure you should control what you can and let what happens happen.

Who hits me pretty well and consistently varies from year to year. I've had a lot of trouble lately with Mike Devereaux of Baltimore. I'm not sure why, but of course he's a good hitter and hits everybody well. Dave Valle of Seattle also hits about .400 off me, even though he hit only about .180 off the league last year. Once, somebody asked me who I had a lot of success against, and I said Sal Bando. I could hardly get him out at all after that.

I've had a lot of bad games, where I just didn't have it and got shelled early, but I always feel bad when I think the fans came to see me and didn't get their money's worth. I felt real bad about doing so poorly against the Yankees at Arlington going for my three hundredth win, but that wasn't the worst. In one home opener for the Astros in the mid-'80s, St. Louis knocked me out of the box in the second or third inning after six or so runs, and the young reliever we brought in couldn't do anything either. We wound up losing by what looked like a football score, and I felt terrible. Opening night should be just another game in a 162–game schedule, but I've never looked at it that way. It's always an honor to be chosen to pitch the opener and there's so much anticipation and excitement that you hate to lose, let alone get routed like that. Nobody remembers what happened a week later except you, but I want the fans to be glad they came out to the game.

14

Opinions, Opinions

A quarter of a century in big league baseball ought to give me the right to have a few opinions on the game. The only question is whether that gives me the right to express them. Well, you've for sure got a right to ignore 'em, so if you're not curious, just skip ahead. Otherwise, here are a few:

Putting On a Game Face

I know a lot of players, especially pitchers, start getting their game face on a day ahead of when they're going to pitch. I don't. I get focused and prepared, but my work comes in the four or five days between starts. I find myself more jovial and relaxed than ever just before going out to warm up before a game. That's the time I feel best because I've worked hard and am confident that I'm prepared. If I'm not at my best and worried about something, then that's a different deal. But usually when I go out there to warm up, all the preparation is behind me and I have a job to do. Once I start to concentrate on that, then my game face goes on.

The actual pitching is a reward for everything I did on the off days to get ready. The win and the adulation are not as much a reward to me as the pitching itself—going out there and being able to be effective because of the preparation. So once I've started warming up, I'm all business. I've seen other pitchers joke around and talk to the hitters because they're in control of their game and things are going right. I never do that, because I know things can change with one pitch, and I'm not going to leave the mound blaming it on losing my intensity.

That makes it pretty hard on me if I have a bad outing. The opportunity and the enjoyment of pitching are lost when I get knocked out early. The last time that happened I was so disgusted with myself that I went straight to the weight room and started lifting, preparing for my next start.

The Strikeout Record

I'm not one to ever say that a record, especially one of mine, can't be broken. If I can set one, why can't someone else break it? But if I have one that's likely to stand longer than the rest, it's the career strikeout record. First of all, not many people are going to come along and be able to pitch five thousand innings. And not only will he have to log all those innings, he'll have to maintain a style that allows him to strike out at least a hitter per inning.

The way they use pitchers nowadays, with longer times off between starts and quicker use of relievers, not many pitchers are piling up those kinds of innings. For years with the Angels I pitched on a four-day rotation. Unless that becomes a tradition again, you won't see anyone with enough innings to threaten the strikeout record.

A Pet Peeve

I have a problem with people in baseball who aren't baseball people. They make decisions about a pitcher, but they have never known what it is to stand on that mound when your arm's killing you or when you're not sure you can get a guy out and the game's riding on it. They don't know what it is to be in a slump and wonder if you're ever going to get out of it, or to know that everyone else thinks it's more than a slump and that you're on your way out of the game. They don't know what it is to be on the road when you have problems at home and are finding it tough to keep focused on your job. (Well, maybe they know that kind of frustration, but they're not contending with such a physically dangerous occupation as we are.)

More and more front office people are college grads—which is okay—but too many of them get their jobs through some sort of connection or relation. Maybe they were big fans, but that doesn't give them enough empathy with the players. I'm not saying every exec has to be a former ballplayer, but I hate to see it going totally the other way.

Worse are pitching coaches who've never pitched. That would be like me trying to become a hitting coach. I understand the principles and could teach to a point, but I don't really understand what goes on in a guy's mind—and that's a big part of this game.

Racial Tension

When I was growing up I went to high school with Mexicans and whites; the blacks had their own schools. We never thought much about integration until it started happening after I graduated. My parents were not prejudiced, but I was not exposed to too many blacks, so race just wasn't an issue with me. The racial tension of the 1960s was something I saw on the news and didn't understand. At that time in Texas the Mexicans were probably as discriminated against as anyone, with many whites considering them inferior common laborers. It didn't take me long to see that that was wrong.

I never took the view that any racial group was inferior or should know and keep its place. I've played with and against many blacks over the years, and it gets to where I don't think we notice each other's color after a while. I've roomed with blacks and have had Latino and black friends I consider as close as any Anglos.

There is racism in the big leagues, just like there is anywhere. As long as you have people you'll have a few who don't think straight. Of course I've found that racism knows no color either. There are blacks and people of other races who are racist too. But there's not a whole lot of it in baseball anymore.

One thing I don't like is when someone gets criticized and blames it on racism. Too often, that's just a cop-out. There are always people going around looking for it, and when you're looking for something you can usually find it. I've played with people like that, and I've played with others who never give it a thought. A lot of it has to do with their backgrounds, their attitudes toward life in general, and whether they have a chip on their shoulder. Again, you learn a lot about people by just listening.

The Designated Hitter

On this issue I have to say I prefer the National League. I think pitchers ought to have to hit and that it makes for a more interesting game. Of course, that comes from a guy with two home runs in a career and a lifetime batting average of .110!

The DH gives a pitcher an opportunity to win more ball games, get more decisions, and pitch more innings—which is what you get paid for—so you know I'm not being selfish in my opinion. The DH also gives a pitcher a little more offensive power, but then he has to face a better lineup too.

My Own Hitting

I could have been a better hitter if I would have had someone to work with me and had the time to invest in it. Still, I never would have been a great hitter. People don't understand why pitchers don't put more time into batting practice, and I'm not sure myself. Maybe someday some organization will emphasize it, and their pitchers will start producing at the plate, and it will become popular. It's just one more part of the game to concern yourself with, but it really won't make you a better pitcher. So even though I prefer pitchers hitting, I don't mind not having to worry about it in the American League. When I was in the National League I never took batting practice except the day I pitched. Then I just basically used batting practice as a way to get loose and to get some bunting work in.

When I was younger I liked the hitting part of the game, but as I got older I realized how much effort goes into a guy staying on top of it enough to face big league pitching. I didn't get hung up with the ego aspect of it.

Umpires

There are still too many incompetent umpires in the big leagues, but of course none of them are going to find out who I think they are. Baseball hasn't done a great job in two areas of umpiring: first, in making sure those guys are in shape, and second, in making sure that their personalities don't come into play on the field.

Seeing those guys overweight and out of shape is a bad image for baseball. I know they don't make the kind of money the players do, but still they have time to work out and they ought to do it. They ought to be mobile enough to get into position quickly and really see a play, even one in the alley. Did a guy catch the ball or trap it? Did it go over the fence or through it? Every play can affect the outcome of the game, so you want the fairest call possible.

I'm not saying they don't have tough jobs, because they do. And I know the pay is not the best, especially in the minors. But with as few umpiring jobs as there are and all the guys who'd love to have them, baseball ought to have tougher requirements and force those guys to stay in shape.

There are several umpires who do work out. We sometimes see them in the hotel weight rooms or even in some of the clubhouses. You feel that a guy takes a little pride in his appearance and his work when he does that.

Their travel schedules are worse than the players', but at least nowadays their schedules include some time off. Umpires have the winter off and have a lot of the benefits that the players have, but they will always have the worst travel schedules.

Television has brought out the worst in some of the personalities. It's okay when an ump wants to have fun and be a little dramatic or flashy when he makes a call, but when there's a disagreement and the umpire becomes the aggressor, like Joe West has done in the National League, something is wrong. West has been reprimanded several times, but he still antagonizes people and tries to intimidate them.

One area where I've fallen short over the years is in controlling my emotions on the mound. That will make some people laugh, because I have this image of being calm, cool, and collected, even when I pitch a no-hitter. But too often I let the umpires know when I think they have missed a call. I might glare at them or stomp around the mound between pitches, stuff like that. I don't mean to show them up, and sometimes I'll even apologize after the game. They usually understand. I wouldn't want to be shown up in a game either. It's just that I get so focused that it irritates me when I don't get a call and really believe it's wrong. Normally I won't talk to an umpire or expect him to talk to me unless I want an explanation for a balk call or a rule interpretation.

The only thing I ask of umpires is that they be consistent. There are some who are better ball-and-strike men than others, but I sure wouldn't ever put into print which was which. What a pitcher wants is a guy to establish his strike zone and not change it as the game goes on. If you're giving me the high strike early (which you rarely get in the National League), then give it to me in the eighth and ninth too. If you're not going to give me the low-and-away fastball off the corner, then don't give it to the other guy. I just want to know where I stand.

Just like pitchers, umpires have their good and bad days, and that can be frustrating. There's always a gray area where a call could go either way. Sometimes your veteran and star players get the edge there. If a hitter is known for having a great eye and he takes a close pitch, he might get the call. If he's a rookie and he takes a close pitch from me, I might get the call. The only way I can control the gray area is to make sure I haven't made an umpire mad or barked at him or showed him up. They don't like that, and I wouldn't either if I were back there. There can't be a tougher job anywhere. Every call you make makes one team happy and the other mad.

In the National League I'm convinced the strike zone has gotten smaller. You hardly ever see a strike called on a pitch above the waist. Some say the zone is below the thighs to the shins. I don't know how low it goes, but I know it's awfully small. The rule book says it's armpits to the top of the knees, but everybody knows you won't get a pitch that high called a strike and that you can get a lot of calls at the bottom of the knees.

I understand the commissioner wants the strike zone larger. That would sure get my vote.

I think umpires should all be under one jurisdiction. In other words, there shouldn't be American League and National League umpires. They should officiate in either league, and that would help their travel schedules even more. If a crew is in Houston and there's an open date when the Rangers are playing, they've got just a short hop. That would also help standardize the strike zones and a few other rule details. There would be fewer personality conflicts because you would see each crew less often.

Interleague Play

There's nothing wrong with the alignment of the leagues, but because of tradition baseball is slow to make any changes. Each league is fighting for its identity, and that's why the umpiring is separate when it doesn't need to be and would be better off not. The separation of the leagues and divisions is not needed anymore. Football, basketball, and even the NCAA have shown that interleague play has increased interest.

If a team was having a real bad year, it would be good for their gate to have not just the great teams and stars from their own league come to town, but the best in all of baseball. It's not a burning desire of mine and I won't picket for it, but I don't think interleague play would hurt.

The Best

I know this will get me into trouble with a lot of great, great stars, but the most talented player I ever played against was Willie Mays. Everybody knows he was a five-point player. A lot has been made of his ability to run, throw, field, hit for average, and hit with power. He didn't have a weakness in any facet of the game, and he found all kinds of ways to beat you. He was also enthusiastic and fun to watch. You could tell he loved the game and the fans.

Besides all that, Willie had longevity. He was the elite of the elite.

Today Barry Bonds of the Pirates may be the best player in the game, but when I left the National League I thought he was short on one ingredient: attitude. And I'm not sure that's changed. He has the most raw talent, but selfishness could keep him from being the best player in the game.

In our league I'd have to lean toward Ken Griffey, Jr. of Seattle. He and Bonds are something to watch, but it's interesting because they're from the new generation of ballplayers. I want to see what they make of their skills, what kind of drive they have, and whether they learn the game through the mastery of little things. I won't get into comparing my own teammates here, but I will later.

Cal Ripken of Baltimore is another outstanding player, but mostly because he's made so much of himself without having great natural talent. He's big and strong and has good eye-hand coordination, but he's not fast and may not have great range. Still, he's in the category of the special player and is one of the best in the game because he really knows how to play. Of course he hasn't missed a game in years, and there are advantages to that.

The best pitcher in the game today? Orel Hershiser of the Dodgers was before he got hurt. That scoreless-inning streak in '88 and his playoff and World Series work that year may never be matched. Dwight Gooden's awful tough for the Mets.

In the American League, and maybe all of baseball, Roger Clemens of the Red Sox has to be the best. It would be unfair for me to compare him with the best in the National League because I've been gone long enough, but of the people I see often, he's the best. He's a tough customer and he does all the things you want a front-liner to do. He doesn't walk many. He gives you the innings. He doesn't give up many hits. He's right there for you every time. If he has a bad game, he bounces back. That's a key. He's playing in a rough town, too. Boston fans are well educated and knowledgeable, and here's this Texas-raised boy (that may be why I'm partial to him) who says what he thinks, is fiery, taunts the hitters, and argues with the umpires. He's got to be good to back that up and still be accepted in a university town. He's one of the new breed of players.

15

Today's Ballplayer

*B*aseball looks easy to the spectator. The rules aren't complicated, and lots of people have enough skill to fool around with the game. But when you listen to veteran big leaguers, not just us dinosaurs in our forties, you hear them talk about really learning the game. It's the little intricacies that make the difference between winning and losing. It can take years to learn it all, and growing up is part of the process.

Kids come into big league baseball with all this raw talent nowadays, and they've got bodies that won't quit. They've got speed, endurance, great arms, quickness, reflexes—everything but brains and attitude. For instance, ask a rookie pitcher how he's going to be judged, what's the ultimate rule? He'll tell you it's his won-loss record and whether he wins twenty games.

When he matures he'll know his job is to give his team a chance to win the ball game. The point is to keep the other guys off the bases or at least off the plate so your guys can get a lead. If I do that, I'm happy whether I get the win or somebody else does. I see less of that attitude in baseball today than I ever have. Hitters are less willing to sacrifice themselves to get the runner over. They're worried about how many hits they're going to get. They know that their earning power is based on statistics, but that's no way to win ball games. I've even seen hitters look at the manager in the dugout after getting a bunt sign as if to say that they couldn't believe it. That's sad.

Sometimes I try to counsel young relievers and get them thinking about what they'll do in different game situations. They look at me like they have no idea what I'm talking about. They'll say, "I'm gonna go in there and throw my curve," or "I'm gonna try to strike 'em out," as if that's what they get paid for and that's what got them here, so that's all they think about. That's how ball games are lost. They really don't understand, and a major part of baseball strategy has been lost.

In the old days there were a lot more players who spent several years in the minors really learning the game. By the time they got to the big leagues their talent may have still been in question, but they had a better idea of how to play. It was as if they had been to baseball college. Now if you've got the talent, someone assumes you can overcome your limited knowledge of strategy.

Some modern ballplayers think that they're entitled to their money just because they were born with talent. Some think they're entitled to be seated ahead of other people, to cut ahead in lines, to have somebody give them something for nothing just because of who they are. I don't understand that mentality. I don't care if you're a doctor, a lawyer, or an Indian chief, you should not be treated any differently than anybody else.

Some proprietors try to give me a free car wash or free parking or even a free meal in a restaurant. I know they're trying to be nice and generous, but first off, I don't need comps. I wish they'd park a laborer's car for free and give him a break. When it happens to me in a restaurant, I always insist on paying unless that creates a scene. I tell them, "I didn't come in here for a comp deal. You can't afford to be giving away free meals." I want to pay just like anybody else. If they want to do something nice, they should give to others in need. I'd rather they just come over and tell me they appreciate my stopping in and that they hope I enjoyed it and will come back.

If you're a starting pitcher in the majors and you stay healthy, you will make a lot of money in a short time. Where's the incentive? It's unbelievable. When I broke into the big leagues you had to excel if you even wanted to make a living. During my first three years with the Mets I didn't make a living, I survived.

The young guys on the Rangers pitching staff are a good group. They work hard and they're willing to condition their bodies. If I have one criticism it's that sometimes they lose sight of their goals. I want to ask them what it is exactly that they're trying to accomplish. When you're in the weight room, you shouldn't be just building muscle or staying in shape, although that's good. Anything that doesn't go into making you a better pitcher ought to be cut out of your regimen. Have a plan. Be committed. Get focused.

I'd love it if one rookie would come to me and say, "I've made the team and I want to do well. What do I need to do?"

I'd tell him it's a lot of work, but it's also fairly simple. Learn the game by studying it. Know what separates the average player from the good player. You'll see some players at this level who are just exceptionally gifted athletes. They're going to stand above everybody and there's nothing you can do about that. Then you've got guys who have just run-of-the-mill big league talent, which is no small thing. It already sets them apart from minor leaguers and tens of thousands of other guys who only dream of playing in the majors. Then you look at the Pete Roses and the Don Suttons and the Cal Ripkens and you ask yourself, how did these guys with run-of-the-mill talent or even less make themselves into outstanding Hall-of-Fame-type players? When you get a handle on that, you're on your way to doing well.

The answer is that it was their hearts and their drive and their intellects. They wanted to become the best ballplayers they could, so they put in extra work. They put in the time on fundamentals, played to their strengths, and worked on their weaknesses. They anticipated situations and made mental as well as physical commitments. Anybody can commit to physical exertion for a limited period. The man who can commit himself to mental discipline has to be alert constantly.

One thing that really disgusts me with the modern player is when he shows off. These guys who hit a home run and then stand in the box and flip their bat away like they're really something just make you want to put the first pitch in their ear the next time around. They might hit one out and then almost walk around the bases, pumping their fist or trying some other way to draw attention to themselves. You don't see me pumping my arms or pointing at guys when I strike them out. I've seen pitchers blow on their finger like it's a smoking pistol after a strikeout. That's bush league.

Sometimes a little emotion, if it's real and spontaneous, is refreshing. I smiled after my seventh no-hitter; I just couldn't help it. I was so happy it had come at Arlington Stadium and that everything worked well after how bad I felt before the game. But usually, even after an achievement like that, I don't do anything that rubs it in to the other team or makes it look like I think I'm hot stuff.

When Carlton Fisk hit that dramatic extra-inning home run in the World Series years ago, it was moving to see him waving and using body English to try to keep it from going foul. That was real. But how many times in all the years since have you seen Carlton do more than clap on the field?

When Kirk Gibson hit that game-winning homer in game one of the 1988 World Series, coming off the bench hardly able to walk, no one begrudged his little fist pumping celebration as he circled the bases. But that was for the situation, not for himself.

The young ballplayers do that all the time in normal games. It's become widespread, and it's horrible, but they think nothing of it. They grew up watching Rickey Henderson and Reggie

Jackson and those guys doing it on ESPN and highlight shows, showing up the other team. And those are two guys with talent who didn't need to do that stuff.

Fisk wasn't admiring his homer. Gibson wasn't admiring his homer. They were pulling for their teams, trying to win, knowing how important their runs were. We had a guy come into Arlington with Seattle who was hitting under .200. I mean he was in a terrible slump and hadn't hit a homer for about six weeks. Well, he finally connects off one of our guys, and it's one of those shots that you know is gone when it hits the bat. He stands at home plate and flips his bat away like it was a weapon and he was Ted Williams or somebody. I was thinking, *What in the world is goin' on?*

That's when you wish Bob Gibson or Don Drysdale was pitching for you, because that guy would pay dearly for a stunt like that the next time up. The best revenge is success anyway, so even though I might not throw at a bat flipper, he'll sure be facing the best I've got to offer next time. With nobody out and nobody on I'll still go after him like we're tied in the bottom of an extra-inning World Series game with a man in scoring position. That's the way I pitched to Pete Rose when he was going for the National League career hit record. If Pete was going to break the record off me, he was going to earn it.

You won't see me ragging on a guy during a game either. Some guys are good at razzing and hollering. I don't think there's any profit in screaming at umpires from the bench either. It's a thankless job and every call is a judgment. If they're wrong, they're wrong, and you're not going to change that.

Mike Scott of the Astros was one of the most talented pitchers I ever played with as far as being big and strong and being able to throw. He knew what he was doing and was one of the premier big league pitchers during the last few years when I was with Houston.

When he was on the mound, he was a committed pitcher. He'd do whatever it took to win. But off the mound he was one of the laziest pitchers I have ever seen. He was blessed with natural strength and ability, and he took it as far as it would take him. He developed that split-finger fastball that made him almost unhittable in 1986 when he won the Cy Young Award and all that. He had people convinced he was scuffing the ball, which distracted them and made him even more effective, whether he was actually doing it or not. But he never did anything to enhance himself physically. Would never work. Nothing. Didn't run. Didn't lift. Had terrible eating habits. All he cared about was playing golf.

Now he has retired before his time due to an injury. Who am I to say the injury could have been prevented? I don't know. Just seems to me a guy who keeps himself in shape can either avoid a lot of serious injuries or bounce back from them. I always liked Mike, but I can't say it surprised me that his career didn't last as long as I felt it should have. When I used to tease him about not working out or about eating junk food, he'd say something like, "You think I want to be pitching 'til I'm forty? No way. I'll be out on the links."

Well, a fella's got the rest of his life for that. There's only so much golf you can play. While he's young and healthy, he should take advantage of the opportunities he has. And being in shape wouldn't have just allowed him to pitch longer. He would have been even better than he was, and when you're talking about Mike Scott being better, you're talking about an exciting thing. He was fabulous as it was. Just think of him being a complete pitcher; who knows what he might have accomplished?

Mike was a good-natured guy and could take my teasing. Sometimes we'd be sitting around harassing each other about habits and work and stuff, and he'd make fun of me for being a hick, working with cows and horses and all. I needled him about his inability to work and that he probably didn't know anything about animals or even a shovel or how to fix a flat tire. I said, "Mike, tell me, have you ever had a job?"

He looked at me funny, so I pressed him. I said, "Mike, I want you to tell me. Have you ever in your life had a real honest-to-goodness job?"

The other guys were hooting because they could see he was trying to think. "You haven't!" somebody said.

"I have a job," he muttered.

I said, "What's your job?"

"I play baseball."

"That's no job. You said it yourself. 'I *play*.' Have you ever had a *real* job, one where you had to get up in the morning and be somewhere at seven-thirty or eight o'clock? Where you had thirty minutes for lunch and didn't get off until five? Where you had to actually do something, and you got paid hourly?" Now we had an audience, so I kept pushing. "Have you ever had one of those?"

"Once," Mike said.

"Once? What was it?"

He told me that when he played in a college summer league they provided jobs for the guys because they couldn't pay them. They played for the local team at night and had jobs during the day.

"So what was *your* job?"

"I worked in a warehouse. I'd get there at nine and had to stay there 'til noon. Once in a while someone would call and have me put something in a box and tape it up and ship it out."

We were laughing. That was the only real job he had ever held in his life, and that's the case with a lot of ballplayers. They don't really know what it is to have to work. Because of that, they don't have a concept of what it means to be committed to your job or being in a situation where if you don't work you don't get paid, and if you don't get paid you don't make ends meet.

I'll never forget a player in the '70s who usually hit over .300 and was one of those elite, gifted athletes. He had a beautiful swing and could crush the ball, was a great base runner and a heads-up player. He made good money and was an All-Star, but he hardly ever took batting practice. Knowing how tough this game is and how hard it is to hit .300, you tell me: If a guy like that works hard, what happens? Could he have hit .400? Would he have been a Hall of Famer? There's no telling how great he could have been.

That lack of work ethic is why you see so many guys come in and out of baseball and make tremendous dollars for a short time and then wind up with very little. They take the same approach to their money that they took toward their jobs, and they don't plan for the future. If they are careful with the money they do receive, they can set *themselves* up for life, but most of them don't. There are a lot of real working people out there who won't make in a lifetime what some journeymen ballplayers make in a few years. But what have they got to show for it when they're out of the game?

Many of them end up declaring bankruptcy and leaving people holding the bag, then they say they got dealt a bad hand. The thing is, they had an opportunity and they didn't take advantage of it. All our lives we hear that old line about putting something away for a rainy day, but not too many ballplayers actually do it. They listen to the wrong people, the wrong financial advisers. They want to make a quick killing, a fast buck. They had no respect for their money so they spent it, thinking it would be a never-ending deal. They weren't prepared for the kinds of resources they got, and now they have to scratch for a living just like anybody else. You hate to see that happen.

I'm not the kind of a guy to give advice to the kids on the Rangers. I like this team, and occasionally I'll be asked for my opinion. But I low-key it. They have to learn on their own. They know I'm here and they can ask me anything: about baseball, money, life, whatever. I figure nobody listens to advice unless they ask for it, and a lot of the time they don't listen to that either.

I'm impressed that the Rangers ballplayers for the most part are hard workers and dedicated to conditioning. I do want to see them focus on what's really important, preparing to get every edge they can. The game is so competitive today and there is so much balance; that's why you see a last-place team beating a first-place team on a given night.

The Rangers had one of the best hitting clubs in the majors in 1991. Now if all the young guys can have the pride and commitment it takes to be excellent and not look at their careers as just a means to generate revenue, we might finally turn a corner and play up to the potential that's been here for the last few years. Arlington is ready for a winner, and I get asked all the time about whether the Rangers can really do it. Let me tell you about a few of the front-liners, and you decide.

16
The New Rangers

My only hesitation about talking about our current ball club is that things change so quickly. By the time you read this we could have traded away some of these players and have a new one that will make all the difference. But that's the hazard of being in a profession like mine.

I also need to apologize in advance to the players I don't name here. I'm sticking with the basic starting lineup from last season, but I know as well as anyone that it's the whole roster that makes a club a winner. As a pitcher it's great to be able to say that the team I'm with is one of the most potent offensive clubs in the big leagues.

I think the only reason we didn't win our division last year was because we had so many injuries to our pitching staff. We just didn't pitch on the level we needed to for us to be contenders, even though we had a fourteen-game winning streak early and started a seven-game streak a couple of weeks later. We also had an eight-game losing streak, but four of those were by one run, and two of those were in extra innings (one of which was eighteen innings long). Not much later we won ten of thirteen games and actually spent a good bit of the season in first place. But we just weren't consistent enough in the second half, and, as I said, our pitchers were hurt. When you look at our list of transactions for the season, pitcher after pitcher is going on or coming off the disabled list, going into surgery, or going on rehab assignment. That makes it hard to develop momentum.

In a way, all those injuries to our pitching staff can work for us. A lot of young kids who wouldn't have otherwise gotten big league experience were pressed into service. Now they know what it's like and what they're up against. I looked forward to spring training because so many of the younger pitchers can look good after even only a year or two in the majors. They don't have that raw rookie look to them anymore. Maybe they haven't had any huge success yet, but they'll come in as veterans, a little more relaxed with a better idea of what it takes to succeed. If they're willing to keep learning and keep working, and—you knew this was coming—stay focused, we could be a team to contend with. We've sure got the bats to back us up.

The ball club was probably looking to a major trade to improve the pitching, but unless they were ready to give up one of our truly great hitters, we're likely going to have the same basic lineup. I'm not optimistic about a deal that would bring us another front-line starter. I'd hate to see them dismantle the offense to improve the pitching staff.

Every club needs a guy who can give you 225–250 innings, and that didn't happen for us last year. Bobby Witt is the kind of pitcher who could be a workhorse like that, but he only started sixteen games in '91 because of injuries. He pitched a four-hit shutout over Cleveland in April but went on the disabled list in May with a rotator cuff tear. In September he had arthroscopic surgery to remove a bone spur from his elbow. If he comes back strong, he could be a good one for us. He's a strikeout pitcher with twenty-two games of ten or more K's.

Kevin Brown had the most starts (33) and innings (210) and was third in strikeouts and fourth in wins. He didn't complete any games and his innings were the lowest by a staff leader since 1973. He did allow a lot of base runners (averaging more than fourteen per nine innings), but if he becomes more durable, he might be a guy we can count on for a lot of innings.

I should be able to contribute the way I have the past few years, and if I can stay off the disabled list I will increase my innings pitched. But they probably won't count on me to take the biggest share of innings. The club probably would hope I could go 175–200 innings, but I wouldn't mind shooting for 225 if I'm healthy.

Jose Guzman led us in wins last year with thirteen and an ERA of 3.08 even though he wasn't recalled from the minors until late in May. He was the American League Comeback Player of the Year after having been out with an injury since 1988. He pitched two two-hitters, including a complete game shutout. He's only the eighth pitcher in big league history to win at least ten games in a season, then not pitch for two seasons, and win at least ten in his first year back. He was remarkable, but since they weren't counting on him coming back at all, they probably won't expect him to log a huge number of innings. Whatever we can get out of him will be great, and if he's strong, who knows?

You look at the hitters on this team and you wonder how we could ever lose a ball game. But winning also takes good defense. That's a problem for us. We made too many errors and too often didn't make the big plays that would have kept us in ball games.

At catcher we platooned Geno Petralli, a lefthanded hitter, and Mike Stanley, who hit righty, until Ivan Rodriguez joined us in June. In October both Petralli and Stanley were granted free agency, and Rodriguez looks like he could be one of the best catching prospects ever. He started 80 percent of our last hundred games, and at age nineteen was one of the youngest Rangers ever.

He played his first big league game for us in Chicago on the day he got married. He also singled and threw out two runners. The next day he became the first teenager to catch for a pitcher over forty years old in a big league game when he and I were the battery against the White Sox. He hit three homers in six games and wound up hitting .264. He's going to be a great one and has the chance to be another Benito Santiago.

My guess is he'll start 90 percent of our games. He'll have to learn how to handle the pitchers, which is always tough for a kid. He speaks very little English too, so he's going to have to learn the language, learn the league, learn the hitters, and learn to take charge. If anybody can do it, he can. It'll come with experience.

At first base we have one of the best hitters in the league, Rafael Palmiero. He and second baseman Julio Franco battled for the league batting title until the last few weeks when Palmiero fell off to finish at .322 and Franco won it with a .341. Palmiero has a pretty swing, a lot like Billy Williams used to have with the Cubs and like Dave Justice has now with the Braves. You either have that swing or you don't; it's not something that can be taught.

Palmiero also has a little more power than Franco with twenty-six homers and eighty-eight runs batted in, compared to Julio's fifteen and seventy-eight. Rafael is no Kent Hrbek or Keith Hernandez with the glove, but he's no Cecil Fielder either. He's got a great attitude and works hard to make himself a complete ballplayer, not just a hitter. He's matured and does a good job for being fairly new to the position. He came up as an outfielder with the Cubs. They don't have a thing to show for trading him to us now.

Palmiero led the majors in doubles and was second in total bases, runs, and extra-base hits. He was fifth in the American

League in multi-hit games. He and Ruben Sierra were tied for third in the big leagues with 203 hits.

Julio Franco at second, besides being the batting champion, knows how to run the bases and play the offensive part of the game. You can't keep a hitter like that out of the lineup, but frankly he hurts us defensively. He makes an awful lot of errors, and I doubt he's going to improve because his approach to catching ground balls is not very good fundamentally. He bends at the waist instead of the knees and he catches the ball too far back. He makes outstanding plays once in a while because he's both quick and fast and knows what he should do, but he hasn't got the correct approach to play his position. He was the All-Star second baseman, but it was because of his hitting. It's the normal, routine plays that make you or break you, and even *Sports Illustrated* said, "There's no way the Rangers can win a championship with as poor a defensive player as Franco playing second base."

That magazine was speculating that we'd trade Julio for pitching help, but that's a tough call. I don't know that it makes sense to trade away the batting champion, even if he's not the best fielder. There's been some talk about hiding him in the outfield, but I don't know if they'd really do that. I don't mean to put him down, but I think he likes to hit more than he likes to work at shoring up his defense. And he's quite a hitter.

At third base we had Steve Beuchele, who I thought was the best defensive third baseman in baseball and was having one of his best years offensively. But he was traded to Pittsburgh for a minor league pitcher and a player to be named later. It wasn't a popular trade with the fans or in the clubhouse, because he was one of the team leaders.

But the Rangers had Dean Palmer, a minor league slugger with incredible power. He had twenty-two homers at Oklahoma

City in the first part of the season, so they figured he was ready for third base. The two big question marks on him are whether he can handle the position defensively and can he make enough contact at the plate. He hit fifteen homers for us, so the potential is there, but he hit only .187 and has a lot of improving to do in the field.

I do think he can work on the fielding and that he has the rookie jitters behind him. He has the confidence that he's played third base on a regular basis in the big leagues. The verdict's still out on him, but he's got the potential.

Most clubs try out their minor league prospects late in the season when the farm system schedules are over and the big league club is out of the race. The only problem with that is that you bring up a bunch of kids and then you find yourself fighting for second or third place and you can't afford to drop any farther in the standings. It's a lot easier to sell your ball club to the fans the next season if you finished a respectable second place than it is if you were way out of the running and had a lineup with six unfamiliar names in it the last few weeks. So it's a no-win situation. These kids need the work and the experience, but sometimes the club can't afford to give it to them.

Shortstop is going to be up for grabs, and we'll probably start whoever has won the job in spring training. Jeff Kunkel tore up a knee in spring training last year and was out for the year. Jeff Huson started about half the games for us until he went on the disabled list with a tendon tear in his knee in August. Then we brought up Jose Hernandez from Tulsa, who started thirty-five games. He was four-for-four in his first official at-bats in the majors and hit over .300 for the first dozen games, but he fell off to .184 by the end of the season. I was glad to see the Rangers pick up free agent Dickie Thon, who had been with the Phillies. He's a guy who, if he returns to form, could really help us. We'll just have to see who emerges there.

We were a little unsettled in left field too. At first they thought Jack Daugherty would be the answer, but he played less than sixty games because of injuries and an appendectomy. He hit over .300 in his last seventeen games. When he was out Kevin Reimer played a lot of left field. He hit .269 with twenty homers, had a five-hit game against Kansas City in June, and hit nine homers in August. For the year he hit a home run for every twenty at-bats. We did a lot of platooning in left, but we need to get consistent there.

In center we had Juan Gonzalez, who led the team in home runs with twenty-seven and had 102 RBI. He's only twenty-two years old and is the youngest Ranger ever to hit twenty home runs in a season. He was the eighteenth youngest ever in the majors to drive in a hundred runs. He was hurt early in the season, but finished strong. Gary Pettis, the former Golden Glove winner, played some center for us because of his defensive ability, but his hitting is down, so we'll probably be going with Gonzalez.

Ruben Sierra in right field is one of those franchise players who doesn't come along very often. He's a great natural hitter and wound up at .307 with twenty-five homers and 116 RBI. He made the All-Star team for the second time and finished high in the voting for MVP. He had four four-hit games and drove in five runs in a game three times. He hit safely in 123 games.

When I first came to the Rangers I liked his potential, but he was not a good fielder and took a lot of criticism for it. He's worked on that and he's improved considerably. He's one of the anchors on the Rangers now. Ruben would like to win an MVP, and I don't blame him. He's got all the tools. In 1989 he lost a close MVP race to Robin Yount and thought he should have won it.

The last two years Cecil Fielder of Detroit has finished second in the MVP balloting. Talk about a one-dimensional player. He's a huge guy with a big bat, but he's not much on the field. He's so strong he doesn't even have to hit the ball well to hit it out. I usually pitch him away and then try to surprise him inside once in a while. But you don't want to get behind on him because then you have to give him a better pitch. As a ball club we've had a fair amount of success getting him out. He's always among the leaders in homers and strikeouts.

In a tough situation, I'd rather see one of our three top hitters at the plate: Sierra, Franco, or Palmiero. If I had to choose one, I'd have to go with Ruben. He'll strike out more often than Julio or Rafael, but he's the man you want up there when you need the big hit. He's our biggest RBI guy.

No matter who you talk to in the big leagues, they'll tell you that their club could win if it got some breaks and stayed healthy. Well, with the Rangers that's true. We've sure got the horses.

17
As for Me

*T*he Texas Rangers are the right kind of a ball club for me to finish my career with. There's a lot of offense, the possibility of some good pitching, I like the manager, and unless the ballpark were right up the road from Alvin, it couldn't be more convenient. Management's been good to me, and the fans are the greatest. There's something about how Texans take to one of their own. It's a real love affair between a guy who'd rather pitch before the home folks than anywhere else in the world.

In fact, one of the local sportswriters, who must have thought I might be getting too old or tired or feeble to keep up with the pace, speculated that maybe I should only pitch at home. Can you imagine? No road trips. No travel. No way that would work. I'd be all out of sync and rhythm and wouldn't pitch on a regular schedule.

It happened last year that I was on the disabled list a couple of times when the team was on the road, and I came off the list when they got home. Also, if I pitched the last game of a home stand, I might do my next day's workout in Arlington and not join the club on the road until the next day. I appreciate those kinds of privileges and think I've earned them, but I also think accommodating me a little like that is good for the club. If I'm healthy and in shape and rested, I do better.

I've so far surpassed any expectations I've ever had about longevity that I just take it a day at a time the way everybody else does. I know that an injury could stop me, and I also know that age is bound to catch up with me one of these days. But when? I shouldn't be able to do what I do now, so who's to say I can't still do it when I'm fifty?

I'd like to say this year is it, or next year for sure, but I've been saying that for a long time. I just don't want to say it anymore. I'll decide based on how I feel and whether I really believe I can help the club. If I don't think so or if they don't think so, I've got plenty to keep me busy.

The aging process is affecting me the way it does a lot of people, with aches and pains and stiffness, but for the most part it hasn't affected my pitching. I've given it every chance to catch up with me by throwing a lot more pitches than most, so I can only credit my staying power to genetics, mechanics, and conditioning.

One thing I'm glad of, and that is that I haven't lost my drive to pitch. That's a big part of my success. It would be real easy to sit back and enjoy all the records, and no one anywhere would begrudge me the pleasure. They'd say I've earned it and have nothing more to prove. But I've still got that competitive drive when I'm on the field. If I lost that, I'd quit real quick, because I'm convinced you can't survive at this level without it. You can lose a little of your physical power and compensate with drive, but without the drive it doesn't make any difference what kind of ability you have. You're not going to get far until you have a burning desire to excel.

Now after having said all that, I realize that this very well could be my last season, and it wouldn't surprise me a lot if it is. The wear and tear physically and mentally of trying to hold up under the demands makes me not want to think of the year after this. I have to walk away from it at some point.

In the summer of 1991 we signed a two-year extension that gives the club an option for the second year, 1993. Whether I play that second year or not, once I'm through as a player I'm committed to the ten-year personal services contract—which I'm more than happy to fulfill.

There are a lot of things we'd like to do as a family and that Ruth and I would like to do and haven't been able to because of all the travel. We'd like to see the country in the spring and summer when we're not on someone else's schedule. Think of it: my springs and summers have been booked solid for twenty-five years.

In some ways my schedule now is harder on Ruth than it's ever been. There are more demands on my time, more obligations to the public, all the commercial stuff—she'll be as happy as I am when that's all behind us. I've felt it necessary to take advantage of all the opportunities that have come to me with the attention from the three hundred wins and the five thousand strikeouts and the last two no-hitters. But the prospect of having a week to myself someday without having to plan for it months in advance, that looks pretty good.

You probably won't see me doing color work on television or anything like that. It isn't that I don't have anything to say or that I couldn't learn to be comfortable doing that. It's just that I have no desire to travel as part of a job. If I'm traveling, I want it to be with my wife and family, just going somewhere because we want to when we want to, not hurrying or worrying. I've always been a homebody. I like to be at home every night if I can. I like to sleep in my own bed. Life on the road, as I've said, is only glamorous to people who've never done it.

When the baseball life *is* finally over, it's going to be an adjustment for everybody in our family. One thing I'm sure of is that I will be through playing by the time Reese and Wendy are out of high school. I like the idea of being around here while they're still in school.

The only goal I ever really had was to be successful in whatever I was doing. There were things I wanted to acquire, and baseball has made that possible. I always wanted a ranch, and I still dream of putting together a spread that could run five or six hundred cows in one location. I'm in the process of putting that together, but I'll get serious about it when I free up some time. I've always been attracted to an area in south Texas where I can spend a lot of time doing what I want to do, operating a ranch on a day-to-day basis without being required to be there every minute.

I don't sit around reflecting on my career, and I probably never will. The reason I don't now is because I'm still in it. I don't want to live in the past. I get a lot of satisfaction out of what I have accomplished and knowing that it's brought joy to people, but when it's over, I'll just move on.

One thing I don't want to do is wait until I can't get the ball to the plate before I know it's time to hang it up. It's a bitter pill to swallow when you realize you can't get the job done any longer, and every player handles it differently. You see a lot of guys retire and live off the glow of that until it wears off, then they want to make a comeback. They watch television and they think they can hit the new pitchers or get out the new hitters. It's sad to see them try to come back. You'll never see me doing that. Once I decide it's over, it'll be over.

I can say I want to be prepared to deal with how much I'll miss the game, but I suppose it's like thinking you're prepared for a loved one's death. There's no doubt in my mind that I'll miss baseball a lot. You don't have something dominate your life this long and then walk away from it without regrets.

People are always asking me if I think about the Hall of Fame. I really don't, and I hope people know me well enough by now to know that I'm being truthful. The subject is brought up more and more each year as guys younger than me are being elected. People used to debate whether I'd make it. Now they pretty much assume I will. I don't think about it one way or the other. I believe you can only control what you can control, and since Hall of Famers are chosen by people voting, I'll leave it at that. If they think I'm deserving, I'll make it. If they don't, I won't.

I can live with that. Either way, I'll always be able to look in the mirror and know that the guy looking back gave the game and the fans and his ball club everything he had to give for as long as he could.

Appendix: Extra Innings

Lynn Nolan (Nolan) Ryan, Jr.

Born: January 31, 1947   Height: 6'2"   Weight: 212   Bats: Right   Throws: Right

Birthplace/Residence:	Born in Refugio, TX...Raised and lives in Alvin, TX.
Major League Service:	24 years, 101 days
How Acquired:	Signed as a free agent, December 7, 1988.

In 1991, NOLAN RYAN (12-6, 2.91) ranked 3rd in the American League in strikeouts, compiled the league's 5th best earned run average (2.91), and tied for the 7th highest winning percentage (.667)...Led the Rangers' staff in ERA, shutouts (2), and strikeouts and was 2nd in wins (12), starts (27), complete games (2), and innings (173)...Recorded the A.L.'s best ratios for fewest hits (5.3) and baserunners (9.3) and most strikeouts (10.56) per 9 innings... Held the opposition to major league lows in batting average at .173 (102–594), slugging percentage at .285 (169–594), and on-base percentage at .263 (179–680)...His ERA was his 2nd lowest in the last 10 seasons (2.76 in 1987), the lowest for a Texas qualifier since RICK HONEYCUTT (2.42) in 1983, and 7th lowest in club history (min. 162 innings pitched).

VICTORIES: His 12 wins were the most for a pitcher, 44 or older, since the Yankees' TOMMY JOHN (13) in 1987...Was just the 6th time that a pitcher, 44 or older has won as many as 12 games...The others:

WINS	PITCHER	TEAM	YEAR	AGE
18	Jack Quinn	Philadelphia (A.L.)	1928	45
16	Phil Niekro	New York (A.L.)	1984	45
16	Phil Niekro	New York (A.L.)	1985	46
13	Tommy John	New York (A.L.)	1987	44
12	Satchel Paige	St. Louis (A.L.)	1952	46

Of the above group, only Quinn (2.90) had a lower ERA...Overall, has 61 wins since turning 40, 5th all-time behind Niekro (121), Quinn (89), CY YOUNG (76), and WARREN SPAHN (75)...Was the 20th time has won 10 or more games, 2nd most in history, one behind DON SUTTON...Finished 6 games over .500 to match best record ever with 1974 (22-16) and 1989 (16-10).

STRIKEOUTS: His 203 strikeouts marked 15th time with 200+ strikeouts and 23rd time with 100+ strikeouts, extending own records...Was his 22nd consecutive year with 100 or more K's, one more than Sutton...Had his string of 4 straight league strikeout titles (2 N.L./2 A.L.) ended...Previous record for strikeouts by a pitcher, 44 or older, was 149 by Niekro in 1985...Fanned 10 or more 6 times to bring career total to 213, 115 more than 2nd place SANDY KOUFAX...Tied his own Rangers' team mark with 16 strikeouts in no-hitter on May 1 vs. Toronto, his 26th game of 15+ K's...Set a club mark with 7 consecutive strikeouts on July 7 against California...Recorded his 5500th strikeout by fanning Seattle's TINO MARTINEZ on Sept. 30 at Arlington...Has fanned 1145 different batters in career, adding 25 1st-time victims in 1991.

LOW-HIT/LOW-RUN GAMES: Pitched his 7th career no-hitter on May 1 against Toronto at Arlington...Has 3 more no-hitters than any pitcher in history...Has been the oldest pitcher to ever throw a no-hitter with each of last 2 gems (June 11, 1990 at Oakland)...Threw 122 pitches and allowed walks to KELLY GRUBER in the 1st and JOE CARTER in the 7th, matching fewest walks ever in his no-hitters...Fanned ROBERTO ALOMAR for final out and 16th strikeout, 2nd most in any of his no-hitters...Was his 19th low-hit game...Other complete game was also a shutout, a 6-hitter vs. Chicago on June 11...Retired 1st 18 batters and had no-hitter for 7 innings on July 7 vs. California before DAVE WINFIELD singled to lead off the 8th...Overall, did not allow a run in 7 starts with a pair of combined shutouts in addition to 2 complete games...Allowed 2 or fewer runs 15 times and 2 or less hits on 11 occasions.

MISCELLANEOUS: His 27 starts and 173 innings were fewest in a full season since 1971 with the Mets...Worked 7 or more innings 14 times...Was the A.L.'s Player of the Week for Apr. 29-May 5 after no-hitter...Was 2-2, 3.94 (13 er/29.2 ip) over 1st 4 starts, then went 1-1, 1.40 (3 er/19.1 ip) in next 3 outings before going on the d.l. with a strained muscle in back of right shoulder on May 14...Was activated on May 29, losing 1st outing to give a 3-4, 3.57 mark...Beginning June 6, was 9-2, 2.62 (35 er/120 ip) in final 19 starts...Was 4-1, 2.22 (17 er/69 ip) in 1st 10 games of this span before being disabled for a 2nd time from July 29-Aug. 18 with more shoulder strain...Upon return, was 5-1, 3.18 (18 er/51 ip) in final 9 outings...After losing to Kansas City on Aug. 24, was 4-0 in last 7 starts...Was 10-4 in 20 home starts, 6-0 in last 9 games after losing to Toronto on July 18...Did not allow a homer in last 9 starts after Detroit's TRAVIS FRYMAN went deep on July 28...Issued just .62 hrs/9 innings, the 10th best ratio in the league.

CAREER: Has a major league record of 314-278 in 25 seasons...Is the all-time leader in strikeouts (5511) and walks (2686) and ranks among the leaders in starts (3rd, 733), losses (3rd, one behind WALTER JOHNSON), shutouts (T8th, 61), innings (10th, 5163.1), wins (T13th with GAYLORD PERRY), and ERA (18th, 3.15)...Set a major league mark on July 23 by making his 545th straight start without a relief appearance...Has now gone 554 games since last relief outing on July 28, 1974.

In 3 seasons with Texas, is 41-25 with a 3.20 ERA (219 er/616.1 ip) and 736 strikeouts...His .621 winning percentage is best in team history (50 or more decisions) while his 3.20 ERA is 2nd lowest behind BERT BLYLEVEN (2.74)...Is also on the Rangers' all-time list in strikeouts (4th), shutouts (7th, 6), wins (9th), and innings (10th)...With his 1st appearance in 1992, will have played in majors in 26 different seasons, tying DEACON McGUIRE and TOMMY JOHN for the most seasons played.

300-GAME WINNERS

511—Cy Young	342—Tim Keefe	311—Tom Seaver
416—Walter Johnson	329—Steve Carlton	308—Hoss Radbourn
373—Christy Mathewson	327—John Clarkson	307—Mickey Welch
373—Grover Alexander	324—Don Sutton	305—Eddie Plank
363—Warren Spahn	318—Phil Niekro	300—Lefty Grove
361—Kid Nichols	314—Gaylord Perry	300—Early Wynn
361—Pud Glavin	**314—NOLAN RYAN**	

RYAN'S ROUTINE: Nolan Ryan follows a workout routine that begins after he finishes pitching a game. The sequence varies, depending on personal commitments.

Post-game: Ices right arm, 20-25 minutes...Rides Lifecycle, 30 minutes.

Next morning: Heavy weight work (50,000 to 55,000 pounds) for upper and lower body with medium dumbbells and weight machine.

Afternoon after game: Abdominal work, 15 varieties of lifts, crunches and sit ups, 40 minutes...Light dumbbell program, 20 minutes...Forward and backward 40-yard sprints, 15-20 minutes...Throws football and baseball, as tolerance allows...Rides Lifecycle or swims, 20 minutes (if stiff).

Two days after game: Duplicates first day routine except for weight work... Long toss with football, 10-15 minutes...Long toss one-hop drill with baseball, 10-15 minutes...Flat-ground work with fastball, working on fundamentals and skills at distance of 35 feet, 15 minutes.

Three days after game: Duplicates entire first day routine...Loosens up throwing football...Works off the bullpen mound at full speed, 10-15 minutes.

Four days after game: "Acute" rest day...Abbreviated heavy weights, light dumbbells, stretching, abdominal work and running as necessary.

Pre-game: Duplicates fourth day routine with weight work limited to 5,000-10,000 pounds...Throws football with catcher Mike Stanley...Three or four hard outfield sprints 20 minutes before game...Long toss with bullpen catcher, 4-5 minutes...Warm up in bullpen, 8-10 minutes...Returns to clubhouse, towels off...Takes the mound after the national anthem.

YEAR	CLUB	W-L	ERA	G	GS	CG	SHO	SV	IP	H	R	ER	BB	SO
1965	Marion-1	3-6	4.38	13	12	2	1	0	78.0	61	47	38	56	115
1966	Greenville	*17.2	2.51	*29	28	9	5	0	183.0	109	59	51	*127	*272
	Williamsport	0-2	0.95	3	3	0	0	0	19.0	9	6	2	12	35
	New York (NL)	0-1	15.00	2	1	0	0	0	3.0	5	5	5	3	6
1967	Winter Haven-2	0-0	2.25	1	1	0	0	0	4.0	1	1	1	2	5
	Jacksonville	1-0	0.00	3	0	0	0	0	7.0	3	1	0	3	18
1968	New York (NL)	6-9	3.09	21	18	3	0	0	134.0	93	50	46	75	133
1969	New York (NL)	6-3	3.54	25	10	2	0	1	89.0	60	38	35	53	92
1970	New York (NL)	7-11	3.41	27	19	5	2	1	132.0	86	59	50	97	125
1971	New York (NL)-3	10-14	3.97	30	26	3	0	0	152.0	125	78	67	116	137
1972	California	19-16	2.28	39	39	20	*9	0	284.0	166	80	72	*157	*329
1973	California	21-16	2.87	41	39	26	4	1	326.0	238	113	104	*162	*383
1974	California	22-16	2.89	42	41	26	3	0	*333.0	221	127	107	*202	*367
1975	California	14-12	3.45	28	28	10	5	0	198.0	152	90	76	132	186
1976	California	17-*18	3.36	39	39	21	*7	0	284.0	193	117	106	*183	*327
1977	California	19-16	2.77	37	37	#22	4	0	299.0	198	110	92	*204	*341
1978	California	10-13	3.71	31	31	14	3	0	235.0	183	106	97	*148	*260
1979	California-4	16-14	3.59	34	34	17	#5	0	223.0	169	104	89	114	*223
1980	Houston	11-10	3.35	35	35	4	2	0	234.0	205	100	87	*98	200
1981	Houston	11-5	*1.69	21	21	5	3	0	149.0	99	34	28	68	140
1982	Houston	16-12	3.16	35	35	10	3	0	250.1	196	100	88	*109	245
1983	Houston	14-9	2.98	29	29	5	2	0	196.1	134	74	65	101	183
1984	Houston	12-11	3.04	30	30	5	2	0	183.2	143	78	62	69	197
1985	Houston	10-12	3.80	35	35	4	0	0	232.0	205	108	98	95	209
1986	Houston	12-8	3.34	30	30	1	0	0	178.0	119	72	66	82	194
1987	Houston	8-16	*2.76	34	34	0	0	0	211.2	154	75	65	87	*270
1988	Houston-5	12-11	3.52	33	33	4	1	0	220.0	186	98	86	87	*228
1989	Texas	16-10	3.20	32	32	6	2	0	239.1	162	96	85	98	*301
1990	Texas	13-9	3.44	30	30	5	2	0	204.0	137	86	78	74	*232
1991	Texas	12-6	2.91	27	27	2	2	0	173.0	102	58	56	72	203
A.L. Totals		179-146	3.09	380	377	169	46	1	2798.1	1921	1087	962	1546	3152
N.L. Totals		135-132	3.23	387	356	51	15	2	2365.0	1810	969	848	1140	2359
M.L. Totals		314-278	3.15	767	733	220	61	3	5163.1	3731	2056	1810	2686	5511

MAJOR LEAGUE	AVG	AB	H	HR	RBI
Hitting Totals	.110	852	94	2	33

* - Led League   # - Tied for league lead
1-Selected by New York Mets organization in June '65 free agent draft (10th round, regular phase)...Signed by Red Murff on 6/26/65.
2-On military list, Jan.3-May 13, '67.
3-Acquired by California from New York Mets with pitcher Don Rose, Catcher Francisco Estrada, and outfielder Leroy Stanton in deal for infielder Jim Fregosi on 12/10/71.
4-Granted free agency on 11/1/79...Signed by Houston as a free agent on 11/19/79.
5-Granted free agency on 11/1/88...Signed by Texas as a free agent on 12/7/88.

DIVISIONAL SERIES RECORD

YEAR	CLUB	W-L	ERA	G	GS	CG	SHO	SV	IP	H	R	ER	BB	SO
1981	Hou. vs. L.A.	1-1	1.80	2	2	1	0	0	15.0	6	4	3	3	14

CHAMPIONSHIP SERIES RECORD

YEAR	CLUB	W-L	ERA	G	GS	CG	SHO	SV	IP	H	R	ER	BB	SO
1969	N.Y. vs. Atl.	1-0	2.57	1	0	0	0	0	7.0	3	2	2	2	7
1979	Cal. vs. Balt.	0-0	1.29	1	1	0	0	0	7.0	4	3	1	3	8
1980	Hou. vs. Phil.	0-0	5.40	2	2	0	0	0	13.1	16	8	8	3	14
1986	Hou. vs. N.Y.	0-1	3.86	2	2	0	0	0	14.0	9	6	6	1	17
L.C.S. Totals		1-1	3.70	6	5	0	0	0	41.1	32	19	17	9	46

WORLD SERIES RECORD

YEAR	CLUB	W-L	ERA	G	GS	CG	SHO	SV	IP	H	R	ER	BB	SO
1969	N.Y. vs. Balt.	0-0	0.00	1	0	0	0	1	2.1	1	0	0	2	3

ALL-STAR GAME RECORD

YEAR	CLUB	W-L	ERA	G	GS	CG	SHO	SV	IP	H	R	ER	BB	SO
1972	A.L. at Atl.		Did not Play											
1973	A.L. at K.C.	0-0	9.00	1	0	0	0	0	2.0	2	2	2	2	2
1975	A.L. at Mil.		Did not Play											
1979	A.L. at Sea.	0-0	13.50	1	1	0	0	0	2.0	5	3	3	1	2
1981	N.L. at Cle.	0-0	0.00	1	0	0	0	0	1.0	0	0	0	0	1
1985	N.L. at Minn.	0-0	0.00	1	0	0	0	0	3.0	2	0	0	2	2
1989	A.L. at Cal.	1-0	0.00	1	0	0	0	0	2.0	1	0	0	0	3
A.S.G. Totals		1-0	4.50	5	1	0	0	0	10.0	10	5	5	5	10

Named to 1977 A.L. squad to replace Frank Tanana, but declined.

A.L. CAREER BY PARK THRU 1991

CLUB	W-L-S	ERA	G	IP	H	ER	CLUB	W-L-S	ERA	G	IP	H	ER
Bal.	4-10-0	4.21	15	98.1	75	46	Cal.	85-57-1	2.37	159	1259.0	785	331
Bos.	2-8-0	4.92	13	78.2	75	43	Chi.(O)	5-10-0	5.35	17	112.2	88	67
Cle.	4-5-0	4.22	10	64.0	61	30	Chi.(N)	0-0-0	0.00	1	5.0	1	0
Det.	7-2-0	2.47	10	83.2	54	23	K.C.(M)	0-0-0	3.00	1	6.0	5	2
Mil.	4-5-0	3.76	10	76.2	64	32	K.C.(R)	9-6-0	3.00	18	129.0	98	43
N.Y.(Y)	2-2-0	5.87	6	30.2	35	20	Min.(MS)	8-5-0	3.27	14	118.1	89	43
N.Y.(Shea)	1-2-0	3.66	3	19.2	18	8	Min.(M)	1-0-0	1.29	1	7.0	6	1
Tor.(Ex)	3-1-0	2.53	4	32.0	23	9	Oak.	5-6-0	3.27	13	99.0	65	36
Tor.(Sky)	0-1-0	2.92	2	12.1	7	4	Sea.	7-3-0	3.06	11	79.1	43	27
							Tex.	32-23-0	3.65	72	486.1	329	197

N.Y.(Y) = Yankee Stadium
N.Y.(Shea) = Shea Stadium ('74-'75)
Tor.(Ex) = Exhibition Stadium
Tor.(Sky) = Sky Dome

Chi.(O) = Old Comiskey Park
Chi.(N) = New Comiskey Park
K.C.(M) = Municipal Stadium
K.C.(R) = Royals Stadium
Min.(MS) = Metropolitan Stadium
Min.(M) = Metrodome

1991 AND CAREER PITCHING BREAKDOWN

CLUB	1991 W-L-S	ERA	G	IP	H	ER	CAREER W-L-S	ERA	G	IP	H	ER
Baltimore	3-0-0	1.40	3	19.1	8	3	8-16-0	4.11	28	186.1	147	85
Boston	1-0-0	3.86	1	7.0	3	3	9-14-0	3.48	28	204.1	151	79
Cleveland	0-1-0	5.40	1	8.1	8	5	12-12-0	3.55	26	190.1	146	75
Detroit	1-0-0	1.86	2	9.2	3	2	16-6-0	2.27	26	202.0	122	51
Milwaukee	0-1-0	6.43	1	7.0	9	5	12-10-0	3.01	25	191.1	128	64
New York	0-0-0	2.00	1	9.0	4	2	12-8-0	3.61	25	169.2	136	68
Toronto	1-2-0	2.22	4	28.1	12	7	7-6-0	2.36	16	126.0	79	33
Vs. East	6-4-0	2.74	13	88.2	47	27	76-72-0	3.22	174	1270.0	909	455
California	2-0-0	1.88	2	14.1	8	3	5-3-0	1.76	8	66.1	35	13
Chicago	1-0-0	1.89	3	19.0	13	4	21-15-1	3.21	44	314.0	210	112
Kansas City	1-1-0	4.50	3	14.0	14	7	24-13-0	2.57	42	315.0	221	90
Minnesota	1-1-0	4.91	2	11.0	7	6	20-9-0	2.71	34	272.1	185	82
Oakland	0-0-0	4.50	2	12.0	5	6	11-16-0	2.91	32	241.0	150	78
Seattle	1-0-0	1.93	2	14.0	8	3	11-5-0	3.48	20	144.2	86	56
Texas	—	—	—	—	—	—	11-13-0	3.92	26	174.1	125	76
Vs. West	6-2-0	3.09	14	84.1	55	29	103-74-1	2.99	206	1527.2	1012	507
Pre A.S.G.	5-4-0	2.71	14	96.1	52	29	174-142-2	3.16	419	2739.1	2077	962
Post A.S.G.	7-2-0	3.17	13	76.2	50	27	140-136-1	3.15	348	2423.0	1654	848
Home	10-4-0	3.08	20	131.2	75	45	182-128-2	2.73	404	2865.0	1907	870
Road	2-2-0	2.40	7	41.1	27	11	132-150-1	3.68	363	2297.1	1824	940
Day	3-0-0	1.90	6	42.2	23	9	82-68-1	3.39	210	1315.2	995	496
Night	9-6-0	3.25	21	130.1	79	47	232-210-2	3.07	557	3846.2	2736	1314
As Starter	12-6-0	2.91	27	173.0	102	56	308-277-0	3.15	733	5102.1	3688	1783
As Reliever	—	—	—	—	—	—	6-1-3	4.05	34	60.0	43	27
April	2-2-0	3.94	4	29.2	23	13	50-34-1	3.17	106	693.0	481	244
May	1-2-0	3.09	4	23.1	8	8	57-47-1	3.05	129	905.2	622	307
June	1-0-0	1.20	4	30.0	17	4	51-43-0	3.14	125	857.2	640	299
July	3-1-0	3.00	6	39.0	19	13	46-66-0	3.55	135	908.2	692	358
August	2-1-0	3.75	3	12.0	10	5	49-48-0	3.11	129	878.2	648	304
Sept./Oct.	3-0-0	3.00	6	39.0	25	13	61-40-1	2.92	143	918.2	648	298

CAREER LOW-HIT GAMES

No Hitters (7): May 15, 1973 at Kansas City (3-0); July 15, 1973 at Detroit (6-0); September 28, 1974 vs. Minnesota (4-0); June 1, 1975 vs. Baltimore (1-0); September 26, 1981 vs. Los Angeles (5-0); June 11, 1990 at Oakland (5-0); May 1, 1991 vs. Toronto (3-0).

One Hitters (12): April 18, 1970 vs Philadelphia (7-0); July 9, 1972 vs. Boston (3-0); August 29, 1973 vs. New York Yankees (5-0); June 27, 1974 vs. Texas (5-0); April 15, 1977 vs. Seattle (7-0); May 5, 1978 vs. Cleveland (5-0); July 13, 1979 vs. New York Yankees (6-1); August 11, 1982 at San Diego (3-0); August 3, 1983 at San Diego (1-0); April 23, 1989 at Toronto (4-1); June 3, 1989 at Seattle (6-1); April 26, 1990 vs. Chicago (1-0).

Combined One Hitters (2): June 19, 1980 vs. St. Louis, Ryan (7 ip) and Joe Sambito (2 ip) (2-0); July 22, 1986 vs. Montreal, Ryan (9.1 ip) and Dave Smith (0.2 ip) (1-0).

Two Hitters (19): (2 New York Mets; 13 California; 4 Houston), latest on August 31, 1982 at New York Mets.

Three Hitters (30): (5 New York Mets; 19 California; 3 Houston; 3 Texas), latest on Aug. 28, 1990 at California.

Four Hitters (27): (1 New York Mets; 21 California; 4 Houston; 1 Texas), latest on Sep. 24, 1990 vs. California.

LONGEST WINNING STREAKS

8 games: April 27-July 13, 1983
7 games, twice: August 29-September 27, 1973; August 31-October 3, 1976
6 games, 3 times: July 16-August 31, 1982; May 6-June 17, 1984; June 22-July 31, 1990

STRIKEOUT HIGHS

19, 4 times: June 14, 1974 vs. Boston; August 12, 1974 vs. Boston; August 20, 1974 vs. Detroit; June 8, 1977 vs. Toronto
18, once: September 10, 1976 at Chicago White Sox
17, 3 times: September 30, 1972 vs. Minnesota; July 15, 1973 at Detroit; August 18, 1976 at Detroit.
16, 8 times: latest on May 1, 1991 vs. Toronto
15, 10 times: latest on Aug. 17, 1990 vs. Chicago

NOLAN RYAN'S MAJOR LEAGUE RECORDS

STRIKEOUT RECORDS

1. Most Strikeouts, Major Leagues-5,511.
2. Most Strikeouts, Season, Major and American League-383, California, 1973.
3. Most Strikeouts, Season, Major and American League, Right-handed Pitcher-383, California, 1973.
4. Most Years, 100 or More Strikeouts, Major Leagues-23, New York Mets, 1968, 1970, 1971; California 1972-79; Houston, 1980-88; Texas, 1989-91.
5. Most Consecutive Years, 100 or More Strikeouts-22, New York Mets, 1970-71; California, 1972-79; Houston, 1980-88; Texas, 1989-91.
6. Most Years, 200 or More Strikeouts, Major Leagues-15, California, 1972-79, except 1975; Houston, 1980, 1982, 1985, 1987, 1988; Texas-1989-91.
7. Most Years, 200 or More Strikeouts, American League-10, California, 1972-79, except 1975; Texas, 1989-91.
8. Most Years, 300 or More Strikeouts, Major and American League-6, California, 1972, 1973, 1974, 1976, 1977; Texas, 1989.
9. Most Strikeouts, Losing Pitcher, Extra-Inning Game, Major and American League-19, California, August 20, 1974, 11 innings, lost 1-0.
10. Most Times, 15 or More Strikeouts, Major Leagues-26, New York Mets, 1970 (1), 1971 (1); California, 1972 (4), 1973 (2), 1974 (6), 1976 (3), 1977 (2), 1979 (1); Houston, 1987 (1); Texas, 1989 (1), 1990 (2), 1991 (1).
11. Most Times, 15 or More Strikeouts, Game, American League-23, California, 1972-79; Texas, 1989-91.
12. Most Times, 10 or More Strikeouts, Game, Major Leagues-213, 67 in National League, New York & Houston, 13 Years, 1966, 1968-71, 1980-88; 146 in American League, California & Texas, 11 Years, 1972-79, 1989-91.
13. Most Times, 10 or More Strikeouts, Game, American League-146, California & Texas, 11 Years, 1972-79, 1989-91.
14. Most Times, 10 or More Strikeouts, Game, Season-23, California, 1973.
15. Three Strikeouts, Inning, on Nine Pitched Balls*-New York Mets, April 19, 1968, 3rd inning; California, July 9, 1972, 2nd inning.
16. Most Consecutive Strikeouts, Game, American League-8*, California, July 9, 1972; California, July 15, 1973.
17. Most Strikeouts, Two Consecutive Games, Major and American League-32*, California, August 7 (13), August 12 (19), 1974, 17 innings.
18. Most Strikeouts, Three Consecutive Games, Major and American League-47, California, August 12 (19), August 16 (9), August 20 (19), 1974, 27.1 innings.

NO-HIT AND LOW-HIT GAME RECORDS

19. Most No-Hitters Pitched, Major Leagues-7, California, 1973 (2), 1974, 1975; Texas, 1990, 1991.
20. Most No-Hitters Pitched, American League-6, California, 1973 (2), 1974, 1975; Texas, 1990, 1991.
21. Most No-Hitters Pitched Season-2*, California, May 15, & July 15, 1973.
22. Oldest Pitcher To Throw No-Hitter-44 yrs., 4 mos., 1 day, May 1, 1991 vs Toronto.
23. Most Teams, Throwing No-Hitter-3, California (4); Houston; Texas (2).
24. Most Different Decades, Throwing No-I litter 0, 1070s, 1000s, 1000s.
25. Longest Span Between Throwing No-Hitters-8 yrs., 8 mos., 16 days, Sept. 26, 1981 until June 11, 1990.
26. Most Low-Hit (No-Hit and One-Hit) Games, Season, American League-3*, California, 1973.
27. Most Low-Hit (No-Hit and One-Hit) Games, Career, Major League-19.
28. Most One-Hit Games, Career, Major League-12*.

BASE ON BALLS RECORDS

29. Most Bases on Balls, Major Leagues-2689.
30. Most Years Leading Majors in Most Bases on Balls-8, California, 1972, 1973, 1974, 1976, 1977, 1978; Houston, 1980, 1982.
31. Most Years Leading American League in Most Bases on Balls-6, California, 1972, 1973, 1974, 1976, 1977, 1978.

MISCELLANEOUS RECORDS

32. Most Clubs Shut Out (Won or Tied), Season, Major and American League-8*, California, 1972.
33. Most Years Leading Major Leagues in Most Wild Pitches-6*, California, 1972, 1977, 1978; Houston, 1981, 1986; Texas, 1989.
34. Most Years Leading Amercian League in Most Wild Pitches-4, California, 1972, 1977, 1978; Texas, 1989.
35. Most Wild Pitches, Major Leagues-265.
36. Most Years Leading American League in Most Errors, Pitcher-4*, California, 1975, 1976, 1977 (tied), 1978.

37. Highest Strikeout Average Per Nine Innings, Season-11.48, Houston, 1987, 270 Strikeouts, 211.2 Innings.
38. Highest Strikeout Average Per Nine Innings, Career-9.61, 25 Seasons, 1966, 1968-91, 5511 Strikeouts, 5163.1 Innings.
39. Lowest Hits Allowed Average Per Nine Innings, Season-5.26, California, 1972, 166 Hits, 284 Innings.
40. Lowest Hits Allowed Average Per Nine Innings, Career-6.50, 25 Seasons, 1966, 1968-91, 3731 Hits, 5163.1 Innings.

CHAMPIONSHIP SERIES RECORDS

41. Most Hits Allowed, Five Game Series, National League-16, Houston, 1980.
42. Most Strikeouts, Total Series,-46*, New York Mets, 1969; California, 1979; Houston, 1980, 1986.
43. Most Strikeouts, Game Relief Pitcher-7, New York Mets, October 6, 1969, Pitched Seven Innings.
44. Most Consecutive Strikeouts, Game-4*, California, October 3, 1979.
45. Most Consecutive Strikeouts, Start of Game-4*, California, October 3, 1979.
46. Highest Fielding Percentage, Pitcher, With Most Chances Accepted, Five Game Series, National League-1.000*, Houston, 1980, Four Chances Accepted.
47. Most Assists, Pitcher, Five Game Series, National League-3*, Houston, 1980.
48. Most Chances Accepted, Pitcher, Five Game Series, National League-4*, Houston, 1980.

*Ties Record

RYAN'S CAREER
314 VICTORIES

NO. .. DATE .... TEAM .... SCORE .... LOSING PITCHER

WITH NEW YORK METS

1 .. 4/14/68 .. Houston (A) .... 4-2 .... Larry Dierker
2 .. 5/2/68 .. Philadelphia (H) ... 3-0 ...... Woodie Fryman
3 .. 5/7/68 .... St. Louis (A) .... 4-1 .... Nellie Briles
4 .. 5/14/68 .. Cincinnati (H) .... 3-2 .... Milt Pappas
5 .. 6/7/68 .... San Francisco (A) 4-0 .... Ray Sadecki
6 .. 6/23/68 .. Los Angeles (H) ... 5-4 .... Bill Singer
7 .. 4/20/69 .. *St. Louis (A) .... 11-3 .... Nellie Briles
8 .. 4/29/69 .. *Montreal (A) .... 2-0 .... Mudcat Grant
9 .. 6/20/69 .. St. Louis (H) .... 4-3 .... Bob Gibson
10 .. 8/5/69 .. Cincinnati (A) .... 10-1 .... Jerry Arrigo
11 .. 9/7/69 .... *Philadelphia (H) .. 9-3 ...... Billy Champion
12 .. 9/10/69 .. Montreal (H) .... 7-1 .... Howie Reed
13 .. 4/18/70 .. Philadelphia (H) ... 7-0 .... Jim Bunning
14 .. 4/30/70 .. San Francisco (A) 4-1 .... Mike McCormack
15 .. 5/24/70 .. Chicago (H) .... 3-1 .... Joe Decker
16 .. 5/30/70 .. Houston (H) .... 4-3 .... Larry Dierker
17 .. 6/24/70 .. Chicago (A) .... 6-1 ...... Archie Reynolds
18 .. 8/4/70 .. Chicago (H) .... 4-0 .... Joe Decker
19 .. 9/22/70 .. *Philadelphia (A) .. 7-6 .... Dick Selma
20 .. 4/23/71 .. *Chicago (A) .... 7-6 .... Ron Tompkins
21 .. 4/29/71 .. St. Louis (A) .... 7-0 .... Jerry Reuss
22 .. 5/4/71 .. Chicago (H) .... 2-1 .... Milt Pappas
23 .. 5/11/71 .. Houston (H) .... 8-1 .... Larry Dierker
24 .. 5/21/71 .. Atlanta (H) .... 6-2 .... Pat Jarvis
25 .. 5/29/71 .. San Diego (A) ...... 2-1 .... Tom Phoebus
26 .. 6/25/71 .. Montreal (A) .... 4-1 .... Claude Raymond
27 .. 6/30/71 .. Pittsburgh (H) .... 4-0 .... Steve Blass
28 .. 8/7/71 .. Atlanta (A) .... 20-6 .... Ron Reed
29 .. 9/23/71 .. Chicago (A) .... 5-4 .... Juan Pizarro

WIN NUMBER 1
APRIL 14, 1968

NEW YORK 4,   HOUSTON 0

NEW YORK	ab	r	h	rbi	HOUSTON	ab	r	h	rbi
Har'lson ss	4	0	0	0	Davis cf	3	0	0	0
Boswell 2b	5	1	1	0	Morgan 2b	2	0	1	0
Agee cf	3	2	2	0	Gotay 2b	1	0	1	0
Swoboda rf	3	1	1	0	King c	4	0	0	0
Shamsky lf	3	0	2	2	Staub 1b	4	0	1	0
Jones lf	1	0	1	1	Wynn lf	4	0	1	0
Kranep'l 1b	4	0	0	0	Miller rf	3	0	0	0
Buchek 3b	4	0	1	0	As'monte 3b	3	0	0	0
Grote c	4	0	1	0	Torres ss	3	0	0	0
Ryan p	3	0	0	0	Rader ph	1	0	0	0
Frisella p	1	0	0	0	Dierker p	0	0	0	0
					Thomas ph	1	0	1	0
					Cuellar p	0	0	0	0
					Ray p	0	0	0	0
					Murrell ph	1	0	0	0
					Coombs p	0	0	0	0
Totals	**35**	**4**	**9**	**3**	**Totals**	**30**	**0**	**5**	**0**

New York	0 1 0	1 0 0	0 2 0 — 4
Houston	0 0 0	0 0 0	0 0 0 — 0

New York	IP	H	R	ER	BB	SO
Ryan (W. 1—0)	6 ⅔	3	0	0	2	8
Frisella	2 ⅓	2	0	0	2	3
Houston	**IP**	**H**	**R**	**ER**	**BB**	**SO**
Dierker (L. 1—1)	6	6	2	2	2	3
Cuellar	1*	3	2	1	0	1
Ray	1	0	0	0	0	1
Coombs	1	0	0	0	0	1

*Pitched to four batters in eighth.

E—Morgan 2. DP—Houston 1. LOB—New York 7, Houston 8, 2B—Shamsky, SB—Morgan. SH—Dierker. HBP—By Dierker (Agee). U—Gorman, Sudol, Weyer and Williams. T—2.51. A—15,290.

WITH CALIFORNIA ANGELS

30 .. 4/18/72 .. Minnesota (H) ...... 2-0 .... Jim Perry
31 .. 5/5/72 .... Milwaukee (H) ...... 4-0 .... Ken Brett
32 .. 5/26/72 .. Kansas City (H) .... 10-5 .... Jim Rooker
33 .. 5/30/72 .. Chicago (H) .... 6-0 .... Stan Bahnsen
34 .. 6/7/72 .... Detroit (A) .... 5-1 .... Joe Niekro
35 .. 6/14/72 .. Cleveland (H) ...... 4-3 .... Milt Wilcox
36 .. 6/23/72 .. Oakland (A) .... 2-1 .... Dave Hamilton
37 .. 6/27/72 .. Minnesota (A) .... 3-1 .... Jim Perry
38 .. 7/1/72 .... Oakland (H) .... 5-3 .... Dave Hamilton
39 .. 7/5/72 .... Milwaukee (H) ...... 1-0 ..... Earl Stephenson
40 .. 7/9/72 .... Boston (H) .... 3-0 .... Sonny Siebert
41 .. 7/27/72 .. Texas (H) .... 5-0 .... Mike Paul
42 .. 8/22/72 .. Baltimore (A) .... 2-0 .... Dave McNally
43 .. 8/27/72 .. Cleveland (H) .... 1-0 .... Phil Hennigan
44 .. 8/31/72 .. Detroit (H) .... 4-0 ...... Woodie Fryman
45 .. 9/4/72 .... Oakland (A) .... 2-1 .... Joe Horlen
46 .. 9/21/72 .. Kansas City (H) .... 4-2 .... Roger Nelson
47 .. 9/25/72 .. Texas (A) .... 2-1 .... Dick Bosman
48 .. 9/30/72 .. Minnesota (H) .... 3-2 .... Dave Goltz
49 .. 4/6/73 .... Kansas City (A) .... 3-2 .... Steve Busby
50 .. 4/11/73 .. Minnesota (H) .... 4-1 .... Bill Hands
51 .. 4/18/73 .. Minnesota (A) .... 3-2 .... Bert Blyleven
52 .. 5/2/73 .... Detroit (A) .... 5-3 .... Lerrin LaGrow
53 .. 5/15/73 .. Kansas City (A) .. 3-0 . Bruce Dal Canton
54 .. 5/19/73 .. Texas (H) .... 9-1 .... Rich Hand
55 .. 6/7/73 .... Detroit (H) .... 3-0 ...... Woodie Fryman
56 .. 6/16/73 .. New York (H) .... 5-2 .... Pat Dobson
57 .. 6/25/73 .. Kansas City (H) .... 5-2 .... Ken Wright
58 .. 7/7/73 .... Cleveland (A) .... 3-1 .... Gaylord Perry
59 .. 7/15/73 .. Detroit (H) .... 6-0 .... Jim Perry
60 .. 8/2/73 .... Texas (H) .... 3-2 .... Sonny Siebert
61 .. 8/7/73 .... Milwaukee (A) ...... 6-5 .... Chris Short
62 .. 8/17/73 .. Detroit (H) .... 10-2 .... Woodie Fryman
63 .. 8/29/73 .. New York (H) .... 5-0 .... Doc Medich
64 .. 9/3/73 .... Oakland (H) .... 3-1 .... John Odom
65 .. 9/11/73 .. Chicago (H) .... 3-1 .... Wilbur Wood
66 .. 9/15/73 .. Kansas City (H) .... 3-1 .... Gene Garber
67 .. 9/19/73 .. Texas (A) .... 6-2 .... Pete Broberg
68 .. 9/23/73 .. Minnesota (A) ...... 15-7 .... Joe Decker
69 .. 9/27/73 .. Minnesota (H) ...... 5-4 .... Bill Campbell
70 .. 4/5/74 .... Chicago (A) .... 8-2 .... Wilbur Wood
71 .. 4/12/74 .. Chicago (H) .... 15-1 .... Terry Forster
72 .. 4/30/74 .. Boston (A) .... 16-6 . Reggie Cleveland
73 .. 5/10/74 .. Kansas City (H) .... 2-1 .... Paul Splittorff
74 .. 5/19/74 .. Minnesota (A) .... 4-2 .... Bert Blyleven
75 .. 5/23/74 .. Kansas City (A) .... 3-1 ... Bruce Dal Canton
76 .. 6/1/74 .... Detroit (H) .... 4-1 .... Joe Coleman
77 .. 6/18/74 .. New York (H) .... 3-0 .... Dick Tidrow

WIN NUMBER 50
APRIL 11, 1973
CALIFORNIA 4, MINNESOTA 1

MINNESOTA	ab	r	h	rbi	CALIFORNIA	ab	r	h	rbi
Hisle cf	5	0	1	1	Alomar 2b	3	1	0	0
Carew 2b	4	0	1	0	Valentine ss	4	0	2	1
Darwin rf	4	0	1	0	Pinson rf	4	1	2	2
Oliva dh	4	0	0	0	McCraw lf	4	0	0	0
Lis 1b	3	0	0	0	Oliver dh	4	0	0	0
Braun 3b	2	0	1	0	Steph'son c	4	0	1	0
T'mpson ss	3	0	0	0	Berry cf	3	1	2	0
Roof c	2	0	0	0	Spencer 1b	3	1	2	1
Brye ph	1	0	0	0	Meoli 3b	2	0	0	0
Mit'rwald c	1	0	0	0	Ryan p	0	0	0	0
Holt lf	3	1	1	0					
Hands p	0	0	0	0					
Decker p	0	0	0	0					
Totals	32	1	5	1	Totals	31	4	9	4

Minnesota	000	000	100 — 1
California	101	020	000 — 4

Minnesota	IP	H	R	ER	BB	SO
Hands (L. 1—1)	5	7	4	4	0	3
Decker	3	2	0	0	1	1
California	IP	H	R	ER	BB	SO
Ryan (W. 2—0)	9	5	1	1	5	11

E—Hisle, Alomar DP—California 1. LOB—Minnesota 9, California 5. 2B—Hisle, Spencer. 3B—Holt. HR—Pinson (1). SH—Alomar. WP—Decker. PB—Stephenson. U—Springstead, Luciano, Phillips and Brinkman. T—2:07. A—6,946.

78 .. 6/22/74 .. Texas (A) .... 7-4 .... Jim Bibby
79 .. 6/27/74 .. Texas (H) .... 5-0 .... Jackie Brown
80 .. 7/15/74 .. Cleveland (A) .... 4-2 .... Steve Arlin
81 .. 7/20/74 .. Baltimore (A) .... 2-0 .... Wayne Garland
82 .. 7/28/74 .. *Minnesota (H) ...... 12-9 ..... Tom Burgmeier
83 .. 8/3/74 .... Kansas City (A) .... 4-3 .... Paul Splittorff
84 .. 8/12/74 .. Boston (H) .... 4-2 .... Roger Moret
85 .. 8/16/74 .. Milwaukee (H) ...... 7-3 .... Clyde Wright
86 .. 8/30/74 .. Milwaukee (A) ...... 9-2 .... Kevin Kobel
87 .. 9/7/74 .... Chicago (H) .... 3-1 .... Jack Kucek
88 .. 9/11/74 .. Kansas City (H) .... 3-2 .... Al Fitzmorris
89 .. 9/15/74 .. Chicago (A) .... 6-2 .... Jack Kucek
90 .. 9/24/74 .. Kansas City (A) .... 9-3 .... Paul Splittorff
91 .. 9/28/74 .. Minnesota (H) .... 4-0 .... Joe Decker
92 .. 4/7/75 .... Kansas City (H) .... 3-2 .... Steve Mingori
93 .. 4/11/75 .. Chicago (H) .... 5-0 .... Claude Osteen
94 .. 4/15/75 .. Minnesota (A) .... 7-3 .... Dave Goltz
95 .. 4/20/75 .. Chicago (A) .... 8-4 .... Claude Osteen
96 .. 5/3/75 .... Texas (A) .... 4-2 .... Jackie Brown

WIN NUMBER 100
JUNE 1, 1975
CALIFORNIA 1, BALTIMORE 0

BALTIMORE	ab	r	h	rbi	CALIFORNIA	ab	r	h	rbi
Sing'ton rf	4	0	0	0	Remy 2b	3	0	1	0
Shopay cf	3	0	0	0	Rivers cf	4	1	1	0
Bumbry lf	4	0	0	0	Harper dh	4	0	1	0
Baylor dh	2	0	0	0	Chalk 3b	3	0	2	1
Davis dh	2	0	0	0	Llenas lf	3	0	1	0
Grich 2b	2	0	0	0	Nettles lf	0	0	0	0
May 1b	3	0	0	0	Stanton rf	2	0	1	0
Robinson 3b	3	0	0	0	Bochte 1b	3	0	1	0
Hendricks c	3	0	0	0	Rodriguez c	3	0	0	0
Belanger ss	2	0	0	0	Smith ss	2	0	1	0
Grimsley p	0	0	0	0	Ryan p	0	0	0	0
Garland p	0	0	0	0					
Totals	28	0	0	0	Totals	27	1	9	1

Baltimore			000	000	000 — 0
California			001	000	00x — 1

Baltimore	IP	H	R	ER	BB	SO
Grimsley (L. 1—7)	3 1/3	8	1	1	0	1
Garland	4 2/3	1	0	0	1	1
California	IP	H	R	ER	BB	SO
Ryan (W. 9—3)	9	0	0	0	4	9

E—Smith. DP—Baltimore 2.LOB—Baltimore 5, California 5. SB—Belanger. SH—Stanton, Remy. U—Morgenweck, Soar, Denkinger and Barnett. T—2:01. A—18,492.

97 .. 5/8/75 .... Oakland (A) .... 5-0 .... Dave Hamilton
98 .. 5/13/75 .. New York (H) .... 5-0 .... Doc Medich
99 .. 5/18/75 .. Baltimore (A) .... 5-1 .... Mike Torrez
100 .. 6/1/75 ... Baltimore (H) .... 1-0 .... Ross Grimsley
101 .. 6/6/75 ... Milwaukee (H) ...... 6-0 .... Jim Slaton
102 .. 7/26/75 . Minnesota (H) ...... 5-0 .... Vic Albury
103 .. 7/30/75 . Chicago (H) .... 5-4 .... Jim Kaat
104 .. 8/20/75 . Milwaukee (A) ...... 6-1 .... Jim Slaton
105 .. 8/24/75 . New York (A) .... 4-3 .... Tippy Martinez
106 .. 4/15/76 . Kansas City (A) .... 5-1 .... Paul Splittorff
107 .. 4/20/76 . Baltimore (H) .... 5-0 ..... Doyle Alexander
108 .. 5/1/76 ... Cleveland (A) .... 6-1 .... Pat Dobson
109 .. 6/1/76 ... Minnesota (A) ...... 6-4 .... Pete Redfern
110 .. 6/15/76 . Milwaukee (H) ...... 1-0 .... Jim Colburn
111 .. 6/19/76 . Boston (H) .... 5-3 .... Rick Wise
112 .. 7/7/76 ... Cleveland (H) .... 2-0 .... Rick Waits
113 .. 7/30/76 . Chicago (H) .... 3-0 .... Ken Brett
114 .. 8/4/76 ... Texas (A) .... 9-6 .... Nellie Briles
115 .. 8/18/76 . Detroit (A) .... 5-4 .... John Hiller
116 .. 8/31/76 . Detroit (H) .... 6-3 .... Vern Ruhle
117 .. 9/5/76 ... Oakland (H) .... 3-2 .... Stan Bahnsen
118 .. 9/10/76 . Chicago (A) .... 3-2 .... Bart Johnson

119 .. 9/15/76 .. Kansas City (H) .... 2-1 .... Doug Bird
120 .. 9/20/76 .. Texas (H) .... 1-0 .... Bert Blyleven
121 .. 9/29/76 .. Chicago (H) .... 3-0 .... Ken Brett
122 .. 10/3/76 .. Oakland (A) .... 1-0 .... Mike Torrez
123 .. 4/7/77 .... Seattle (A) .... 2-0 .... Enrique Romo
124 .. 4/15/77 .. Seattle (H) .... 7-0 .... Glenn Abbott
125 .. 4/25/77 .. Oakland (H) .... 11-6 .... Doc Medich
126 .. 5/6/77 .... Boston (A) .... 8-4 .... Luis Tiant
127 .. 5/10/77 .. Kansas City (A) .... 6-1 .... Paul Splittorff
128 .. 5/19/77 .. Minnesota (H) ...... 5-3 .... Dave Goltz
129 .. 5/24/77 .. Detroit (A) .... 2-1 .... John Hiller
130 .. 5/29/77 .. Toronto (A) .... 3-2 .... Dave Lemanczyk
131 .. 6/12/77 .. Cleveland (H) .... 11-4 .... Pat Dobson
132 .. 6/29/77 .. Kansas City (H) .... 7-0 .... Jim Colborn
133 .. 7/4/77 .... Oakland (H) .... 4-2 .... Rick Langford
134 .. 7/12/77 .. Minnesota (H) ...... 3-0 .. Paul Thormodsgard
135 .. 7/16/77 .. Seattle (H) .... 5-4 .... Enrique Romo
136 .. 7/25/77 .. Seattle (A) .... 4-3 .... Dick Pole
137 .. 8/3/77 .... New York (H) .... 5-3 .... Ron Guidry
138 .. 8/8/77 .... Kansas City (A) .... 6-4 .... Andy Hassler
139 .. 8/13/77 .. New York (A) .... 6-5 .... Sparky Lyle
140 .. 9/3/77 .... Cleveland (A) .... 3-2 .... Wayne Garland
141 .. 9/8/77 .... Chicago (H) .... 2-0 .... Francisco Barrios
142 .. 4/29/78 .. Toronto (H) .... 5-0 .... Dave Lemanczyk
143 .. 5/5/78 .... Cleveland (H) .... 5-0 .... Rick Wise
144 .. 5/23/78 .. Chicago (H) .... 5-4 .... Jim Willoughby
145 .. 7/19/78 .. Cleveland (H) .... 3-0 .... Rick Wise
146 .. 7/23/78 .. Detroit (A) .... 4-3 .... Jim Slaton
147 .. 8/11/78 .. Seattle (H) .... 3-1 .... Byron McLaughlin
148 .. 9/10/78 .. Kansas City (H) .... 13-3 .... Paul Splittorff
149 .. 9/19/78 .. Minnesota (A) ...... 4-1 .... Roger Erickson
150 .. 9/24/78 .. Chicago (A) .... 7-3 .... Francisco Barrios
151 .. 10/1/78 .. Chicago (H) .... 5-4 .... Francisco Barrios
152 .. 4/11/79 .. Minnesota (H) ...... 11-2 .... Dave Goltz
153 .. 4/17/79 .. Minnesota (A) ...... 6-0 .... Dave Goltz
154 .. 4/21/79 .. Oakland (H) .... 13-1 .... Matt Keough
155 .. 5/2/79 .... New York (H) .... 1-0 .... Ron Guidry
156 .. 5/20/79 .. Chicago (H) .... 4-0 .... Ross Baumgarten
157 .. 5/30/79 .. Seattle (A) .... 3-2 .... Shane Rawley
158 .. 6/9/79 .... Detroit (H) .... 9-1 .... Dave Rozema
159 .. 6/14/79 .. Toronto (A) .... 10-2 .... Phil Huffman
160 .. 6/18/79 .. Texas (H) .... 5-0 .... Fergie Jenkins
161 .. 7/1/79 .... Kansas City (A) .... 14-2 .... Paul Splittorff
162 .. 7/9/79 .... Boston (H) .... 6-0 .... Mike Torrez
163 .. 7/13/79 .. New York (H) .... 6-1 .... Luis Tiant
164 .. 8/18/79 .. Toronto (H) .... 7-5 ..... Tom Underwood
165 .. 9/3/79 .... Chicago (H) .... 6-5 ... Ross Baumgarten
166 .. 9/7/79 .... Milwaukee (H) ...... 6-3 .... Bill Travers
167 .. 9/24/79 .. Kansas City (H) .... 4-3 .... Larry Gura

WIN NUMBER 150
SEPTEMBER 24, 1978

CALIFORNIA 7, CHICAGO 3

CALIFORNIA	ab	r	h	rbi	CHICAGO	ab	r	h	rbi
R.Miller cf	5	1	2	2	Chappas ss	2	0	0	0
Landr'x rf	5	0	1	0	Molinaro rf	4	0	0	0
Lansford 3b	5	1	2	2	Lemon cf	2	0	0	1
Baylor dh	5	1	1	1	Johnson dh	4	0	1	0
Rudi lf	3	1	1	0	Garr lf	4	1	1	0
J'son 1b	4	1	1	0	Soderh'm 3b	3	0	0	0
Downing c	4	1	2	1	Bell 3b	1	0	0	0
Grich 2b	3	1	1	1	Squires 1b	4	1	1	0
Anderson ss	2	0	0	0	Foley c	3	1	2	2
Ryan p	0	0	0	0	Pryor 2b	3	0	0	0
Hartzell p	0	0	0	0	Barrios p	0	0	0	0
					Schueler p	0	0	0	0
Totals	**36**	**7**	**11**	**7**	**Totals**	**30**	**3**	**5**	**3**

California	2 0 0	0 0 5	0 0 0 — 7
Chicago	0 1 0	0 1 1	0 0 0 — 3

California	IP	H	R	ER	BB	SO
Ryan (W.9—13)	7	5	3	3	5	6
Hartzell	2	0	0	0	0	0
Chicago	**IP**	**H**	**R**	**ER**	**BB**	**SO**
Barrios (L.9—14)*	5	10	7	7	2	2
Schueler	4	1	0	0	1	0

*Pitched to five batters in sixth.

E—Lansford DP—California 1 LOB—California 6, Chicago 8 2B—R. Miller, Squires, 3B—Landreaux HR—Lansford (7), Baylor (33), SB—Molinaro—Lemon, Jackson SH—Pryor, Anderson SF—Lemon, HBP—By Ryan (Chappas). U—DiMuro, Barnett, McKean and Voltaggio T—2:32 A—12,621.

WITH HOUSTON ASTROS

168 .. 4/22/80 .. Cincinnati (H) .... 8-0 .... Frank Pastore
169 .. 5/18/80 .. Philadelphia (H) ... 3-0 .... Randy Lerch
170 .. 5/28/80 .. San Diego (H) ...... 1-0 .... Rick Wise
171 .. 6/14/80 .. Pittsburgh (A) .... 7-3 .... Don Robinson
172 .. 6/19/80 .. St. Louis (H) .... 2-0 .... Bob Sykes
173 .. 8/4/80 .. San Francisco (H) 4-2 . Alan Hargesheimer
174 .. 8/14/80 .. San Diego (A) ...... 2-1 .... John Curtis
175 .. 8/19/80 .. Pittsburgh (H) ...... 5-2 ...... John Candelaria
176 .. 8/24/80 .. Chicago (H) .... 2-1 .... Bill Caudill
177 .. 9/25/80 .. Atlanta (A) .... 4-2 .... Phil Niekro
178 .. 9/30/80 .. Atlanta (H) .... 7-3 ..... Doyle Alexander
179 .. 4/15/81 .. Atlanta (A) .... 2-0 .... Tommy Boggs
180 .. 5/11/81 .. Cincinnati (H) .... 5-0 .... Mike LaCross
181 .. 5/16/81 .. Chicago (H) .... 6-1 .... Randy Martz
182 .. 5/26/81 .. San Diego (H) ...... 1-0 .. Juan Eichelberger
183 .. 6/5/81 .... New York (H) .... 3-0 .... Randy Jones
184 .. 8/14/81 .. San Diego (A) ...... 5-1 .... Tim Lollar

185 .. 8/19/81 .. Montreal (H) .... 9-1 ..... Scott Sanderson
186 .. 9/4/81 .... Montreal (A) .... 5-0 .... Bill Gullickson
187 .. 9/20/81 .. San Francisco (A) 7-3 .... Gary Lavalle
188 .. 9/26/81 .. Los Angeles (H) ... 5-0 .... Ted Power
189 .. 10/1/81 .. Cincinnati (A) .... 8-1 .... Bruce Berenyi
190 .. 4/26/82 .. St. Louis (A) .... 6-2 .... John Martin
191 .. 5/1/82 .... Pittsburgh (A) .... 6-3 .... Paul Moskau
192 .. 5/11/82 .. Pittsburgh (A) .... 4-2 .... Tom Griffin
193 .. 5/28/82 .. New York (A) .... 8-3 .... Randy Jones
194 .. 6/2/82 .... Montreal (A) .... 6-4 ..... Scott Sanderson
195 .. 6/18/82 .. San Diego (H) ...... 7-2 .... Chris Welch
196 .. 6/28/82 .. Atlanta (A) .... 6-2 .... Rick Mahler
197 .. 7/4/82 .... Los Angeles (A) .... 3-0 .... Jerry Reuss
198 .. 7/16/82 .. Pittsburgh (H) ...... 4-2 .... Larry McWilliams
199 .. 7/21/82 .. Chicago (A) .... 2-1 .... Allen Ripley
200 .. 7/27/82 .. Cincinnati (H) .... 3-2 ..... Charlie Leibrandt
201 .. 8/11/82 .. San Diego (A) .... 3-0 .... Eric Show
202 .. 8/21/82 .. Montreal (H) .... 5-3 .... Ray Burris
203 .. 8/31/82 .. New York (A) .... 4-0 .... Ed Lynch
204 .. 9/15/82 .. Atlanta (A) .... 5-4 .... Tommy Boggs
205 .. 9/26/82 .. Cincinnati (A) .... 4-0 .... Bob Shirley
206 .. 4/17/83 .. Montreal (H) .... 6-3 .... Bill Gullickson

WIN NUMBER 200
JULY 27, 1982

HOUSTON 3, CINNCINATI 2

CINCINNATI	ab	r	h	rbi	HOUSTON	ab	r	h	rbi
Lawless 2b	4	0	1	0	Thon ss	4	1	1	0
Miller lf	3	1	1	0	Scott cf	4	1	2	1
Cedeno cf	4	0	1	1	Knight 1b	3	1	2	1
Driessen 1b	3	0	0	0	Cruz lf	4	0	1	0
H'seholder rf	4	1	1	0	Garner 2b	4	0	0	0
Kr'chichl 3b	4	0	0	0	Howe 3b	3	0	0	0
Oester ss	4	0	1	1	Puhl rf	4	0	2	1
Trevino c	3	0	0	0	Pujos c	3	0	1	0
Leibrandt p	3	0	0	0	Ryan p	2	0	0	0
Kern p	0	0	0	0					
Totals	**32**	**2**	**5**	**2**	**Totals**	**31**	**3**	**9**	**3**

Cincinnati	1 0 0	1 0 0	0 0 0 — 2
Houston	1 0 1	0 0 0	0 1 x — 3

Cincinnati	IP	H	R	ER	BB	SO
Leibrandt (L. 3—6)	7 1/3	8	3	3	1	2
Kern	2/3	1	0	0	1	1
Houston	**IP**	**H**	**R**	**ER**	**BB**	**SO**
Ryan (W. 11—9)	9	5	2	1	2	13

Game—winning RBI—Puhl.
E—Ryan, Trevino, Milner. LOB—Cincinnati 5, Houston 8. 2B—Cedeno, Scott, Knight, Oester, SB—Thon, Scott 2, Knight, Lawless 2, Milner. SH—Pujols, Ryan, T—2:17. A—19,009.

WIN NUMBER 250
AUGUST 27, 1986

HOUSTON 7,   CHICAGO 1

CHICAGO	ab	r	h	rbi
Mumphrey cf	4	0	1	0
Sandberg 2b	4	0	0	0
Bosley lf	4	1	1	0
Moreland 1b	3	0	0	0
Francona rf	3	0	1	0
Dunston ss	4	0	0	0
Speier 3b	3	0	0	1
Martin c	2	0	0	0
J. Davis ph-c	1	0	0	0
Moyer p	0	0	0	0
R. Davis p	0	0	0	0
Trillo ph	1	0	0	0
Trout p	0	0	0	0
Dernier ph	1	0	1	0
Gumpert p	0	0	0	0
Totals	**30**	**1**	**4**	**1**

HOUSTON	ab	r	h	rbi
Hatcher cf	4	1	1	0
Pankovits 2b	3	2	1	2
Garner 3b	5	1	4	2
G. Davis 1b	3	0	0	1
Bass rf	4	1	2	1
Cruz lf	4	0	1	1
Ashby c	3	1	1	0
Thon ss	3	1	1	0
Ryan p	2	0	0	0
Ruhl ph	1	0	0	0
Kerfeld p	1	0	0	0
Totals	**33**	**7**	**11**	**7**

Chicago	000 000	100	— 1	
Houston	003 300	10x	— 7	

Chicago	IP	H	R	ER	BB	SO
Moyer (L. 5—4)	3 ⅓	5	5	5	3	1
R. Davis	1 ⅔	2	1	1	0	0
Trout	2	4	1	1	2	1
Gumpert	1	0	0	0	0	1
Houston	**IP**	**H**	**R**	**ER**	**BB**	**SO**
Ryan (W. 9—8)	6	1	0	0	2	5
Kerfeld (Save 6)	3	3	1	1	3	5

Game-winning RBI—Garner.
E—None. DP—Chicago 1. LOB—Chicago 5, Houston 8.
SB—Hatcher, Ashby, Thon, Pankovits, Garner, Bass,
Dernier. SF—G. Davis. Balk—Moyer. T—2:39. A—24, 198.

207 .. 4/27/83 .. Montreal (A) .... 4-2 ..... Scott Sanderson
208 .. 5/2/83 .... New York (A) .... 3-2 .... Mike Torrez
209 .. 6/12/83 .. San Diego (H) .... 2-0 .... Eric Show
210 .. 6/17/83 .. San Diego (A) .... 4-1 .... Eric Show
211 .. 6/28/83 .. Atlanta (A) .... 4-3 .... Terry Forster
212 .. 7/2/83 .... Los Angeles (H) .... 3-1 .... Joe Beckwith
213 .. 7/8/83 .... New York (A) .... 6-3 .... Mike Torrez
214 .. 7/13/83 .. Montreal (H) .... 9-4 .... Charlie Lea
215 .. 8/3/83 .... San Diego (A) .... 1-0 .... Tim Lollar
216 .. 8/7/83 .... San Francisco (A) 2-1 .... Greg Minton
217 .. 8/12/83 .. San Francisco (H) 5-2 .... Renie Martin
218 .. 9/1/83 .... Pittsburgh (H) .... 3-0 .... Cecilio Guante
219 .. 9/20/83 .. Los Angeles (A) .... 15-2 ..... Alejandro Pena
220 .. 4/4/84 .... Montreal (H) .... 8-2 .... Bill Gullickson
221 .. 5/6/84 .... New York (A) .... 10-1 ..... Dwight Gooden
222 .. 5/11/84 .. Chicago (H) .... 3-1 .... Dick Ruthven
223 .. 5/16/84 .. Pittsburgh (A) .... 1-0 ...... John Candelaria

224 .. 5/21/84 .. St. Louis (A) .... 3-2 .... Bob Forsch
225 .. 5/26/84 .. Pittsburgh (H) ...... 2-0 .... Jose DeLeon
226 .. 6/17/84 .. Los Angeles (H) ... 1-0 .... Bob Welch
227 .. 7/24/84 .. San Francisco (A) 10-3 .... Mark Davis
228 .. 8/3/84 .... San Diego (H) ...... 6-2 .... Eric Show
229 .. 8/12/84 .. Cincinnati (A) .... 6-1 ..... Andy McGaffigan
230 .. 8/22/84 .. Chicago (A) .... 8-3 .... Dick Ruthven
231 .. 9/5/84 .... San Francisco (A) 4-1 .... Randy Lerch
232 .. 4/9/85 .... Los Angeles (H) ... 2-1Fernando Valenzuela
233 .. 4/14/85 .. Philadelphia (H) ... 5-3 .... Steve Carlton
234 .. 5/18/85 .. St. Louis (H) .... 6-5 .... Kurt Kepshire
235 .. 5/24/85 .. Chicago (A) .... 6-2 .... Dick Ruthven
236 .. 5/29/85 .. Pittsburgh (H) ...... 8-3 .... Ray Krawczyk
237 .. 6/8/85 .... San Francisco (H) 4-1 .... Bill Laskey
238 .. 6/12/85 .. San Diego (H) ...... 3-2 .... Eric Show
239 .. 6/17/85 .. Atlanta (A) .... 4-3 .... Steve Shields
240 .. 8/28/85 .. Chicago (H) .... 3-0 .... Jay Baller
241 .. 10/5/85 .. San Diego (A) .... 9-3 .... Ed Wojna
242 .. 4/12/86 .. Atlanta (H) .... 4-3 .... Rick Mahler
243 .. 4/16/86 .. San Francisco (A) 4-1 .... Roger Mason
244 .. 4/25/86 .. Cincinnati (H) .... 3-1 .... Tom Browning
245 .. 6/24/86 .. Cincinnati (H) .... 8-4 .... Tom Browning
246 .. 7/8/86 .... Montreal (A) .... 4-1 .... Jay Tibbs
247 .. 7/12/86 .. Philadelphia (H) ... 4-3 .... Shane Rawley
248 .. 7/27/86 .. Philadelphia (A) ... 3-2 .... Kevin Gross
249 .. 8/12/86 .. Los Angeles (H) ... 3-0 .... Rick Honeycutt
250 .. 8/27/86 .. Chicago (H) .... 7-1 .... Jamie Moyer
251 .. 9/8/86 .... Cincinnati (H) .... 3-1 .... Chris Welsh
252 .. 9/24/86 .. San Francisco (H) 6-0 .... Mike LaCoss
253 .. 10/3/86 .. Atlanta (H) .... 6-2 .... Jim Acker
254 .. 4/8/87 .... Los Angeles (H) ... 7-3 .... Matt Young
255 .. 5/1/87 .... Atlanta (A) .... 12-3 ...... Rick Mahler
256 .. 6/7/87 .... San Francisco (H) 3-0 ..... Atlee Hammaker
257 .. 6/12/87 .. Los Angeles (A) ... 5-1 .... Bob Welch
258 .. 8/18/87 .. St. Louis (H) .... 4-0 .... Danny Cox
259 .. 9/4/87 .... Pittsburgh (H) ...... 5-1 .... Mike Bielecki
260 .. 9/8/87 .... San Francisco (H) 4-2 ..... Atlee Hammaker
261 .. 9/14/87 .. Los Angeles (A) ... 8-1 .... Shawn Hillegas
262 .. 4/12/88 .. Atlanta (A) .... 8-3 .... Zane Smith
263 .. 4/17/88 .. Cincinnati (H) .... 5-3 .... Danny Jackson
264 .. 5/13/88 .. Chicago (H) .... 8-2 .... Jamie Moyer
265 .. 5/18/88 .. Pittsburgh (H) ...... 4-2 .... Doug Drabek
266 .. 5/29/88 .. Chicago (A) .... 7-1 .... Jamie Moyer
267 .. 7/9/88 .... New York (H) .... 6-3 .... Rick Aguilera
268 .. 7/21/88 .. Philadelphia (H) ... 2-0 .... Mike Maddux
269 .. 7/27/88 .. San Diego (A) .... 4-1 .... Ed Whitson
270 .. 8/15/88 .. San Diego (H) ...... 7-3 .... Andy Hawkins
271 .. 9/3/88 .... St. Louis (H) .... 10-1 .. Larry McWilliams
272 .. 9/8/88 .... Los Angeles (A) ... 2-1 .... John Tudor
273 .. 9/14/88 .. Cincinnati (A) .... 7-1 .... Danny Jackson

WITH TEXAS RANGERS

274 .. 4/12/89 .. Milwaukee (A) ...... 8-1 .... Bill Wegman
275 .. 4/23/89 .. Toronto (A) .... 4-1 .... Todd Stottlemyre
276 .. 4/30/89 .. Boston (H) .... 2-1 .... Roger Clemens
277 .. 5/11/89 .. Kansas City (A) .... 6-3 .... Mark Gubicza
278 .. 5/23/89 .. Kansas City (H) .... 10-8 .... Luis Aquino
279 .. 6/3/89 .... Seattle (A) .... 6-1 .... Clint Zavaras
280 .. 6/8/89 .... Chicago (H) .... 11-7 .... Eric King
281 .. 6/14/89 .. California (H) .... 5-1 .... Chuck Finley
282 .. 6/25/89 .. Cleveland (H) .... 4-2 .... Tom Candiotti
283 .. 7/6/89 .... California (A) .... 3-0 .... Kirk McCaskill
284 .. 7/20/89 .. New York (H) .... 6-2 .... Andy Hawkins
285 .. 7/30/89 .. Milwaukee (H) ...... 9-3 .... Don August
286 .. 8/10/89 .. Detroit (H) .... 4-1 ...... Doyle Alexander
287 .. 8/16/89 .. Seattle (A) .... 3-1 ...... Scott Bankhead
288 .. 9/2/89 .... Kansas City (H) .... 6-3 .... Terry Leach
289 .. 9/30/89 .. California (A) .... 2-0 .... Chuck Finley
290 .. 4/9/90 .... Toronto (H) .... 4-2 .... Todd Stottlemyre
291 .. 4/14/90 .. New York (A) .... 8-4 .... Andy Hawkins
292 .. 4/20/90 .. New York (H) .... 6-5 ...... Lee Guetterman
293 .. 4/26/90 .. Chicago (H) .... 1-0 .... Melido Perez
294 .. 6/11/90 .. Oakland (A) .... 5-0 .... Scott Sanderson
295 .. 6/22/90 .. Seattle (H) .... 5-2 .... Matt Young
296 .. 6/27/90 .. Minnesota (A) .... 9-2 .... Kevin Tapani
297 .. 7/7/90 .... Boston (H) .... 7-4 .... Mike Boddicker
298 .. 7/14/90 .. Detroit (A) .... 5-3 .... Jeff Robinson
299 .. 7/20/90 .. Detroit (H) .... 5-3 .... Steve Searcy
300 .. 7/31/90 .. Milwaukee (A) ...... 11-3 .... Chris Bosio
301 .. 8/22/90 .. Seattle (H) .... 5-4 .... Bill Swift
302 .. 9/3/90 .... Cleveland (H) .... 6-2 .... Mike Walker
303 .. 4/14/91 .. Baltimore (H) .... 15-3 .... Jeff Robinson
304 .. 4/20/91 .. Baltimore (A) .... 1-0 .... Jose Mesa
305 .. 5/1/91 .... Toronto (H) .... 3-0 .... Jimmy Key
306 .. 6/11/91 .. Chicago (H) .... 2-0 .... Alex Fernandez
307 .. 7/7/91 .... California (H) .... 7-0 .... Chuck Finley
308 .. 7/23/91 .. Boston (H) .... 5-4 .... Greg Harris
309 .. 7/28/91 .. Detroit (H) .... 10-6 .... Frank Tanana
310 .. 8/19/91 .. Baltimore (H) .... 4-1 .... Mike Mussina
311 .. 8/30/91 .. Kansas City (H) .... 6-2 .... Mike Boddicker
312 .. 9/12/91 .. Minnesota (H) .... 4-3 .... Jack Morris
313 .. 9/19/91 .. California (H) .... 10-3 .... Chuck Finley
314 .. 9/25/91 .. Seattle (A) .... 7-1 .... Rich Delucia

* = relief appearance

WIN NUMBER 300
AUGUST 27, 1986

TEXAS 11,   MILWAUKEE 3

TEXAS	ab	r	h	bi	MILWAUKEE	ab	r	h	bi
Huson ss	4	0	1	2	Molitor 1b	5	2	3	0
Daugherty ph	1	1	1	1	Yount cf	5	1	1	1
Green ss	0	0	0	0	Sheffield 3b	4	0	0	0
Franco 2b	5	1	1	4	DParker dh	4	0	1	0
Palmeiro 1b	5	0	2	0	Vaughn lf	4	0	0	0
Sierra rf	5	2	3	0	Gantner 2b	3	0	2	1
Baines dh	5	1	1	0	Felder rf	3	0	0	0
Incaviglia lf	3	2	2	2	COBrien c	3	0	0	0
Petrali c	2	1	0	1	Hamilton ph	1	0	0	0
Buechele 3b	4	2	2	1	Spiers ss	4	0	0	0
Pettis cf	3	1	0	0					
Totals	37	11	13	11	Totals	36	3	7	2

Texas	000 041 006	—11
Milwaukee	001 000 020	— 3

E—Buechele, Franco 2, Knudson. DP—Milwaukee 1.
LOB—Texas 3, Milwaukee 8. 2B—Sierra. 3B—Yount,
Huson, Palmeiro. HR—Incaviglia (17), Franco (7). SB—
Gantner (7). S—Pettis. SF—Petralli.

Texas	IP	H	R	ER	BB	SO
Ryan (W 11–4).....	7⅔	6	3	1	2	8
Arnsberg S3).......	1⅓	1	0	0	0	0
Milwaukee						
Bosio (L4–9)......	5⅓	6	5	5	1	1
Mirabella.........	2⅔	4	2	2	1	1
Knudson.........	0	1	2	1	0	0
Fossas...........	1	2	2	2	0	1

Mirabella pitched to 2 batters in the 9th, Knudson pitched
to 2 batters in the 9th.
WP—Ryan. Umpires—Home, Clark; First, Hirschbeck;
Second, Roe; Third, Phillips. T—3:05. A—51,533.

RYAN'S SEVEN CAREER NO-HITTERS

NO-HITTER NUMBER 1
MAY 15, 1973
CALIFORNIA 3, KANSAS CITY 0

CALIFORNIA	ab	r	h	bi	KANSAS CITY	ab	r	h	bi
Pinson lf	5	1	2	0	Patek ss	4	0	0	0
Alomar 2b	4	0	0	0	Hovley rf	3	0	0	0
Valentine cf	4	0	1	0	Otis cf	4	0	0	0
Robinson dh	3	1	1	0	Mayberry 1b	3	0	0	0
Oliver rf	4	1	2	2	Rojas 2b	3	0	0	0
Berry rf	0	0	0	0	Kirkpatr'k dh-c	3	0	0	0
Gallagher 3b	4	0	2	1	Pinella lf	3	0	0	0
Spencer 1b	4	0	1	0	Schaal 3b	2	0	0	0
Meoli ss	4	0	1	0	Taylor c	1	0	0	0
Torborg c	4	0	1	0	Hopkins ph	1	0	0	0
Ryan p	0	0	0	0	Dal Canton p	0	0	0	0
					Garber p	0	0	0	0
Totals	36	3	11	3	Totals	27	0	0	0

California	2 0 0	0 0 1	0 0 0 — 3
Kansas City	0 0 0	0 0 0	0 0 0 — 0

DP—Kansas City 1. LOB—California 8, Kansas City 3. HR—Oliver (4). SB—Hovley. S—Alomar.

California	IP	H	R	ER	BB	SO
Ryan (W 5—3)	9	0	0	0	3	12
Kansas City						
Dal Canton (L 2—2)	5 2/3	8	3	3	1	0
Garber	3 1/3	3	0	0	0	0

T—2:54. A—9,265.

MAY 15, 1973 AT KANSAS CITY—CALIFORNIA 3, KANSAS CITY 0

Nolan Ryan chalked up the first of his major league record seven no-hitters for the California Angels as he stopped the Kansas City Royals for the first hitless game by an Angel righthander in the club's history. Ryan finished with 12 strikeouts as he recorded at least one whiff in every inning except the fifth. The only close call of the game came in the eighth inning when Royals pinch hitter Gail Hopkins hit a looping liner into left field which shortstop Rudy Meoli came up with on a running over-the-shoulder catch with his back to the plate. The Angels and Ryan got all the offensive support they needed from right-fielder Bob Oliver, two of the three RBI with a solo home run and a single.

California	2 0 0	0 0 1	0 0 0 —	3 11 0
Kansas City	0 0 0	0 0 0	0 0 0 —	0 0 0

Ryan and Torborg. Dal Canton, Garber (6) and Taylor, Kirkpatrick. WP—Ryan (5—3) LP—Dal Canton (2—2).

Ryan Pitching Line: 9 IP 0 H 0 R 0 ER 3 BB 12 SO

NO-HITTER NUMBER 2
JULY 15, 1973
CALIFORNIA 6, DETROIT 0

CALIFORNIA	ab	r	h	bi	DETROIT	ab	r	h	bi
Alomar 2b	5	0	2	0	Northrup lf	4	0	0	0
Pinson rf	4	0	0	1	M. Stanley cf	3	0	0	0
McCraw lf	2	0	0	0	G. Brown dh	2	0	0	0
Lienas ph	1	0	1	2	Cash 1b	4	0	0	0
Stanton lf	0	1	0	0	Sims c	3	0	0	0
Epstein 1b	3	1	1	0	McAuliffe 2b	3	0	0	0
Oliver dh	3	1	1	1	Sharon rf	2	0	0	0
Berry cf	3	0	0	0	A.Rodriguez 3b	3	0	0	0
Gallagher 3b	4	0	2	2	E.Brinkman ss	3	0	0	0
Meoli ss	4	1	1	0	J.Perry p	0	0	0	0
Kusnyer c	3	2	1	0	Scherman p	0	0	0	0
Ryan p	0	0	0	0	B.Miller p	0	0	0	0
					Farmer p	0	0	0	0
Totals	32	6	9	6	Totals	27	0	0	0

California	0 0 1	0 0 0	0 5 0 — 6
Detroit	0 0 0	0 0 0	0 0 0 — 0

DP—Detroit 2, LOB—California 5, Detroit 4. 2B—Epstein, Meoli. SF—Pinson.

California	IP	H	R	ER	BB	SO
Ryan (W 11—11)	9	0	0	0	4	17
Detroit						
J.Perry (L 9—9)	7 1/3	5	3	3	3	2
Scherman	1/3	0	0	0	0	0
B.Miller	0	2	3	3	1	0
Farmer	1 1/3	2	0	0	1	0

T—2:21. A—41,411.

JULY 15, 1973 AT DETROIT—CALIFORNIA 6, DETROIT 0

The "easiest" no-hitter for Ryan in terms of scores as he turned in his second no-hitter of the 1973 campaign, again on the road, by stopping the Detroit Tigers 6–0. Ryan had 17 strikeouts for the game with 16 of them coming in the first seven innings. However, his arm stiffened up somewhat in the top of the eighth as the Angels batted around while scoring five runs to break open a close game. Ryan had to rely on no special defensive accomplishments to preserve the no-hitter as he became the fifth man in history to throw two no-hitters in a season.

California	0 0 1	0 0 0	0 5 0 —	6 9 0
Detroit	0 0 0	0 0 0	0 0 0 —	0 0 0

Ryan and Kusnyer. J.Perry, Scherman (8), Miller (8), Farmer (8) and Sims. WP—Ryan (11—11). LP—J. Perry (9—9).

Ryan Pitching Line: 9 IP 0 H 0 R 0 ER 4 BB 17 SO

NO-HITTER NUMBER 3
SEPTEMBER 28, 1974
CALIFORNIA 4, MINNESOTA 0

MINNESOTA	ab	r	h	bi	CALIFORNIA	ab	r	h	bi
Brye cf	2	0	0	0	M.Nettles cf	4	1	2	3
Carew 2b	2	0	0	0	D.Doyle 2b	4	0	1	0
Braun 3b	3	0	0	0	Bochte 1b	3	0	0	1
Darwin rf	4	0	0	0	Lahoud dh	4	0	1	0
Oliva dh	3	0	0	0	Stanton rf	4	0	1	0
Hisle lf	3	0	0	0	Chalk 3b	2	1	0	0
Bourque 1b	3	0	0	0	Balaz lf	2	1	1	0
Killebrew ph	0	0	0	0	Meoli ss	2	1	1	0
Terrell pr	0	0	0	0	Egan c	2	0	0	0
Gomez ss	2	0	0	0	Ryan p	0	0	0	0
Soderholm ss	2	0	0	0					
Borgmann c	3	0	0	0					
Decker p	0	0	0	0					
Butler p	0	0	0	0					
Totals	27	0	0	0	Totals	27	4	7	4

Minnesota	0 0 0	0 0 0	0 0 0 — 0
California	0 0 2	2 0 0	0 0 x — 4

E—Braun. LOB—Minnesota 8, California 4. 2B—Meoli, Balaz. SB—M.Nettles. S—Egan. SF—Bochte.

Minnesota	IP	H	R	ER	BB	SO
Decker (L 16—14)	2 ²/₃	4	2	1	0	1
Butler	5 ¹/₃	3	2	2	3	8
California						
Ryan (W 22—16)	9	0	0	0	8	15

T—2:22. A—10,872.

NO-HITTER NUMBER 4
JUNE 1, 1975
CALIFORNIA 1, BALTIMORE 0

BALTIMORE	ab	r	h	bi	CALIFORNIA	ab	r	h	bi
Singleton rf	4	0	0	0	Remy 2b	3	0	1	0
Shopay cf	3	0	0	0	Rivers cf	4	1	1	0
Bumbry lf	4	0	0	0	Harper dh	4	0	1	0
Baylor dh	2	0	0	0	Chalk 3b	3	0	2	1
Davis dh	2	0	0	0	Llenas lf	3	0	1	0
Grich 2b	2	0	0	0	M.Nettles lf	0	0	0	0
May 1b	3	0	0	0	Stanton rf	2	0	1	0
Robinson 3b	3	0	0	0	Bochte 1b	3	0	1	0
Hendricks c	3	0	0	0	Rodriguez c	3	0	0	0
Belanger ss	2	0	0	0	Smith ss	2	0	1	0
Grimsley p	0	0	0	0	Ryan p	0	0	0	0
Garland p	0	0	0	0					
Totals	28	0	0	0	Totals	27	1	9	1

Baltimore	0 0 0	0 0 0	0 0 0 — 0
California	0 0 1	0 0 0	0 0 x — 1

E—Smith. DP—Baltimore 2. LOB—Baltimore 5, California 5. SB—Belanger. S—Stanton, Remy.

Baltimore	IP	H	R	ER	BB	SO
Grimsley (L 1—7)	3 ¹/₃	8	1	1	0	1
Garland	4 ²/₃	1	0	0	1	1
California						
Ryan (W 9—3)	9	0	0	0	4	9

T—2:01. A—18,492.

SEPTEMBER 28, 1974 AT ANAHEIM—CALIFORNIA 4, MINNESOTA 0

Nolan Ryan makes the most of his final start of the 1974 campaign by ringing up his third career no-hitter to raise his final record to 22–16 at the expense of Minnesota Twins, 4–0. Ryan started in splended fashion as his first seven pitches were strikes and he struck out the side in both the first and second innings. He finished the game with 15 strikeouts, but also had to contend with no less than eight walks—seven of them in the first five innings. The Angels won it with two runs in both the third and fourth innings with centerfielder Morris Nettles driving home three of them.

Minnesota	0 0 0	0 0 0	0 0 0 —	0 0 2
California	0 0 2	2 0 0	0 0 x —	4 7 0

Decker, Butler (3) and Borgmann. Ryan and Egan. WP—Ryan (22—16). LP—Decker (16—14).

Ryan Pitching Line: 9 IP   0 H   0 R 0 ER 8 BB 15 SO

JUNE 1, 1975 AT ANAHEIM—CALIFORNIA 1, BALTIMORE 0

Nolan Ryan moved into a tie with Dodger great Sandy Koufax as he fired the fourth no-hitter of his career in nipping the Baltimore Orioles 1—0. Making his 12th start of the season, Ryan polished off the Orioles with nine strikeouts as he came up with his fourth no-hit effort in the period of 109 starts. The only offensive output in the game came in the bottom of the third when Angel third baseman Dave Chalk singled home Mickey Rivers.

Baltimore	0 0 0	0 0 0	0 0 0 —	0 0 0
California	0 0 1	0 0 0	0 0 0 —	1 9 1

Grimsley, Garland (4) and Hendricks. Ryan and Rodriguez. WP—Ryan (9—3). LP—Grimsley (1—7).

Ryan Pitching Line: 9 IP   0 H   0 R 0 ER 4 BB   9 SO

NO-HITTER NUMBER 5
SEPTEMBER 26, 1981
HOUSTON 5, LOS ANGELES 0

LOS ANGELES	ab	r	h	bi	HOUSTON	ab	r	h	bi
Lopes 2b	3	0	0	0	Puhl rf	4	1	1	0
Smith ph	1	0	0	0	Garner 2b	4	0	2	1
Landreaux cf	3	0	0	0	T.Scott cf	5	1	0	0
Baker lf	4	0	0	0	Cruz lf	4	1	3	1
Garvey 1b	2	0	0	0	Ashby c	4	0	1	2
Guerrero 3b	3	0	0	0	Howe 3b	4	0	0	0
Scioscia c	3	0	0	0	Spilman 1b	2	0	0	0
Roenicke rf	3	0	0	0	Pittman ph	1	0	1	0
Thomas ss	2	0	0	0	Walling 1b	0	1	0	0
Power p	1	0	0	0	Reynolds ss	4	1	2	1
Goltz p	0	0	0	0	Ryan p	2	0	1	0
Perconte ph	1	0	0	0					
Forster p	0	0	0	0					
Johnstone ph	1	0	0	0					
Stewart p	0	0	0	0					
Howe p	0	0	0	0					
Totals	27	0	0	0	Totals	34	5	11	5

Los Angeles	000	000	000 —	0
Houston	002	000	03x —	5

E—Thomas. LOB—Los Angeles 3, Houston 12. 2B—Cruz, Reynolds. 3B—Reynolds. SB—Garner, Garvey, Thomas, Cruz. S—Ryan.

Los Angeles	IP	H	R	ER	BB	SO
Power (L 1—3)	3 1/3	6	2	1	3	1
Goltz	2/3	0	0	0	0	0
Forster	3	2	0	0	1	2
Stewart	1/3	2	3	3	2	0
Howe	2/3	1	0	0	0	0
Houston						
Ryan (W 10—5)	9	0	0	0	3	11

T—2:01. A—18,492.

SEPTEMBER 26, 1981 AT HOUSTON—HOUSTON 5, LOS ANGELES 0

History was made as Nolan Ryan became the first man in the history of the sport to pitch five no-hitters in his career as he notched a crucial 5—0 win over the Los Angeles Dodgers. Ryan wound up with 11 strikeouts (the 135th in his career fanned 10 or more men in a game) while walking only three. He threw a total of 129 pitches (52 balls, 77 strikes). Ryan stood at 10 strikeouts through the opening six innings, but set down only one more the rest of the way as he retired the final 19 batters in a row. Catcher Alan Ashby gave the Astros a 2—0 lead with a two-run single in the third and then Houston wrapped up the win with three more in the eighth.

Los Angeles	000	000	000 —	0	0 1
Houston	002	000	03x —	5	11 0

Power, Goltz (4), Forster (5), Stewart (8), Howe (8) and Scioscia. Ryan and Ashby. WP—Ryan (10—5), LP—Power (1—3).

Ryan Pitching Line: 9 IP   0 H   0 R 0 ER 3 BB 11 SO

NO-HITTER NUMBER 6
JUNE 11, 1990
TEXAS 5, OAKLAND 0

TEXAS	ab	r	h	bi	OAKLAND	ab	r	h	bi
Pettis cf	5	1	2	0	R.Hend'son lf	4	0	0	0
Palmeiro 1b	4	1	0	0	Randolph 2b	4	0	0	0
Franco 2b	4	2	2	4	Jennings 1b	3	0	0	0
Sierra rf	3	0	1	0	Hassey dh	3	0	0	0
Baines dh	4	0	1	0	Jose rf	3	0	0	0
Incaviglia lf	4	0	1	0	D.Hend'son cf	3	0	0	0
JoRussell c	3	1	1	1	Quirk c	2	0	0	0
Buechele 3b	4	0	0	0	Lansford ph	1	0	0	0
Huson ss	3	0	1	0	Steinbach c	0	0	0	0
					Weiss ss	2	0	0	0
					Gallego 3b	1	0	0	0
					Phelps ph	1	0	0	0
Totals	34	5	9	5	Totals	27	0	0	0

Texas	210	020	000 — 5
Oakland	000	000	000 — 0

LOB—Texas 6, Oakland 2. HR—Franco 2 (6), JoRussell (2). SB—Pettis (20), Sierra (5), Weiss (5).

Texas	IP	H	R	ER	BB	SO
Ryan (W 5—3)	9	0	0	0	2	14
Oakland						
Sanderson (L 7—3)	6	8	5	5	2	3
Norris	2	1	0	0	2	3
Nelson	1	0	0	0	0	0

WP—Norris.
T—2:49. A—33,436.

JUNE 11, 1990 AT OAKLAND—TEXAS 5, OAKLAND 0

Nolan Ryan accomplished several milestones with the sixth no-hitter of his major league career. At the age of 43 years, 4 months, 12 days, he became the oldest pitcher to ever throw a no-hitter while also becoming the first to reach that achievement in three different decades and with three different teams. Ryan was making just his second start since coming off the disabled list and was still bothered by the lower back trouble that had sidelined him for nearly three weeks. He allowed only two baserunners, walks to Walt Weiss in the third and Mike Gallego in the sixth, while fanning 14 and throwing 132 pitches. The Rangers offense was provided by a pair of 2-run homers by Julio Franco and a solo blast by John Russell, who was catching Ryan for the first time ever.

Texas	210	020	000 —	5	9 0
Oakland	000	000	000 —	0	0 0

Ryan and Russell. Sanderson, Norris (7), Nelson (9) and Quirk, Steinbach (9). WP—Ryan (5—3), LP—Sanderson (7—3).

Ryan Pitching Line: 9 IP   0 H   0 R 0 ER 2 BB 14 SO

NO-HITTER NUMBER 7
MAY 1, 1991
TEXAS 3, TORONTO 0

TORONTO	AB	R	H	BI	TEXAS	AB	R	H	BI
White cf	4	0	0	0	Pettis cf	4	1	1	0
R. Alomar 2b	4	0	0	0	Daugherty lf	4	0	1	0
Gruber 3b	2	0	0	0	Palmeiro 1b	4	1	2	0
Carter lf	2	0	0	0	Sierra rf	4	1	1	2
Olerud 1b	3	0	0	0	Franco 2b	4	0	0	0
Whiten rf	3	0	0	0	Gonzalez dh	3	0	1	0
G. Hill dh	3	0	0	0	Stanley c	3	0	1	0
Myers c	3	0	0	0	Buechele 3b	4	0	1	0
M. Lee ss	3	0	0	0	Huson ss	2	0	0	0
Totals	27	0	0	0	Totals	32	3	8	2

Toronto	000	000	000	—	0
Texas	003	000	00x	—	3

E: Gruber (2), Myers (1), M. Lee (5), Palmeiro (1). LOB: Toronto 2, Texas 8, 2B: Gonzalez (3), Stanley (1), HR: Sierra (5). RBIs: Sierra 2 (15). SB: Pettis (8). CS: Gonzalez (1). S: Huson.

Toronto	IP	H	R	ER	BB	SO
Key (L 4—1)	6	5	3	3	1	5
MacDonald	1	2	0	0	0	2
Fraser	1	1	0	0	0	0
Texas	**IP**	**H**	**R**	**ER**	**BB**	**SO**
Ryan (W 3—2)	9	0	0	0	2	16

HBP: by Fraser (Gonzalez).
Umpires: Home, Tschida; First, Coble; Second, Shulock; Third, Johnson.T:2.25. A: 33,439.

MAY 1, 1991 AT ARLINGTON—TEXAS 3, TORONTO 0

On Arlington Appreciation Night, Nolan Ryan gave 33,439 fans the thrill of a lifetime with perhaps the most dominating performance in any of his seven no-hitters. He retired 27 of 29 batters, issuing walks to Kelly Gruber in the first and Joe Carter in the seventh while tying his own club record of 16 strikeouts, his second most ever in a no-hitter. The closest that Toronto came to a hit was in the sixth inning on a shallow fly ball by Manuel Lee that Gary Pettis charged and caught at knee-level. He recorded at least one strikeout in every inning and fanned Roberto Alomar to end the game on his 122nd pitch. Ruben Sierra hit a two-run homer for the Rangers. It was the first no-hitter ever pitched by a Ranger at Arlington Stadium.

Toronto	000	000	000	—	0 0 3
Texas	003	000	00x	—	3 8 1

Key, MacDonald (7), Fraser (8) and Myers. Ryan and Stanley. WP—Ryan (3—2). LP—Key (4—1).

Ryan Pitching Line: 9 IP   0 H   0 R 0 ER   2 BB   16 SO

RYAN'S 5,511 CAREER STRIKEOUTS

1	Sept. 11, 1966	Pat Jarvis	Braves
2	Sept. 11, 1966	Eddie Mathews	Braves
3	Sept. 11, 1966	Dennis Menke	Braves
4	Sept. 18, 1966	Rusty Staub	Astros
5	Sept. 18, 1966	Bob Aspromonte	Astros
6	Sept. 18, 1966	Bob Bruce	Astros
7	April 14, 1968	Ron Davis	Astros
8	April 14, 1968	Joe Morgan	Astros
9	April 14, 1968	Hal King	Astros
10	April 14, 1968	Jim Wynn	Astros
11	April 14, 1968	Norm Miller	Astros
12	April 14, 1968	Hector Torres	Astros
13	April 14, 1968	Ron Davis	Astros
14	April 14, 1968	Rusty Staub	Astros
15	April 19, 1968	Wes Parker	Dodgers
16	April 19, 1968	Zolio Versalles	Dodgers
17	April 19, 1968	Willie Davis	Dodgers
18	April 19, 1968	Ron Fairly	Dodgers
19	April 19, 1968	Claude Osteen	Dodgers
20	April 19, 1968	Wes Parker	Dodgers
21	April 19, 1968	Zolio Versalles	Dodgers
22	April 19, 1968	Ricky Colavito	Dodgers
23	April 19, 1968	Claude Osteen	Dodgers
24	April 19, 1968	Jim Lefebvre	Dodgers
25	April 19, 1968	Claude Osteen	Dodgers
26	April 27, 1968	Tony Perez	Reds
27	April 27, 1968	Johnny Bench	Reds
28	April 27, 1968	Leo Cardenas	Reds
29	April 27, 1968	Mack Jones	Reds
30	April 27, 1968	Vada Pinson	Reds
31	April 27, 1968	Milt Pappas	Reds
32	April 27, 1968	Pete Rose	Reds
33	May 2, 1968	Cookie Rojas	Phillies
34	May 2, 1968	Johnny Callison	Phillies
35	May 2, 1968	Tony Gonzalez	Phillies
36	May 2, 1968	Bill White	Phillies
37	May 2, 1968	Tony Taylor	Phillies
38	May 2, 1968	Johnny Callison	Phillies
39	May 2, 1968	Woodie Fryman	Phillies
40	May 2, 1968	Johnny Callison	Phillies

41	May 2, 1968	Don Lock	Phillies
42	May 2, 1968	Tony Taylor	Phillies
43	May 7, 1968	Lou Brock	Cardinals
44	May 7, 1968	Bob Tolan	Cardinals
45	May 7, 1968	Tim McCarver	Cardinals
46	May 7, 1968	Nellie Briles	Cardinals
47	May 7, 1968	Mike Shannon	Cardinals
48	May 7, 1968	Dick Schofield	Cardinals
49	May 7, 1968	Dave Ricketts	Cardinals
50	May 7, 1968	Johnny Edwards	Cardinals
51	May 14, 1968	Pete Rose	Reds
52	May 14, 1968	Alex Johnson	Reds
53	May 14, 1968	Johnny Bench	Reds
54	May 14, 1968	Vada Pinson	Reds
55	May 14, 1968	Lee May	Reds
56	May 14, 1968	Leo Cardenas	Reds
57	May 14, 1968	Mel Queen	Reds
58	May 14, 1968	Alex Johnson	Reds
59	May 14, 1968	Tony Perez	Reds
60	May 14, 1968	Alex Johnson	Reds
61	May 14, 1968	Vada Pinson	Reds
62	May 14, 1968	Tony Perez	Reds
63	May 14, 1968	Lee May	Reds
64	May 14, 1968	Johnny Bench	Reds
65	May 19, 1968	Sonny Jackson	Braves
66	May 19, 1968	Hank Aaron	Braves
67	May 19, 1968	Ron Reed	Braves
68	May 19, 1968	Tito Francona	Braves
69	May 19, 1968	Sonny Jackson	Braves
70	May 19, 1968	Tito Francona	Braves
71	May 19, 1968	Sandy Valdespino	Braves
72	May 24, 1968	Bob Tillman	Braves
73	May 24, 1968	Felipe Alou	Braves
74	May 24, 1968	Joe Torre	Braves
75	June 1, 1968	Lou Brock	Cardinals
76	June 1, 1968	Roger Maris	Cardinals
77	June 1, 1968	Ray Washburn	Cardinals
78	June 1, 1968	Mike Shannon	Cardinals
79	June 1, 1968	Orlando Cepada	Cardinals
80	June 1, 1968	Bob Tolan	Cardinals
81	June 1, 1968	Dick Schofield	Cardinals
82	June 7, 1968	Frank Johnson	Giants
83	June 7, 1968	Dave Marshall	Giants
84	June 7, 1968	Al Oliver	Giants
85	June 7, 1968	Bob Barton	Giants
86	June 7, 1968	Frank Johnson	Giants
87	June 7, 1968	Jim Davenport	Giants
88	June 7, 1968	Jack Hiatt	Giants
89	June 12, 1968	Zolio Versalles	Dodgers
90	June 12, 1968	Don Drysdale	Dodgers
91	June 12, 1968	Wes Parker	Dodgers
92	June 18, 1968	Dick Simpson	Astros
93	June 18, 1968	Doug Rader	Astros
94	June 18, 1968	Bob Watson	Astros
95	June 18, 1968	Hector Torres	Astros
96	June 18, 1968	Dick Simpson	Astros
97	June 18, 1968	Bob Watson	Astros
98	June 18, 1968	Ron Brand	Astros
99	June 18, 1968	Hector Torres	Astros
100	June 18, 1968	Denny Lemaster	Astros
101	June 18, 1968	Ron Brand	Astros
102	June 18, 1968	Dick Simpson	Astros
103	June 18, 1968	Denny Lemaster	Astros
104	June 23, 1968	Paul Popovich	Dodgers
105	June 23, 1968	Jim Lefebvre	Dodgers
106	June 23, 1968	Zolio Versalles	Dodgers
107	June 23, 1968	Wes Parker	Dodgers
108	June 23, 1968	Zolio Versalles	Dodgers
109	June 23, 1968	Bill Singer	Dodgers
110	June 28, 1968	Bob Watson	Astros
111	June 28, 1968	Larry Dierker	Astros
112	June 28, 1968	Dick Simpson	Astros
113	June 28, 1968	Rusty Staub	Astros
114	June 28, 1968	Jim Wynn	Astros
115	June 28, 1968	Dennis Menke	Astros
116	July 3, 1968	Willie Stargell	Pirates
117	July 3, 1968	Matty Alou	Pirates
118	July 3, 1968	Donn Clendenon	Pirates
119	July 3, 1968	Steve Blass	Pirates
120	July 3, 1968	Donn Clendenon	Pirates
121	July 15, 1968	Cookie Rojas	Phillies
122	July 15, 1968	Roberto Pena	Phillies
123	July 15, 1968	John Briggs	Phillies
124	July 15, 1968	Cookie Rojas	Phillies
125	July 15, 1968	Johnny Callison	Phillies
126	July 15, 1968	Cookie Rojas	Phillies
127	July 15, 1968	Cookie Rojas	Phillies
128	July 24, 1968	Mike Lum	Braves
129	July 24, 1968	Marty Martinez	Braves
130	July 29, 1968	Lou Brock	Cardinals
131	July 29, 1968	Curt Flood	Cardinals
132	July 29, 1968	Roger Maris	Cardinals
133	July 29, 1968	Orlando Cepada	Cardinals
134	July 29, 1968	Ray Washburn	Cardinals
135	July 29, 1968	Ray Washburn	Cardinals
136	July 29, 1968	Mike Shannon	Cardinals
137	Sept. 3, 1968	Mike Lum	Braves
138	Sept. 3, 1968	Deron Johnson	Braves
139	Sept. 10, 1968	Ron Santo	Cubs
140	April 9, 1969	Manny Mota	Expos
141	April 9, 1969	Floyd Wicker	Expos
142	April 14, 1969	Deron Johnson	Phillies
143	April 16, 1969	Fred Patek	Pirates
144	April 16, 1969	Bob Moose	Pirates
145	April 20, 1969	Mike Shannon	Cardinals
146	April 20, 1969	Nellie Briles	Cardinals
147	April 20, 1969	Lou Brock	Cardinals
148	April 20, 1969	Joe Hague	Cardinals
149	April 29, 1969	John Bateman	Expos
150	April 29, 1969	Don Bosch	Expos
151	April 29, 1969	Ty Cline	Expos
152	April 29, 1969	John Bateman	Expos

153	April 29, 1969	Mack Jones	Expos
154	April 29, 1969	Coco Laboy	Expos
155	April 29, 1969	Gary Sutherland	Expos
156	May 3, 1969	Ernie Banks	Cubs
157	May 3, 1969	Don Young	Cubs
158	May 3, 1969	Billy Williams	Cubs
159	May 3, 1969	Willie Smith	Cubs
160	June 11, 1969	Bobby Bonds	Giants
161	June 17, 1969	John Briggs	Phillies
162	June 17, 1969	Larry Hisle	Phillies
163	June 17, 1969	Terry Harmon	Phillies
164	June 17, 1969	Grant Jackson	Phillies
165	June 20, 1969	Curt Flood	Cardinals
166	June 20, 1969	Mike Shannon	Cardinals
167	June 20, 1969	Bob Gibson	Cardinals
168	June 25, 1969	Larry Hisle	Phillies
169	June 25, 1969	John Briggs	Phillies
170	June 25, 1969	Rick Joseph	Phillies
171	June 25, 1969	Gene Stone	Phillies
172	June 25, 1969	Ron Stone	Phillies
173	June 25, 1969	Lowell Palmer	Phillies
174	June 25, 1969	Larry Hisle	Phillies
175	June 25, 1969	John Briggs	Phillies
176	June 25, 1969	Lowell Palmer	Phillies
177	June 25, 1969	Gene Stone	Phillies
178	July 1, 1969	Joe Torre	Cardinals
179	July 1, 1969	Steve Huntz	Cardinals
180	July 1, 1969	Steve Carlton	Cardinals
181	July 1, 1969	Steve Carlton	Cardinals
182	July 13, 1969	Kevin Collins	Expos
183	July 13, 1969	Bob Bailey	Expos
184	July 13, 1969	Kevin Collins	Expos
185	July 27, 1969	Jerry Arrigo	Reds
186	July 27, 1969	Tony Perez	Reds
187	July 27, 1969	Lee May	Reds
188	July 27, 1969	Johnny Bench	Reds
189	July 30, 1969	Joe Morgan	Astros
190	July 30, 1969	Norm Miller	Astros
191	July 30, 1969	Curt Blefary	Astros
192	July 30, 1969	Doug Rader	Astros
193	July 30, 1969	Jim Wynn	Astros
194	July 30, 1969	Norm Miller	Astros
195	July 30, 1969	Curt Blefary	Astros
196	August 5, 1969	Lee May	Reds
197	August 5, 1969	Pat Corrales	Reds
198	August 5, 1969	Pete Rose	Reds
199	August 5, 1969	Bob Tolan	Reds
200	August 5, 1969	Tony Perez	Reds
201	August 5, 1969	Jim Stewart	Reds
202	August 5, 1969	Johnny Bench	Reds
203	Sept. 3, 1969	Andy Kosco	Dodgers
204	Sept. 3, 1969	Ted Sizemore	Dodgers
205	Sept. 7, 1969	Dave Watkins	Phillies
206	Sept. 7, 1969	Cookie Rojas	Phillies
207	Sept. 7, 1969	Tony Taylor	Phillies
208	Sept. 10, 1969	Ty Cline	Expos
209	Sept. 10, 1969	Angel Hermoso	Expos
210	Sept. 10, 1969	Howie Reed	Expos
211	Sept. 10, 1969	Ron Fairly	Expos
212	Sept. 10, 1969	Ty Cline	Expos
213	Sept. 10, 1969	Mack Jones	Expos
214	Sept. 10, 1969	Coco Laboy	Expos
215	Sept. 10, 1969	John Bateman	Expos
216	Sept. 10, 1969	Jim Fairey	Expos
217	Sept. 10, 1969	Rusty Staub	Expos
218	Sept. 10, 1969	Coco Laboy	Expos
219	Sept. 14, 1969	Willie Stargell	Pirates
220	Sept. 14, 1969	Steve Blass	Pirates
221	Sept. 14, 1969	Roberto Clemente	Pirates
222	Sept. 14, 1969	Fred Patek	Pirates
223	Sept. 14, 1969	Steve Blass	Pirates
224	Sept. 14, 1969	Willie Stargell	Pirates
225	Sept. 14, 1969	Roberto Clemente	Pirates
226	Sept. 19, 1969	Willie Stargell	Pirates
227	Sept. 19, 1969	Bob Veale	Pirates
228	Sept. 28, 1969	John Briggs	Phillies
229	Sept. 28, 1969	Ron Stone	Phillies
230	Sept. 28, 1969	Johnny Callison	Phillies
231	Oct. 1, 1969	Don Young	Cubs
232	April 18, 1970	John Briggs	Phillies
233	April 18, 1970	Deron Johnson	Phillies
234	April 18, 1970	Larry Hisle	Phillies
235	April 18, 1970	Ron Stone	Phillies
236	April 18, 1970	John Briggs	Phillies
237	April 18, 1970	Deron Johnson	Phillies
238	April 18, 1970	Tim McCarver	Phillies
239	April 18, 1970	Larry Bowa	Phillies
240	April 18, 1970	Jim Bunning	Phillies
241	April 18, 1970	John Briggs	Phillies
242	April 18, 1970	Tim McCarver	Phillies
243	April 18, 1970	Larry Hisle	Phillies
244	April 18, 1970	Ron Stone	Phillies
245	April 18, 1970	Larry Bowa	Phillies
246	April 18, 1970	Deron Johnson	Phillies
247	April 24, 1970	Maury Wills	Dodgers
248	April 24, 1970	Bill Buckner	Dodgers
249	April 24, 1970	Claude Osteen	Dodgers
250	April 24, 1970	Willie Crawford	Dodgers
251	April 24, 1970	Bill Grabarkewitz	Dodgers
252	April 30, 1970	Bobby Bonds	Giants
253	April 30, 1970	Dick Dietz	Giants
254	April 30, 1970	Bob Taylor	Giants
255	April 30, 1970	Bobby Bonds	Giants
256	April 30, 1970	Dick Dietz	Giants
257	April 30, 1970	Bob Taylor	Giants
258	April 30, 1970	Steve Whitaker	Giants
259	April 30, 1970	Dick Dietz	Giants
260	May 5, 1970	Von Joshua	Dodgers
261	May 5, 1970	Willie Crawford	Dodgers
262	May 5, 1970	Bill Grabarkewitz	Dodgers
263	May 5, 1970	Sandy Vance	Dodgers
264	May 5, 1970	Bill Grabarkewitz	Dodgers

265	May 10, 1970	Bob Burda	Giants
266	May 10, 1970	Juan Marichal	Giants
267	May 24, 1970	Billy Williams	Cubs
268	May 24, 1970	Ron Santo	Cubs
269	May 24, 1970	Jim Hickman	Cubs
270	May 24, 1970	Jack Hiatt	Cubs
271	May 24, 1970	Joe Decker	Cubs
272	May 24, 1970	Cleo James	Cubs
273	May 24, 1970	Jimmie Hall	Cubs
274	May 24, 1970	Willie Smith	Cubs
275	May 30, 1970	Jim Wynn	Astros
276	May 30, 1970	Norm Miller	Astros
277	May 30, 1970	Dennis Menke	Astros
278	May 30, 1970	Joe Pepitone	Astros
279	May 30, 1970	Doug Rader	Astros
280	May 30, 1970	Jim Wynn	Astros
281	May 30, 1970	Dennis Menke	Astros
282	May 30, 1970	Joe Pepitone	Astros
283	May 30, 1970	Doug Rader	Astros
284	May 30, 1970	Johnny Edwards	Astros
285	May 30, 1970	Larry Dierker	Astros
286	June 5, 1970	Bernie Carbo	Reds
287	June 5, 1970	Bob Tolan	Reds
288	June 5, 1970	Lee May	Reds
289	June 5, 1970	Bernie Carbo	Reds
290	June 5, 1970	Dave Concepcion	Reds
291	June 5, 1970	Jim McGlothlin	Reds
292	June 17, 1970	Bernie Carbo	Reds
293	June 24, 1970	Willie Smith	Cubs
294	June 24, 1970	Willie Smith	Cubs
295	July 14, 1970	Ron Hunt	Giants
296	July 14, 1970	Ken Henderson	Giants
297	July 14, 1970	Jim Ray Hart	Giants
298	July 14, 1970	Frank Johnson	Giants
299	July 14, 1970	Rich Robertson	Giants
300	July 14, 1970	Bobby Bonds	Giants
301	July 14, 1970	Rich Robertson	Giants
302	July 22, 1970	Clarence Gaston	Padres
303	August 4, 1970	Ron Santo	Cubs
304	August 4, 1970	Joe Pepitone	Cubs
305	August 4, 1970	Johnny Callison	Cubs
306	August 4, 1970	Randy Hundley	Cubs
307	August 4, 1970	Joe Decker	Cubs
308	August 4, 1970	Jim Hickman	Cubs
309	August 4, 1970	Randy Hundley	Cubs
310	August 4, 1970	Joe Decker	Cubs
311	August 4, 1970	Ron Santo	Cubs
312	August 4, 1970	Jim Hickman	Cubs
313	August 4, 1970	Joe Pepitone	Cubs
314	August 4, 1970	Willie Smith	Cubs
315	August 4, 1970	Joe Pepitone	Cubs
316	August 9, 1970	Fred Patek	Pirates
317	August 9, 1970	Roberto Clemente	Pirates
318	August 9, 1970	Manny Sanguillen	Pirates
319	August 9, 1970	Fred Patek	Pirates
320	August 9, 1970	Roberto Clemente	Pirates
321	August 9, 1970	Luke Walker	Pirates
322	August 9, 1970	Fred Patek	Pirates
323	August 9, 1970	Bob Robertson	Pirates
324	August 9, 1970	Manny Sanguillen	Pirates
325	August 9, 1970	Luke Walker	Pirates
326	August 14, 1970	Felix Millan	Braves
327	August 14, 1970	Clete Boyer	Braves
328	August 14, 1970	Ron Reed	Braves
329	August 25, 1970	Mike Lum	Braves
330	August 25, 1970	Clete Boyer	Braves
331	August 25, 1970	Pat Jarvis	Braves
332	August 30, 1970	John Mayberry	Astros
333	August 30, 1970	Jesus Alou	Astros
334	August 30, 1970	Doug Rader	Astros
335	Sept. 4, 1970	Jim Hickman	Cubs
336	Sept. 4, 1970	Bill Hands	Cubs
337	Sept. 4, 1970	Bill Hands	Cubs
338	Sept. 9, 1970	Larry Bowa	Phillies
339	Sept. 9, 1970	John Briggs	Phillies
340	Sept. 9, 1970	Scott Reid	Phillies
341	Sept. 9, 1970	Barry Lersch	Phillies
342	Sept. 9, 1970	Denny Doyle	Phillies
343	Sept. 9, 1970	John Briggs	Phillies
344	Sept. 9, 1970	Don Money	Phillies
345	Sept. 9, 1970	Scott Reid	Phillies
346	Sept. 9, 1970	Tim McCarver	Phillies
347	Sept. 9, 1970	Barry Lersch	Phillies
348	Sept. 9, 1970	Larry Bowa	Phillies
349	Sept. 9, 1970	Scott Reid	Phillies
350	Sept. 9, 1970	Denny Doyle	Phillies
351	Sept. 14, 1970	John Bateman	Expos
352	Sept. 27, 1970	Dock Ellis	Pirates
353	Sept. 27, 1970	Al Oliver	Pirates
354	Sept. 30, 1970	Paul Popovich	Cubs
355	Sept. 30, 1970	Don Kessinger	Cubs
356	Sept. 30, 1970	Willie Smith	Cubs
357	April 23, 1971	Billy Williams	Cubs
358	April 23, 1971	Joe Pepitone	Cubs
359	April 23, 1971	Paul Popovich	Cubs
360	April 29, 1971	Lou Brock	Cardinals
361	April 29, 1971	Leron Lee	Cardinals
362	April 29, 1971	Jerry Reuss	Cardinals
363	April 29, 1971	Leron Lee	Cardinals
364	April 29, 1971	Jerry Reuss	Cardinals
365	May 4, 1971	Glen Beckert	Cubs
366	May 4, 1971	Ron Santo	Cubs
367	May 4, 1971	Johnny Callison	Cubs
368	May 4, 1971	Ernie Banks	Cubs
369	May 4, 1971	Joe Pepitone	Cubs
370	May 4, 1971	Billy Williams	Cubs
371	May 4, 1971	Ernie Banks	Cubs
372	May 11, 1971	Joe Morgan	Astros
373	May 11, 1971	Cesar Cedeno	Astros
374	May 11, 1971	Rich Chiles	Astros
375	May 11, 1971	Dennis Menke	Astros
376	May 11, 1971	Larry Dierker	Astros

377	May 11, 1971	Rich Chiles	Astros
378	May 11, 1971	Rich Chiles	Astros
379	May 11, 1971	Cesar Cedeno	Astros
380	May 16, 1971	Vic Davalillo	Pirates
381	May 16, 1971	Roberto Clemente	Pirates
382	May 16, 1971	Gene Alley	Pirates
383	May 16, 1971	Roberto Clemente	Pirates
384	May 21, 1971	Sonny Jackson	Braves
385	May 21, 1971	Marty Perez	Braves
386	May 21, 1971	Ralph Garr	Braves
387	May 21, 1971	Hank Aaron	Braves
388	May 21, 1971	Marty Perez	Braves
389	May 21, 1971	Pat Jarvis	Braves
390	May 21, 1971	Clete Boyer	Braves
391	May 29, 1971	Don Mason	Padres
392	May 29, 1971	Ollie Brown	Padres
393	May 29, 1971	Ed Spiezio	Padres
394	May 29, 1971	Fred Kendall	Padres
395	May 29, 1971	Tom Phoebus	Padres
396	May 29, 1971	Clarence Gaston	Padres
397	May 29, 1971	Ivan Murrell	Padres
398	May 29, 1971	Tom Phoebus	Padres
399	May 29, 1971	Clarence Gaston	Padres
400	May 29, 1971	Nate Colbert	Padres
401	May 29, 1971	Ollie Brown	Padres
402	May 29, 1971	Ivan Murrell	Padres
403	May 29, 1971	Fred Kendall	Padres
404	May 29, 1971	Angel Bravo	Padres
405	May 29, 1971	Clarence Gaston	Padres
406	May 29, 1971	Ivan Murrell	Padres
407	June 5, 1971	Maury Wills	Dodgers
408	June 5, 1971	Duke Sims	Dodgers
409	June 5, 1971	Willie Davis	Dodgers
410	June 5, 1971	Von Joshua	Dodgers
411	June 10, 1971	Enzo Hernandez	Padres
412	June 10, 1971	Clarence Gaston	Padres
413	June 10, 1971	Ed Spiezio	Padres
414	June 10, 1971	Dave Campbell	Padres
415	June 15, 1971	Dick Allen	Dodgers
416	June 15, 1971	Jim Lefebvre	Dodgers
417	June 15, 1971	Tom Haller	Dodgers
418	June 15, 1971	Al Downing	Dodgers
419	June 15, 1971	Willie Crawford	Dodgers
420	June 15, 1971	Al Downing	Dodgers
421	June 15, 1971	Willie Davis	Dodgers
422	June 15, 1971	Tom Haller	Dodgers
423	June 15, 1971	Maury Wills	Dodgers
424	June 20, 1971	Willie Montanez	Phillies
425	June 20, 1971	Oscar Gamble	Phillies
426	June 20, 1971	Ron Stone	Phillies
427	June 20, 1971	Deron Johnson	Phillies
428	June 20, 1971	Barry Lersch	Phillies
429	June 20, 1971	Barry Lersch	Phillies
430	June 20, 1971	Ron Stone	Phillies
431	June 25, 1971	Ron Fairly	Expos
432	June 25, 1971	John Bateman	Expos
433	June 25, 1971	Rusty Staub	Expos
434	June 25, 1971	Ron Fairly	Expos
435	June 25, 1971	John Bateman	Expos
436	June 25, 1971	Jim Fairey	Expos
437	June 25, 1971	Stan Swanson	Expos
438	June 25, 1971	John Bateman	Expos
439	June 25, 1971	Jim Gosger	Expos
440	June 25, 1971	Stan Swanson	Expos
441	June 30, 1971	Willie Stargell	Pirates
442	June 30, 1971	Al Oliver	Pirates
443	June 30, 1971	Vic Davalillo	Pirates
444	June 30, 1971	Willie Stargell	Pirates
445	June 30, 1971	Al Oliver	Pirates
446	June 30, 1971	Bob Robertson	Pirates
447	June 30, 1971	Richie Hebner	Pirates
448	June 30, 1971	Willie Stargell	Pirates
449	June 30, 1971	Charlie Sands	Pirates
450	July 5, 1971	Rich Hacker	Expos
451	July 5, 1971	Bob Bailey	Expos
452	July 5, 1971	Ron Fairly	Expos
453	July 5, 1971	Dave McDonald	Expos
454	July 5, 1971	John Strohmayer	Expos
455	July 11, 1971	Pete Rose	Reds
456	July 11, 1971	Bernie Carbo	Reds
457	July 16, 1971	Johnny Edwards	Astros
458	July 16, 1971	Jack Billingham	Astros
459	July 23, 1971	Roger Metzger	Astros
460	July 29, 1971	Ted Simmons	Cardinals
461	July 29, 1971	Lou Brock	Cardinals
462	July 29, 1971	Jerry Reuss	Cardinals
463	August 3, 1971	Tony Perez	Reds
464	August 3, 1971	Pat Corrales	Reds
465	August 3, 1971	Wayne Simpson	Reds
466	August 7, 1971	Zolio Versalles	Braves
467	August 7, 1971	Ron Reed	Braves
468	August 7, 1971	Mike Lum	Braves
469	August 7, 1971	Ron Reed	Braves
470	August 7, 1971	Ron Reed	Braves
471	August 7, 1971	Oscar Brown	Braves
472	August 7, 1971	Ralph Garr	Braves
473	August 12, 1971	Larry Stahl	Padres
474	August 31, 1971	Ted Sizemore	Cardinals
475	August 31, 1971	Ted Simmons	Cardinals
476	August 31, 1971	Joe Hague	Cardinals
477	August 31, 1971	Jose Cruz	Cardinals
478	August 31, 1971	Jerry Reuss	Cardinals
479	August 31, 1971	Lou Brock	Cardinals
480	August 31, 1971	Joe Torre	Cardinals
481	August 31, 1971	Jose Cruz	Cardinals
482	August 31, 1971	Dal Maxvill	Cardinals
483	August 31, 1971	Jerry Reuss	Cardinals
484	August 31, 1971	Lou Brock	Cardinals
485	August 31, 1971	Matty Alou	Cardinals
486	Sept. 5, 1971	Deron Johnson	Phillies
487	Sept. 5, 1971	Oscar Gamble	Phillies
488	Sept. 14, 1971	John Strohmayer	Expos

489	Sept. 23, 1971	Pat Bourque	Cubs
490	Sept. 23, 1971	Gene Hiser	Cubs
491	Sept. 23, 1971	Frank Fernandez	Cubs
492	Sept. 23, 1971	Gene Hiser	Cubs
493	Sept. 23, 1971	Paul Popovich	Cubs
494	April 18, 1972	Danny Thompson	Twins
495	April 18, 1972	Rod Carew	Twins
496	April 18, 1972	Charlie Manuel	Twins
497	April 18, 1972	Jim Perry	Twins
498	April 18, 1972	Danny Thompson	Twins
499	April 18, 1972	Rod Carew	Twins
500	April 18, 1972	Charlie Manuel	Twins
501	April 18, 1972	Rick Dempsey	Twins
502	April 18, 1972	Steve Braun	Twins
503	April 18, 1972	Rod Carew	Twins
504	April 23, 1972	Hal King	Rangers
505	April 23, 1972	Dave Nelson	Rangers
506	April 28, 1972	Don Buford	Orioles
507	April 28, 1972	Boog Powell	Orioles
508	April 28, 1972	Jim Palmer	Orioles
509	May 5, 1972	Davey May	Brewers
510	May 5, 1972	Billy Conigliaro	Brewers
511	May 5, 1972	Darrell Porter	Brewers
512	May 5, 1972	Ken Brett	Brewers
513	May 5, 1972	Davey May	Brewers
514	May 5, 1972	George Scott	Brewers
515	May 5, 1972	Darrell Porter	Brewers
516	May 5, 1972	Brock Davis	Brewers
517	May 5, 1972	Billy Conigliaro	Brewers
518	May 5, 1972	Darrell Porter	Brewers
519	May 5, 1972	Rick Auerbach	Brewers
520	May 5, 1972	Bill Voss	Brewers
521	May 5, 1972	Davey May	Brewers
522	May 5, 1972	George Scott	Brewers
523	May 10, 1972	Reggie Smith	Red Sox
524	May 10, 1972	Rick Miller	Red Sox
525	May 10, 1972	Carlton Fisk	Red Sox
526	May 10, 1972	Marty Pattin	Red Sox
527	May 10, 1972	Rick Miller	Red Sox
528	May 15, 1972	Angel Mangual	A's
529	May 15, 1972	Bert Campaneris	A's
530	May 15, 1972	Reggie Jackson	A's
531	May 22, 1972	Reggie Jackson	A's
532	May 22, 1972	Dave Duncan	A's
533	May 22, 1972	Reggie Jackson	A's
534	May 22, 1972	Larry Brown	A's
535	May 22, 1972	Sal Bando	A's
536	May 22, 1972	Bert Campaneris	A's
537	May 26, 1972	Paul Schaal	Royals
538	May 26, 1972	Steve Hovley	Royals
539	May 30, 1972	Bill Melton	White Sox
540	May 30, 1972	Jay Johnstone	White Sox
541	May 30, 1972	Stan Bahnsen	White Sox
542	May 30, 1972	Rich Morales	White Sox
543	May 30, 1972	Walt Williams	White Sox
544	May 30, 1972	Pat Kelly	White Sox
545	May 30, 1972	Ed Herrmann	White Sox
546	May 30, 1972	Rich Morales	White Sox
547	May 30, 1972	Jorge Orta	White Sox
548	May 30, 1972	Carlos May	White Sox
549	June 3, 1972	Tom McCraw	Indians
550	June 3, 1972	Eddie Leon	Indians
551	June 3, 1972	Lou Camilli	Indians
552	June 3, 1972	Alex Johnson	Indians
553	June 7, 1972	Mickey Stanley	Tigers
554	June 7, 1972	Ed Brinkman	Tigers
555	June 7, 1972	Joe Niekro	Tigers
556	June 7, 1972	Gates Brown	Tigers
557	June 7, 1972	Willie Horton	Tigers
558	June 11, 1972	Danny Cater	Red Sox
559	June 14, 1972	Jack Brohammer	Indians
560	June 14, 1972	Eddie Leon	Indians
561	June 14, 1972	Jack Brohammer	Indians
562	June 14, 1972	Alex Johnson	Indians
563	June 14, 1972	Chris Chambliss	Indians
564	June 14, 1972	Ray Fosse	Indians
565	June 14, 1972	Graig Nettles	Indians
566	June 18, 1972	Dick McAuliffe	Tigers
567	June 18, 1972	Bill Freehan	Tigers
568	June 18, 1972	Mickey Lolich	Tigers
569	June 18, 1972	Aurelio Rodriguez	Tigers
570	June 18, 1972	Jim Northrup	Tigers
571	June 18, 1972	Dick McAuliffe	Tigers
572	June 18, 1972	Bill Freehan	Tigers
573	June 18, 1972	Mickey Stanley	Tigers
574	June 18, 1972	Ed Brinkman	Tigers
575	June 23, 1972	Bert Campaneris	A's
576	June 23, 1972	Mike Epstein	A's
577	June 23, 1972	Dave Duncan	A's
578	June 23, 1972	Angel Mangual	A's
579	June 23, 1972	Tim Cullen	A's
580	June 23, 1972	Dave Hamilton	A's
581	June 23, 1972	Bert Campaneris	A's
582	June 23, 1972	Reggie Jackson	A's
583	June 23, 1972	Angel Mangual	A's
584	June 23, 1972	Mike Epstein	A's
585	June 27, 1972	Cesar Tovar	Twins
586	June 27, 1972	Rod Carew	Twins
587	June 27, 1972	Jim Perry	Twins
588	June 27, 1972	Charlie Manuel	Twins
589	June 27, 1972	Cesar Tovar	Twins
590	June 27, 1972	Rod Carew	Twins
591	June 27, 1972	Jim Nettles	Twins
592	July 1, 1972	Joe Rudi	A's
593	July 1, 1972	Reggie Jackson	A's
594	July 1, 1972	Dave Duncan	A's
595	July 1, 1972	Tim Cullen	A's
596	July 1, 1972	Dave Hamilton	A's
597	July 1, 1972	Bert Campaneris	A's
598	July 1, 1972	Reggie Jackson	A's
599	July 1, 1972	Sal Bando	A's
600	July 1, 1972	Dave Duncan	A's

601	July 1, 1972	Tim Cullen	A's
602	July 1, 1972	Sal Bando	A's
603	July 1, 1972	Dave Duncan	A's
604	July 1, 1972	Bill Voss	A's
605	July 1, 1972	Sal Bando	A's
606	July 1, 1972	Dave Duncan	A's
607	July 1, 1972	Adrian Garrett	A's
608	July 5, 1972	Earl Stephenson	Brewers
609	July 5, 1972	John Briggs	Brewers
610	July 5, 1972	Rick Auerbach	Brewers
611	July 5, 1972	Earl Stephenson	Brewers
612	July 5, 1972	John Briggs	Brewers
613	July 5, 1972	Earl Stephenson	Brewers
614	July 5, 1972	Ellie Rodriguez	Brewers
615	July 5, 1972	Bob Heise	Brewers
616	July 9, 1972	Doug Griffin	Red Sox
617	July 9, 1972	Reggie Smith	Red Sox
618	July 9, 1972	Rico Petrocelli	Red Sox
619	July 9, 1972	Carlton Fisk	Red Sox
620	July 9, 1972	Bob Burda	Red Sox
621	July 9, 1972	Juan Beniquez	Red Sox
622	July 9, 1972	Sonny Siebert	Red Sox
623	July 9, 1972	Tommy Harper	Red Sox
624	July 9, 1972	Doug Griffin	Red Sox
625	July 9, 1972	Carlton Fisk	Red Sox
626	July 9, 1972	Juan Beniquez	Red Sox
627	July 9, 1972	Sonny Siebert	Red Sox
628	July 9, 1972	Carlton Fisk	Red Sox
629	July 9, 1972	Bob Burda	Red Sox
630	July 9, 1972	Ben Oglivie	Red Sox
631	July 9, 1972	Tommy Harper	Red Sox
632	July 14, 1972	Rick Auerbach	Brewers
633	July 14, 1972	Ron Clark	Brewers
634	July 14, 1972	John Felske	Brewers
635	July 14, 1972	Jim Lonborg	Brewers
636	July 14, 1972	John Felske	Brewers
637	July 14, 1972	George Scott	Brewers
638	July 14, 1972	Dave May	Brewers
639	July 14, 1972	Dave May	Brewers
640	July 18, 1972	Rico Petrocelli	Red Sox
641	July 18, 1972	Carlton Fisk	Red Sox
642	July 18, 1972	Doug Griffin	Red Sox
643	July 18, 1972	Rico Petrocelli	Red Sox
644	July 18, 1972	John Kennedy	Red Sox
645	July 18, 1972	Sonny Siebert	Red Sox
646	July 18, 1972	Tommy Harper	Red Sox
647	July 22, 1972	Johnny Callison	Yankees
648	July 22, 1972	Roy White	Yankees
649	July 22, 1972	Bernie Allen	Yankees
650	July 27, 1972	Dave Nelson	Rangers
651	July 27, 1972	Rich Billings	Rangers
652	July 27, 1972	Ted Ford	Rangers
653	July 27, 1972	Jim Mason	Rangers
654	July 27, 1972	Vic Harris	Rangers
655	July 27, 1972	Mike Paul	Rangers
656	July 27, 1972	Ted Ford	Rangers
657	July 27, 1972	Jim Mason	Rangers
658	July 27, 1972	Vic Harris	Rangers
659	July 27, 1972	Dalton Jones	Rangers
660	July 27, 1972	Dave Nelson	Rangers
661	July 27, 1972	Rich Billings	Rangers
662	July 27, 1972	Jim Mason	Rangers
663	July 27, 1972	Ted Ford	Rangers
664	July 31, 1972	Steve Hovley	Royals
665	July 31, 1972	Fred Patek	Royals
666	July 31, 1972	Roger Nelson	Royals
667	July 31, 1972	Cookie Rojas	Royals
668	July 31, 1972	Ed Kirkpatrick	Royals
669	July 31, 1972	Paul Schaal	Royals
670	July 31, 1972	Roger Nelson	Royals
671	July 31, 1972	Steve Hovley	Royals
672	July 31, 1972	Lou Piniella	Royals
673	July 31, 1972	Paul Schaal	Royals
674	July 31, 1972	Roger Nelson	Royals
675	August 4, 1972	Ed Kirkpatrick	Royals
676	August 4, 1972	John Mayberry	Royals
677	August 4, 1972	Bruce DalCanton	Royals
678	August 4, 1972	Paul Schaal	Royals
679	August 4, 1972	Fred Patek	Royals
680	August 4, 1972	Bruce DalCanton	Royals
681	August 4, 1972	John Mayberry	Royals
682	August 4, 1972	Bruce DalCanton	Royals
683	August 9, 1972	Pat Kelly	White Sox
684	August 9, 1972	Jay Johnstone	White Sox
685	August 9, 1972	Carlos May	White Sox
686	August 9, 1972	Ed Spiezio	White Sox
687	August 9, 1972	Wilbur Wood	White Sox
688	August 9, 1972	Ed Spiezio	White Sox
689	August 9, 1972	Mike Andrews	White Sox
690	August 9, 1972	Luis Alvarado	White Sox
691	August 9, 1972	Wilbur Wood	White Sox
692	August 13, 1972	Jim Nettles	Twins
693	August 13, 1972	Danny Thompson	Twins
694	August 13, 1972	Jim Nettles	Twins
695	August 13, 1972	Harmon Killebrew	Twins
696	August 13, 1972	Danny Thompson	Twins
697	August 13, 1972	Bobby Darwin	Twins
698	August 13, 1972	Glenn Borgmann	Twins
699	August 13, 1972	Dick Woodson	Twins
700	August 13, 1972	Jim Nettles	Twins
701	August 18, 1972	Gates Brown	Tigers
702	August 18, 1972	Bill Freehan	Tigers
703	August 18, 1972	Bill Freehan	Tigers
704	August 18, 1972	Aurelio Rodriguez	Tigers
705	August 18, 1972	Ed Brinkman	Tigers
706	August 22, 1972	Johnny Oates	Orioles
707	August 22, 1972	Tommy Davis	Orioles
708	August 22, 1972	Don Baylor	Orioles
709	August 22, 1972	Davey Johnson	Orioles
710	August 22, 1972	Johnny Oates	Orioles
711	August 22, 1972	Dave McNally	Orioles
712	August 22, 1972	Tommy Davis	Orioles

713 ...... August 22, 1972 . Don Baylor .... Orioles
714 ...... August 22, 1972 . Davey Johnson .... Orioles
715 ...... August 22, 1972 . Boog Powell .... Orioles
716 ...... August 22, 1972 . Davey Johnson .... Orioles
717 ...... August 27, 1972 . Chris Chambliss ...... Indians
718 ...... August 27, 1972 . Del Unser .... Indians
719 ...... August 27, 1972 . Buddy Bell .... Indians
720 ...... August 27, 1972 . Jack Brohammer ..... Indians
721 ...... August 27, 1972 . Chris Chambliss ...... Indians
722 ...... August 27, 1972 . Frank Duffy .... Indians
723 ...... August 27, 1972 . Milt Wilcox .... Indians
724 ...... August 27, 1972 . Graig Nettles .... Indians
725 ...... August 27, 1972 . Phil Hennigan .... Indians
726 ...... August 27, 1972 . Phil Hennigan .... Indians
727 ...... August 31, 1972 . Aurelio Rodriguez ..... Tigers
728 ...... August 31, 1972 . Duke Sims .... Tigers
729 ...... August 31, 1972 . Duke Sims .... Tigers
730 ...... August 31, 1972 . Aurelio Rodriguez ..... Tigers
731 ...... August 31, 1972 . Jim Northrup .... Tigers
732 ...... August 31, 1972 . Norm Cash .... Tigers
733 ...... August 31, 1972 . Aurelio Rodriguez ..... Tigers
734 ...... August 31, 1972 . Jim Northrup .... Tigers
735 ...... August 31, 1972 . Willie Horton .... Tigers
736 ...... August 31, 1972 . Norm Cash .... Tigers
737 ...... Sept. 4, 1972 ...... Dal Maxvill .... A's
738 ...... Sept. 4, 1972 ...... Joe Horlen .... A's
739 ...... Sept. 4, 1972 ...... Matty Alou .... A's
740 ...... Sept. 4, 1972 ...... Mike Epstein .... A's
741 ...... Sept. 4, 1972 ...... Dave Duncan .... A's
742 ...... Sept. 4, 1972 ...... Reggie Jackson .... A's
743 ...... Sept. 4, 1972 ...... Mike Hegan .... A's
744 ...... Sept. 4, 1972 ...... Don Mincher .... A's
745 ...... Sept. 4, 1972 ...... Joe Rudi .... A's
746 ...... Sept. 4, 1972 ...... Matty Alou .... A's
747 ...... Sept. 4, 1972 ...... Gene Tenace .... A's
748 ...... Sept. 8, 1972 ...... Carlos May .... White Sox
749 ...... Sept. 8, 1972 ...... Stan Bahnsen .... White Sox
750 ...... Sept. 8, 1972 ...... Dick Allen .... White Sox
751 ...... Sept. 8, 1972 ...... Carlos May .... White Sox
752 ...... Sept. 8, 1972 ...... Pat Kelly .... White Sox
753 ...... Sept. 8, 1972 ...... Rick Reichardt .... White Sox
754 ...... Sept. 12, 1972 .... Ted Ford .... Rangers
755 ...... Sept. 12, 1972 .... Rich Billings .... Rangers
756 ...... Sept. 12, 1972 .... Bill Gogolewski ..... Rangers
757 ...... Sept. 12, 1972 .... Toby Harrah .... Rangers
758 ...... Sept. 12, 1972 .... Larry Biittner .... Rangers
759 ...... Sept. 12, 1972 .... Rich Billings .... Rangers
760 ...... Sept. 12, 1972 .... Joe Lovitto .... Rangers
761 ...... Sept. 12, 1972 .... Bill Fahey .... Rangers
762 ...... Sept. 12, 1972 .... Bill Gogolewski ..... Rangers
763 ...... Sept. 12, 1972 .... Ted Ford .... Rangers
764 ...... Sept. 12, 1972 .... Joe Lovitto .... Rangers
765 ...... Sept. 12, 1972 .... Bill Gogolewski ..... Rangers
766 ...... Sept. 12, 1972 .... Toby Harrah .... Rangers
767 ...... Sept. 12, 1972 .... Dalton Jones .... Rangers
768 ...... Sept. 12, 1972 .... Vic Harris .... Rangers

769 ...... Sept. 16, 1972 .... Pat Kelly .... White Sox
770 ...... Sept. 16, 1972 .... Dick Allen .... White Sox
771 ...... Sept. 16, 1972 .... Rick Reichardt .... White Sox
772 ...... Sept. 16, 1972 .... Rich Morales ...... White Sox
773 ...... Sept. 16, 1972 .... Rick Reichardt .... White Sox
774 ...... Sept. 16, 1972 .... Stan Bahnsen .... White Sox
775 ...... Sept. 16, 1972 .... Ed Herrmann ...... White Sox
776 ...... Sept. 16, 1972 .... Stan Bahnsen .... White Sox
777 ...... Sept. 16, 1972 .... Carlos May .... White Sox
778 ...... Sept. 16, 1972 .... Buddy Bradford .. White Sox
779 ...... Sept. 16, 1972 .... Ed Spiezio .... White Sox
780 ...... Sept. 21, 1972 .... Paul Schaal .... Royals
781 ...... Sept. 21, 1972 .... Steve Hovley .... Royals
782 ...... Sept. 21, 1972 .... Lou Piniella .... Royals
783 ...... Sept. 21, 1972 .... Roger Nelson .... Royals
784 ...... Sept. 25, 1972 .... Vic Harris .... Rangers
785 ...... Sept. 25, 1972 .... Dick Bosman .... Rangers
786 ...... Sept. 25, 1972 .... Jim Mason .... Rangers
787 ...... Sept. 25, 1972 .... Tom Grieve .... Rangers
788 ...... Sept. 25, 1972 .... Dalton Jones .... Rangers
789 ...... Sept. 25, 1972 .... Vic Harris .... Rangers
790 ...... Sept. 25, 1972 .... Dave Nelson .... Rangers
791 ...... Sept. 25, 1972 .... Ted Ford .... Rangers
792 ...... Sept. 25, 1972 .... Tom Grieve .... Rangers
793 ...... Sept. 25, 1972 .... Ted Ford .... Rangers
794 ...... Sept. 25, 1972 .... Dalton Jones .... Rangers
795 ...... Sept. 25, 1972 .... Rich Billings .... Rangers
796 ...... Sept. 30, 1972 .... Steve Braun .... Twins
797 ...... Sept. 30, 1972 .... Bobby Darwin .... Twins
798 ...... Sept. 30, 1972 .... Glenn Borgmann .... Twins
799 ...... Sept. 30, 1972 .... Rick Renick .... Twins
800 ...... Sept. 30, 1972 .... Dave Goltz .... Twins
801 ...... Sept. 30, 1972 .... Danny Thompson ...... Twins
802 ...... Sept. 30, 1972 .... Bobby Darwin .... Twins
803 ...... Sept. 30, 1972 .... Steve Brye .... Twins
804 ...... Sept. 30, 1972 .... Rick Renick .... Twins
805 ...... Sept. 30, 1972 .... Charlie Manuel .... Twins
806 ...... Sept. 30, 1972 .... Danny Thompson ...... Twins
807 ...... Sept. 30, 1972 .... Steve Braun .... Twins
808 ...... Sept. 30, 1972 .... Harmon Killebrew ...... Twins
809 ...... Sept. 30, 1972 .... Bobby Darwin .... Twins
810 ...... Sept. 30, 1972 .... Glenn Borgmann .... Twins
811 ...... Sept. 30, 1972 .... Rick Renick .... Twins
812 ...... Sept. 30, 1972 .... Rick Renick .... Twins
813 ...... Oct. 4, 1972 .... Angel Mangual .... A's
814 ...... Oct. 4, 1972 .... John Odom .... A's
815 ...... Oct. 4, 1972 .... Ted Kubiak .... A's
816 ...... Oct. 4, 1972 .... Angel Mangual .... A's
817 ...... Oct. 4, 1972 .... Dave Duncan .... A's
818 ...... Oct. 4, 1972 .... Angel Mangual .... A's
819 ...... Oct. 4, 1972 .... Dal Maxvill .... A's
820 ...... Oct. 4, 1972 .... Ted Kubiak .... A's
821 ...... Oct. 4, 1972 .... Matty Alou .... A's
822 ...... Oct. 4, 1972 .... Larry Haney .... A's
823 ...... April 6, 1973 .... Fred Patek .... Royals
824 ...... April 6, 1973 .... Amos Otis .... Royals

825	April 6, 1973	Hal McRae	Royals
826	April 6, 1973	Paul Schaal	Royals
827	April 6, 1973	Fred Patek	Royals
828	April 6, 1973	John Mayberry	Royals
829	April 6, 1973	Jerry May	Royals
830	April 6, 1973	Amos Otis	Royals
831	April 6, 1973	Paul Schaal	Royals
832	April 6, 1973	Amos Otis	Royals
833	April 6, 1973	John Mayberry	Royals
834	April 6, 1973	Hal McRae	Royals
835	April 11, 1973	Larry Hisle	Twins
836	April 11, 1973	Phil Roof	Twins
837	April 11, 1973	Larry Hisle	Twins
838	April 11, 1973	Steve Braun	Twins
839	April 11, 1973	Phil Roof	Twins
840	April 11, 1973	Jim Holt	Twins
841	April 11, 1973	Steve Brye	Twins
842	April 11, 1973	Joe Lis	Twins
843	April 11, 1973	George Mitterwald	Twins
844	April 11, 1973	Jim Holt	Twins
845	April 11, 1973	Larry Hisle	Twins
846	April 18, 1973	Bobby Darwin	Twins
847	April 18, 1973	George Mitterwald	Twins
848	April 18, 1973	Rod Carew	Twins
849	April 18, 1973	Harmon Killebrew	Twins
850	April 18, 1973	Tony Oliva	Twins
851	April 18, 1973	Danny Thompson	Twins
852	April 18, 1973	George Mitterwald	Twins
853	April 18, 1973	Larry Hisle	Twins
854	April 18, 1973	Harmon Killebrew	Twins
855	April 18, 1973	Tony Oliva	Twins
856	April 18, 1973	Jim Holt	Twins
857	April 18, 1973	Larry Hisle	Twins
858	April 18, 1973	Rod Carew	Twins
859	April 18, 1973	Bobby Darwin	Twins
860	April 22, 1973	Bert Campaneris	A's
861	April 22, 1973	Bill North	A's
862	April 22, 1973	Gene Tenace	A's
863	April 22, 1973	Bert Campaneris	A's
864	April 22, 1973	Joe Rudi	A's
865	April 22, 1973	Sal Bando	A's
866	April 22, 1973	Gene Tenace	A's
867	April 22, 1973	Ray Fosse	A's
868	April 22, 1973	Joe Rudi	A's
869	April 27, 1973	Charlie Spikes	Indians
870	April 27, 1973	Ron Lolich	Indians
871	April 27, 1973	Dave Duncan	Indians
872	April 27, 1973	Leo Cardenas	Indians
873	April 27, 1973	Jack Brohammer	Indians
874	April 27, 1973	Dave Duncan	Indians
875	April 27, 1973	George Hendrick	Indians
876	April 27, 1973	Leo Cardenas	Indians
877	May 2, 1973	Mickey Stanley	Tigers
878	May 2, 1973	Aurelio Rodriguez	Tigers
879	May 2, 1973	Bill Freehan	Tigers
880	May 2, 1973	Ed Brinkman	Tigers
881	May 2, 1973	Ed Brinkman	Tigers
882	May 2, 1973	Bill Freehan	Tigers
883	May 2, 1973	Ed Brinkman	Tigers
884	May 6, 1973	Don Baylor	Orioles
885	May 6, 1973	Al Bumbry	Orioles
886	May 6, 1973	Earl Williams	Orioles
887	May 6, 1973	Don Baylor	Orioles
888	May 6, 1973	Brooks Robinson	Orioles
889	May 12, 1973	John Jeter	White Sox
890	May 12, 1973	Dick Allen	White Sox
891	May 12, 1973	Bill Melton	White Sox
892	May 12, 1973	Ken Henderson	White Sox
893	May 15, 1973	Fred Patek	Royals
894	May 15, 1973	Amos Otis	Royals
895	May 15, 1973	John Mayberry	Royals
896	May 15, 1973	Lou Piniella	Royals
897	May 15, 1973	Paul Schaal	Royals
898	May 15, 1973	Fred Patek	Royals
899	May 15, 1973	John Mayberry	Royals
900	May 15, 1973	Paul Schaal	Royals
901	May 15, 1973	Carl Taylor	Royals
902	May 15, 1973	John Mayberry	Royals
903	May 15, 1973	Ed Kirkpatrick	Royals
904	May 15, 1973	Steve Hovley	Royals
905	May 19, 1973	Dave Nelson	Rangers
906	May 19, 1973	Joe Lovitto	Rangers
907	May 19, 1973	Alex Johnson	Rangers
908	May 19, 1973	Vic Harris	Rangers
909	May 19, 1973	Dave Nelson	Rangers
910	May 19, 1973	Larry Biittner	Rangers
911	May 19, 1973	Jim Mason	Rangers
912	May 19, 1973	Dave Nelson	Rangers
913	May 19, 1973	Alex Johnson	Rangers
914	May 19, 1973	Jeff Burroughs	Rangers
915	May 19, 1973	Dave Nelson	Rangers
916	May 19, 1973	Alex Johnson	Rangers
917	May 24, 1973	Bill Melton	White Sox
918	May 24, 1973	Rick Reichardt	White Sox
919	May 24, 1973	Jorge Orta	White Sox
920	May 24, 1973	Eddie Leon	White Sox
921	May 24, 1973	Ed Herrmann	White Sox
922	May 24, 1973	Jorge Orta	White Sox
923	May 24, 1973	Ken Henderson	White Sox
924	May 24, 1973	Bill Melton	White Sox
925	May 24, 1973	Carlos May	White Sox
926	May 24, 1973	Jorge Orta	White Sox
927	May 24, 1973	Eddie Leon	White Sox
928	May 24, 1973	Pat Kelly	White Sox
929	May 24, 1973	Dick Allen	White Sox
930	May 29, 1973	Rick Miller	Red Sox
931	May 29, 1973	Danny Cater	Red Sox
932	May 29, 1973	Reggie Smith	Red Sox
933	May 29, 1973	John Kennedy	Red Sox
934	May 29, 1973	Danny Cater	Red Sox
935	May 29, 1973	John Kennedy	Red Sox
936	May 29, 1973	Rick Miller	Red Sox

937	May 29, 1973	Carlton Fisk	Red Sox
938	May 29, 1973	Orlando Cepada	Red Sox
939	May 29, 1973	Rico Petrocelli	Red Sox
940	June 2, 1973	Roy White	Yankees
941	June 2, 1973	Graig Nettles	Yankees
942	June 2, 1973	Thurman Munson	Yankees
943	June 2, 1973	Horace Clarke	Yankees
944	June 2, 1973	Gene Michael	Yankees
945	June 2, 1973	Horace Clarke	Yankees
946	June 7, 1973	Duke Sims	Tigers
947	June 7, 1973	Dick McAuliffe	Tigers
948	June 7, 1973	Ed Brinkman	Tigers
949	June 7, 1973	Aurelio Rodriguez	Tigers
950	June 7, 1973	Jim Northrup	Tigers
951	June 7, 1973	Bill Freehan	Tigers
952	June 7, 1973	Norm Cash	Tigers
953	June 12, 1973	Luis Aparcio	Red Sox
954	June 12, 1973	Rico Petrocelli	Red Sox
955	June 12, 1973	John Kennedy	Red Sox
956	June 12, 1973	Rick Miller	Red Sox
957	June 12, 1973	Carlton Fisk	Red Sox
958	June 12, 1973	Carl Yastrzemski	Red Sox
959	June 12, 1973	Tommy Harper	Red Sox
960	June 12, 1973	Carlton Fisk	Red Sox
961	June 12, 1973	Reggie Smith	Red Sox
962	June 16, 1973	Roy White	Yankees
963	June 16, 1973	Bobby Murcer	Yankees
964	June 16, 1973	Jim Hart	Yankees
965	June 16, 1973	Thurman Munson	Yankees
966	June 16, 1973	Gene Michael	Yankees
967	June 16, 1973	Roy White	Yankees
968	June 16, 1973	Thurman Munson	Yankees
969	June 16, 1973	Horace Clarke	Yankees
970	June 16, 1973	Thurman Munson	Yankees
971	June 16, 1973	Roy White	Yankees
972	June 20, 1973	Carlos May	White Sox
973	June 20, 1973	Ed Herrmann	White Sox
974	June 20, 1973	Dick Allen	White Sox
975	June 20, 1973	Carlos May	White Sox
976	June 20, 1973	Eddie Leon	White Sox
977	June 20, 1973	Eddie Leon	White Sox
978	June 25, 1973	Ed Kirkpatrick	Royals
979	June 25, 1973	Lou Piniella	Royals
980	June 25, 1973	Fran Healy	Royals
981	June 25, 1973	Steve Hovley	Royals
982	June 25, 1973	Frank White	Royals
983	June 25, 1973	Ed Kirkpatrick	Royals
984	June 25, 1973	Lou Piniella	Royals
985	June 25, 1973	Paul Schaal	Royals
986	June 25, 1973	Frank White	Royals
987	June 29, 1973	Rod Carew	Twins
988	June 29, 1973	Jerry Terrell	Twins
989	June 29, 1973	Joe Lis	Twins
990	June 29, 1973	George Mitterwald	Twins
991	June 29, 1973	Steve Braun	Twins
992	June 29, 1973	Jim Holt	Twins
993	June 29, 1973	Rod Carew	Twins
994	June 29, 1973	Bobby Darwin	Twins
995	June 29, 1973	Larry Hisle	Twins
996	June 29, 1973	Joe Lis	Twins
997	June 29, 1973	Rod Carew	Twins
998	June 29, 1973	Joe Lis	Twins
999	July 3, 1973	Bill North	A's
1000	July 3, 1973	Sal Bando	A's
1001	July 3, 1973	Reggie Jackson	A's
1002	July 3, 1973	Joe Rudi	A's
1003	July 3, 1973	Dick Green	A's
1004	July 3, 1973	Gene Tenace	A's
1005	July 3, 1973	Dick Green	A's
1006	July 3, 1973	Reggie Jackson	A's
1007	July 3, 1973	Burt Campaneris	A's
1008	July 3, 1973	Mike Hegan	A's
1009	July 7, 1973	John Ellis	Indians
1010	July 7, 1973	John Lowenstein	Indians
1011	July 7, 1973	Leo Cardenas	Indians
1012	July 7, 1973	Charlie Spikes	Indians
1013	July 7, 1973	John Lowenstein	Indians
1014	July 7, 1973	Chris Chambliss	Indians
1015	July 11, 1973	Al Bumbry	Orioles
1016	July 11, 1973	Brooks Robinson	Orioles
1017	July 11, 1973	Boog Powell	Orioles
1018	July 11, 1973	Earl Williams	Orioles
1019	July 11, 1973	Mark Belanger	Orioles
1020	July 11, 1973	Al Bumbry	Orioles
1021	July 11, 1973	Boog Powell	Orioles
1022	July 11, 1973	Earl Williams	Orioles
1023	July 11, 1973	Bobby Grich	Orioles
1024	July 11, 1973	Mark Belanger	Orioles
1025	July 11, 1973	Al Bumbry	Orioles
1026	July 15, 1973	Mickey Stanley	Tigers
1027	July 15, 1973	Norm Cash	Tigers
1028	July 15, 1973	Duke Sims	Tigers
1029	July 15, 1973	Dick McAuliffe	Tigers
1030	July 15, 1973	Dick Sharon	Tigers
1031	July 15, 1973	Aurelio Rodriguez	Tigers
1032	July 15, 1973	Jim Northrup	Tigers
1033	July 15, 1973	Gates Brown	Tigers
1034	July 15, 1973	Norm Cash	Tigers
1035	July 15, 1973	Duke Sims	Tigers
1036	July 15, 1973	Dick McAuliffe	Tigers
1037	July 15, 1973	Aurelio Rodriguez	Tigers
1038	July 15, 1973	Mickey Stanley	Tigers
1039	July 15, 1973	Duke Sims	Tigers
1040	July 15, 1973	Dick McAuliffe	Tigers
1041	July 15, 1973	Dick Sharon	Tigers
1042	July 15, 1973	Ed Brinkman	Tigers
1043	July 19, 1973	Al Bumbry	Orioles
1044	July 19, 1973	Boog Powell	Orioles
1045	July 19, 1973	Earl Williams	Orioles
1046	July 19, 1973	Terry Crowley	Orioles
1047	July 19, 1973	Brooks Robinson	Orioles
1048	July 19, 1973	Al Bumbry	Orioles

1049 .... July 19, 1973 ...... Mark Belanger .... Orioles	1105 .... August 17, 1973 . Al Kaline .... Tigers
1050 .... July 19, 1973 ...... Al Bumbry .... Orioles	1106 .... August 17, 1973 . Bill Freehan .... Tigers
1051 .... July 19, 1973 ...... Rich Coggins .... Orioles	1107 .... August 17, 1973 . Ed Brinkman .... Tigers
1052 .... July 19, 1973 ...... Earl Williams .... Orioles	1108 .... August 17, 1973 . Jim Northrup .... Tigers
1053 .... July 19, 1973 ...... Al Bumbry .... Orioles	1109 .... August 17, 1973 . Dick Sharon .... Tigers
1054 .... July 19, 1973 ...... Rich Coggins .... Orioles	1110 .... August 17, 1973 . Norm Cash .... Tigers
1055 .... July 19, 1973 ...... Earl Williams .... Orioles	1111 .... August 21, 1973 . Bob Coluccio .... Brewers
1056 .... July 26, 1973 ...... Bill Sudakis .... Rangers	1112 .... August 21, 1973 . Darrell Porter .... Brewers
1057 .... July 26, 1973 ...... Larry Biittner .... Rangers	1113 .... August 21, 1973 . John Briggs .... Brewers
1058 .... July 26, 1973 ...... Bill Sudakis .... Rangers	1114 .... August 21, 1973 . Tim Johnson .... Brewers
1059 .... July 29, 1973 ...... Fred Patek .... Royals	1115 .... August 21, 1973 . Pedro Garcia .... Brewers
1060 .... July 29, 1973 ...... Rich Reichardt .... Royals	1116 .... August 21, 1973 . Don Money .... Brewers
1061 .... July 29, 1973 ...... Carl Taylor .... Royals	1117 .... August 21, 1973 . Darrell Porter .... Brewers
1062 .... August 2, 1973 ... Alex Johnson .... Rangers	1118 .... August 21, 1973 . Davey May .... Brewers
1063 .... August 2, 1973 ... Jeff Burroughs ...... Rangers	1119 .... August 25, 1973 . Rick Miller .... Red Sox
1064 .... August 2, 1973 ... Larry Biittner .... Rangers	1120 .... August 25, 1973 . Mario Guerrero ..... Red Sox
1065 .... August 2, 1973 ... Rich Billings .... Rangers	1121 .... August 25, 1973 . Orlando Cepada ... Red Sox
1066 .... August 2, 1973 ... Jim Spencer .... Rangers	1122 .... August 25, 1973 . Carlton Fisk .... Red Sox
1067 .... August 2, 1973 ... Bill Sudakis .... Rangers	1123 .... August 25, 1973 . Ben Oglivie .... Red Sox
1068 .... August 2, 1973 ... Dave Nelson .... Rangers	1124 .... August 25, 1973 . Cecil Cooper .... Red Sox
1069 .... August 2, 1973 ... Alex Johnson .... Rangers	1125 .... August 25, 1973 . Doug Griffin .... Red Sox
1070 .... August 2, 1973 ... Bill Sudakis .... Rangers	1126 .... August 25, 1973 . Mario Guerrero ..... Red Sox
1071 .... August 2, 1973 ... Alex Johnson .... Rangers	1127 .... August 29, 1973 . Ron Blomberg ...... Yankees
1072 .... August 2, 1973 ... Jim Spencer .... Rangers	1128 .... August 29, 1973 . Mike Hegan .... Yankees
1073 .... August 7, 1973 ... George Scott .... Brewers	1129 .... August 29, 1973 . Horace Clarke ...... Yankees
1074 .... August 7, 1973 ... George Scott .... Brewers	1130 .... August 29, 1973 . Thurman Munson . Yankees
1075 .... August 7, 1973 ... John Felske .... Brewers	1131 .... August 29, 1973 . Bobby Murcer .... Yankees
1076 .... August 7, 1973 ... Ellie Rodriguez ..... Brewers	1132 .... August 29, 1973 . Gene Michael .... Yankees
1077 .... August 7, 1973 ... Tim Johnson .... Brewers	1133 .... August 29, 1973 . Graig Nettles .... Yankees
1078 .... August 7, 1973 ... Pedro Garcia .... Brewers	1134 .... August 29, 1973 . Mike Hegan .... Yankees
1079 .... August 7, 1973 ... John Vukovich ...... Brewers	1135 .... August 29, 1973 . Gene Michael .... Yankees
1080 .... August 7, 1973 ... John Briggs .... Brewers	1136 .... August 29, 1973 . Roy White .... Yankees
1081 .... August 7, 1973 ... Bob Coluccio .... Brewers	1137 .... Sept. 3, 1973 ...... Bill North .... A's
1082 .... August 7, 1973 ... John Felske .... Brewers	1138 .... Sept. 3, 1973 ...... Bert Campaneris .... A's
1083 .... August 7, 1973 ... George Scott .... Brewers	1139 .... Sept. 3, 1973 ...... Sal Bando .... A's
1084 .... August 7, 1973 ... John Felske .... Brewers	1140 .... Sept. 3, 1973 ...... Reggie Jackson .... A's
1085 .... August 7, 1973 ... Bob Coluccio .... Brewers	1141 .... Sept. 3, 1973 ...... Gene Tenace .... A's
1086 .... August 11, 1973 . Mario Guerrero ..... Red Sox	1142 .... Sept. 3, 1973 ...... Dick Green .... A's
1087 .... August 11, 1973 . Rico Petrocelli .... Red Sox	1143 .... Sept. 3, 1973 ...... Bill North .... A's
1088 .... August 11, 1973 . Carlton Fisk .... Red Sox	1144 .... Sept. 3, 1973 ...... Bert Campaneris .... A's
1009 .... August 11, 1973 . Ben Oglivie .... Red Sox	1145 .... Sept. 3, 1973 ...... Pat Dourque .... A's
1090 .... August 11, 1973 . Orlando Cepada ... Red Sox	1146 .... Sept. 3, 1973 ...... Dick Green .... A's
1091 .... August 11, 1973 . Carlton Fisk .... Red Sox	1147 .... Sept. 3, 1973 ...... Gene Tenace .... A's
1092 .... August 11, 1973 . Ben Oglivie .... Red Sox	1148 .... Sept. 3, 1973 ...... Deron Johnson .... A's
1093 .... August 11, 1973 . Tommy Harper ...... Red Sox	1149 .... Sept. 11 1973 ...... Pat Kelly .... White Sox
1094 .... August 11, 1973 . Mario Guerrero ..... Red Sox	1150 .... Sept. 11 1973 ...... Jorge Orta .... White Sox
1095 .... August 11, 1973 . Carlton Fisk .... Red Sox	1151 .... Sept. 11 1973 ...... Sam Ewing .... White Sox
1096 .... August 11, 1973 . Rico Petrocelli .... Red Sox	1152 .... Sept. 11, 1973 .... Brian Downing .... White Sox
1097 .... August 11, 1973 . Doug Griffin .... Red Sox	1153 .... Sept. 11, 1973 .... Carlos May .... White Sox
1098 .... August 17, 1973 . Gates Brown .... Tigers	1154 .... Sept. 11, 1973 .... Sam Ewing .... White Sox
1099 .... August 17, 1973 . Dick McAuliffe .... Tigers	1155 .... Sept. 11, 1973 .... Sam Ewing .... White Sox
1100 .... August 17, 1973 . Bill Freehan .... Tigers	1156 .... Sept. 11, 1973 .... Luis Alvarado ..... White Sox
1101 .... August 17, 1973 . Aurelio Rodriguez ..... Tigers	1157 .... Sept. 11, 1973 .... Bill Sharp .... White Sox
1102 .... August 17, 1973 . Norm Cash .... Tigers	1158 .... Sept. 11, 1973 .... Pat Kelly .... White Sox
1103 .... August 17, 1973 . Aurelio Rodriguez ..... Tigers	1159 .... Sept. 11, 1973 .... Bucky Dent .... White Sox
1104 .... August 17, 1973 . Ed Brinkman .... Tigers	1160 .... Sept. 11, 1973 .... Sam Ewing .... White Sox

1161 .... Sept. 15, 1973 .... Amos Otis .... Royals	1217 .... April 12, 1974 ..... Carlos May .... White Sox
1162 .... Sept. 15, 1973 .... Steve Hovley .... Royals	1218 .... April 16, 1974 ..... Steve Braun .... Twins
1163 .... Sept. 15, 1973 .... Amos Otis .... Royals	1219 .... April 16, 1974 ..... Sergio Ferrer .... Twins
1164 .... Sept. 15, 1973 .... John Mayberry .... Royals	1220 .... April 16, 1974 ..... Bobby Darwin .... Twins
1165 .... Sept. 15, 1973 .... Fred Patek .... Royals	1221 .... April 16, 1974 ..... Steve Braun .... Twins
1166 .... Sept. 15, 1973 .... John Mayberry .... Royals	1222 .... April 16, 1974 ..... Larry Hisle .... Twins
1167 .... Sept. 15, 1973 .... Hal McRae .... Royals	1223 .... April 16, 1974 ..... Rod Carew .... Twins
1168 .... Sept. 15, 1973 .... Ed Kirkpatrick .... Royals	1224 .... April 16, 1974 ..... Bobby Darwin .... Twins
1169 .... Sept. 15, 1973 .... Fred Patek .... Royals	1225 .... April 16, 1974 ..... Larry Hisle .... Twins
1170 .... Sept. 15, 1973 .... Gail Hopkins .... Royals	1226 .... April 16, 1974 ..... Glenn Borgmann ... Twins
1171 .... Sept. 19, 1973 .... Jim Mason .... Rangers	1227 .... April 16, 1974 ..... Jerry Terrell .... Twins
1172 .... Sept. 19, 1973 .... Bill Sudakis .... Rangers	1228 .... April 16, 1974 ..... Jerry Terrell .... Twins
1173 .... Sept. 19, 1973 .... Jim Mason .... Rangers	1229 .... April 20, 1974 ..... Bill North .... A's
1174 .... Sept. 19, 1973 .... Bill Sudakis .... Rangers	1230 .... April 20, 1974 ..... Joe Rudi .... A's
1175 .... Sept. 19, 1973 .... Rich Billings .... Rangers	1231 .... April 20, 1974 ..... Gene Tenace .... A's
1176 .... Sept. 19, 1973 .... Bill Sudakis .... Rangers	1232 .... April 20, 1974 ..... Ted Kubiak .... A's
1177 .... Sept. 19, 1973 .... Bill Madlock .... Rangers	1233 .... April 20, 1974 ..... Bill North .... A's
1178 .... Sept. 23, 1973 .... Rod Carew .... Twins	1234 .... April 20, 1974 ..... Sal Bando .... A's
1179 .... Sept. 23, 1973 .... Craig Kusick .... Twins	1235 .... April 26, 1974 ..... Oscar Gamble .... Indians
1180 .... Sept. 23, 1973 .... Larry Hisle .... Twins	1236 .... April 26, 1974 ..... Dave Duncan .... Indians
1181 .... Sept. 23, 1973 .... Jerry Terrell .... Twins	1237 .... April 26, 1974 ..... Charlie Spikes .... Indians
1182 .... Sept. 23, 1973 .... Jim Holt .... Twins	1238 .... April 26, 1974 ..... Leron Lee .... Indians
1183 .... Sept. 23, 1973 .... Jerry Terrell .... Twins	1239 .... April 26, 1974 ..... Dave Duncan .... Indians
1184 .... Sept. 23, 1973 .... Glenn Borgmann .... Twins	1240 .... April 26, 1974 ..... Oscar Gamble .... Indians
1185 .... Sept. 23, 1973 .... Larry Hisle .... Twins	1241 .... April 26, 1974 ..... George Hendrick ..... Indians
1186 .... Sept. 23, 1973 .... Jerry Terrell .... Twins	1242 .... April 30, 1974 ..... Cecil Cooper .... Red Sox
1187 .... Sept. 23, 1973 .... Steve Brye .... Twins	1243 .... April 30, 1974 ..... Rico Petrocelli .... Red Sox
1188 .... Sept. 23, 1973 .... Craig Kusick .... Twins	1244 .... April 30, 1974 ..... Rick Miller .... Red Sox
1189 .... Sept. 23, 1973 .... Larry Hisle .... Twins	1245 .... April 30, 1974 ..... Cecil Cooper .... Red Sox
1190 .... Sept. 27, 1973 .... Jim Holt .... Twins	1246 .... April 30, 1974 ..... Rico Petrocelli .... Red Sox
1191 .... Sept. 27, 1973 .... George Mitterwald ..... Twins	1247 .... April 30, 1974 ..... Cecil Cooper .... Red Sox
1192 .... Sept. 27, 1973 .... Mike Adams .... Twins	1248 .... April 30, 1974 ..... Rico Petrocelli .... Red Sox
1193 .... Sept. 27, 1973 .... Rod Carew .... Twins	1249 .... April 30, 1974 ..... Dwight Evans .... Red Sox
1194 .... Sept. 27, 1973 .... Tony Oliva .... Twins	1250 .... April 30, 1974 ..... Carlton Fisk .... Red Sox
1195 .... Sept. 27, 1973 .... Jim Holt .... Twins	1251 .... April 30, 1974 ..... Rick Miller .... Red Sox
1196 .... Sept. 27, 1973 .... Mike Adams .... Twins	1252 .... April 30, 1974 ..... Jaun Beniquez .. Red Sox
1197 .... Sept. 27, 1973 .... Jerry Terrell .... Twins	1253 .... April 30, 1974 ..... Rico Petrocelli .... Red Sox
1198 .... Sept. 27, 1973 .... Steve Brye .... Twins	1254 .... April 30, 1974 ..... Dwight Evans .... Red Sox
1199 .... Sept. 27, 1973 .... Rod Carew .... Twins	1255 .... April 30, 1974 ..... Bob Montgomery .. Red Sox
1200 .... Sept. 27, 1973 .... Harmon Killebrew ...... Twins	1256 .... April 30, 1974 ..... John Kennedy .... Red Sox
1201 .... Sept. 27, 1973 .... Rod Carew .... Twins	1257 .... May 5, 1974 .... Ellie Hendricks .... Orioles
1202 .... Sept. 27, 1973 .... Harmon Killebrew ...... Twins	1258 .... May 5, 1974 .... Al Bumbry .... Orioles
1203 .... Sept. 27, 1973 .... George Mitterwald ..... Twins	1259 .... May 5, 1974 .... Boog Powell .... Orioles
1204 .... Sept. 27, 1973 .... Steve Brye .... Twins	1260 .... May 5, 1974 .... Ellie Hendricks .... Orioles
1205 .... Sept. 27, 1973 .... Rich Reese .... Twins	1261 .... May 5, 1974 .... Al Bumbry .... Orioles
1206 .... April 5, 1974 ...... Bill Melton .... White Sox	1262 .... May 5, 1974 .... Boog Powell .... Orioles
1207 .... April 5, 1974 ...... Jorge Orta .... White Sox	1263 .... May 10, 1974 ...... Fred Patek .... Royals
1208 .... April 5, 1974 .... Pat Kelly .... White Sox	1264 .... May 10, 1974 ...... Jim Wohlford .... Royals
1209 .... April 5, 1974 ...... Dick Allen .... White Sox	1265 .... May 10, 1974 ...... Vada Pinson .... Royals
1210 .... April 5, 1974 .... Carlos May .... White Sox	1266 .... May 10, 1974 ...... George Brett .... Royals
1211 .... April 9, 1974 ...... Toby Harrah .... Rangers	1267 .... May 10, 1974 ...... Jim Wohlford .... Royals
1212 .... April 12, 1974 ..... Ed Herrmann ..... White Sox	1268 .... May 10, 1974 ...... John Mayberry .... Royals
1213 .... April 12, 1974 ..... Ron Santo .... White Sox	1269 .... May 10, 1974 ...... Fran Healy .... Royals
1214 .... April 12, 1974 ..... Ron Santo .... White Sox	1270 .... May 10, 1974 ...... George Brett .... Royals
1215 .... April 12, 1974 ..... Ken Henderson .. White Sox	1271 .... May 10, 1974 ...... Jim Wohlford .... Royals
1216 .... April 12, 1974 ..... Bucky Dent .... White Sox	1272 .... May 10, 1974 ...... Hal McRae .... Royals

1273	May 15, 1974	Mike Hargrove	Rangers
1274	May 15, 1974	Larry Brown	Rangers
1275	May 15, 1974	Toby Harrah	Rangers
1276	May 15, 1974	Mike Hargrove	Rangers
1277	May 15, 1974	Jim Sundberg	Rangers
1278	May 15, 1974	Jeff Burroughs	Rangers
1279	May 19, 1974	Larry Hisle	Twins
1280	May 19, 1974	Tony Oliva	Twins
1281	May 19, 1974	Eric Soderholm	Twins
1282	May 19, 1974	Glenn Borgmann	Twins
1283	May 19, 1974	Tony Oliva	Twins
1284	May 19, 1974	Harmon Killebrew	Twins
1285	May 19, 1974	Bobby Darwin	Twins
1286	May 19, 1974	Eric Soderholm	Twins
1287	May 19, 1974	Joe Lis	Twins
1288	May 19, 1974	Larry Hisle	Twins
1289	May 19, 1974	Jerry Terrell	Twins
1290	May 19, 1974	Jim Holt	Twins
1291	May 23, 1974	John Mayberry	Royals
1292	May 23, 1974	Fred Patek	Royals
1293	May 23, 1974	Jim Wohlford	Royals
1294	May 23, 1974	Amos Otis	Royals
1295	May 23, 1974	Richie Scheinblum	Royals
1296	May 23, 1974	Fran Healy	Royals
1297	May 27, 1974	Davey May	Brewers
1298	May 27, 1974	Bob Hansen	Brewers
1299	May 27, 1974	John Briggs	Brewers
1300	May 27, 1974	Bob Hansen	Brewers
1301	May 27, 1974	Bob Coluccio	Brewers
1302	May 27, 1974	George Scott	Brewers
1303	May 27, 1974	Bob Hansen	Brewers
1304	May 27, 1974	Don Money	Brewers
1305	June 1, 1974	Mickey Stanley	Tigers
1306	June 1, 1974	Norm Cash	Tigers
1307	June 1, 1974	Aurelio Rodriguez	Tigers
1308	June 1, 1974	Gary Sutherland	Tigers
1309	June 1, 1974	Jim Northrup	Tigers
1310	June 1, 1974	Ben Oglivie	Tigers
1311	June 1, 1974	Jim Northrup	Tigers
1312	June 1, 1974	Norm Cash	Tigers
1313	June 1, 1974	Aurelio Rodriguez	Tigers
1314	June 1, 1974	Ben Oglivie	Tigers
1315	June 1, 1974	Gates Brown	Tigers
1316	June 5, 1974	Darrell Porter	Brewers
1317	June 5, 1974	Rob Ellis	Brewers
1318	June 5, 1974	Robin Yount	Brewers
1319	June 5, 1974	Davey May	Brewers
1320	June 5, 1974	Robin Yount	Brewers
1321	June 9, 1974	Al Kaline	Tigers
1322	June 9, 1974	Willie Horton	Tigers
1323	June 9, 1974	Bill Freehan	Tigers
1324	June 9, 1974	Gerry Moses	Tigers
1325	June 9, 1974	Al Kaline	Tigers
1326	June 9, 1974	Bill Freehan	Tigers
1327	June 14, 1974	Cecil Cooper	Red Sox
1328	June 14, 1974	Rick Miller	Red Sox
1329	June 14, 1974	Bernie Carbo	Red Sox
1330	June 14, 1974	Terry Hughes	Red Sox
1331	June 14, 1974	Cecil Cooper	Red Sox
1332	June 14, 1974	Rick Miller	Red Sox
1333	June 14, 1974	Dick McAuliffe	Red Sox
1334	June 14, 1974	Mario Guerrero	Red Sox
1335	June 14, 1974	Cecil Cooper	Red Sox
1336	June 14, 1974	Rick Miller	Red Sox
1337	June 14, 1974	Bernie Carbo	Red Sox
1338	June 14, 1974	Rico Petrocelli	Red Sox
1339	June 14, 1974	Cecil Cooper	Red Sox
1340	June 14, 1974	Bernie Carbo	Red Sox
1341	June 14, 1974	Cecil Cooper	Red Sox
1342	June 14, 1974	Dick McAuliffe	Red Sox
1343	June 14, 1974	Carl Yastrzemski	Red Sox
1344	June 14, 1974	Rick Burleson	Red Sox
1345	June 14, 1974	Cecil Cooper	Red Sox
1346	June 18, 1974	Elliott Maddox	Yankees
1347	June 18, 1974	Bobby Murcer	Yankees
1348	June 18, 1974	Jim Mason	Yankees
1349	June 18, 1974	Graig Nettles	Yankees
1350	June 18, 1974	Thurman Munson	Yankees
1351	June 18, 1974	Jim Mason	Yankees
1352	June 18, 1974	Graig Nettles	Yankees
1353	June 22, 1974	Dave Nelson	Rangers
1354	June 22, 1974	Tom Grieve	Rangers
1355	June 22, 1974	Jim Sundberg	Rangers
1356	June 22, 1974	Alex Johnson	Rangers
1357	June 22, 1974	Mike Hargrove	Rangers
1358	June 22, 1974	Toby Harrah	Rangers
1359	June 22, 1974	Dave Nelson	Rangers
1360	June 22, 1974	Alex Johnson	Rangers
1361	June 22, 1974	Tom Grieve	Rangers
1362	June 22, 1974	Toby Harrah	Rangers
1363	June 27, 1974	Dave Nelson	Rangers
1364	June 27, 1974	Jim Spencer	Rangers
1365	June 27, 1974	Lenny Randle	Rangers
1366	June 27, 1974	Toby Harrah	Rangers
1367	June 27, 1974	Jeff Burroughs	Rangers
1368	June 27, 1974	Jim Spencer	Rangers
1369	July 1, 1974	Bert Campaneris	A's
1370	July 1, 1974	Angel Mangual	A's
1371	July 1, 1974	Larry Haney	A's
1372	July 1, 1974	Bill North	A's
1373	July 1, 1974	Angel Mangual	A's
1374	July 1, 1974	Bill North	A's
1375	July 1, 1974	Bert Campaneris	A's
1376	July 1, 1974	Joe Rudi	A's
1377	July 1, 1974	Larry Haney	A's
1378	July 1, 1974	Pat Bourque	A's
1379	July 5, 1974	John Ellis	Indians
1380	July 5, 1974	Charlie Spikes	Indians
1381	July 5, 1974	Dave Duncan	Indians
1382	July 5, 1974	Charlie Spikes	Indians
1383	July 5, 1974	Frank Duffy	Indians
1384	July 5, 1974	John Lowenstein	Indians

1385 .... July 5, 1974 .... John Ellis .... Indians	1441 ... August 7, 1974 ... Jorge Orta .... White Sox
1386 .... July 5, 1974 .... Charlie Spikes .... Indians	1442 ... August 7, 1974 ... Ken Henderson .. White Sox
1387 .... July 10, 1974 ...... Al Bumbry .... Orioles	1443 ... August 7, 1974 ... Bill Melton .... White Sox
1388 .... July 10, 1974 ...... Bobby Grich .... Orioles	1444 ... August 7, 1974 ... Bill Sharp .... White Sox
1389 .... July 10, 1974 ...... Don Baylor .... Orioles	1445 ... August 7, 1974 ... Brian Downing .... White Sox
1390 .... July 10, 1974 ...... Ellie Hendricks .... Orioles	1446 ... August 7, 1974 ... Jorge Orta .... White Sox
1391 .... July 15, 1974 ...... John Lowenstein ..... Indians	1447 ... August 12, 1974 . Cecil Cooper .... Red Sox
1392 .... July 15, 1974 ...... Dave Duncan .... Indians	1448 ... August 12, 1974 . Rico Petrocelli .... Red Sox
1393 .... July 15, 1974 ...... Charlie Spikes .... Indians	1449 ... August 12, 1974 . Carl Yastrzemski . Red Sox
1394 .... July 15, 1974 ...... John Lowenstein ..... Indians	1450 ... August 12, 1974 . Dwight Evans .... Red Sox
1395 .... July 15, 1974 ...... John Ellis .... Indians	1451 ... August 12, 1974 . Doug Griffin .... Red Sox
1396 .... July 15, 1974 ...... Buddy Bell .... Indians	1452 ... August 12, 1974 . Bob Montgomery .. Red Sox
1397 .... July 15, 1974 ...... Dave Duncan .... Indians	1453 ... August 12, 1974 . Rico Petrocelli .... Red Sox
1398 .... July 15, 1974 ...... Oscar Gamble .... Indians	1454 ... August 12, 1974 . Dwight Evans .... Red Sox
1399 .... July 20, 1974 ...... Bobby Grich .... Orioles	1455 ... August 12, 1974 . Rick Miller .... Red Sox
1400 .... July 20, 1974 ...... Brooks Robinson ..... Orioles	1456 ... August 12, 1974 . Bob Montgomery .. Red Sox
1401 .... July 20, 1974 ...... Rich Coggins .... Orioles	1457 ... August 12, 1974 . Rico Petrocelli .... Red Sox
1402 .... July 20, 1974 ...... Al Bumbry .... Orioles	1458 ... August 12, 1974 . Dwight Evans .... Red Sox
1403 .... July 20, 1974 ...... Bobby Grich .... Orioles	1459 ... August 12, 1974 . Rick Miller .... Red Sox
1404 .... July 20, 1974 ...... Boog Powell .... Orioles	1460 ... August 12, 1974 . Bob Montgomery .. Red Sox
1405 .... July 20, 1974 ...... Ellie Hendricks .... Orioles	1461 ... August 12, 1974 . Jaun Beniquez ...... Red Sox
1406 .... July 20, 1974 ...... Al Bumbry .... Orioles	1462 ... August 12, 1974 . Cecil Cooper .... Red Sox
1407 .... July 25, 1974 ...... Tony Solaita .... Royals	1463 ... August 12, 1974 . Rico Petrocelli .... Red Sox
1408 .... July 25, 1974 ...... Vada Pinson .... Royals	1464 ... August 12, 1974 . Rick Miller .... Red Sox
1409 .... July 25, 1974 ...... George Brett .... Royals	1465 ... August 12, 1974 . Bernie Carbo .... Red Sox
1410 .... July 25, 1974 ...... John Mayberry .... Royals	1466 ... August 16, 1974 . Don Money .... Brewers
1411 .... July 25, 1974 ...... Vada Pinson .... Royals	1467 ... August 16, 1974 . John Briggs .... Brewers
1412 .... July 25, 1974 ...... Fred Patek .... Royals	1468 ... August 16, 1974 . Robin Yount .... Brewers
1413 .... July 25, 1974 ...... Fred Patek .... Royals	1469 ... August 16, 1974 . Pedro Garcia .... Brewers
1414 .... July 25, 1974 ...... Fran Healy .... Royals	1470 ... August 16, 1974 . Davey May .... Brewers
1415 .... July 25, 1974 ...... Amos Otis .... Royals	1471 ... August 16, 1974 . Don Money .... Brewers
1416 .... July 28, 1974 ...... Steve Braun .... Twins	1472 ... August 16, 1974 . John Briggs .... Brewers
1417 .... July 30, 1974 ...... Jorge Orta .... White Sox	1473 ... August 16, 1974 . Robin Yount .... Brewers
1418 .... July 30, 1974 ...... Bill Sharp .... White Sox	1474 ... August 16, 1974 . John Briggs .... Brewers
1419 .... July 30, 1974 ...... Ed Herrmann ..... White Sox	1475 ... August 20, 1974 . Jim Nettles .... Tigers
1420 .... July 30, 1974 ...... Jorge Orta .... White Sox	1476 ... August 20, 1974 . Aurelio Rodriguez ..... Tigers
1421 .... July 30, 1974 ...... Ken Henderson .. White Sox	1477 ... August 20, 1974 . Dick Sharon .... Tigers
1422 .... July 30, 1974 ...... Jorge Orta .... White Sox	1478 ... August 20, 1974 . Ron LeFlore .... Tigers
1423 .... July 30, 1974 ...... Bill Sharp .... White Sox	1479 ... August 20, 1974 . Tom Veryzer .... Tigers
1424 .... July 30, 1974 ...... Dick Allen .... White Sox	1480 ... August 20, 1974 . Dick Sharon .... Tigers
1425 .... August 3, 1974 ... Fred Patek .... Royals	1481 ... August 20, 1974 . Ron LeFlore .... Tigers
1426 .... August 3, 1974 ... Tony Solaita .... Royals	1482 ... August 20, 1974 . Bill Freehan .... Tigers
1427 .... August 3, 1974 ... Jim Wohlford .... Royals	1483 ... August 20, 1974 . Jim Nettles .... Tigers
1428 .... August 3, 1974 ... George Brett .... Royals	1484 ... August 20, 1974 . Aurelio Rodriguez ..... Tigers
1429 .... August 3, 1974 ... Fran Healy .... Royals	1485 ... August 20, 1974 . Tom Veryzer .... Tigers
1430 .... August 3, 1974 ... Amos Otis .... Royals	1486 ... August 20, 1974 . Ron LeFlore .... Tigers
1431 .... August 3, 1974 ... Jim Wohlford .... Royals	1487 ... August 20, 1974 . Gary Sutherland .... Tigers
1432 .... August 3, 1974 ... Cookie Rojas .... Royals	1488 ... August 20, 1974 . Ben Oglivie .... Tigers
1433 .... August 3, 1974 ... Fran Healy .... Royals	1489 ... August 20, 1974 . Bill Freehan .... Tigers
1434 .... August 7, 1974 ... Pat Kelly .... White Sox	1490 ... August 20, 1974 . Jim Nettles .... Tigers
1435 .... August 7, 1974 ... Jorge Orta .... White Sox	1491 ... August 20, 1974 . Dick Sharon .... Tigers
1436 .... August 7, 1974 ... Dick Allen .... White Sox	1492 ... August 20, 1974 . Gene Lamont .... Tigers
1437 .... August 7, 1974 ... Ken Henderson .. White Sox	1493 ... August 20, 1974 . Ron LeFlore .... Tigers
1438 .... August 7, 1974 ... Jorge Orta .... White Sox	1494 ... August 25, 1974 . Chris Chambliss ... Yankees
1439 .... August 7, 1974 ... Dick Allen .... White Sox	1495 ... August 25, 1974 . Roy White .... Yankees
1440 .... August 7, 1974 ... Brian Downing .... White Sox	1496 ... August 25, 1974 . Elliott Maddox .... Yankees

1497	August 25, 1974	Ron Blomberg	Yankees
1498	August 25, 1974	Thurman Munson	Yankees
1499	August 25, 1974	Jim Mason	Yankees
1500	August 25, 1974	Sandy Alomar	Yankees
1501	August 30, 1974	Tim Johnson	Brewers
1502	August 30, 1974	George Scott	Brewers
1503	August 30, 1974	John Briggs	Brewers
1504	August 30, 1974	Darrell Porter	Brewers
1505	August 30, 1974	Mike Hegan	Brewers
1506	August 30, 1974	Don Money	Brewers
1507	August 30, 1974	John Briggs	Brewers
1508	August 30, 1974	Mike Hegan	Brewers
1509	August 30, 1974	Don Money	Brewers
1510	Sept. 3, 1974	Gene Tenace	A's
1511	Sept. 3, 1974	Gene Tenace	A's
1512	Sept. 7, 1974	Brian Downing	White Sox
1513	Sept. 7, 1974	Lee Richard	White Sox
1514	Sept. 7, 1974	Brian Downing	White Sox
1515	Sept. 7, 1974	Pat Kelly	White Sox
1516	Sept. 7, 1974	Bill Sharp	White Sox
1517	Sept. 7, 1974	Jorge Orta	White Sox
1518	Sept. 7, 1974	Ken Henderson	White Sox
1519	Sept. 7, 1974	Brian Downing	White Sox
1520	Sept. 7, 1974	Carlos May	White Sox
1521	Sept. 11, 1974	Fred Patek	Royals
1522	Sept. 11, 1974	Jim Wohlford	Royals
1523	Sept. 11, 1974	Frank White	Royals
1524	Sept. 11, 1974	Vada Pinson	Royals
1525	Sept. 11, 1974	Hal McRae	Royals
1526	Sept. 11, 1974	Jim Wohlford	Royals
1527	Sept. 11, 1974	Al Cowens	Royals
1528	Sept. 11, 1974	Frank White	Royals
1529	Sept. 11, 1974	Jim Wohlford	Royals
1530	Sept. 11, 1974	Al Cowens	Royals
1531	Sept. 11, 1974	Frank White	Royals
1532	Sept. 11, 1974	Buck Martinez	Royals
1533	Sept. 11, 1974	George Brett	Royals
1534	Sept. 11, 1974	Tony Solaita	Royals
1535	Sept. 11, 1974	Vada Pinson	Royals
1536	Sept. 15, 1974	Ken Henderson	White Sox
1537	Sept. 15, 1974	Lee Richard	White Sox
1538	Sept. 15, 1974	Carlos May	White Sox
1539	Sept. 15, 1974	Lee Richard	White Sox
1540	Sept. 15, 1974	Tony Muser	White Sox
1541	Sept. 15, 1974	Ken Henderson	White Sox
1542	Sept. 15, 1974	Bill Stein	White Sox
1543	Sept. 20, 1974	Pat Bourque	Twins
1544	Sept. 20, 1974	Danny Thompson	Twins
1545	Sept. 20, 1974	Glenn Borgmann	Twins
1546	Sept. 20, 1974	Steve Braun	Twins
1547	Sept. 20, 1974	Rod Carew	Twins
1548	Sept. 20, 1974	Pat Bourque	Twins
1549	Sept. 24, 1974	Al Cowens	Royals
1550	Sept. 24, 1974	George Brett	Royals
1551	Sept. 24, 1974	Tony Solaita	Royals
1552	Sept. 24, 1974	Amos Otis	Royals
1553	Sept. 24, 1974	Tony Solaita	Royals
1554	Sept. 24, 1974	Frank White	Royals
1555	Sept. 24, 1974	Buck Martinez	Royals
1556	Sept. 24, 1974	Vada Pinson	Royals
1557	Sept. 24, 1974	Amos Otis	Royals
1558	Sept. 28, 1974	Steve Brye	Twins
1559	Sept. 28, 1974	Rod Carew	Twins
1560	Sept. 28, 1974	Bobby Darwin	Twins
1561	Sept. 28, 1974	Larry Hisle	Twins
1562	Sept. 28, 1974	Pat Bourque	Twins
1563	Sept. 28, 1974	Luis Gomez	Twins
1564	Sept. 28, 1974	Bobby Darwin	Twins
1565	Sept. 28, 1974	Pat Bourque	Twins
1566	Sept. 28, 1974	Bobby Darwin	Twins
1567	Sept. 28, 1974	Larry Hisle	Twins
1568	Sept. 28, 1974	Pat Bourque	Twins
1569	Sept. 28, 1974	Rod Carew	Twins
1570	Sept. 28, 1974	Steve Braun	Twins
1571	Sept. 28, 1974	Larry Hisle	Twins
1572	Sept. 28, 1974	Eric Soderholm	Twins
1573	April 7, 1975	Fred Patek	Royals
1574	April 7, 1975	Hal McRae	Royals
1575	April 7, 1975	Harmon Killebrew	Royals
1576	April 7, 1975	John Mayberry	Royals
1577	April 7, 1975	Hal McRae	Royals
1578	April 7, 1975	Harmon Killebrew	Royals
1579	April 7, 1975	Fred Patek	Royals
1580	April 7, 1975	Harmon Killebrew	Royals
1581	April 7, 1975	George Brett	Royals
1582	April 7, 1975	Cookie Rojas	Royals
1583	April 7, 1975	Hal McRae	Royals
1584	April 7, 1975	Harmon Killebrew	Royals
1585	April 11, 1975	Jorge Orta	White Sox
1586	April 11, 1975	Deron Johnson	White Sox
1587	April 11, 1975	Bucky Dent	White Sox
1588	April 11, 1975	Brian Downing	White Sox
1589	April 11, 1975	Nyls Nyman	White Sox
1590	April 11, 1975	Ken Henderson	White Sox
1591	April 11, 1975	Deron Johnson	White Sox
1592	April 11, 1975	Brian Downing	White Sox
1593	April 11, 1975	Bill Melton	White Sox
1594	April 11, 1975	Ken Henderson	White Sox
1595	April 15, 1975	Glenn Borgmann	Twins
1596	April 15, 1975	Bobby Darwin	Twins
1597	April 15, 1975	Glenn Borgmann	Twins
1598	April 15, 1975	Bobby Darwin	Twins
1599	April 15, 1975	Steve Braun	Twins
1600	April 15, 1975	Lyman Bostock	Twins
1601	April 15, 1975	Larry Hisle	Twins
1602	April 20, 1975	Ken Henderson	White Sox
1603	April 20, 1975	Pete Varney	White Sox
1604	April 20, 1975	Pete Varney	White Sox
1605	April 20, 1975	Deron Johnson	White Sox
1606	April 20, 1975	Pat Kelly	White Sox
1607	April 20, 1975	Pat Kelly	White Sox
1608	April 24, 1975	Willie Davis	Rangers

1609 .... April 24, 1975 ..... Mike Hargrove ...... Rangers		1665 .... June 1, 1975 .... Ken Singleton .... Orioles	
1610 .... April 24, 1975 ..... Roy Howell .... Rangers		1666 .... June 1, 1975 .... Al Bumbry .... Orioles	
1611 .... April 24, 1975 ..... Willie Davis ..... Rangers		1667 .... June 1, 1975 .... Mark Belanger .... Orioles	
1612 .... April 24, 1975 ..... Jeff Burroughs ...... Rangers		1668 .... June 1, 1975 .... Bobby Grich .... Orioles	
1613 .... April 24, 1975 ..... Jim Sundberg .... Rangers		1669 .... June 6, 1975 .... Bill Sharp .... Brewers	
1614 .... April 24, 1975 ..... Cesar Tovar .... Rangers		1670 .... June 6, 1975 .... George Scott .... Brewers	
1615 .... April 24, 1975 ..... Jeff Burroughs ...... Rangers		1671 .... June 6, 1975 .... Bill Sharp .... Brewers	
1616 .... May 3, 1975 .... Jeff Burroughs ...... Rangers		1672 .... June 6, 1975 .... Kurt Bevacqua ...... Brewers	
1617 .... May 3, 1975 .... Roy Howell .... Rangers		1673 .... June 6, 1975 .... Robin Yount .... Brewers	
1618 .... May 3, 1975 .... Willie Davis .... Rangers		1674 .... June 6, 1975 .... Sixto Lezcano ...... Brewers	
1619 .... May 3, 1975 .... Lenny Randle .... Rangers		1675 .... June 10, 1975 ..... Elliott Maddox .... Yankees	
1620 .... May 3, 1975 .... Roy Smalley .... Rangers		1676 .... June 10, 1975 ..... Roy White .... Yankees	
1621 .... May 3, 1975 .... Cesar Tovar .... Rangers		1677 .... June 10, 1975 ..... Chris Chambliss ... Yankees	
1622 .... May 3, 1975 .... Willie Davis .... Rangers		1678 .... June 10, 1975 .... Ed Herrmann .... Yankees	
1623 .... May 3, 1975 .... Mike Hargrove ...... Rangers		1679 .... June 10, 1975 ..... Sandy Alomar .... Yankees	
1624 .... May 3, 1975 .... Joe Lovitto .... Rangers		1680 .... June 14, 1975 ..... Sixto Lezcano .... Brewers	
1625 .... May 8, 1975 .... Bill North .... A's		1681 .... June 14, 1975 ..... Gorman Thomas ... Brewers	
1626 .... May 8, 1975 .... Bert Campaneris .... A's		1682 .... June 14, 1975 ..... Robin Yount .... Brewers	
1627 .... May 8, 1975 .... Joe Rudi .... A's		1683 .... June 14, 1975 ..... Tim Johnson .... Brewers	
1628 .... May 8, 1975 .... Larry Haney .... A's		1684 .... June 14, 1975 ..... Gorman Thomas ... Brewers	
1629 .... May 8, 1975 .... Gene Tenace .... A's		1685 .... June 14, 1975 ..... Sixto Lezcano .... Brewers	
1630 .... May 8, 1975 .... Claudell Washington ..... A's		1686 .... June 14, 1975 ..... George Scott .... Brewers	
1631 .... May 8, 1975 .... Joe Rudi .... A's		1687 .... June 14, 1975 ..... Hank Aaron .... Brewers	
1632 .... May 8, 1975 .... Billy Williams .... A's		1688 .... June 14, 1975 ..... Darrell Porter .... Brewers	
1633 .... May 8, 1975 .... Bill North .... A's		1689 .... June 14, 1975 ..... Pedro Garcia .... Brewers	
1634 .... May 8, 1975 .... Charlie Sands .... A's		1690 .... June 14, 1975 ..... Tim Johnson .... Brewers	
1635 .... May 13, 1975 ..... Graig Nettles .... Yankees		1691 .... June 14, 1975 ..... Robin Yount .... Brewers	
1636 .... May 13, 1975 ..... Sandy Alomar .... Yankees		1692 .... June 18, 1975 ..... George Brett .... Royals	
1637 .... May 13, 1975 ..... Bobby Bonds .... Yankees		1693 .... June 18, 1975 ..... Amos Otis .... Royals	
1638 .... May 13, 1975 ..... Chris Chambliss ... Yankees		1694 .... June 29, 1975 .... Phil Garner .... A's	
1639 .... May 13, 1975 ..... Fred Stanley .... Yankees		1695 .... June 29, 1975 .... Gene Tenace .... A's	
1640 .... May 13, 1975 ..... Elliott Maddox .... Yankees		1696 .... June 29, 1975 .... Claudell Washington ..... A's	
1641 .... May 13, 1975 ..... Elliott Maddox .... Yankees		1697 .... June 29, 1975 .... Reggie Jackson .... A's	
1642 .... May 18, 1975 ..... Ken Singleton .... Orioles		1698 .... July 3, 1975 .... Eric Soderholm .... Twins	
1643 .... May 18, 1975 ..... Mark Belanger .... Orioles		1699 .... July 3, 1975 .... Rod Carew .... Twins	
1644 .... May 18, 1975 ..... Al Bumbry .... Orioles		1700 .... July 3, 1975 .... Jerry Terrell .... Twins	
1645 .... May 18, 1975 ..... Dave Duncan .... Orioles		1701 .... July 3, 1975 .... Lyman Bostock .... Twins	
1646 .... May 18, 1975 ..... Al Bumbry .... Orioles		1702 .... July 3, 1975 .... Glenn Borgmann ...... Twins	
1647 .... May 23, 1975 ..... Jim Rice .... Red Sox		1703 .... July 3, 1975 .... Dan Ford .... Twins	
1648 .... May 23, 1975 ..... Dwight Evans .... Red Sox		1704 .... July 3, 1975 .... Steve Braun .... Twins	
1649 .... May 23, 1975 ..... Rico Petrocelli .... Red Sox		1705 .... July 3, 1975 .... Tom Kelly .... Twins	
1650 .... May 23, 1975 ..... Dwight Evans .... Red Sox		1706 .... July 8, 1975 .... Ken Singleton .... Orioles	
1651 .... May 23, 1975 ..... Jim Rice .... Red Sox		1707 .... July 8, 1975 .... Bobby Grich .... Orioles	
1652 .... May 23, 1975 ..... Fred Lynn .... Red Sox		1708 .... July 8, 1975 .... Ellie Hendricks .... Orioles	
1653 .... May 23, 1975 ..... Rico Petrocelli .... Red Sox		1709 .... July 8, 1975 .... Lee May .... Orioles	
1654 .... May 28, 1975 ..... Buddy Bell .... Indians		1710 .... July 8, 1975 .... Paul Blair .... Orioles	
1655 .... May 28, 1975 ..... Charlie Spikes .... Indians		1711 .... July 12, 1975 ...... Duane Kuiper .... Indians	
1656 .... May 28, 1975 ..... Oscar Gamble .... Indians		1712 .... July 12, 1975 ...... Boog Powell .... Indians	
1657 .... May 28, 1975 ..... Alan Ashby .... Indians		1713 .... July 12, 1975 ...... Buddy Bell .... Indians	
1658 .... May 28, 1975 ..... George Hendrick ..... Indians		1714 .... July 12, 1975 ...... John Lowenstein ..... Indians	
1659 .... May 28, 1975 ..... Boog Powell .... Indians		1715 .... July 12, 1975 ...... Rick Manning .... Indians	
1660 .... June 1, 1975 .... Tom Shopay .... Orioles		1716 .... July 12, 1975 ...... Buddy Bell .... Indians	
1661 .... June 1, 1975 .... Al Bumbry .... Orioles		1717 .... July 18, 1975 ...... Bobby Darwin .... Brewers	
1662 .... June 1, 1975 .... Lee May .... Orioles		1718 .... July 18, 1975 ...... Charlie Moore .... Brewers	
1663 .... June 1, 1975 .... Ken Singleton .... Orioles		1719 .... July 18, 1975 ...... Bobby Darwin .... Brewers	
1664 .... June 1, 1975 .... Al Bumbry .... Orioles		1720 .... July 18, 1975 ...... Charlie Moore .... Brewers	

1721 .... July 18, 1975 ...... Sixto Lezcano .... Brewers	1777 .... April 20, 1976 ...... Al Bumbry .... Orioles
1722 .... July 18, 1975 ...... Don Money .... Brewers	1778 .... April 20, 1976 ..... Royle Stillman .... Orioles
1723 .... July 22, 1975 ...... Don Baylor .... Orioles	1779 .... April 20, 1976 ..... Mark Belanger .... Orioles
1724 .... July 22, 1975 ...... Mark Belanger .... Orioles	1780 .... April 20, 1976 ..... Al Bumbry .... Orioles
1725 .... July 26, 1975 ...... John Briggs .... Twins	1781 .... April 20, 1976 ..... Ellie Hendricks .... Orioles
1726 .... July 26, 1975 ...... Dan Ford .... Twins	1782 .... April 20, 1976 ..... Brooks Robinson ..... Orioles
1727 .... July 30, 1975 ...... Jorge Orta .... White Sox	1783 .... April 20, 1976 ..... Al Bumbry .... Orioles
1728 .... July 30, 1975 ...... Carlos May .... White Sox	1784 .... April 20, 1976 ..... Paul Blair .... Orioles
1729 .... July 30, 1975 ...... Ken Henderson .. White Sox	1785 .... April 20, 1976 ..... Bobby Grich .... Orioles
1730 .... July 30, 1975 ...... Bill Melton .... White Sox	1786 .... April 20, 1976 ..... Ken Singleton .... Orioles
1731 .... July 30, 1975 ...... Bucky Dent .... White Sox	1787 .... April 27, 1976 ..... Tommy Harper .... Orioles
1732 .... August 3, 1975 ... Jeff Burroughs ...... Rangers	1788 .... April 27, 1976 ..... Paul Blair .... Orioles
1733 .... August 3, 1975 ... Toby Harrah .... Rangers	1789 .... April 27, 1976 ..... Andres Mora .... Orioles
1734 .... August 3, 1975 ... Tom Grieve .... Rangers	1790 .... April 27, 1976 ..... Doug DeCinces .... Orioles
1735 .... August 3, 1975 ... Roy Howell .... Rangers	1791 .... April 27, 1976 ..... Paul Blair .... Orioles
1736 .... August 3, 1975 ... Jim Sundberg .... Rangers	1792 .... April 27, 1976 ..... Andres Mora .... Orioles
1737 .... August 3, 1975 ... Dave Moates .... Rangers	1793 .... April 27, 1976 ..... Ken Singleton .... Orioles
1738 .... August 3, 1975 ... Lenny Randle .... Rangers	1794 .... April 27, 1976 ..... Ellie Hendricks .... Orioles
1739 .... August 3, 1975 ... Tom Grieve .... Rangers	1795 .... April 27, 1976 ..... Mark Belanger .... Orioles
1740 .... August 3, 1975 ... Jim Sundberg .... Rangers	1796 .... April 27, 1976 ..... Andres Mora .... Orioles
1741 .... August 8, 1975 ... Fred Stanley .... Yankees	1797 .... April 27, 1976 ..... Mark Belanger .... Orioles
1742 .... August 20, 1975 . Bob Mitchell .... Brewers	1798 .... May 1, 1976 .... Duane Kuiper .... Indians
1743 .... August 20, 1975 . Bill Sharp .... Brewers	1799 .... May 1, 1976 .... Charlie Spikes .... Indians
1744 .... August 20, 1975 . Kurt Bevacqua .... Brewers	1800 .... May 1, 1976 .... Alan Ashby .... Indians
1745 .... August 20, 1975 . Gorman Thomas ... Brewers	1801 .... May 1, 1976 .... Buddy Bell .... Indians
1746 .... August 20, 1975 . Mike Hegan .... Brewers	1802 .... May 1, 1976 .... Rick Manning .... Indians
1747 .... August 20, 1975 . Kurt Bevacqua .... Brewers	1803 .... May 1, 1976 .... Duane Kuiper .... Indians
1748 .... August 20, 1975 . Bob Mitchell .... Brewers	1804 .... May 5, 1976 .... Roy White .... Yankees
1749 .... August 20, 1975 . Gorman Thomas ... Brewers	1805 .... May 5, 1976 .... Lou Piniella .... Yankees
1750 .... August 20, 1975 . Bob Sheldon .... Brewers	1806 .... May 5, 1976 .... Graig Nettles .... Yankees
1751 .... August 24, 1975 . Thurman Munson . Yankees	1807 .... May 5, 1976 .... Jim Mason .... Yankees
1752 .... August 24, 1975 . Graig Nettles .... Yankees	1808 .... May 5, 1976 .... Roy White .... Yankees
1753 .... August 24, 1975 . Walt Williams .... Yankees	1809 .... May 5, 1976 .... Lou Piniella .... Yankees
1754 .... August 24, 1975 . Sandy Alomar .... Yankees	1810 .... May 5, 1976 .... Graig Nettles .... Yankees
1755 .... August 24, 1975 . Thurman Munson . Yankees	1811 .... May 5, 1976 .... Willie Randolph .... Yankees
1756 .... August 24, 1975 . Rich Coggins .... Yankees	1812 .... May 10, 1976 ...... Bill North .... A's
1757 .... August 24, 1975 . Sandy Alomar .... Yankees	1813 .... May 10, 1976 ...... Sal Bando .... A's
1758 .... August 24, 1975 . Ed Herrmann .... Yankees	1814 .... May 10, 1976 ...... Billy Williams .... A's
1759 .... April 10, 1976 ..... Gene Tenace .... A's	1815 .... May 10, 1976 ...... Phil Garner .... A's
1760 .... April 10, 1976 ..... Phil Garner .... A's	1816 .... May 10, 1976 ...... Joe Rudi .... A's
1761 .... April 10, 1976 ..... Claudell Washington ..... A's	1817 .... May 10, 1976 ...... Sal Bando .... A's
1762 .... April 10, 1976 ..... Gene Tenace .... A's	1818 .... May 10, 1976 ...... Phil Garner .... A's
1763 .... April 10, 1976 ..... Claudell Washington ..... A's	1819 .... May 10, 1976 ...... Bill North .... A's
1764 .... April 10, 1976 ..... Don Baylor .... A's	1820 .... May 10, 1976 ...... Sal Bando .... A's
1765 .... April 10, 1976 ..... Sal Bando .... A's	1821 .... May 10, 1976 ...... Billy Williams .... A's
1766 .... April 15, 1976 ..... Fran Healy .... Royals	1822 .... May 10, 1976 ...... Phil Garner .... A's
1767 .... April 15, 1976 ..... Amos Otis .... Royals	1823 .... May 10, 1976 ...... Billy Williams .... A's
1768 .... April 15, 1976 ..... George Brett .... Royals	1824 .... May 14, 1976 ...... Lyman Bostock .... Twins
1769 .... April 15, 1976 ..... Fran Healy .... Royals	1825 .... May 14, 1976 ...... Dan Ford .... Twins
1770 .... April 15, 1976 ..... Jim Wohlford .... Royals	1826 .... May 14, 1976 ...... Danny Thompson ...... Twins
1771 .... April 15, 1976 ..... Frank White .... Royals	1827 .... May 14, 1976 ...... Rod Carew .... Twins
1772 .... April 15, 1976 ..... Amos Otis .... Royals	1828 .... May 14, 1976 ...... Dan Ford .... Twins
1773 .... April 15, 1976 ..... Fran Healy .... Royals	1829 .... May 18, 1976 ...... Rich Coggins ...... White Sox
1774 .... April 15, 1976 ..... Jamie Quirk .... Royals	1830 .... May 18, 1976 ...... Jorge Orta .... White Sox
1775 .... April 20, 1976 ..... Royle Stillman .... Orioles	1831 .... May 18, 1976 ...... Jack Brohamer ... White Sox
1776 .... April 20, 1976 ..... Brooks Robinson ..... Orioles	1832 .... May 18, 1976 ...... Rich Coggins ...... White Sox

1833	May 18, 1976	Jim Spencer	White Sox
1834	May 18, 1976	Bill Stein	White Sox
1835	May 18, 1976	Jorge Orta	White Sox
1836	May 18, 1976	Bill Stein	White Sox
1837	May 18, 1976	Rich Coggins	White Sox
1838	May 23, 1976	Jeff Burroughs	Rangers
1839	May 28, 1976	Fred Patek	Royals
1840	May 28, 1976	Amos Otis	Royals
1841	May 28, 1976	George Brett	Royals
1842	May 28, 1976	Fred Patek	Royals
1843	May 28, 1976	Amos Otis	Royals
1844	June 1, 1976	Tony Oliva	Twins
1845	June 1, 1976	Lyman Bostock	Twins
1846	June 1, 1976	Craig Kusick	Twins
1847	June 1, 1976	Jerry Terrell	Twins
1848	June 1, 1976	Dan Ford	Twins
1849	June 1, 1976	Lyman Bostock	Twins
1850	June 1, 1976	Larry Hisle	Twins
1851	June 6, 1976	Fred Lynn	Red Sox
1852	June 6, 1976	Rick Burleson	Red Sox
1853	June 6, 1976	Jim Rice	Red Sox
1854	June 11, 1976	Alex Johnson	Tigers
1855	June 11, 1976	Jason Thompson	Tigers
1856	June 11, 1976	Ben Oglivie	Tigers
1857	June 11, 1976	Ron LeFlore	Tigers
1858	June 11, 1976	Pedro Garcia	Tigers
1859	June 11, 1976	Alex Johnson	Tigers
1860	June 11, 1976	Chuck Scrivener	Tigers
1861	June 11, 1976	Ron LeFlore	Tigers
1862	June 11, 1976	Alex Johnson	Tigers
1863	June 15, 1976	George Scott	Brewers
1864	June 15, 1976	Jim Rosario	Brewers
1865	June 15, 1976	Gary Sutherland	Brewers
1866	June 15, 1976	Jim Rosario	Brewers
1867	June 15, 1976	Bernie Carbo	Brewers
1868	June 15, 1976	Robin Yount	Brewers
1869	June 15, 1976	Darrell Porter	Brewers
1870	June 15, 1976	Hank Aaron	Brewers
1871	June 15, 1976	Don Money	Brewers
1872	June 19, 1976	Rick Miller	Red Sox
1873	June 19, 1976	Rick Miller	Red Sox
1874	June 19, 1976	Dwight Evans	Red Sox
1875	June 19, 1976	Carl Yastrzemski	Red Sox
1876	June 19, 1976	Rico Petrocelli	Red Sox
1877	June 19, 1976	Dwight Evans	Red Sox
1878	June 19, 1976	Fred Lynn	Red Sox
1879	June 19, 1976	Jim Rice	Red Sox
1880	June 19, 1976	Rico Petrocelli	Red Sox
1881	June 19, 1976	Rick Miller	Red Sox
1882	June 19, 1976	Dwight Evans	Red Sox
1883	June 19, 1976	Jim Rice	Red Sox
1884	June 19, 1976	Carlton Fisk	Red Sox
1885	June 19, 1976	Rico Petrocelli	Red Sox
1886	June 19, 1976	Rick Burleson	Red Sox
1887	June 26, 1976	George Brett	Royals
1888	June 26, 1976	Fred Patek	Royals
1889	June 26, 1976	Frank White	Royals
1890	June 26, 1976	Amos Otis	Royals
1891	June 26, 1976	Tony Solaita	Royals
1892	June 26, 1976	Bob Stinson	Royals
1893	June 26, 1976	Frank White	Royals
1894	June 26, 1976	Gerorge Brett	Royals
1895	July 3, 1976	Roy Smalley	Twins
1896	July 3, 1976	Rod Carew	Twins
1897	July 3, 1976	Larry Hisle	Twins
1898	July 3, 1976	Bob Randall	Twins
1899	July 3, 1976	Roy Smalley	Twins
1900	July 3, 1976	Lyman Bostock	Twins
1901	July 3, 1976	Larry Hisle	Twins
1902	July 3, 1976	Lyman Bostock	Twins
1903	July 7, 1976	George Hendrick	Indians
1904	July 7, 1976	Buddy Bell	Indians
1905	July 7, 1976	Larvell Blanks	Indians
1906	July 7, 1976	Rico Carty	Indians
1907	July 7, 1976	Duane Kuiper	Indians
1908	July 7, 1976	Larvell Blanks	Indians
1909	July 7, 1976	Rick Manning	Indians
1910	July 7, 1976	George Hendrick	Indians
1911	July 7, 1976	Orlando Gonzalez	Indians
1912	July 7, 1976	Duane Kuiper	Indians
1913	July 11, 1976	Bobby Grich	Orioles
1914	July 11, 1976	Lee May	Orioles
1915	July 11, 1976	Bobby Grich	Orioles
1916	July 11, 1976	Ken Singleton	Orioles
1917	July 11, 1976	Brooks Robinson	Orioles
1918	July 11, 1976	Rick Dempsey	Orioles
1919	July 11, 1976	Tim Nordbrook	Orioles
1920	July 11, 1976	Ken Singleton	Orioles
1921	July 11, 1976	Rick Dempsey	Orioles
1922	July 11, 1976	Tony Muser	Orioles
1923	July 11, 1976	Brooks Robinson	Orioles
1924	July 11, 1976	Paul Blair	Orioles
1925	July 16, 1976	Terry Crowley	Orioles
1926	July 16, 1976	Dave Duncan	Orioles
1927	July 16, 1976	Tony Muser	Orioles
1928	July 16, 1976	Reggie Jackson	Orioles
1929	July 16, 1976	Dave Duncan	Orioles
1930	July 16, 1976	Ken Singleton	Orioles
1931	July 16, 1976	Reggie Jackson	Orioles
1932	July 16, 1976	Terry Crowley	Orioles
1933	July 21, 1976	Rick Manning	Indians
1934	July 21, 1976	George Hendrick	Indians
1935	July 21, 1976	Rick Manning	Indians
1936	July 26, 1976	Tom Poquette	Royals
1937	July 26, 1976	Jamie Quirk	Royals
1938	July 26, 1976	Frank White	Royals
1939	July 26, 1976	Tom Poquette	Royals
1940	July 26, 1976	Jamie Quirk	Royals
1941	July 26, 1976	Fred Patek	Royals
1942	July 26, 1976	Frank White	Royals
1943	July 30, 1976	Jim Spencer	White Sox
1944	July 30, 1976	Jack Brohamer	White Sox

1945 .... July 30, 1976 ...... Bucky Dent .... White Sox	2001 .... August 31, 1976 . Dan Meyer .... Tigers
1946 .... July 30, 1976 ...... Jim Essian .... White Sox	2002 .... August 31, 1976 . Rusty Staub .... Tigers
1947 .... July 30, 1976 ...... Jerry Hairston ..... White Sox	2003 .... August 31, 1976 . Pedro Garcia .... Tigers
1948 .... July 30, 1976 ...... Jorge Orta .... White Sox	2004 .... August 31, 1976 . Ron LeFlore .... Tigers
1949 .... July 30, 1976 ...... Bill Stein .... White Sox	2005 .... August 31, 1976 . Ben Oglivie .... Tigers
1950 .... July 30, 1976 ...... Jorge Orta .... White Sox	2006 .... August 31, 1976 . Jason Thompson ...... Tigers
1951 .... July 30, 1976 ...... Jerry Hairston ..... White Sox	2007 .... August 31, 1976 . Dan Meyer .... Tigers
1952 .... July 30, 1976 ...... Ralph Garr .... White Sox	2008 .... August 31, 1976 . Phil Mankowski .... Tigers
1953 .... August 4, 1976 .... Tom Grieve .... Rangers	2009 .... August 31, 1976 . Ron LeFlore .... Tigers
1954 .... August 4, 1976 ... Lenny Randle ..... Rangers	2010 .... August 31, 1976 . Ron LeFlore .... Tigers
1955 .... August 4, 1976 ... Juan Beniquez ..... Rangers	2011 .... Sept. 5, 1976 ...... Bill North .... A's
1956 .... August 4, 1976 ... Jeff Burroughs ..... Rangers	2012 .... Sept. 5, 1976 ...... Claudell Washington ..... A's
1957 .... August 4, 1976 ... Lenny Randle .... Rangers	2013 .... Sept. 5, 1976 .... Joe Rudi .... A's
1958 .... August 8, 1976 ... Bill North .... A's	2014 .... Sept. 5, 1976 ...... Willie McCovey .... A's
1959 .... August 8, 1976 ... Jeff Newman .... A's	2015 .... Sept. 5, 1976 ...... Don Baylor .... A's
1960 .... August 8, 1976 ... Bill North .... A's	2016 .... Sept. 5, 1976 ...... Bert Campaneris .... A's
1961 .... August 8, 1976 ... Bert Campaneris .... A's	2017 .... Sept. 5, 1976 .... Claudell Washington ..... A's
1962 .... August 8, 1976 ... Jeff Newman .... A's	2018 .... Sept. 5, 1976 ...... Sal Bando .... A's
1963 .... August 8, 1976 ... Joe Rudi .... A's	2019 .... Sept. 10, 1976 ..... Bill Stein .... White Sox
1964 .... August 8, 1976 ... Gene Tenace .... A's	2020 .... Sept. 10, 1976 ..... Sam Ewing .... White Sox
1965 .... August 8, 1976 ... Billy Williams .... A's	2021 .... Sept. 10, 1976 ..... Chet Lemon .... White Sox
1966 .... August 12, 1976 . Denny Doyle .... Red Sox	2022 .... Sept. 10, 1976 ..... Bucky Dent .... White Sox
1967 .... August 12, 1976 . Carl Yastrzemski .. Red Sox	2023 .... Sept. 10, 1976 ..... Jim Essian .... White Sox
1968 .... August 12, 1976 . Jim Rice .... Red Sox	2024 .... Sept. 10, 1976 ,,,, Jim Spencer .... White Sox
1969 .... August 12, 1976 . Cecil Cooper .... Red Sox	2025 .... Sept. 10, 1976 ..... Sam Ewing .... White Sox
1970 .... August 12, 1976 . Carlton Fisk .... Red Sox	2026 .... Sept. 10, 1976 ..... Chet Lemon .... White Sox
1971 .... August 12, 1976 . Butch Hobson .... Red Sox	2027 .... Sept. 10, 1976 ..... Alan Bannister .... White Sox
1972 .... August 12, 1976 . Rick Burleson .... Red Sox	2028 .... Sept. 10, 1976 ..... Ralph Garr .... White Sox
1973 .... August 12, 1976 . Jim Rice .... Red Sox	2029 .... Sept. 10, 1976 ..... Bill Stein .... White Sox
1974 .... August 12, 1976 . Cecil Cooper .... Red Sox	2030 .... Sept. 10, 1976 ..... Jorge Orta .... White Sox
1975 .... August 18, 1976 . Ron LeFlore .... Tigers	2031 .... Sept. 10, 1976 ..... Sam Ewing .... White Sox
1976 .... August 18, 1976 . Willie Horton .... Tigers	2032 .... Sept. 10, 1976 ..... Ralph Garr .... White Sox
1977 .... August 18, 1976 . Jason Thompson ...... Tigers	2033 .... Sept. 10, 1976 ..... Bill Stein .... White Sox
1978 .... August 18, 1976 . Aurelio Rodriguez ..... Tigers	2034 .... Sept. 10, 1976 ..... Jim Spencer .... White Sox
1979 .... August 18, 1976 . Tom Veryzer .... Tigers	2035 .... Sept. 10, 1976 ..... Jorge Orta ,......... White Sox
1980 .... August 18, 1976 . Willie Horton .... Tigers	2036 .... Sept. 10, 1976 ..... Sam Ewing .... White Sox
1981 .... August 18, 1976 . Jason Thompson ...... Tigers	2037 .... Sept. 15, 1976 ..... Hal McRae .... Royals
1982 .... August 18, 1976 . Ron LeFlore .... Tigers	2038 .... Sept. 15, 1976 ..... Bob Stinson .... Royals
1983 .... August 18, 1976 . Rusty Staub .... Tigers	2039 .... Sept. 15, 1976 ..... Fred Patek .... Royals
1984 .... August 18, 1976 . Jason Thompson ...... Tigers	2040 .... Sept. 15, 1976 ..... Hal McRae .... Royals
1985 .... August 18, 1976 . John Wockenfuss ..... Tigers	2041 .... Sept. 15, 1976 .... Al Cowens .... Royals
1986 .... August 18, 1976 . Ben Oglivie .... Tigers	2042 .... Sept. 15, 1976 ..... Frank White .... Royals
1987 .... August 18, 1976 . Ron LeFlore .... Tigers	2043 .... Sept. 15, 1976 ..... Hal McRae .... Royals
1988 .... August 18, 1976 . Willie Horton .... Tigers	2044 .... Sept. 15, 1976 ..... Al Cowens .... Royals
1989 .... August 18, 1976 . Tom Veryzer .... Tigers	2045 .... Sept. 15, 1976 ..... Tom Poquette .... Royals
1990 .... August 18, 1976 . Ron LeFlore .... Tigers	2046 .... Sept. 20, 1976 ..... Lenny Randle .... Rangers
1991 .... August 18, 1976 . Willie Horton .... Tigers	2047 .... Sept. 20, 1976 .... Jim Sundberg .... Rangers
1992 .... August 23, 1976 . Denny Doyle .... Red Sox	2048 .... Sept. 20, 1976 .... Jeff Burroughs ...... Rangers
1993 .... August 23, 1976 . Fred Lynn .... Red Sox	2049 .... Sept. 20, 1976 .... Gene Clines .... Rangers
1994 .... August 23, 1976 . Carl Yastrzemski .. Red Sox	2050 .... Sept. 25, 1976 .... Rod Carew .... Twins
1995 .... August 23, 1976 . Cecil Cooper .... Red Sox	2051 .... Sept. 25, 1976 .... Lyman Bostock .... Twins
1996 .... August 23, 1976 . Denny Doyle .... Red Sox	2052 .... Sept. 25, 1976 .... Butch Wynegar .... Twins
1997 .... August 23, 1976 . Fred Lynn .... Red Sox	2053 .... Sept. 25, 1976 .... Larry Hisle .... Twins
1998 .... August 23, 1976 . Cecil Cooper .... Red Sox	2054 .... Sept. 25, 1976 .... Mike Cubbage .... Twins
1999 .... August 28, 1976 . Willie Randolph .... Yankees	2055 .... Sept. 25, 1976 .... Roy Smalley .... Twins
2000 .... August 31, 1976 . Ron LeFlore .... Tigers	2056 .... Sept. 25, 1976 .... Butch Wynegar .... Twins

2057 .... Sept. 25, 1976 .... Dan Ford .... Twins
2058 .... Sept. 25, 1976 .... Bob Randall .... Twins
2059 .... Sept. 25, 1976 .... Steve Braun .... Twins
2060 .... Sept. 25, 1976 .... Roy Smalley .... Twins
2061 .... Sept. 29, 1976 .... Alan Bannister .... White Sox
2062 .... Sept. 29, 1976 .... Bill Stein .... White Sox
2063 .... Sept. 29, 1976 .... Alan Bannister .... White Sox
2064 .... Sept. 29, 1976 .... Chet Lemon ...... White Sox
2065 .... Sept. 29, 1976 .... Jim Essian .... White Sox
2066 .... Sept. 29, 1976 .... Ralph Garr .... White Sox
2067 .... Sept. 29, 1976 .... Jorge Orta .... White Sox
2068 .... Sept. 29, 1976 .... Chet Lemon ...... White Sox
2069 .... Sept. 29, 1976 .... Bucky Dent .... White Sox
2070 .... Sept. 29, 1976 .... Alan Bannister .... White Sox
2071 .... Sept. 29, 1976 .... Jerry Hairston ..... White Sox
2072 .... October 3, 1976 .. Dennis Walling .... A's
2073 .... October 3, 1976 .. Wayne Gross .... A's
2074 .... October 3, 1976 .. Jim Holt .... A's
2075 .... October 3, 1976 .. Matt Alexander .... A's
2076 .... October 3, 1976 .. Jeff Newman .... A's
2077 .... October 3, 1976 .. Ron Fairly .... A's
2078 .... October 3, 1976 .. Ken McMullen .... A's
2079 .... October 3, 1976 .. Matt Alexander .... A's
2080 .... October 3, 1976 .. Jeff Newman .... A's
2081 .... October 3, 1976 .. Tommy Sandt .... A's
2082 .... October 3, 1976 .. Dennis Walling .... A's
2083 .... October 3, 1976 .. Jim Holt .... A's
2084 .... October 3, 1976 .. Bill North .... A's
2085 .... October 3, 1976 .. Phil Garner .... A's
2086 .... April 7, 1977 ...... Dave Collins .... Mariners
2087 .... April 7, 1977 ...... Lee Stanton .... Mariners
2088 .... April 7, 1977 ...... Craig Reynolds ..... Mariners
2089 .... April 7, 1977 ...... Dave Collins .... Mariners
2090 .... April 7, 1977 ...... Bill Stein .... Mariners
2091 .... April 7, 1977 ...... Lee Stanton .... Mariners
2092 .... April 11, 1977 ..... Rodney Scott .... A's
2093 .... April 11, 1977 ..... Tony Armas .... A's
2094 .... April 11, 1977 ..... Rodney Scott .... A's
2095 .... April 11, 1977 ..... Mitchell Page .... A's
2096 .... April 11, 1977 ..... Wayne Gross .... A's
2097 .... April 11, 1977 ..... Tony Armas .... A's
2098 .... April 11, 1977 ..... Rob Picciolo .... A's
2099 .... April 11, 1977 ..... Bill North .... A's
2100 .... April 11, 1977 ..... Rich McKinney .... A's
2101 .... April 11, 1977 ..... Jeff Newman .... A's
2102 .... April 11, 1977 ..... Wayne Gross .... A's
2103 .... April 15, 1977 ..... Dave Collins .... Mariners
2104 .... April 15, 1977 ..... Bob Stinson .... Mariners
2105 .... April 15, 1977 ..... Ruppert Jones ...... Mariners
2106 .... April 15, 1977 ..... Dan Meyer .... Mariners
2107 .... April 15, 1977 ..... Carlos Lopez .... Mariners
2108 .... April 15, 1977 ..... Carlos Lopez .... Mariners
2109 .... April 15, 1977 ..... Ruppert Jones ...... Mariners
2110 .... April 15, 1977 ..... Bill Stein .... Mariners
2111 .... April 20, 1977 ..... Alan Bannister .... White Sox
2112 .... April 20, 1977 ..... Tim Nordbrook .... White Sox

2113 .... April 20, 1977 ..... Richie Zisk .... White Sox
2114 .... April 20, 1977 ..... Oscar Gamble .... White Sox
2115 .... April 20, 1977 ..... Chet Lemon ...... White Sox
2116 .... April 20, 1977 ..... Chet Lemon ...... White Sox
2117 .... April 25, 1977 ..... Dick Allen .... A's
2118 .... April 25, 1977 ..... Rob Picciolo .... A's
2119 .... April 25, 1977 ..... Rodney Scott .... A's
2120 .... April 25, 1977 ..... Mitchell Page .... A's
2121 .... April 30, 1977 ..... Mark Belanger .... Orioles
2122 .... April 30, 1977 ..... Ken Singleton .... Orioles
2123 .... April 30, 1977 ..... Larry Harlow .... Orioles
2124 .... April 30, 1977 ..... Ken Singleton .... Orioles
2125 .... April 30, 1977 ..... Lee May .... Orioles
2126 .... April 30, 1977 ..... Eddie Murray .... Orioles
2127 .... April 30, 1977 ..... Larry Harlow .... Orioles
2128 .... April 30, 1977 ..... Rick Dempsey .... Orioles
2129 .... April 30, 1977 ..... Al Bumbry .... Orioles
2130 .... April 30, 1977 ..... Mark Belanger .... Orioles
2131 .... April 30, 1977 ..... Al Bumbry .... Orioles
2132 .... April 30, 1977 ..... Ken Singleton .... Orioles
2133 .... April 30, 1977 ..... Larry Harlow .... Orioles
2134 .... May 6, 1977 .... Bernie Carbo .... Red Sox
2135 .... May 6, 1977 .... Denny Doyle .... Red Sox
2136 .... May 6, 1977 .... George Scott .... Red Sox
2137 .... May 6, 1977 .... Dwight Evans .... Red Sox
2138 .... May 6, 1977 .... Butch Hobson .... Red Sox
2139 .... May 6, 1977 .... Steve Dillard .... Red Sox
2140 .... May 6, 1977 .... Bernie Carbo .... Red Sox
2141 .... May 6, 1977 .... Jim Rice .... Red Sox
2142 .... May 6, 1977 .... Denny Doyle .... Red Sox
2143 .... May 6, 1977 .... Butch Hobson .... Red Sox
2144 .... May 6, 1977 .... Bernie Carbo .... Red Sox
2145 .... May 6, 1977 .... Denny Doyle .... Red Sox
2146 .... May 6, 1977 .... Carlton Fisk .... Red Sox
2147 .... May 6, 1977 .... Dwight Evans .... Red Sox
2148 .... May 6, 1977 .... Jim Rice .... Red Sox
2149 .... May 10, 1977 ...... Tom Poquette .... Royals
2150 .... May 10, 1977 ...... Amos Otis .... Royals
2151 .... May 10, 1977 ...... Fred Patek .... Royals
2152 .... May 10, 1977 ...... Darrell Porter .... Royals
2153 .... May 10, 1977 ...... Amos Otis .... Royals
2154 .... May 10, 1977 ...... Pete Lacock .... Royals
2155 .... May 14, 1977 ...... Reggie Jackson .... Yankees
2156 .... May 14, 1977 ...... Chris Chambliss ... Yankees
2157 .... May 14, 1977 ...... Roy White .... Yankees
2158 .... May 14, 1977 ...... Graig Nettles .... Yankees
2159 .... May 14, 1977 ...... Carlos May .... Yankees
2160 .... May 14, 1977 ...... Bucky Dent .... Yankees
2161 .... May 14, 1977 ...... Reggie Jackson .... Yankees
2162 .... May 14, 1977 ...... Bucky Dent .... Yankees
2163 .... May 19, 1977 ..... Dan Ford .... Twins
2164 .... May 19, 1977 ..... Butch Wynegar .... Twins
2165 .... May 19, 1977 ...... Rod Carew .... Twins
2166 .... May 19, 1977 ...... Roy Smalley .... Twins
2167 .... May 19, 1977 ...... Rod Carew .... Twins
2168 .... May 19, 1977 ...... Lyman Bostock .... Twins

2169 .... May 19, 1977 ...... Rich Chiles .... Twins	2225 .... June 8, 1977 .... Roy Howell .... Blue Jays
2170 .... May 19, 1977 ...... Dan Ford .... Twins	2226 .... June 8, 1977 ...... Otto Velez .... Blue Jays
2171 .... May 19, 1977 ...... Roy Smalley .... Twins	2227 .... June 8, 1977 .... Dave McKay .... Blue Jays
2172 .... May 19, 1977 ...... Lyman Bostock .... Twins	2228 .... June 8, 1977 .... Ernie Whitt .... Blue Jays
2173 .... May 19, 1977 ...... Larry Hisle .... Twins	2229 .... June 12, 1977 ..... Bruce Bochte .... Indians
2174 .... May 19, 1977 ...... Butch Wynegar .... Twins	2230 .... June 12, 1977 ..... Buddy Bell .... Indians
2175 .... May 24, 1977 ...... Tito Fuentes .... Tigers	2231 .... June 12, 1977 ..... John Lowenstein ..... Indians
2176 .... May 24, 1977 ...... Rusty Staub .... Tigers	2232 .... June 12, 1977 ..... Bruce Bochte .... Indians
2177 .... May 24, 1977 ...... Steve Kemp .... Tigers	2233 .... June 12, 1977 ..... Frank Duffy .... Indians
2178 .... May 24, 1977 ...... Mickey Stanley .... Tigers	2234 .... June 12, 1977 ..... Duane Kuiper .... Indians
2179 .... May 24, 1977 ...... Tito Fuentes .... Tigers	2235 .... June 12, 1977 ..... Paul Dade .... Indians
2180 .... May 24, 1977 ...... Steve Kemp .... Tigers	2236 .... June 12, 1977 ..... Buddy Bell .... Indians
2181 .... May 24, 1977 ...... Tom Veryzer .... Tigers	2237 .... June 12, 1977 ..... John Lowenstein ..... Indians
2182 .... May 24, 1977 ...... Rusty Staub .... Tigers	2238 .... June 12, 1977 ..... Bill Melton .... Indians
2183 .... May 24, 1977 ...... Steve Kemp .... Tigers	2239 .... June 16, 1977 ..... Roy Smalley .... Twins
2184 .... May 24, 1977 ...... Milt May .... Tigers	2240 .... June 16, 1977 ..... Lyman Bostock .... Twins
2185 .... May 24, 1977 ...... Mickey Stanley .... Tigers	2241 .... June 16, 1977 ..... Glenn Adams .... Twins
2186 .... May 24, 1977 ...... Ron LeFlore .... Tigers	2242 .... June 16, 1977 ..... Rich Chiles .... Twins
2187 .... May 29, 1977 ...... John Scott ...... Blue Jays	2243 .... June 16, 1977 ..... Butch Wynegar .... Twins
2188 .... May 29, 1977 ...... Alan Ashby .... Blue Jays	2244 .... June 16, 1977 ..... Rob Wilfong .... Twins
2189 .... May 29, 1977 ...... Sam Ewing .... Blue Jays	2245 .... June 16, 1977 ..... Glenn Adams .... Twins
2190 .... May 29, 1977 ...... Doug Ault .... Blue Jays	2246 .... June 16, 1977 ..... Roy Smalley .... Twins
2191 .... May 29, 1977 ...... Hector Torres ...... Blue Jays	2247 .... June 16, 1977 ..... Butch Wynegar .... Twins
2192 .... May 29, 1977 ...... Otto Velez .... Blue Jays	2248 .... June 16, 1977 ..... Rob Wilfong .... Twins
2193 .... May 29, 1977 ...... Sam Ewing .... Blue Jays	2249 .... June 16, 1977 ..... Rod Carew .... Twins
2194 .... May 29, 1977 ...... Doug Ault .... Blue Jays	2250 .... June 16, 1977 ..... Lyman Bostock .... Twins
2195 .... May 29, 1977 ...... Hector Torres ...... Blue Jays	2251 .... June 16, 1977 ..... Rich Chiles .... Twins
2196 .... May 29, 1977 ...... Otto Velez .... Blue Jays	2252 .... June 16, 1977 ..... Roy Smalley .... Twins
2197 .... May 29, 1977 ...... Doug Ault .... Blue Jays	2253 .... June 21, 1977 ..... Jorge Orta .... White Sox
2198 .... May 29, 1977 ...... Ernie Whitt .... Blue Jays	2254 .... June 21, 1977 ..... Royle Stillman .... White Sox
2199 .... June 4, 1977 ...... Ron LeFlore .... Tigers	2255 .... June 21, 1977 ..... Chet Lemon .... White Sox
2200 .... June 4, 1977 ...... Jason Thompson ...... Tigers	2256 .... June 21, 1977 ..... Oscar Gamble .... White Sox
2201 .... June 4, 1977 ...... Phil Mankowski .... Tigers	2257 .... June 21, 1977 ..... Ralph Garr .... White Sox
2202 .... June 4, 1977 ...... Tom Veryzer .... Tigers	2258 .... June 21, 1977 ..... Alan Bannister .... White Sox
2203 .... June 4, 1977 ...... Tito Fuentes .... Tigers	2259 .... June 21, 1977 ..... Jorge Orta .... White Sox
2204 .... June 4, 1977 ...... Tim Corcoran .... Tigers	2260 .... June 21, 1977 ..... Royle Stillman .... White Sox
2205 .... June 4, 1977 ...... Jason Thompson ...... Tigers	2261 .... June 21, 1977 ..... Chet Lemon .... White Sox
2206 .... June 4, 1977 ...... Ben Oglivie .... Tigers	2262 .... June 25, 1977 ..... Juan Beniquez ..... Rangers
2207 .... June 4, 1977 ...... Tim Corcoran .... Tigers	2263 .... June 25, 1977 ..... Ken Henderson ..... Rangers
2208 .... June 4, 1977 ...... Tom Veryzer .... Tigers	2264 .... June 25, 1977 ..... Bump Wills .... Rangers
2209 .... June 4, 1977 ...... Tito Fuentes .... Tigers	2265 .... June 25, 1977 ..... Jim Sundberg ...... Rangers
2210 .... June 8, 1977 ...... John Scott .... Blue Jays	2266 .... June 25, 1977 ..... Bert Campaneris ... Rangers
2211 .... June 8, 1977 ...... Otto Velez .... Blue Jays	2267 .... June 25, 1977 ..... C. Washington ..... Rangers
2212 .... June 8, 1977 ...... Ron Fairly .... Blue Jays	2268 .... June 25, 1977 ..... Ken Henderson ..... Rangers
2213 .... June 8, 1977 ...... Al Woods .... Blue Jays	2269 .... June 25, 1977 ..... Toby Harrah .... Rangers
2214 .... June 8, 1977 ...... Alan Ashby .... Blue Jays	2270 .... June 25, 1977 ..... Bump Wills .... Rangers
2215 .... June 8, 1977 ...... Dave McKay .... Blue Jays	2271 .... June 25, 1977 ..... Jim Sundberg .... Rangers
2216 .... June 8, 1977 ...... Bob Bailor .... Blue Jays	2272 .... June 25, 1977 ..... C. Washington ...... Rangers
2217 .... June 8, 1977 ...... Roy Howell .... Blue Jays	2273 .... June 25, 1977 ..... Ken Henderson ..... Rangers
2218 .... June 8, 1977 ...... Otto Velez .... Blue Jays	2274 .... June 29, 1977 ..... George Brett .... Royals
2219 .... June 8, 1977 ...... Ron Fairly .... Blue Jays	2275 .... June 29, 1977 ..... Darrell Porter .... Royals
2220 .... June 8, 1977 ...... Al Woods .... Blue Jays	2276 .... June 29, 1977 ..... Fred Patek .... Royals
2221 .... June 8, 1977 ...... Alan Ashby .... Blue Jays	2277 .... June 29, 1977 ..... Tom Poquette .... Royals
2222 .... June 8, 1977 ...... Dave McKay .... Blue Jays	2278 .... June 29, 1977 ..... Darrell Porter .... Royals
2223 .... June 8, 1977 ...... Otto Velez .... Blue Jays	2279 .... June 29, 1977 ..... Frank White .... Royals
2224 .... June 8, 1977 ...... Al Woods .... Blue Jays	2280 .... June 29, 1977 ..... Tom Poquette .... Royals

2281 .... June 29, 1977 ..... John Mayberry .... Royals
2282 .... June 29, 1977 ..... Dave Nelson .... Royals
2283 .... June 29, 1977 ..... Tom Poquette .... Royals
2284 .... June 29, 1977 ..... Hal McRae .... Royals
2285 .... June 29, 1977 ..... Darrell Porter .... Royals
2286 .... July 4, 1977 .... Matt Alexander .... A's
2287 .... July 4, 1977 .... Tony Armas .... A's
2288 .... July 4, 1977 .... Earl Williams .... A's
2289 .... July 4, 1977 .... Mike Jorgensen .... A's
2290 .... July 4, 1977 .... Willie Crawford .... A's
2291 .... July 4, 1977 .... Mitchell Page .... A's
2292 .... July 4, 1977 .... Earl Williams .... A's
2293 .... July 4, 1977 .... Mike Jorgensen .... A's
2294 .... July 4, 1977 .... Tony Armas .... A's
2295 .... July 4, 1977 .... Marty Perez .... A's
2296 .... July 4, 1977 .... Wayne Gross .... A's
2297 .... July 8, 1977 .... Mike Hargrove ...... Rangers
2298 .... July 8, 1977 .... Bump Wills .... Rangers
2299 .... July 8, 1977 .... Willie Horton .... Rangers
2300 .... July 12, 1977 ...... Roy Smalley .... Twins
2301 .... July 12, 1977 ...... Rod Carew .... Twins
2302 .... July 12, 1977 ...... Roy Smalley .... Twins
2303 .... July 12, 1977 ...... Rod Carew .... Twins
2304 .... July 12, 1977 ...... Roy Smalley .... Twins
2305 .... July 12, 1977 ...... Rob Wilfong .... Twins
2306 .... July 12, 1977 ...... Larry Hisle .... Twins
2307 .... July 12, 1977 .... Glenn Adams .... Twins
2308 .... July 16, 1977 ...... Dave Collins .... Mariners
2309 .... July 16, 1977 ...... Dan Meyer .... Mariners
2310 .... July 16, 1977 ...... Lee Stanton .... Mariners
2311 .... July 16, 1977 ...... Steve Braun .... Mariners
2312 .... July 16, 1977 ...... Julio Cruz .... Mariners
2313 .... July 16, 1977 ...... Dave Collins .... Mariners
2314 .... July 16, 1977 ...... Dan Meyer .... Mariners
2315 .... July 16, 1977 ...... Lee Stanton .... Mariners
2316 .... July 16, 1977 ...... Lee Stanton .... Mariners
2317 .... July 16, 1977 .... Bill Stein .... Mariners
2318 .... July 16, 1977 ...... Ruppert Jones ...... Mariners
2319 .... July 16, 1977 ...... Dan Meyer .... Mariners
2320 .... July 21, 1977 ...... Rod Carew .... Twins
2321 .... July 21, 1977 ...... Rob Wilfong .... Twins
2322 .... July 21, 1977 ...... Roy Smalley .... Twins
2323 .... July 21, 1977 ...... Rob Wilfong .... Twins
2324 .... July 25, 1977 ...... Julio Cruz .... Mariners
2325 .... July 25, 1977 ...... Dave Collins .... Mariners
2326 .... July 25, 1977 ...... Lee Stanton .... Mariners
2327 .... July 25, 1977 ...... Ruppert Jones ...... Mariners
2328 .... July 25, 1977 ...... Bill Stein .... Mariners
2329 .... July 25, 1977 ...... Lee Stanton .... Mariners
2330 .... July 25, 1977 ...... Craig Reynolds ..... Mariners
2331 .... July 25, 1977 ...... Lee Stanton .... Mariners
2332 .... July 25, 1977 ...... Ruppert Jones ...... Mariners
2333 .... July 25, 1977 ...... Dave Collins .... Mariners
2334 .... July 30, 1977 ...... Jim Rice .... Red Sox
2335 .... July 30, 1977 ...... George Scott .... Red Sox
2336 .... July 30, 1977 ...... Rick Burleson .... Red Sox
2337 .... July 30, 1977 ...... Fred Lynn .... Red Sox
2338 .... July 30, 1977 ...... Carlton Fisk .... Red Sox
2339 .... July 30, 1977 ...... Denny Doyle .... Red Sox
2340 .... August 3, 1977 ... Bucky Dent .... Yankees
2341 .... August 3, 1977 ... Roy White .... Yankees
2342 .... August 3, 1977 ... Chris Chambliss ... Yankees
2343 .... August 8, 1977 ... Joe Lahoud .... Royals
2344 .... August 8, 1977 ... Joe Lahoud .... Royals
2345 .... August 8, 1977 ... Tom Poquette .... Royals
2346 .... August 13, 1977 . Willie Randolph ...... Yankees
2347 .... August 13, 1977 . Reggie Jackson .... Yankees
2348 .... August 13, 1977 . Carlos May .... Yankees
2349 .... August 13, 1977 . George Zeber .... Yankees
2350 .... August 13, 1977 . Mickey Klutts .... Yankees
2351 .... August 13, 1977 . Roy White .... Yankees
2352 .... August 13, 1977 . Thurman Munson . Yankees
2353 .... August 13, 1977 . Reggie Jackson .... Yankees
2354 .... August 13, 1977 . Mickey Rivers .... Yankees
2355 .... August 13, 1977 . Thurman Munson . Yankees
2356 .... August 13, 1977 . Reggie Jackson .... Yankees
2357 .... August 19, 1977 . Doug Ault .... Blue Jays
2358 .... August 19, 1977 . Dave McKay .... Blue Jays
2359 .... August 19, 1977 . Ron Fairly .... Blue Jays
2360 .... August 19, 1977 . Doug Ault .... Blue Jays
2361 .... August 19, 1977 . Dave McKay .... Blue Jays
2362 .... August 19, 1977 . Ron Fairly .... Blue Jays
2363 .... August 19, 1977 . Sam Ewing .... Blue Jays
2364 .... August 19, 1977 . Al Woods .... Blue Jays
2365 .... August 19, 1977 . Doug Ault .... Blue Jays
2366 .... August 19, 1977 . Steve Staggs ..... Blue Jays
2367 .... August 19, 1977 . Roy Howell .... Blue Jays
2368 .... August 19, 1977 . Doug Ault .... Blue Jays
2369 .... August 19, 1977 . Sam Ewing .... Blue Jays
2370 .... August 24, 1977 . Paul Dade .... Indians
2371 .... August 24, 1977 . Duane Kuiper .... Indians
2372 .... August 24, 1977 . Bruce Bochte .... Indians
2373 .... August 24, 1977 . Larvell Blanks .... Indians
2374 .... August 24, 1977 . Andre Thornton .... Indians
2375 .... August 24, 1977 . Bruce Bochte .... Indians
2376 .... August 24, 1977 . Ray Fosse .... Indians
2377 .... August 24, 1977 . Paul Dade .... Indians
2378 .... August 24, 1977 . Larvell Blanks .... Indians
2379 .... August 24, 1977 . Ray Fosse .... Indians
2380 .... August 29, 1977 . Mark Belanger .... Orioles
2381 .... August 29, 1977 . Eddie Murray .... Orioles
2382 .... August 29, 1977 . Pat Kelly .... Orioles
2383 .... August 29, 1977 . Ken Singleton .... Orioles
2384 .... August 29, 1977 . Eddie Murray .... Orioles
2385 .... August 29, 1977 . Doug DeCinces .... Orioles
2386 .... August 29, 1977 . Billy Smith .... Orioles
2387 .... August 29, 1977 . Mark Belanger .... Orioles
2388 .... August 29, 1977 . Doug DeCinces .... Orioles
2389 .... August 29, 1977 . Billy Smith .... Orioles
2390 .... August 29, 1977 . Doug DeCinces .... Orioles
2391 .... Sept. 3, 1977 ...... Andre Thornton .... Indians
2392 .... Sept. 3, 1977 ...... Rico Carty .... Indians

2393	Sept. 3, 1977	Paul Dade	Indians
2394	Sept. 3, 1977	Bruce Bochte	Indians
2395	Sept. 3, 1977	Larvell Blanks	Indians
2396	Sept. 3, 1977	Jim Norris	Indians
2397	Sept. 3, 1977	Paul Dade	Indians
2398	Sept. 8, 1977	Oscar Gamble	White Sox
2399	Sept. 8, 1977	Jim Essian	White Sox
2400	Sept. 8, 1977	Jorge Orta	White Sox
2401	Sept. 8, 1977	Richie Zisk	White Sox
2402	Sept. 8, 1977	Alan Bannister	White Sox
2403	Sept. 12, 1977	C. Washington	Rangers
2404	Sept. 12, 1977	Toby Harrah	Rangers
2405	Sept. 12, 1977	Tom Grieve	Rangers
2406	Sept. 12, 1977	Mike Hargrove	Rangers
2407	Sept. 12, 1977	C. Washington	Rangers
2408	Sept. 12, 1977	Toby Harrah	Rangers
2409	Sept. 12, 1977	Willie Horton	Rangers
2410	Sept. 12, 1977	C. Washington	Rangers
2411	Sept. 12, 1977	Mike Hargrove	Rangers
2412	Sept. 19, 1977	C. Washington	Rangers
2413	Sept. 19, 1977	Dave May	Rangers
2414	Sept. 19, 1977	Ken Henderson	Rangers
2415	Sept. 19, 1977	Jim Sundberg	Rangers
2416	Sept. 19, 1977	Toby Harrah	Rangers
2417	Sept. 25, 1977	Clint Hurdle	Royals
2418	Sept. 25, 1977	Joe Lahoud	Royals
2419	Sept. 25, 1977	Darrell Porter	Royals
2420	Sept. 25, 1977	Bob Heise	Royals
2421	Sept. 25, 1977	Joe Lahoud	Royals
2422	Sept. 25, 1977	Pete Lacock	Royals
2423	Sept. 25, 1977	U.L. Washington	Royals
2424	Sept. 25, 1977	Willie Wilson	Royals
2425	Sept. 25, 1977	Dave Nelson	Royals
2426	Sept. 25, 1977	Clint Hurdle	Royals
2427	April 8, 1978	Miguel Dilone	A's
2428	April 8, 1978	Tony Armas	A's
2429	April 8, 1978	Dave Revering	A's
2430	April 8, 1978	Jim Essian	A's
2431	April 8, 1978	Wayne Gross	A's
2432	April 8, 1978	Miguel Dilone	A's
2433	April 8, 1978	Gary Thomasson	A's
2434	April 8, 1978	Tony Armas	A's
2435	April 8, 1978	Dave Revering	A's
2436	April 8, 1978	Wayne Gross	A's
2437	April 8, 1978	Steve Staggs	A's
2438	April 8, 1978	Bill North	A's
2439	April 8, 1978	Tony Armas	A's
2440	April 13, 1978	Willie Norwood	Twins
2441	April 13, 1978	Glenn Adams	Twins
2442	April 13, 1978	Butch Wynegar	Twins
2443	April 13, 1978	Dan Ford	Twins
2444	April 13, 1978	Bob Randall	Twins
2445	April 13, 1978	Glenn Adams	Twins
2446	April 13, 1978	Mike Cubbage	Twins
2447	April 13, 1978	Roy Smalley	Twins
2448	April 13, 1978	Glenn Adams	Twins
2449	April 13, 1978	Dan Ford	Twins
2450	April 13, 1978	Hosken Powell	Twins
2451	April 13, 1978	Bob Randall	Twins
2452	April 18, 1978	Bob Stinson	Mariners
2453	April 18, 1978	John Hale	Mariners
2454	April 18, 1978	John Hale	Mariners
2455	April 18, 1978	Julio Cruz	Mariners
2456	April 18, 1978	Bob Stinson	Mariners
2457	April 18, 1978	Ruppert Jones	Mariners
2458	April 18, 1978	Dan Meyer	Mariners
2459	April 18, 1978	Lee Stanton	Mariners
2460	April 24, 1978	Ruppert Jones	Mariners
2461	April 24, 1978	Dan Meyer	Mariners
2462	April 24, 1978	John Hale	Mariners
2463	April 24, 1978	Craig Reynolds	Mariners
2464	April 24, 1978	Julio Cruz	Mariners
2465	April 24, 1978	Bob Stinson	Mariners
2466	April 24, 1978	Ruppert Jones	Mariners
2467	April 24, 1978	Bill Stein	Mariners
2468	April 24, 1978	Craig Reynolds	Mariners
2469	April 24, 1978	Julio Cruz	Mariners
2470	April 24, 1978	John Hale	Mariners
2471	April 24, 1978	Bob Stinson	Mariners
2472	April 24, 1978	Lee Stanton	Mariners
2473	April 24, 1978	Bill Stein	Mariners
2474	April 24, 1978	Craig Reynolds	Mariners
2475	April 29, 1978	Roy Howell	Blue Jays
2476	April 29, 1978	Luis Gomez	Blue Jays
2477	April 29, 1978	Roy Howell	Blue Jays
2478	April 29, 1978	Rick Cerone	Blue Jays
2479	April 29, 1978	Garth Iorg	Blue Jays
2480	April 29, 1978	Luis Gomez	Blue Jays
2481	April 29, 1978	Bob Bailor	Blue Jays
2482	April 29, 1978	Tim Johnson	Blue Jays
2483	April 29, 1978	Sam Ewing	Blue Jays
2484	April 29, 1978	John Mayberry	Blue Jays
2485	April 29, 1978	Rick Cerone	Blue Jays
2486	May 5, 1978	Buddy Bell	Indians
2487	May 5, 1978	John Grubb	Indians
2488	May 5, 1978	Larvell Blanks	Indians
2489	May 5, 1978	Paul Dade	Indians
2490	May 5, 1978	Buddy Bell	Indians
2491	May 5, 1978	Andre Thornton	Indians
2492	May 5, 1978	Larvell Blanks	Indians
2493	May 5, 1978	Paul Dade	Indians
2494	May 5, 1978	Rick Manning	Indians
2495	May 5, 1978	John Grubb	Indians
2496	May 5, 1978	Larvell Blanks	Indians
2497	May 5, 1978	Ron Pruitt	Indians
2498	May 12, 1978	Willie Horton	Indians
2499	May 12, 1978	Ron Hassey	Indians
2500	May 12, 1978	Buddy Bell	Indians
2501	May 12, 1978	Andre Thornton	Indians
2502	May 12, 1978	Jim Norris	Indians
2503	May 17, 1978	Ron Blomberg	White Sox
2504	May 17, 1978	Bob Molinaro	White Sox

2505 .... May 17, 1978 ...... Ralph Garr .... White Sox	2561 .... July 19, 1978 ...... Gary Alexander .... Indians
2506 .... May 17, 1978 ...... Don Kessinger ... White Sox	2562 .... July 19, 1978 ...... Gary Alexander .... Indians
2507 .... May 17, 1978 ...... Chet Lemon .... White Sox	2563 .... July 19, 1978 ...... Jim Norris .... Indians
2508 .... May 17, 1978 ...... Ron Blomberg .... White Sox	2564 .... July 19, 1978 ...... Duane Kuiper .... Indians
2509 .... May 23, 1978 ...... Jorge Orta .... White Sox	2565 .... July 19, 1978 ...... Rick Manning .... Indians
2510 .... May 23, 1978 ...... Ron Blomberg .... White Sox	2566 .... July 19, 1978 ...... John Grubb .... Indians
2511 .... May 23, 1978 ...... Eric Soderholm .. White Sox	2567 .... July 19, 1978 ...... Andre Thornton ...... Indians
2512 .... May 23, 1978 ...... Bill Naharodny .. White Sox	2568 .... July 19, 1978 ...... Gary Alexander .... Indians
2513 .... May 23, 1978 ...... Eric Soderholm .. White Sox	2569 .... July 23, 1978 ...... Phil Mankowski .... Tigers
2514 .... May 23, 1978 ...... Eric Soderholm .. White Sox	2570 .... July 23, 1978 ...... Rusty Staub .... Tigers
2515 .... May 23, 1978 ...... Bill Naharodny .... White Sox	2571 .... July 23, 1978 ...... Lance Parrish .... Tigers
2516 .... May 28, 1978 ...... Cecil Cooper .... Brewers	2572 .... July 23, 1978 ...... Mark Wagner .... Tigers
2517 .... May 28, 1978 ...... Gorman Thomas ... Brewers	2573 .... July 23, 1978 ...... Phil Mankowski .... Tigers
2518 .... May 28, 1978 ...... Ben Oglivie .... Brewers	2574 .... July 23, 1978 ...... Steve Kemp .... Tigers
2519 .... May 28, 1978 ...... Gorman Thomas ... Brewers	2575 .... July 23, 1978 ...... Lance Parrish .... Tigers
2520 .... May 28, 1978 ...... Don Money .... Brewers	2576 .... July 23, 1978 ...... Tim Corcoran .... Tigers
2521 .... May 28, 1978 ...... Charlie Moore .... Brewers	2577 .... July 23, 1978 ...... Phil Mankowski .... Tigers
2522 .... May 28, 1978 ...... Cecil Cooper .... Brewers	2578 .... July 23, 1978 ...... Steve Kemp .... Tigers
2523 .... May 28, 1978 ...... Sixto Lezcano .... Brewers	2579 .... July 23, 1978 ...... Lance Parrish .... Tigers
2524 .... June 2, 1978 ...... Jerry Remy .... Red Sox	2580 .... July 27, 1978 ...... Ben Oglivie .... Brewers
2525 .... June 2, 1978 ...... Jerry Remy .... Red Sox	2581 .... July 27, 1978 ...... Larry Hisle .... Brewers
2526 .... June 2, 1978 ...... Carlton Fisk .... Red Sox	2582 .... July 27, 1978 ...... Jim Gantner .... Brewers
2527 .... June 2, 1978 ...... Rick Burleson .... Red Sox	2583 .... August 1, 1978 ... Jeff Newman .... A's
2528 .... June 2, 1978 ...... Jim Rice .... Red Sox	2584 .... August 1, 1978 ... Joe Wallis .... A's
2529 .... June 6, 1978 ...... Larry Harlow .... Orioles	2585 .... August 1, 1978 ... Mitchell Page .... A's
2530 .... June 6, 1978 ...... Pat Kelly .... Orioles	2586 .... August 1, 1978 ... Mike Edwards .... A's
2531 .... June 6, 1978 ...... Billy Smith .... Orioles	2587 .... August 1, 1978 ... Dave Revering .... A's
2532 .... June 10, 1978 ..... Reggie Jackson .... Yankees	2588 .... August 1, 1978 ... Joe Wallis .... A's
2533 .... June 10, 1978 ..... Willie Randolph .... Yankees	2589 .... August 1, 1978 ... Willie Horton .... A's
2534 .... June 10, 1978 ..... Reggie Jackson .... Yankees	2590 .... August 1, 1978 ... Tony Armas .... A's
2535 .... June 10, 1978 ..... Graig Nettles .... Yankees	2591 .... August 6, 1978 ... Hosken Powell .... Twins
2536 .... June 10, 1978 ..... Mickey Rivers .... Yankees	2592 .... August 6, 1978 ... Roy Smalley .... Twins
2537 .... June 10, 1978 ..... Roy White .... Yankees	2593 .... August 6, 1978 ... Mike Cubbage .... Twins
2538 .... June 10, 1978 ..... Willie Randolph .... Yankees	2594 .... August 6, 1978 ... Mike Cubbage .... Twins
2539 .... June 10, 1978 ..... Mike Heath .... Yankees	2595 .... August 6, 1978 ... Glenn Adams .... Twins
2540 .... July 5, 1978 .... Clint Hurdle .... Royals	2596 .... August 6, 1978 ... Rich Chiles .... Twins
2541 .... July 9, 1978 .... John Hale .... Mariners	2597 .... August 6, 1978 ... Hosken Powell .... Twins
2542 .... July 9, 1978 .... Tom Paciorek .... Mariners	2598 .... August 6, 1978 ... Roy Smalley .... Twins
2543 .... July 9, 1978 .... Dan Meyer .... Mariners	2599 .... August 6, 1978 ... Dan Ford .... Twins
2544 .... July 9, 1978 .... Bill Stein .... Mariners	2600 .... August 6, 1978 ... Butch Wynegar .... Twins
2545 .... July 9, 1978 .... John Hale .... Mariners	2601 .... August 11, 1978 . Julio Cruz .... Mariners
2546 .... July 14, 1978 ...... Rick Bosetti .... Blue Jays	2602 .... August 11, 1978 . Ruppert Jones ..... Mariners
2547 .... July 14, 1978 ...... Roy Howell .... Blue Jays	2603 .... August 11, 1978 . John Hale .... Mariners
2548 .... July 14, 1978 ...... John Mayberry .... Blue Jays	2604 .... August 11, 1978 . Bob Stinson .... Mariners
2549 .... July 14, 1978 ...... Dave McKay .... Blue Jays	2605 .... August 11, 1978 . Leon Roberts .... Mariners
2550 .... July 14, 1978 ...... Rick Cerone .... Blue Jays	2606 .... August 11, 1978 . John Hale .... Mariners
2551 .... July 14, 1978 ...... Roy Howell .... Blue Jays	2607 .... August 11, 1978 . Bob Stinson .... Mariners
2552 .... July 14, 1978 ...... Rico Carty .... Blue Jays	2608 .... August 11, 1978 . Leon Roberts .... Mariners
2553 .... July 14, 1978 ...... John Mayberry .... Blue Jays	2609 .... August 11, 1978 . Bob Stinson .... Mariners
2554 .... July 14, 1978 ...... Dave McKay .... Blue Jays	2610 .... August 11, 1978 . Bob Robertson ..... Mariners
2555 .... July 14, 1978 ...... Rick Bosetti .... Blue Jays	2611 .... August 16, 1978 . Jerry Remy .... Red Sox
2556 .... July 14, 1978 ...... Dave McKay .... Blue Jays	2612 .... August 16, 1978 . Jim Rice .... Red Sox
2557 .... July 14, 1978 ...... Tommy Hutton .... Blue Jays	2613 .... August 16, 1978 . Fred Lynn .... Red Sox
2558 .... July 14, 1978 ...... Dave McKay .... Blue Jays	2614 .... August 16, 1978 . Garry Hancock ...... Red Sox
2559 .... July 19, 1978 ...... John Grubb .... Indians	2615 .... August 16, 1978 . Dwight Evans .... Red Sox
2560 .... July 19, 1978 ...... Andre Thornton .... Indians	2616 .... August 16, 1978 . Butch Hobson .... Red Sox

2617 .... August 16, 1978 . Rick Burleson .... Red Sox	2673 .... Sept. 24, 1978 .... Ralph Garr .... White Sox
2618 .... August 16, 1978 . Carlton Fisk .... Red Sox	2674 .... October 1, 1978 .. Eric Soderholm .. White Sox
2619 .... August 16, 1978 . Garry Hancock ...... Red Sox	2675 .... October 1, 1978 .. Greg Pryor .... White Sox
2620 .... August 16, 1978 . Dwight Evans .... Red Sox	2676 .... October 1, 1978 .. C.Washington .... White Sox
2621 .... August 16, 1978 . Butch Hobson .... Red Sox	2677 .... October 1, 1978 .. Eric Soderholm .. White Sox
2622 .... August 16, 1978 . Carlton Fisk .... Red Sox	2678 .... October 1, 1978 .. Marv Foley .... White Sox
2623 .... August 16, 1978 . Jim Rice .... Red Sox	2679 .... October 1, 1978 .. Harry Chappas ... White Sox
2624 .... August 20, 1978 . Billy Smith .... Orioles	2680 .... October 1, 1978 .. C. Washington ... White Sox
2625 .... August 20, 1978 . Pat Kelly .... Orioles	2681 .... October 1, 1978 .. Eric Soderholm .. White Sox
2626 .... August 20, 1978 . Ken Singleton .... Orioles	2682 .... October 1, 1978 .. Lamar Johnson .. White Sox
2627 .... August 20, 1978 . Eddie Murray .... Orioles	2683 .... October 1, 1978 .. C. Washington ... White Sox
2628 .... August 20, 1978 . Rick Dempsey .... Orioles	2684 .... October 1, 1978 .. Mike Squires ...... White Sox
2629 .... August 20, 1978 . Billy Smith .... Orioles	2685 .... October 1, 1978 .. Marv Foley .... White Sox
2630 .... August 20, 1978 . Pat Kelly .... Orioles	2686 .... October 1, 1978 .. Ron Blomberg .... White Sox
2631 .... August 20, 1978 . Rick Dempsey .... Orioles	2687 .... April 6, 1979 .... Willie Horton .... Mariners
2632 .... Sept. 6, 1978 ...... John Lowenstein ... Rangers	2688 .... April 11, 1979 .... Butch Wynegar .... Twins
2633 .... Sept. 6, 1978 ..... Bobby Bonds .... Rangers	2689 .... April 11, 1979 .... Rick Sofield .... Twins
2634 .... Sept. 6, 1978 ..... Bump Wills .... Rangers	2690 .... April 11, 1979 .... Willie Norwood .... Twins
2635 .... Sept. 6, 1978 ...... Juan Beniquez ...... Rangers	2691 .... April 11, 1979 .... Roy Smalley .... Twins
2636 .... Sept. 6, 1978 ..... Bump Wills .... Rangers	2692 .... April 11, 1979 .... Butch Wynegar .... Twins
2637 .... Sept. 6, 1978 ..... Richie Zisk .... Rangers	2693 .... April 11, 1979 .... Rob Wilfong .... Twins
2638 .... Sept. 6, 1978 ...... Jim Sundberg .... Rangers	2694 .... April 11, 1979 .... Ron Jackson .... Twins
2639 .... Sept. 6, 1978 ..... Mike Hargrove ..... Rangers	2695 .... April 11, 1979 .... Willie Norwood .... Twins
2640 .... Sept. 6, 1978 ..... Bobby Bonds .... Rangers	2696 .... April 11, 1979 .... Rob Wilfong .... Twins
2641 .... Sept. 10, 1978 ... Hal McRae .... Royals	2697 .... April 11, 1979 .... Rick Sofield .... Twins
2642 .... Sept. 10, 1978 ... Amos Otis .... Royals	2698 .... April 17, 1979 .... Mike Cubbage .... Twins
2643 .... Sept. 10, 1978 .... U.L. Washington ...... Royals	2699 .... April 17, 1979 .... Rob Wilfong .... Twins
2644 .... Sept. 10, 1978 .... Tom Poquette .... Royals	2700 .... April 17, 1979 .... Ken Landreaux .... Twins
2645 .... Sept. 10, 1978 .... Hal McRae .... Royals	2701 .... April 17, 1979 .... Rick Sofield .... Twins
2646 .... Sept. 10, 1978 .... Pete Lacock .... Royals	2702 .... April 17, 1979 .... Mike Cubbage .... Twins
2647 .... Sept. 10, 1978 .... Amos Otis .... Royals	2703 .... April 17, 1979 .... Ken Landreaux .... Twins
2648 .... Sept. 10, 1978 .... Hal McRae .... Royals	2704 .... April 17, 1979 .... Glenn Adams .... Twins
2649 .... Sept. 10, 1978 .... U.L. Washington ...... Royals	2705 .... April 17, 1979 .... Rick Sofield .... Twins
2650 .... Sept. 10, 1978 .... Tom Poquette .... Royals	2706 .... April 17, 1979 .... Roy Smalley .... Twins
2651 .... Sept. 10, 1978 .... Pete Lacock .... Royals	2707 .... April 17, 1979 .... Glenn Adams .... Twins
2652 .... Sept. 10, 1978 .... Willie Wilson .... Royals	2708 .... April 21, 1979 .... Larry Murray .... A's
2653 .... Sept. 15, 1978 .... Al Cowens .... Royals	2709 .... April 21, 1979 .... Mitchell Page .... A's
2654 .... Sept. 15, 1978 .... Fred Patek .... Royals	2710 .... April 21, 1979 .... Wayne Gross .... A's
2655 .... Sept. 15, 1978 .... Pete Lacock .... Royals	2711 .... April 21, 1979 .... Mickey Klutts .... A's
2656 .... Sept. 15, 1978 .... Al Cowens .... Royals	2712 .... April 21, 1979 .... Jim Essian .... A's
2657 .... Sept. 15, 1978 .... Steve Braun .... Royals	2713 .... April 21, 1979 .... Larry Murray .... A's
2658 .... Sept. 19, 1978 .... Mike Cubbage .... Twins	2714 .... April 21, 1979 .... Dave Revering .... A's
2659 .... Sept. 19, 1978 .... Rod Carew .... Twins	2715 .... April 21, 1979 .... Mickey Klutts .... A's
2660 .... Sept. 19, 1978 .... Glenn Adams .... Twins	2716 .... April 21, 1979 .... Mike Edwards .... A's
2661 .... Sept. 19, 1978 .... Dan Ford .... Twins	2717 .... April 21, 1979 .... Larry Murray .... A's
2662 .... Sept. 19, 1978 .... Rich Chiles .... Twins	2718 .... April 21, 1979 .... Jim Essian .... A's
2663 .... Sept. 19, 1978 .... Butch Wynegar .... Twins	2719 .... April 21, 1979 .... Larry Murray .... A's
2664 .... Sept. 19, 1978 .... Roy Smalley .... Twins	2720 .... April 26, 1979 .... Eddie Murray .... Orioles
2665 .... Sept. 19, 1978 .... Rob Wilfong .... Twins	2721 .... April 26, 1979 .... John Lowenstein ..... Orioles
2666 .... Sept. 19, 1978 .... Dan Ford .... Twins	2722 .... May 2, 1979 .... Juan Beniquez ... Yankees
2667 .... Sept. 19, 1978 .... Dan Ford .... Twins	2723 .... May 2, 1979 .... Thurman Munson . Yankees
2668 .... Sept. 24, 1978 .... Chet Lemon .... White Sox	2724 .... May 2, 1979 .... Reggie Jackson .... Yankees
2669 .... Sept. 24, 1978 .... Lamar Johnson .. White Sox	2725 .... May 2, 1979 .... Lou Piniella .... Yankees
2670 .... Sept. 24, 1978 .... Eric Soderholm .. White Sox	2726 .... May 2, 1979 .... Juan Beniquez ...... Yankees
2671 .... Sept. 24, 1978 .... Mike Squires ...... White Sox	2727 .... May 2, 1979 .... Reggie Jackson .... Yankees
2672 .... Sept. 24, 1978 .... Harry Chappas ... White Sox	2728 .... May 2, 1979 .... Graig Nettles .... Yankees

2729 .... May 7, 1979 .... Dwight Evans .... Red Sox	2785 .... June 14, 1979 ..... Danny Ainge .... Blue Jays
2730 .... May 15, 1979 ...... Cecil Cooper .... Brewers	2786 .... June 18, 1979 ..... John Grubb .... Rangers
2731 .... May 15, 1979 ...... Gorman Thomas ... Brewers	2787 .... June 18, 1979 ..... Oscar Gamble .... Rangers
2732 .... May 15, 1979 ...... Ben Oglivie .... Brewers	2788 .... June 18, 1979 ..... Bump Wills .... Rangers
2733 .... May 15, 1979 ...... Gorman Thomas ... Brewers	2789 .... June 18, 1979 ..... Pat Putnam .... Rangers
2734 .... May 15, 1979 ...... Dick Davis .... Brewers	2790 .... June 18, 1979 ..... Nelson Norman ..... Rangers
2735 .... May 15, 1979 ...... Gorman Thomas ... Brewers	2791 .... June 18, 1979 ..... Bump Wills .... Rangers
2736 .... May 15, 1979 ...... Ben Oglivie .... Brewers	2792 .... June 18, 1979 ..... John Grubb .... Rangers
2737 .... May 20, 1979 ...... Ralph Garr .... White Sox	2793 .... June 18, 1979 ..... Eric Soderholm ..... Rangers
2738 .... May 20, 1979 ...... Jorge Orta .... White Sox	2794 .... June 18, 1979 ..... Bump Wills .... Rangers
2739 .... May 20, 1979 ...... Marv Foley .... White Sox	2795 .... June 18, 1979 ..... John Grubb .... Rangers
2740 .... May 20, 1979 ...... C. Washington ... White Sox	2796 .... June 22, 1979 ..... Al Cowens .... Royals
2741 .... May 20, 1979 ...... Chet Lemon ...... White Sox	2797 .... June 22, 1979 ..... Darrell Porter .... Royals
2742 .... May 20, 1979 ...... Eric Soderholm .. White Sox	2798 .... June 22, 1979 ..... George Scott .... Royals
2743 .... May 20, 1979 ...... Greg Pryor .... White Sox	2799 .... June 22, 1979 ..... Pete Lacock .... Royals
2744 .... May 20, 1979 ...... C. Washington ... White Sox	2800 .... June 22, 1979 ..... Al Cowens .... Royals
2745 .... May 20, 1979 ...... Chet Lemon ...... White Sox	2801 .... June 22, 1979 ..... Darrell Porter .... Royals
2746 .... May 20, 1979 ...... Eric Soderholm .. White Sox	2802 .... June 22, 1979 ..... George Scott .... Royals
2747 .... May 20, 1979 ...... Joe Gates .... White Sox	2803 .... June 22, 1979 ..... Willie Wilson .... Royals
2748 .... May 25, 1979 ...... Chet Lemon ...... White Sox	2804 .... June 22, 1979 ..... George Scott .... Royals
2749 .... May 25, 1979 ...... C. Washington ... White Sox	2805 .... June 27, 1979 ..... Pat Putnam .... Rangers
2750 .... May 25, 1979 ...... Chet Lemon .... White Sox	2806 .... June 27, 1979 ..... Bump Wills .... Rangers
2751 .... May 25, 1979 ...... Bill Nahorodny ... White Sox	2807 .... June 27, 1979 ..... John Grubb .... Rangers
2752 .... May 25, 1979 ...... C. Washington ... White Sox	2808 .... June 27, 1979 ..... Dave Roberts .... Rangers
2753 .... May 30, 1979 ...... Julio Cruz .... Mariners	2809 .... June 27, 1979 ..... Bump Wills .... Rangers
2754 .... May 30, 1979 ...... Willie Horton .... Mariners	2810 .... June 27, 1979 ..... Dave Roberts .... Rangers
2755 .... May 30, 1979 ...... Dan Meyer .... Mariners	2811 .... July 1, 1979 .... Steve Braun .... Royals
2756 .... May 30, 1979 ...... Tom Paciorek ...... Mariners	2812 .... July 1, 1979 .... Pete Lacock .... Royals
2757 .... May 30, 1979 ...... Mario Mendoza ..... Mariners	2813 .... July 1, 1979 .... Frank White .... Royals
2758 .... May 30, 1979 ...... Willie Horton .... Mariners	2814 .... July 1, 1979 .... Fred Patek .... Royals
2759 .... May 30, 1979 ...... Leon Roberts .... Mariners	2815 .... July 1, 1979 .... Darrell Porter .... Royals
2760 .... May 30, 1979 ...... Larry Milbourne .... Mariners	2816 .... July 1, 1979 .... Al Cowens .... Royals
2761 .... May 30, 1979 ...... Julio Cruz .... Mariners	2817 .... July 1, 1979 .... Frank White .... Royals
2762 .... May 30, 1979 ...... Bruce Bochte .... Mariners	2818 .... July 1, 1979 .... Willie Wilson .... Royals
2763 .... May 30, 1979 ...... Larry Cox .... Mariners	2819 .... July 1, 1979 .... Frank White .... Royals
2764 .... May 30, 1979 ...... Willie Horton .... Mariners	2820 .... July 1, 1979 .... Pete Lacock .... Royals
2765 .... June 9, 1979 .... Ron LeFlore .... Tigers	2821 .... July 5, 1979 .... Jeff Newman .... A's
2766 .... June 9, 1979 .... Lou Whitaker .... Tigers	2822 .... July 5, 1979 .... Rickey Henderson .... A's
2767 .... June 9, 1979 .... Alan Trammell .... Tigers	2823 .... July 5, 1979 .... Tony Armas .... A's
2768 .... June 9, 1979 .... Ron LeFlore .... Tigers	2824 .... July 5, 1979 .... Tony Armas .... A's
2769 .... June 9, 1979 .... Lou Whitaker .... Tigers	2825 .... July 5, 1979 .... Larry Murray .... A's
2770 .... June 9, 1979 .... Lance Parrish .... Tigers	2826 .... July 9, 1979 .... Jim Rice .... Red Sox
2771 .... June 9, 1979 .... Alan Trammell .... Tigers	2827 .... July 9, 1979 .... Bob Watson .... Red Sox
2772 .... June 9, 1979 .... Ron LeFlore .... Tigers	2828 .... July 9, 1979 .... Butch Hobson ...... Red Sox
2773 .... June 9, 1979 .... Steve Kemp .... Tigers	2829 .... July 9, 1979 .... Bob Montgomery .. Red Sox
2774 .... June 9, 1979 .... Jason Thompson ...... Tigers	2830 .... July 9, 1979 .... Rick Burleson .... Red Sox
2775 .... June 9, 1979 .... Champ Summers ..... Tigers	2831 .... July 9, 1979 .... Jim Rice .... Red Sox
2776 .... June 9, 1979 .... Alan Trammell .... Tigers	2832 .... July 9, 1979 .... Carl Yastrzemski .. Red Sox
2777 .... June 9, 1979 .... Lou Whitaker .... Tigers	2833 .... July 9, 1979 .... Bob Watson .... Red Sox
2778 .... June 9, 1979 .... Steve Kemp .... Tigers	2834 .... July 9, 1979 .... Butch Hobson ...... Red Sox
2779 .... June 9, 1979 .... Rusty Staub .... Tigers	2835 .... July 9, 1979 .... Bob Montgomery .. Red Sox
2780 .... June 9, 1979 .... Jason Thompson ...... Tigers	2836 .... July 9, 1979 .... Jim Rice .... Red Sox
2781 .... June 14, 1979 ..... Danny Ainge .... Blue Jays	2837 .... July 9, 1979 .... Bob Watson .... Red Sox
2782 .... June 14, 1979 ..... Al Woods .... Blue Jays	2838 .... July 13, 1979 ...... Graig Nettles .... Yankees
2783 .... June 14, 1979 ..... Alfredo Griffin ...... Blue Jays	2839 .... July 13, 1979 ...... Lou Piniella .... Yankees
2784 .... June 14, 1979 ..... Bob Davis .... Blue Jays	2840 .... July 13, 1979 ...... Bucky Dent .... Yankees

2841	July 13, 1979	Bobby Murcer	Yankees
2842	July 13, 1979	Thurman Munson	Yankees
2843	July 13, 1979	Graig Nettles	Yankees
2844	July 13, 1979	Lou Piniella	Yankees
2845	July 13, 1979	Willie Randolph	Yankees
2846	July 13, 1979	Chris Chambliss	Yankees
2847	July 21, 1979	Mark Belanger	Orioles
2848	July 21, 1979	Pat Kelly	Orioles
2849	July 21, 1979	Ken Singleton	Orioles
2850	July 21, 1979	Ken Singleton	Orioles
2851	July 21, 1979	Doug DeCinces	Orioles
2852	July 21, 1979	Mark Belanger	Orioles
2853	July 25, 1979	Mickey Rivers	Yankees
2854	July 25, 1979	Willie Randolph	Yankees
2855	August 13, 1979	Lance Parrish	Tigers
2856	August 13, 1979	Steve Kemp	Tigers
2857	August 18, 1979	Joe Cannon	Blue Jays
2858	August 18, 1979	John Mayberry	Blue Jays
2859	August 18, 1979	Danny Ainge	Blue Jays
2860	August 18, 1979	Joe Cannon	Blue Jays
2861	August 18, 1979	Roy Howell	Blue Jays
2862	August 18, 1979	Danny Ainge	Blue Jays
2863	August 18, 1979	Alfredo Griffin	Blue Jays
2864	August 22, 1979	Ron Hassey	Indians
2865	August 26, 1979	Tony Solaita	Blue Jays
2866	August 30, 1979	Bobby Bonds	Indians
2867	August 30, 1979	Bobby Bonds	Indians
2868	August 30, 1979	Jim Norris	Indians
2869	August 30, 1979	Bobby Bonds	Indians
2870	August 30, 1979	Ron Hassey	Indians
2871	Sept. 3, 1979	Thad Bosley	White Sox
2872	Sept. 3, 1979	Chet Lemon	White Sox
2873	Sept. 3, 1979	Chet Lemon	White Sox
2874	Sept. 7, 1979	Gorman Thomas	Brewers
2875	Sept. 7, 1979	Ben Oglivie	Brewers
2876	Sept. 7, 1979	Ben Oglivie	Brewers
2877	Sept. 7, 1979	Charlie Moore	Brewers
2878	Sept. 7, 1979	Paul Molitor	Brewers
2879	Sept. 15, 1979	Don Money	Brewers
2880	Sept. 15, 1979	Gorman Thomas	Brewers
2881	Sept. 15, 1979	Sixto Lezcano	Brewers
2882	Sept. 15, 1979	Jim Gantner	Brewers
2883	Sept. 15, 1979	Paul Molitor	Brewers
2884	Sept. 15, 1979	Ben Oglivie	Brewers
2885	Sept. 15, 1979	Charlie Moore	Brewers
2886	Sept. 15, 1979	Paul Molitor	Brewers
2887	Sept. 15, 1979	Jim Gantner	Brewers
2888	Sept. 15, 1979	Cecil Cooper	Brewers
2889	Sept. 19, 1979	U.L. Washington	Royals
2890	Sept. 19, 1979	George Brett	Royals
2891	Sept. 19, 1979	Amos Otis	Royals
2892	Sept. 19, 1979	U.L. Washington	Royals
2893	Sept. 19, 1979	Frank White	Royals
2894	Sept. 19, 1979	U.L. Washington	Royals
2895	Sept. 19, 1979	Amos Otis	Royals
2896	Sept. 19, 1979	U.L. Washington	Royals
2897	Sept. 19, 1979	Willie Wilson	Royals
2898	Sept. 24, 1979	Hal McRae	Royals
2899	Sept. 24, 1979	Darrell Porter	Royals
2900	Sept. 24, 1979	Hal McRae	Royals
2901	Sept. 24, 1979	Amos Otis	Royals
2902	Sept. 24, 1979	Al Cowens	Royals
2903	Sept. 24, 1979	Frank White	Royals
2904	Sept. 24, 1979	Willie Wilson	Royals
2905	Sept. 24, 1979	Al Cowens	Royals
2906	Sept. 28, 1979	Mickey Rivers	Rangers
2907	Sept. 28, 1979	Al Oliver	Rangers
2908	Sept. 28, 1979	Richie Zisk	Rangers
2909	Sept. 28, 1979	Bump Wills	Rangers
2910	April 12, 1980	Ron Cey	Dodgers
2911	April 12, 1980	Davey Lopes	Dodgers
2912	April 12, 1980	Reggie Smith	Dodgers
2913	April 17, 1980	Bill Russell	Dodgers
2914	April 17, 1980	Don Sutton	Dodgers
2915	April 17, 1980	Dusty Baker	Dodgers
2916	April 17, 1980	Derrel Thomas	Dodgers
2917	April 17, 1980	Reggie Smith	Dodgers
2918	April 22, 1980	Ken Griffey	Reds
2919	April 22, 1980	Dan Driessen	Reds
2920	April 22, 1980	Junior Kennedy	Reds
2921	April 22, 1980	Cesar Geronimo	Reds
2922	April 22, 1980	Junior Kennedy	Reds
2923	April 22, 1980	Cesar Geronimo	Reds
2924	April 22, 1980	Hector Cruz	Reds
2925	April 27, 1980	Mike Jorgensen	Mets
2926	April 27, 1980	Jose Cardenal	Mets
2927	April 27, 1980	Frank Taveras	Mets
2928	April 27, 1980	Ron Hodges	Mets
2929	April 27, 1980	Ray Burris	Mets
2930	May 2, 1980	George Hendrick	Cardinals
2931	May 2, 1980	Tony Scott	Cardinals
2932	May 2, 1980	Tony Scott	Cardinals
2933	May 2, 1980	Bob Forsch	Cardinals
2934	May 2, 1980	Ken Oberkfell	Cardinals
2935	May 2, 1980	Jim Kaat	Cardinals
2936	May 7, 1980	Scott Sanderson	Expos
2937	May 7, 1980	Ron LeFlore	Expos
2938	May 7, 1980	Ken Macha	Expos
2939	May 7, 1980	Tony Bernazard	Expos
2940	May 7, 1980	Scott Sanderson	Expos
2941	May 13, 1980	Warren Cromartie	Expos
2942	May 13, 1980	Tony Bernazard	Expos
2943	May 13, 1980	Gary Carter	Expos
2944	May 13, 1980	Tony Bernazard	Expos
2945	May 13, 1980	Larry Parrish	Expos
2946	May 13, 1980	Tony Bernazard	Expos
2947	May 13, 1980	Ron LeFlore	Expos
2948	May 13, 1980	Rodney Scott	Expos
2949	May 13, 1980	Andre Dawson	Expos
2950	May 18, 1980	Bake McBride	Phillies
2951	May 18, 1980	Greg Luzinski	Phillies
2952	May 18, 1980	Garry Maddox	Phillies

2953 .... May 18, 1980 ...... Randy Lerch .... Phillies
2954 .... May 18, 1980 ...... Bake McBride .... Phillies
2955 .... May 18, 1980 ...... Greg Luzinski .... Phillies
2956 .... May 18, 1980 ...... Mike Schmidt .... Phillies
2957 .... May 18, 1980 ...... Bake McBride .... Phillies
2958 .... May 18, 1980 ...... Mike Schmidt .... Phillies
2959 .... May 18, 1980 ...... Greg Luzinski .... Phillies
2960 .... May 23, 1980 ...... Steve Carlton .... Phillies
2961 .... May 28, 1980 ...... Willie Montanez ...... Padres
2962 .... May 28, 1980 ...... Ozzie Smith .... Padres
2963 .... May 28, 1980 ...... Gene Tenace .... Padres
2964 .... May 28, 1980 ...... Rick Wise .... Padres
2965 .... May 28, 1980 ...... Gene Tenace .... Padres
2966 .... May 28, 1980 ...... Von Joshua .... Padres
2967 .... May 28, 1980 ...... Dave Winfield .... Padres
2968 .... June 2, 1980 .... Willie Montanez ...... Padres
2969 .... June 2, 1980 .... Barry Evans .... Padres
2970 .... June 2, 1980 .... Rick Wise .... Padres
2971 .... June 2, 1980 .... Eric Rasmussen ...... Padres
2972 .... June 8, 1980 .... Bill North .... Giants
2973 .... June 8, 1980 .... Terry Whitfield .... Giants
2974 .... June 8, 1980 .... Rennie Stennett .... Giants
2975 .... June 8, 1980 .... Vida Blue .... Giants
2976 .... June 8, 1980 .... Bill North .... Giants
2977 .... June 8, 1980 .... Terry Whitfield .... Giants
2978 .... June 8, 1980 .... Johnnie LeMaster .... Giants
2979 .... June 8, 1980 .... Bill North .... Giants
2980 .... June 8, 1980 .... Rich Murray .... Giants
2981 .... June 8, 1980 .... Bill North .... Giants
2982 .... June 14, 1980 ..... Mike Easler .... Pirates
2983 .... June 14, 1980 ..... Ed Ott .... Pirates
2984 .... June 14, 1980 ..... Omar Moreno .... Pirates
2985 .... June 19, 1980 ..... Ted Simmons ...... Cardinals
2986 .... June 19, 1980 ..... George Hendrick . Cardinals
2987 .... June 19, 1980 ..... Leon Durhan .... Cardinals
2988 .... June 19, 1980 ..... Tommy Herr .... Cardinals
2989 .... June 19, 1980 ..... Bob Sykes .... Cardinals
2990 .... June 19, 1980 ..... Bob Sykes .... Cardinals
2991 .... June 19, 1980 ..... Terry Kennedy ..... Cardinals
2992 .... June 24, 1980 ..... Rudy Law .... Dodgers
2993 .... June 24, 1980 ..... Ron Cey .... Dodgers
2994 .... June 24, 1980 ..... Ron Cey .... Dodgers
2995 .... June 24, 1980 ..... Davey Lopes .... Dodgers
2996 .... June 24, 1980 ..... Steve Howe .... Dodgers
2997 .... June 29, 1980 ..... Dave Concepcion ...... Reds
2998 .... July 4, 1980 .... Ken Griffey .... Reds
2999 .... July 4, 1980 .... Dan Driessen .... Reds
3000 .... July 4, 1980 .... Cesar Geronimo .... Reds
3001 .... July 4, 1980 .... Dave Concepcion ...... Reds
3002 .... July 4, 1980 .... Dave Collins .... Reds
3003 .... July 4, 1980 .... Ray Knight .... Reds
3004 .... July 10, 1980 ...... Rudy Law .... Dodgers
3005 .... July 10, 1980 ...... Steve Yeager .... Dodgers
3006 .... July 10, 1980 ...... Rudy Law .... Dodgers
3007 .... July 10, 1980 ...... Reggie Smith .... Dodgers
3008 .... July 10, 1980 ...... Steve Yeager .... Dodgers

3009 .... July 10, 1980 ...... Reggie Smith .... Dodgers
3010 .... July 10, 1980 ...... Dusty Baker .... Dodgers
3011 .... July 15, 1980 ...... Del Unser .... Phillies
3012 .... July 15, 1980 ...... Bob Boone .... Phillies
3013 .... July 20, 1980 ...... Rodney Scott .... Expos
3014 .... July 20, 1980 ...... Andre Dawson .... Expos
3015 .... July 20, 1980 ...... Ellis Valentine .... Expos
3016 .... July 20, 1980 ...... Larry Parrish .... Expos
3017 .... July 20, 1980 ...... Ron LeFlore .... Expos
3018 .... July 20, 1980 ...... Ellis Valentine .... Expos
3019 .... July 20, 1980 ...... Steve Rogers .... Expos
3020 .... July 20, 1980 ...... Rodney Scott .... Expos
3021 .... July 20, 1980 ...... Ellis Valentine .... Expos
3022 .... July 20, 1980 ...... Warren Cromartie ..... Expos
3023 .... July 20, 1980 ...... Larry Parrish .... Expos
3024 .... July 25, 1980 ...... Tim Raines .... Expos
3025 .... July 30, 1980 ...... Mike Schmidt .... Phillies
3026 .... July 30, 1980 ...... Manny Trillo .... Phillies
3027 .... July 30, 1980 ...... Lonnie Smith .... Phillies
3028 .... August 4, 1980 ... Larry Herndon .... Giants
3029 .... August 4, 1980 ... Al Hargesheimer ...... Giants
3030 .... August 4, 1980 ... Larry Herndon .... Giants
3031 .... August 4, 1980 ... Rennie Stennett .... Giants
3032 .... August 4, 1980 ... Max Venable .... Giants
3033 .... August 4, 1980 ... Rennie Stennett .... Giants
3034 .... August 4, 1980 ... Terry Whitfield .... Giants
3035 .... August 9, 1980 ... Jerry Mumphrey ...... Padres
3036 .... August 9, 1980 ... John Curtis .... Padres
3037 .... August 9, 1980 ... John D'Acquisto ...... Padres
3038 .... August 14, 1980 . Jerry Mumphrey ...... Padres
3039 .... August 14, 1980 . John Curtis .... Padres
3040 .... August 14, 1980 . Gene Richards .... Padres
3041 .... August 14, 1980 . Jerry Mumphrey ...... Padres
3042 .... August 14, 1980 . Barry Evans .... Padres
3043 .... August 14, 1980 . John Curtis .... Padres
3044 .... August 14, 1980 . Dave Winfield .... Padres
3045 .... August 19, 1980 . Mike Easler .... Pirates
3046 .... August 19, 1980 . Ed Ott .... Pirates
3047 .... August 19, 1980 . John Candelaria ..... Pirates
3048 .... August 19, 1980 . Dave Parker .... Pirates
3049 .... August 19, 1980 . Bill Madlock .... Pirates
3050 .... August 19, 1980 . Ed Ott .... Pirates
3051 .... August 19, 1980 . Omar Moreno .... Pirates
3052 .... August 24, 1980 . Ivan DeJesus .... Cubs
3053 .... August 24, 1980 . Scot Thompson .... Cubs
3054 .... August 24, 1980 . Mike Tyson .... Cubs
3055 .... August 24, 1980 . Doug Capilla .... Cubs
3056 .... August 24, 1980 . Cliff Johnson .... Cubs
3057 .... August 24, 1980 . Steve Dillard .... Cubs
3058 .... August 29, 1980 . Mike Tyson .... Cubs
3059 .... August 29, 1980 . Mike Tyson .... Cubs
3060 .... Sept. 5, 1980 ...... Tony Scott .... Cardinals
3061 .... Sept. 5, 1980 ...... Keith Hernandez . Cardinals
3062 .... Sept. 5, 1980 ...... Dane Iorg .... Cardinals
3063 .... Sept. 5, 1980 ...... Ken Reitz .... Cardinals
3064 .... Sept. 5, 1980 ...... Mike Phillips .... Cardinals

3065	Sept. 5, 1980	Don Hood	Cardinals
3066	Sept. 5, 1980	Ken Reitz	Cardinals
3067	Sept. 5, 1980	George Hendrick	Cardinals
3068	Sept. 5, 1980	Leon Durham	Cardinals
3069	Sept. 10, 1980	Davey Lopes	Dodgers
3070	Sept. 10, 1980	Derrel Thomas	Dodgers
3071	Sept. 10, 1980	Burt Hooton	Dodgers
3072	Sept. 10, 1980	Davey Lopes	Dodgers
3073	Sept. 10, 1980	Derrel Thomas	Dodgers
3074	Sept. 10, 1980	Burt Hooton	Dodgers
3075	Sept. 10, 1980	Jay Johnstone	Dodgers
3076	Sept. 10, 1980	Mike Scioscia	Dodgers
3077	Sept. 10, 1980	Burt Hooton	Dodgers
3078	Sept. 15, 1980	Bob Shirley	Padres
3079	Sept. 15, 1980	Ozzie Smith	Padres
3080	Sept. 15, 1980	Randy Bass	Padres
3081	Sept. 15, 1980	Tim Flannery	Padres
3082	Sept. 20, 1980	Joe Pettini	Giants
3083	Sept. 20, 1980	Ed Whitson	Giants
3084	Sept. 20, 1980	Terry Whitfield	Giants
3085	Sept. 20, 1980	Joe Pettini	Giants
3086	Sept. 20, 1980	Guy Sularz	Giants
3087	Sept. 20, 1980	Johnnie LeMaster	Giants
3088	Sept. 25, 1980	Gary Mathews	Braves
3089	Sept. 25, 1980	Bob Horner	Braves
3090	Sept. 25, 1980	Rafael Ramirez	Braves
3091	Sept. 25, 1980	Phil Niekro	Braves
3092	Sept. 25, 1980	Rafael Ramirez	Braves
3093	Sept. 30, 1980	Gary Mathews	Braves
3094	Sept. 30, 1980	Dale Murphy	Braves
3095	Sept. 30, 1980	Glenn Hubbard	Braves
3096	Sept. 30, 1980	Doyle Alexander	Braves
3097	Sept. 30, 1980	Gary Mathews	Braves
3098	Sept. 30, 1980	Glenn Hubbard	Braves
3099	Sept. 30, 1980	Doyle Alexander	Braves
3100	Sept. 30, 1980	Terry Harper	Braves
3101	October 4, 1980	Rick Monday	Dodgers
3102	October 4, 1980	Joe Ferguson	Dodgers
3103	October 4, 1980	Jerry Reuss	Dodgers
3104	October 4, 1980	Rick Monday	Dodgers
3105	October 4, 1980	Dusty Baker	Dodgers
3106	October 4, 1980	Pedro Guerrero	Dodgers
3107	October 4, 1980	Joe Ferguson	Dodgers
3108	October 4, 1980	Jerry Reuss	Dodgers
3109	October 4, 1980	Jerry Reuss	Dodgers
3110	April 15, 1981	Rafael Ramirez	Braves
3111	April 15, 1981	C. Washington	Braves
3112	April 15, 1981	Glenn Hubbard	Braves
3113	April 15, 1981	Dale Murphy	Braves
3114	April 15, 1981	Rafael Ramirez	Braves
3115	April 15, 1981	C. Washington	Braves
3116	April 15, 1981	Dale Murphy	Braves
3117	April 15, 1981	Mike Lum	Braves
3118	April 15, 1981	Tommy Boggs	Braves
3119	April 25, 1981	Bruce Berenyi	Reds
3120	April 25, 1981	Dave Collins	Reds
3121	April 25, 1981	George Foster	Reds
3122	April 25, 1981	Dan Driessen	Reds
3123	April 25, 1981	Joe Nolan	Reds
3124	April 25, 1981	Ron Oester	Reds
3125	April 25, 1981	Bruce Berenyi	Reds
3126	April 25, 1981	George Foster	Reds
3127	April 25, 1981	Ron Oester	Reds
3128	April 25, 1981	Dave Collins	Reds
3129	May 1, 1981	Rod Scurry	Pirates
3130	May 6, 1981	Tim Blackwell	Cubs
3131	May 6, 1981	Bill Caudill	Cubs
3132	May 6, 1981	Steve Henderson	Cubs
3133	May 11, 1981	Ken Griffey	Reds
3134	May 11, 1981	Dave Concepcion	Reds
3135	May 11, 1981	Johnny Bench	Reds
3136	May 11, 1981	Ron Oester	Reds
3137	May 11, 1981	Ken Griffey	Reds
3138	May 11, 1981	Dave Collins	Reds
3139	May 11, 1981	Dave Concepcion	Reds
3140	May 11, 1981	George Foster	Reds
3141	May 11, 1981	Dave Collins	Reds
3142	May 11, 1981	Ray Knight	Reds
3143	May 11, 1981	Ken Griffey	Reds
3144	May 16, 1981	Steve Henderson	Cubs
3145	May 16, 1981	Ken Reitz	Cubs
3146	May 16, 1981	Tim Blackwell	Cubs
3147	May 16, 1981	Randy Martz	Cubs
3148	May 16, 1981	Steve Henderson	Cubs
3149	May 16, 1981	Randy Martz	Cubs
3150	May 16, 1981	Scot Thompson	Cubs
3151	May 16, 1981	Jim Tracy	Cubs
3152	May 21, 1981	Orlando Sanchez	Cardinals
3153	May 21, 1981	John Martin	Cardinals
3154	May 21, 1981	Garry Templeton	Cardinals
3155	May 21, 1981	Ken Oberkfell	Cardinals
3156	May 21, 1981	Orlando Sanchez	Cardinals
3157	May 21, 1981	John Martin	Cardinals
3158	May 26, 1981	Juan Eichelberger	Padres
3159	May 26, 1981	Broderick Perkins	Padres
3160	May 26, 1981	Terry Kennedy	Padres
3161	May 26, 1981	Juan Eichelberger	Padres
3162	May 26, 1981	Ruppert Jones	Padres
3163	May 26, 1981	Juan Eichelberger	Padres
3164	May 31, 1981	Larry Herndon	Giants
3165	May 31, 1981	Tom Griffin	Giants
3166	May 31, 1981	Darrell Evans	Giants
3167	May 31, 1981	Jerry Martin	Giants
3168	June 5, 1981	Mookie Wilson	Mets
3169	June 5, 1981	Lee Mazzilli	Mets
3170	June 5, 1981	Randy Jones	Mets
3171	June 5, 1981	Mookie Wilson	Mets
3172	June 5, 1981	Frank Taveras	Mets
3173	June 5, 1981	Dave Kingman	Mets
3174	June 5, 1981	Mookie Wilson	Mets
3175	June 5, 1981	Lee Mazzilli	Mets
3176	June 5, 1981	Mookie Wilson	Mets

3177	June 5, 1981	Dave Kingman	Mets	3233	Sept. 26, 1981	Ted Power	Dodgers
3178	June 10, 1981	Luis Aguayo	Phillies	3234	Sept. 26, 1981	Davey Lopes	Dodgers

3177 .... June 5, 1981 .... Dave Kingman .... Mets
3178 .... June 10, 1981 ..... Luis Aguayo .... Phillies
3179 .... June 10, 1981 ..... Steve Carlton .... Phillies
3180 .... June 10, 1981 ..... Pete Rose .... Phillies
3181 .... June 10, 1981 ..... Luis Aguayo .... Phillies
3182 .... June 10, 1981 ..... Steve Carlton .... Phillies
3183 .... June 10, 1981 ..... Pete Rose .... Phillies
3184 .... June 10, 1981 ..... Bob Boone .... Phillies
3185 .... June 10, 1981 ..... Pete Rose .... Phillies
3186 .... August 14, 1981 . Randy Bass .... Padres
3187 .... August 14, 1981 . Gene Richards .... Padres
3188 .... August 14, 1981 . Randy Bass .... Padres
3189 .... August 19, 1981 . Tim Raines .... Expos
3190 .... August 19, 1981 . Rodney Scott .... Expos
3191 .... August 19, 1981 . Andre Dawson .... Expos
3192 .... August 19, 1981 . Tim Wallach .... Expos
3193 .... August 19, 1981 . Mike Phillips .... Expos
3194 .... August 19, 1981 . Scott Sanderson .... Expos
3195 .... August 19, 1981 . Andre Dawson .... Expos
3196 .... August 19, 1981 . Andre Dawson .... Expos
3197 .... August 25, 1981 . Frank Taveras .... Mets
3198 .... August 25, 1981 . Lee Mazzilli .... Mets
3199 .... August 25, 1981 . Greg Harris .... Mets
3200 .... August 25, 1981 . Hubie Brooks .... Mets
3201 .... August 25, 1981 . Mookie Wilson .... Mets
3202 .... August 25, 1981 . Hubie Brooks .... Mets
3203 .... August 25, 1981 . Mike Jorgensen .... Mets
3204 .... August 30, 1981 . Lonnie Smith .... Phillies
3205 .... August 30, 1981 . Dick Davis .... Phillies
3206 .... August 30, 1981 . Dick Davis .... Phillies
3207 .... August 30, 1981 . Luis Aguayo .... Phillies
3208 .... Sept. 4, 1981 ...... John Milner .... Expos
3209 .... Sept. 4, 1981 ...... Bill Gullickson .... Expos
3210 .... Sept. 4, 1981 ...... Tim Raines .... Expos
3211 .... Sept. 4, 1981 ...... Warren Cromartie ..... Expos
3212 .... Sept. 4, 1981 ...... Larry Parrish .... Expos
3213 .... Sept. 4, 1981 ...... Chris Speier .... Expos
3214 .... Sept. 4, 1981 ...... Rowland Office .... Expos
3215 .... Sept. 9, 1981 ...... Ed Miller .... Braves
3216 .... Sept. 9, 1981 ...... Brett Butler .... Braves
3217 .... Sept. 9, 1981 ...... Bruce Benedict .... Braves
3218 .... Sept. 15, 1981 .... Paul Householder ...... Reds
3219 .... Sept. 15, 1981 .... Ray Knight .... Reds
3220 .... Sept. 15, 1981 .... George Foster .... Reds
3221 .... Sept. 15, 1981 .... Charlie Leibrandt .... Reds
3222 .... Sept. 20, 1981 .... Milt May .... Giants
3223 .... Sept. 20, 1981 .... Jack Clark .... Giants
3224 .... Sept. 20, 1981 .... Billy Smith .... Giants
3225 .... Sept. 20, 1981 .... Enos Cabell .... Giants
3226 .... Sept. 20, 1981 .... Jeffrey Leonard .... Giants
3227 .... Sept. 20, 1981 .... Darrell Evans .... Giants
3228 .... Sept. 20, 1981 .... Dave Bergman .... Giants
3229 .... Sept. 20, 1981 .... Jerry Martin .... Giants
3230 .... Sept. 26, 1981 .... Ken Landreaux .... Dodgers
3231 .... Sept. 26, 1981 .... Pedro Guerrero ..... Dodgers
3232 .... Sept. 26, 1981 .... Mike Scioscia .... Dodgers

3233 .... Sept. 26, 1981 .... Ted Power .... Dodgers
3234 .... Sept. 26, 1981 .... Davey Lopes ... Dodgers
3235 .... Sept. 26, 1981 .... Steve Garvey .... Dodgers
3236 .... Sept. 26, 1981 .... Mike Scioscia .... Dodgers
3237 .... Sept. 26, 1981 .... Jack Perconte .... Dodgers
3238 .... Sept. 26, 1981 .... Davey Lopes .... Dodgers
3239 .... Sept. 26, 1981 .... Dusty Baker .... Dodgers
3240 .... Sept. 26, 1981 .... Reggie Smith ... Dodgers
3241 .... October 1, 1981 .... Ken Griffey .... Reds
3242 .... October 1, 1981 .... Dave Concepcion .... Reds
3243 .... October 1, 1981 .. George Foster .... Reds
3244 .... October 1, 1981 .. Ron Oester .... Reds
3245 .... October 1, 1981 .. Bruce Berenyi .... Reds
3246 .... October 1, 1981 .. George Foster .... Reds
3247 .... October 1, 1981 .. Johnny Bench .... Reds
3248 .... October 1, 1981 .. Dave Collins .... Reds
3249 .... October 1, 1981 .. Paul Householder ...... Reds
3250 .... April 6, 1982 .... Tommy Herr .... Cardinals
3251 .... April 6, 1982 .... Bob Forsch .... Cardinals
3252 .... April 6, 1982 .... Darrell Porter ...... Cardinals
3253 .... April 6, 1982 .... Dane Iorg .... Cardinals
3254 .... April 6, 1982 .... Tommy Herr .... Cardinals
3255 .... April 11, 1982 ..... Bob Horner .... Braves
3256 .... April 11, 1982 ..... Rick Mahler .... Braves
3257 .... April 11, 1982 ..... Brett Butler .... Braves
3258 .... April 16, 1982 ..... Brett Butler .... Braves
3259 .... April 16, 1982 ..... Bob Horner .... Braves
3260 .... April 16, 1982 ..... Rufino Linares .... Braves
3261 .... April 16, 1982 ..... Glenn Hubbard .... Braves
3262 .... April 16, 1982 ..... Chris Chambliss ...... Braves
3263 .... April 16, 1982 ..... Rufino Linares .... Braves
3264 .... April 21, 1982 ..... Pedro Guerrero ..... Dodgers
3265 .... April 21, 1982 ..... Ken Landreaux ..... Dodgers
3266 .... April 21, 1982 ..... Steve Garvey .... Dodgers
3267 .... April 21, 1982 ..... Pedro Guerrero ..... Dodgers
3268 .... April 26, 1982 ..... Keith Hernandez . Cardinals
3269 .... April 26, 1982 ..... Mark Littell .... Cardinals
3270 .... April 26, 1982 ..... Jim Kaat .... Cardinals
3271 .... April 26, 1982 ..... Steve Braun .... Cardinals
3272 .... April 26, 1982 ..... George Hendrick . Cardinals
3273 .... May 1, 1982 .... Dale Berra .... Pirates
3274 .... May 1, 1982 .... Cecilio Guante .... Pirates
3275 .... May 1, 1982 .... Bill Madlock .... Pirates
3276 .... May 1, 1982 .... Mike Easler .... Pirates
3277 .... May 7, 1982 .... Bump Wills .... Cubs
3278 .... May 7, 1982 .... Junior Kennedy .... Cubs
3279 .... May 7, 1982 .... Ryne Sandberg .... Cubs
3280 .... May 7, 1982 .... Steve Henderson .... Cubs
3281 .... May 11, 1982 ...... Dave Parker .... Pirates
3282 .... May 11, 1982 ...... Willie Stargell .... Pirates
3283 .... May 11, 1982 ...... Tom Griffin .... Pirates
3284 .... May 11, 1982 ...... Dave Parker .... Pirates
3285 .... May 16, 1982 ...... Keith Moreland .... Cubs
3286 .... May 16, 1982 ...... Doug Bird .... Cubs
3287 .... May 16, 1982 ...... Junior Kennedy .... Cubs
3288 .... May 16, 1982 ...... Larry Cox .... Cubs

3289 .... May 16, 1982 ...... Junior Kennedy .... Cubs			
3290 .... May 16, 1982 ...... Gary Woods .... Cubs			
3291 .... May 22, 1982 ...... Gary Rajsich .... Mets			
3292 .... May 22, 1982 ...... Ron Gardenhire .... Mets			
3293 .... May 22, 1982 ...... Pete Falcone .... Mets			
3294 .... May 22, 1982 ...... Pete Falcone .... Mets			
3295 .... May 22, 1982 ...... George Foster .... Mets			
3296 .... May 22, 1982 ...... Gary Rajsich .... Mets			
3297 .... May 22, 1982 ...... Wally Backman .... Mets			
3298 .... May 22, 1982 ...... Ron Gardenhire .... Mets			
3299 .... May 22, 1982 ...... Gary Rajsich .... Mets			
3300 .... May 22, 1982 ...... Mookie Wilson .... Mets			
3301 .... May 28, 1982 ...... John Stearns .... Mets			
3302 .... May 28, 1982 ...... Dave Kingman .... Mets			
3303 .... May 28, 1982 ...... Gary Rajsich .... Mets			
3304 .... May 28, 1982 ...... Mookie Wilson .... Mets			
3305 .... May 28, 1982 ...... John Stearns .... Mets			
3306 .... May 28, 1982 ...... George Foster .... Mets			
3307 .... May 28, 1982 ...... Dave Kingman .... Mets			
3308 .... May 28, 1982 ...... Gary Rajsich .... Mets			
3309 .... May 28, 1982 ...... Wally Backman .... Mets			
3310 .... May 28, 1982 ...... George Foster .... Mets			
3311 .... May 28, 1982 ...... Dave Kingman .... Mets			
3312 .... June 2, 1982 ...... Andre Dawson .... Expos			
3313 .... June 2, 1982 ...... Andre Dawson .... Expos			
3314 .... June 2, 1982 ...... Warren Cromartie ..... Expos			
3315 .... June 2, 1982 ...... Scott Sanderson .... Expos			
3316 .... June 2, 1982 ...... Warren Cromartie ..... Expos			
3317 .... June 8, 1982 ...... Joe Morgan .... Giants			
3318 .... June 8, 1982 ...... Jim Wohlford .... Giants			
3319 .... June 8, 1982 ...... Reggie Smith .... Giants			
3320 .... June 8, 1982 ...... Tom O'Malley .... Giants			
3321 .... June 13, 1982 ..... Garry Templeton ..... Padres			
3322 .... June 13, 1982 ..... Ruppert Jones .... Padres			
3323 .... June 13, 1982 ..... Tim Flannery .... Padres			
3324 .... June 13, 1982 ..... John Montefusco ..... Padres			
3325 .... June 13, 1982 ..... Alan Wiggins .... Padres			
3326 .... June 13, 1982 ..... Garry Templeton ..... Padres			
3327 .... June 13, 1982 ..... Terry Kennedy .... Padres			
3328 .... June 13, 1982 ..... Luis Salazar .... Padres			
3329 .... June 13, 1982 ..... Sixto Lezcano .... Padres			
3330 .... June 18, 1982 ..... Garry Templeton ..... Padres			
3331 .... June 18, 1982 ..... Ruppert Jones .... Padres			
3332 .... June 18, 1982 ..... Tim Flannery .... Padres			
3333 .... June 18, 1982 ..... Chris Welsh .... Padres			
3334 .... June 18, 1982 ..... Ruppert Jones .... Padres			
3335 .... June 18, 1982 ..... Terry Kennedy .... Padres			
3336 .... June 18, 1982 ..... Chris Welsh .... Padres			
3337 .... June 18, 1982 ..... Terry Kennedy .... Padres			
3338 .... June 18, 1982 ..... Tim Flannery .... Padres			
3339 .... June 18, 1982 ..... Ruppert Jones .... Padres			
3340 .... June 18, 1982 ..... Sixto Lezcano .... Padres			
3341 .... June 23, 1982 ..... Chili Davis .... Giants			
3342 .... June 23, 1982 ..... Dave Bergman .... Giants			
3343 .... June 23, 1982 ..... Chili Davis .... Giants			
3344 .... June 28, 1982 ..... Chris Chambliss ...... Braves			

3345 .... June 28, 1982 ..... Dale Murphy .... Braves
3346 .... June 28, 1982 ..... C. Washington .... Braves
3347 .... June 28, 1982 ..... Dale Murphy .... Braves
3348 .... June 28, 1982 ..... Rafael Ramirez .... Braves
3349 .... June 28, 1982 ..... Rick Mahler .... Braves
3350 .... June 28, 1982 ..... C. Washington .... Braves
3351 .... June 28, 1982 ..... Dale Murphy .... Braves
3352 .... June 28, 1982 ..... Rufino Linares .... Braves
3353 .... June 28, 1982 ..... Bob Horner .... Braves
3354 .... July 4, 1982 .... Steve Sax .... Dodgers
3355 .... July 4, 1982 .... Ron Roenicke .... Dodgers
3356 .... July 4, 1982 .... Ron Cey .... Dodgers
3357 .... July 4, 1982 .... Jorge Orta .... Dodgers
3358 .... July 4, 1982 .... Steve Sax .... Dodgers
3359 .... July 4, 1982 .... Ron Roenicke .... Dodgers
3360 .... July 4, 1982 .... Jorge Orta .... Dodgers
3361 .... July 4, 1982 .... Steve Garvey .... Dodgers
3362 .... July 4, 1982 .... Ron Roenicke .... Dodgers
3363 .... July 4, 1982 .... Ron Cey .... Dodgers
3364 .... July 9, 1982 .... Lonnie Smith .... Cardinals
3365 .... July 9, 1982 .... Tommy Herr .... Cardinals
3366 .... July 9, 1982 .... Ken Oberkfell .... Cardinals
3367 .... July 9, 1982 .... Willie McGee ...... Cardinals
3368 .... July 9, 1982 .... Keith Hernandez . Cardinals
3369 .... July 9, 1982 .... Dave LaPoint .... Cardinals
3370 .... July 9, 1982 .... Dave LaPoint .... Cardinals
3371 .... July 9, 1982 .... Willie McGee ...... Cardinals
3372 .... July 9, 1982 .... Ozzie Smith .... Cardinals
3373 .... July 9, 1982 .... Jeff Lahti .... Cardinals
3374 .... July 16, 1982 ..... Jason Thompson .... Pirates
3375 .... July 16, 1982 ..... Mike Easler .... Pirates
3376 .... July 16, 1982 ..... Larry McWilliams .... Pirates
3377 .... July 16, 1982 ..... Omar Moreno .... Pirates
3378 .... July 16, 1982 ..... Dave Parker .... Pirates
3379 .... July 16, 1982 ..... Mike Easler .... Pirates
3380 .... July 16, 1982 ..... Larry McWilliams ..... Pirates
3381 .... July 16, 1982 ..... Mike Easler .... Pirates
3382 .... July 16, 1982 ..... Tony Pena .... Pirates
3383 .... July 16, 1982 ..... Dave Parker .... Pirates
3384 .... July 16, 1982 ..... Mike Easler .... Pirates
3385 .... July 21, 1982 ..... Ryne Sandberg .... Cubs
3386 .... July 21, 1982 ..... Junior Kennedy .... Cubs
3387 .... July 21, 1982 ..... Keith Moreland .... Cubs
3388 .... July 21, 1982 ..... Allen Ripley .... Cubs
3389 .... July 27, 1982 ..... Paul Householder ...... Reds
3390 .... July 27, 1982 ..... Ron Oester .... Reds
3391 .... July 27, 1982 ..... Charlie Leibrandt .... Reds
3392 .... July 27, 1982 ..... Alex Trevino .... Reds
3393 .... July 27, 1982 ..... Charlie Leibrandt .... Reds
3394 .... July 27, 1982 ..... Cesar Cedeno .... Reds
3395 .... July 27, 1982 ..... Dan Driessen .... Reds
3396 .... July 27, 1982 ..... Paul Householder ...... Reds
3397 .... July 27, 1982 ..... Ron Oester .... Reds
3398 .... July 27, 1982 ..... Alex Trevino .... Reds
3399 .... July 27, 1982 ..... Charlie Leibrandt .... Reds
3400 .... July 27, 1982 ..... Eddie Milner .... Reds

3401	July 27, 1982	Cesar Cedeno	Reds
3402	August 1, 1982	Joe Morgan	Giants
3403	August 1, 1982	Chili Davis	Giants
3404	August 1, 1982	Reggie Smith	Giants
3405	August 1, 1982	Jeffrey Leonard	Giants
3406	August 1, 1982	Milt May	Giants
3407	August 1, 1982	Reggie Smith	Giants
3408	August 6, 1982	Atlee Hammaker	Giants
3409	August 6, 1982	Chili Davis	Giants
3410	August 6, 1982	Duane Kuiper	Giants
3411	August 6, 1982	Jeffrey Leonard	Giants
3412	August 6, 1982	Atlee Hammaker	Giants
3413	August 6, 1982	Chili Davis	Giants
3414	August 6, 1982	Champ Summers	Giants
3415	August 6, 1982	Duane Kuiper	Giants
3416	August 11, 1982	Broderick Perkins	Padres
3417	August 11, 1982	Joe Pittman	Padres
3418	August 11, 1982	Tony Gwynn	Padres
3419	August 11, 1982	Luis Salazar	Padres
3420	August 11, 1982	Terry Kennedy	Padres
3421	August 11, 1982	Terry Kennedy	Padres
3422	August 16, 1982	Tom Lawless	Reds
3423	August 16, 1982	Dan Driessen	Reds
3424	August 16, 1982	Bob Shirley	Reds
3425	August 16, 1982	Tom Lawless	Reds
3426	August 16, 1982	Tom Lawless	Reds
3427	August 16, 1982	Dan Driessen	Reds
3428	August 16, 1982	Paul Householder	Reds
3429	August 21, 1982	Joel Youngblood	Expos
3430	August 21, 1982	Andre Dawson	Expos
3431	August 21, 1982	Andre Dawson	Expos
3432	August 21, 1982	Al Oliver	Expos
3433	August 21, 1982	Warren Cromartie	Expos
3434	August 26, 1982	Andre Dawson	Expos
3435	August 26, 1982	Al Oliver	Expos
3436	August 26, 1982	Bill Gullickson	Expos
3437	August 26, 1982	Tim Raines	Expos
3438	August 26, 1982	Warren Cromartie	Expos
3439	August 26, 1982	Andre Dawson	Expos
3440	August 26, 1982	Doug Flynn	Expos
3441	August 31, 1982	Mookie Wilson	Mets
3442	August 31, 1982	Dave Kingman	Mets
3443	August 31, 1982	Brian Giles	Mets
3444	August 31, 1982	Ed Lynch	Mets
3445	August 31, 1982	Mookie Wilson	Mets
3446	August 31, 1982	Ron Hodges	Mets
3447	August 31, 1982	Ed Lynch	Mets
3448	August 31, 1982	Mike Jorgensen	Mets
3449	August 31, 1982	Mookie Wilson	Mets
3450	Sept. 5, 1982	Ozzie Virgil	Phillies
3451	Sept. 5, 1982	Pete Rose	Phillies
3452	Sept. 5, 1982	Mike Schmidt	Phillies
3453	Sept. 5, 1982	Ozzie Virgil	Phillies
3454	Sept. 5, 1982	Ivan DeJesus	Phillies
3455	Sept. 5, 1982	Len Matuszek	Phillies
3456	Sept. 5, 1982	Pete Rose	Phillies
3457	Sept. 5, 1982	Manny Trillo	Phillies
3458	Sept. 10, 1982	Dusty Baker	Dodgers
3459	Sept. 10, 1982	Rick Monday	Dodgers
3460	Sept. 10, 1982	Bill Russell	Dodgers
3461	Sept. 10, 1982	Burt Hooton	Dodgers
3462	Sept. 10, 1982	Ken Landreaux	Dodgers
3463	Sept. 10, 1982	Steve Garvey	Dodgers
3464	Sept. 10, 1982	Derrel Thomas	Dodgers
3465	Sept. 10, 1982	Mike Scioscia	Dodgers
3466	Sept. 10, 1982	Jose Morales	Dodgers
3467	Sept. 15, 1982	C. Washington	Braves
3468	Sept. 15, 1982	Glenn Hubbard	Braves
3469	Sept. 15, 1982	Terry Harper	Braves
3470	Sept. 15, 1982	Bob Porter	Braves
3471	Sept. 20, 1982	Dale Murphy	Braves
3472	Sept. 20, 1982	C. Washington	Braves
3473	Sept. 20, 1982	Glenn Hubbard	Braves
3474	Sept. 26, 1982	Duane Walker	Reds
3475	Sept. 26, 1982	Dan Driessen	Reds
3476	Sept. 26, 1982	Cesar Cedeno	Reds
3477	Sept. 26, 1982	Bob Shirley	Reds
3478	Sept. 26, 1982	Duane Walker	Reds
3479	Sept. 26, 1982	Bob Shirley	Reds
3480	Sept. 26, 1982	Duane Walker	Reds
3481	Sept. 26, 1982	Paul Householder	Reds
3482	Sept. 26, 1982	Rafael Landestoy	Reds
3483	Sept. 26, 1982	Dave Concepcion	Reds
3484	Sept. 26, 1982	Ron Oester	Reds
3485	October 1, 1982	Duane Walker	Reds
3486	October 1, 1982	Paul Householder	Reds
3487	October 1, 1982	Ron Oester	Reds
3488	October 1, 1982	Rafael Landestoy	Reds
3489	October 1, 1982	Duane Walker	Reds
3490	October 1, 1982	Duane Walker	Reds
3491	October 1, 1982	Bob Shirley	Reds
3492	October 1, 1982	Gary Redus	Reds
3493	October 1, 1982	Duane Walker	Reds
3494	October 1, 1982	Ron Oester	Reds
3495	April 17, 1983	Tim Raines	Expos
3496	April 17, 1983	Andre Dawson	Expos
3497	April 17, 1983	Warren Cromartie	Expos
3498	April 17, 1983	Gary Carter	Expos
3499	April 17, 1983	Terry Francona	Expos
3500	April 17, 1983	Andre Dawson	Expos
3501	April 17, 1983	Warren Cromartie	Expos
3502	April 22, 1983	Dick Ruthven	Phillies
3503	April 22, 1983	Joe Morgan	Phillies
3504	April 22, 1983	Bo Diaz	Phillies
3505	April 27, 1983	Tim Wallach	Expos
3506	April 27, 1983	Tim Blackwell	Expos
3507	April 27, 1983	Bryan Little	Expos
3508	April 27, 1983	Tim Blackwell	Expos
3509	April 27, 1983	Brad Mills	Expos
3510	May 2, 1983	Hubie Brooks	Mets
3511	May 2, 1983	Danny Heep	Mets
3512	May 2, 1983	Wally Backman	Mets

3513 .... May 2, 1983 .... Brian Giles .... Mets		3569 .... July 8, 1983 .... Brian Giles .... Mets	
3514 .... May 2, 1983 .... Mike Torrez .... Mets		3570 .... July 8, 1983 .... Hubie Brooks .... Mets	
3515 .... May 2, 1983 .... Hubie Brooks .... Mets		3571 .... July 8, 1983 .... Keith Hernandez .... Mets	
3516 .... May 2, 1983 .... George Foster .... Mets		3572 .... July 8, 1983 .... Darryl Strawberry .... Mets	
3517 .... May 2, 1983 .... Wally Backman .... Mets		3573 .... July 8, 1983 .... Ron Hodges .... Mets	
3518 .... May 2, 1983 .... Ronn Reynolds .... Mets		3574 .... July 13, 1983 .... Al Oliver .... Expos	
3519 .... May 2, 1983 .... Mike Torrez .... Mets		3575 .... July 13, 1983 .... Terry Francona .... Expos	
3520 .... May 2, 1983 .... Hubie Brooks .... Mets		3576 .... July 13, 1983 .... Andre Dawson .... Expos	
3521 .... May 2, 1983 .... Wally Backman .... Mets		3577 .... July 13, 1983 .... Chris Speier .... Expos	
3522 .... June 7, 1983 .... Chili Davis .... Giants		3578 .... July 13, 1983 .... Bryan Little .... Expos	
3523 .... June 7, 1983 .... Jeffrey Leonard .... Giants		3579 .... July 17, 1983 .... Hubie Brooks .... Mets	
3524 .... June 7, 1983 .... Atlee Hammaker ...... Giants		3580 .... July 17, 1983 .... Darryl Strawberry .... Mets	
3525 .... June 12, 1983 ..... Steve Garvey .... Padres		3581 .... July 17, 1983 .... Keith Hernandez .... Mets	
3526 .... June 12, 1983 ..... Kevin McReynolds .. Padres		3582 .... July 17, 1983 .... Walt Terrell .... Mets	
3527 .... June 12, 1983 ..... Luis Salazar .... Padres		3583 .... July 17, 1983 .... Jose Oquendo .... Mets	
3528 .... June 12, 1983 ..... Eric Show .... Padres		3584 .... July 21, 1983 .... Doug Flynn .... Expos	
3529 .... June 12, 1983 ..... Eric Show .... Padres		3585 .... July 21, 1983 .... Tim Raines .... Expos	
3530 .... June 12, 1983 ..... Steve Garvey .... Padres		3586 .... July 26, 1983 .... Mike Schmidt ... Phillies	
3531 .... June 12, 1983 ..... Kevin McReynolds .. Padres		3587 .... July 26, 1983 .... Joe Lefebvre .... Phillies	
3532 .... June 12, 1983 ..... Luis Salazar .... Padres		3588 .... July 26, 1983 .... Charles Hudson ...... Phillies	
3533 .... June 12, 1983 ..... Mario Ramirez .... Padres		3589 .... July 26, 1983 .... Charles Hudson ...... Phillies	
3534 .... June 12, 1983 ..... Jerry Turner .... Padres		3590 .... July 26, 1983 .... Von Hayes .... Phillies	
3535 .... June 12, 1983 ..... Terry Kennedy .... Padres		3591 .... July 26, 1983 .... Charles Hudson ...... Phillies	
3536 .... June 17, 1983 ..... Kevin McReynolds .. Padres		3592 .... July 30, 1983 .... Dan Driessen .... Reds	
3537 .... June 17, 1983 ..... Eric Show .... Padres		3593 .... July 30, 1983 .... Ron Oester .... Reds	
3538 .... June 17, 1983 ..... Steve Garvey .... Padres		3594 .... July 30, 1983 .... Dan Driessen .... Reds	
3539 .... June 17, 1983 ..... Kevin McReynolds .. Padres		3595 .... July 30, 1983 ...... Duane Walker .... Reds	
3540 .... June 17, 1983 ..... Terry Kennedy .... Padres		3596 .... July 30, 1983 ...... Nick Esasky .... Reds	
3541 .... June 17, 1983 ..... Ruppert Jones .... Padres		3597 .... August 3, 1983 ... Ruppert Jones .... Padres	
3542 .... June 22, 1983 ..... Chris Chambliss ..... Braves		3598 .... August 3, 1983 ... Tim Lollar .... Padres	
3543 .... June 22, 1983 ..... Brett Butler .... Braves		3599 .... August 3, 1983 ... Bobby Brown .... Padres	
3544 .... June 22, 1983 ..... Glenn Hubbard .... Braves		3600 .... August 3, 1983 ... Terry Kennedy .... Padres	
3545 .... June 22, 1983 ..... Jerry Royster .... Braves		3601 .... August 3, 1983 ... Bobby Brown .... Padres	
3546 .... June 22, 1983 ..... Chris Chambliss ..... Braves		3602 .... August 3, 1983 ... Alan Wiggins .... Padres	
3547 .... June 22, 1983 ..... Jerry Royster .... Braves		3603 .... August 3, 1983 ... Terry Kennedy .... Padres	
3548 .... June 22, 1983 ..... C. Washington .... Braves		3604 .... August 3, 1983 ... Luis Salazar .... Padres	
3549 .... June 28, 1983 ..... Craig McMurtry .... Braves		3605 .... August 3, 1983 ... Tim Flannery .... Padres	
3550 .... June 28, 1983 ..... Glenn Hubbard .... Braves		3606 .... August 3, 1983 ... Kurt Bevacqua .... Padres	
3551 .... June 28, 1983 ..... Craig McMurtry .... Braves		3607 .... August 7, 1983 ... Darrell Evans .... Giants	
3552 .... June 28, 1983 ..... Rafael Ramirez .... Braves		3608 .... August 7, 1983 ... Jeffrey Leonard .... Giants	
3553 .... June 28, 1983 ..... Glenn Hubbard .... Braves		3609 .... August 7, 1983 ... Chili Davis .... Giants	
3554 .... July 2, 1983 .... Pedro Guerrero ..... Dodgers		3610 .... August 7, 1983 ... Milt May .... Giants	
3555 .... July 2, 1983 .... Joe Beckwith .... Dodgers		3611 .... August 7, 1983 ... Mike Krukow .... Giants	
3556 .... July 2, 1983 .... Rafael Landestoy .. Dodgers		3612 .... August 7, 1983 ... Chili Davis .... Giants	
3557 .... July 2, 1983 .... Derrel Thomas ...... Dodgers		3613 .... August 7, 1983 ... Milt May .... Giants	
3558 .... July 2, 1983 .... Greg Brock .... Dodgers		3614 .... August 7, 1983 ... Jeffrey Leonard .... Giants	
3559 .... July 2, 1983 .... Mike Marshall .... Dodgers		3615 .... August 12, 1983 . Dave Bergman .... Giants	
3560 .... July 2, 1983 .... Ron Roenicke .... Dodgers		3616 .... August 12, 1983 . Renie Martin .... Giants	
3561 .... July 2, 1983 .... Derrel Thomas ...... Dodgers		3617 .... August 12, 1983 . Chili Davis .... Giants	
3562 .... July 8, 1983 .... Hubie Brooks .... Mets		3618 .... August 12, 1983 . Jack Clark .... Giants	
3563 .... July 8, 1983 .... Keith Hernandez .... Mets		3619 .... August 12, 1983 . Jeffrey Leonard .... Giants	
3564 .... July 8, 1983 .... Brian Giles .... Mets		3620 .... August 17, 1983 . Dave Concepcion .... Reds	
3565 .... July 8, 1983 .... Tom Gorman .... Mets		3621 .... August 17, 1983 . Frank Pastore .... Reds	
3566 .... July 8, 1983 .... Mookie Wilson .... Mets		3622 .... August 17, 1983 . Nick Esasky .... Reds	
3567 .... July 8, 1983 .... Darryl Strawberry .... Mets		3623 .... August 21, 1983 . Dane Iorg .... Cardinals	
3568 .... July 8, 1983 .... Ron Hodges .... Mets		3624 .... August 21, 1983 . Darrell Porter .... Cardinals	

3625 .... August 21, 1983 . Danny Cox .... Cardinals
3626 .... August 21, 1983 . Andy Van Slyke ... Cardinals
3627 .... August 21, 1983 . Darrell Porter .... Cardinals
3628 .... August 26, 1983 . Mel Hall .... Cubs
3629 .... August 26, 1983 . Jody Davis .... Cubs
3630 .... Sept. 1, 1983 ...... Marvell Wynne .... Pirates
3631 .... Sept. 1, 1983 ...... Doug Frobel .... Pirates
3632 .... Sept. 1, 1983 ...... Rafael Belliard .... Pirates
3633 .... Sept. 1, 1983 ...... Lee Mazzilli .... Pirates
3634 .... Sept. 1, 1983 ...... Doug Frobel .... Pirates
3635 .... Sept. 1, 1983 ...... Richie Hebner .... Pirates
3636 .... Sept. 1, 1983 ...... Lee Tunnell .... Pirates
3637 .... Sept. 1, 1983 ...... Lee Mazzilli .... Pirates
3638 .... Sept. 1, 1983 ...... Dale Berra .... Pirates
3639 .... Sept. 1, 1983 ...... Joe Orsulak .... Pirates
3640 .... Sept. 7, 1983 ...... Alan Wiggins .... Padres
3641 .... Sept. 7, 1983 ...... Terry Kennedy .... Padres
3642 .... Sept. 7, 1983 ...... Ruppert Jones .... Padres
3643 .... Sept. 7, 1983 ...... Eric Show .... Padres
3644 .... Sept. 7, 1983 ...... Terry Kennedy .... Padres
3645 .... Sept. 7, 1983 ...... Garry Templeton ..... Padres
3646 .... Sept. 11, 1983 .... Dan Gladden .... Giants
3647 .... Sept. 11, 1983 .... Guy Sularz .... Giants
3648 .... Sept. 11, 1983 .... Atlee Hammaker ...... Giants
3649 .... Sept. 11, 1983 .... Dan Gladden .... Giants
3650 .... Sept. 11, 1983 .... Chili Davis .... Giants
3651 .... Sept. 11, 1983 .... Chris Smith .... Giants
3652 .... Sept. 11, 1983 .... Max Venable .... Giants
3653 .... Sept. 11, 1983 .... Chili Davis .... Giants
3654 .... Sept. 11, 1983 .... Darrell Evans .... Giants
3655 .... Sept. 11, 1983 .... Chris Smith .... Giants
3656 .... Sept. 11, 1983 .... Max Venable .... Giants
3657 .... Sept. 15, 1983 .... Bill Russell .... Dodgers
3658 .... Sept. 15, 1983 .... R.J. Reynolds .... Dodgers
3659 .... Sept. 15, 1983 .... Alejandro Pena ..... Dodgers
3660 .... Sept. 15, 1983 .... R.J. Reynolds .... Dodgers
3661 .... Sept. 15, 1983 .... Alejandro Pena ..... Dodgers
3662 .... Sept. 20, 1983 .... Steve Yeager .... Dodgers
3663 .... Sept. 20, 1983 .... Rafael Landestoy .. Dodgers
3664 .... Sept. 20, 1983 .... Steve Sax .... Dodgers
3665 .... Sept. 20, 1983 .... R.J. Reynolds .... Dodgers
3666 .... Sept. 20, 1983 .... Steve Yeager .... Dodgers
3667 .... Sept. 20, 1983 .... Ken Landreaux ..... Dodgers
3668 .... Sept. 20, 1983 .... Mike Marshall .... Dodgers
3669 .... Sept. 25, 1983 .... Tom O'Malley .... Giants
3670 .... Sept. 25, 1983 .... Joel Youngblood ...... Giants
3671 .... Sept. 25, 1983 .... Chili Davis .... Giants
3672 .... Sept. 25, 1983 .... Chris Smith .... Giants
3673 .... Sept. 29, 1983 .... Glenn Hubbard .... Braves
3674 .... Sept. 29, 1983 .... Rafael Ramirez .... Braves
3675 .... Sept. 29, 1983 .... Craig McMurtry .... Braves
3676 .... Sept. 29, 1983 .... Chris Chambliss ...... Braves
3677 .... Sept. 29, 1983 .... Brett Butler .... Braves
3678 .... April 4, 1984 .... Tim Raines .... Expos
3679 .... April 4, 1984 .... Andre Dawson .... Expos
3680 .... April 4, 1984 .... Argenis Salazar .... Expos

3681 .... April 4, 1984 .... Bill Gullickson .... Expos
3682 .... April 4, 1984 .... Tim Raines .... Expos
3683 .... April 4, 1984 .... Andre Dawson .... Expos
3684 .... April 10, 1984 ..... Joe Lefebvre .... Phillies
3685 .... April 10, 1984 ..... Von Hayes .... Phillies
3686 .... April 10, 1984 ..... Bo Diaz .... Phillies
3687 .... April 10, 1984 ..... Len Matuszek .... Phillies
3688 .... April 10, 1984 ..... Joe Lefebvre .... Phillies
3689 .... April 10, 1984 ..... Juan Samuel .... Phillies
3690 .... April 10, 1984 ..... Mike Schmidt .... Phillies
3691 .... April 10, 1984 ..... Joe Lefebvre .... Phillies
3692 .... April 10, 1984 ..... Von Hayes .... Phillies
3693 .... April 10, 1984 ..... Ivan DeJesus .... Phillies
3694 .... April 10, 1984 ..... John Denny .... Phillies
3695 .... April 15, 1984 ..... Nick Esasky .... Reds
3696 .... April 15, 1984 ..... Dan Bilardello .... Reds
3697 .... April 15, 1984 ..... Joe Price .... Reds
3698 .... April 15, 1984 ..... Eddie Milner .... Reds
3699 .... April 15, 1984 ..... Tony Perez .... Reds
3700 .... April 15, 1984 ..... Dave Parker .... Reds
3701 .... April 15, 1984 ..... Nick Esasky .... Reds
3702 .... April 15, 1984 ..... Joe Price .... Reds
3703 .... April 20, 1984 ..... Bob Horner .... Braves
3704 .... April 20, 1984 ..... C. Washington .... Braves
3705 .... April 25, 1984 ..... Terry Whitfield .... Dodgers
3706 .... April 25, 1984 ..... Pedro Guerrero ..... Dodgers
3707 .... April 25, 1984 ..... Pedro Guerrero ..... Dodgers
3708 .... April 25, 1984 ..... Mike Marshall .... Dodgers
3709 .... May 1, 1984 .... Ron Oester .... Reds
3710 .... May 1, 1984 .... Duane Walker .... Reds
3711 .... May 1, 1984 .... Dave Concepcion .... Reds
3712 .... May 1, 1984 .... Brad Gulden .... Reds
3713 .... May 1, 1984 .... Jeff Russell .... Reds
3714 .... May 1, 1984 .... Duane Walker .... Reds
3715 .... May 1, 1984 .... Dave Parker .... Reds
3716 .... May 1, 1984 .... Brad Gulden .... Reds
3717 .... May 6, 1984 .... Wally Backman .... Mets
3718 .... May 6, 1984 .... Darryl Strawberry .... Mets
3719 .... May 6, 1984 .... Ross Jones .... Mets
3720 .... May 6, 1984 .... Wally Backman .... Mets
3721 .... May 6, 1984 .... Darryl Strawberry .... Mets
3722 .... May 6, 1984 .... Mookie Wilson .... Mets
3723 .... May 6, 1984 .... Darryl Strawberry .... Mets
3724 .... May 11, 1984 ...... Garry Matthews .... Cubs
3725 .... May 11, 1984 ...... Mel Hall .... Cubs
3726 .... May 11, 1984 ...... Jody Davis .... Cubs
3727 .... May 11, 1984 ...... Ryne Sandberg .... Cubs
3728 .... May 11, 1984 ...... Dick Ruthven .... Cubs
3729 .... May 11, 1984 ...... Bob Dernier .... Cubs
3730 .... May 11, 1984 ...... Leon Durham .... Cubs
3731 .... May 11, 1984 ...... Ron Cey .... Cubs
3732 .... May 16, 1984 ...... Jason Thompson ..... Pirates
3733 .... May 16, 1984 ...... Amos Otis .... Pirates
3734 .... May 16, 1984 ...... Jason Thompson ..... Pirates
3735 .... May 16, 1984 ...... Milt May .... Pirates
3736 .... May 16, 1984 ...... Amos Otis .... Pirates

3737 .... May 16, 1984 ...... Jason Thompson ..... Pirates		3793 .... July 24, 1984 ...... Mark Davis .... Giants
3738 .... May 16, 1984 ...... Milt May .... Pirates		3794 .... July 24, 1984 ...... Scot Thompson .... Giants
3739 .... May 16, 1984 ...... Amos Otis .... Pirates		3795 .... July 24, 1984 ...... Joel Youngblood ...... Giants
3740 .... May 16, 1984 ...... Lee Mazzilli .... Pirates		3796 .... July 24, 1984 ...... Chili Davis .... Giants
3741 .... May 16, 1984 ...... Marvell Wynne .... Pirates		3797 .... July 28, 1984 ...... Steve Garvey .... Padres
3742 .... May 16, 1984 ...... Johnny Ray .... Pirates		3798 .... July 28, 1984 ...... Carmelo Martinez .... Padres
3743 .... May 21, 1984 ...... Tommy Herr .... Cardinals		3799 .... July 28, 1984 ...... Luis Salazar .... Padres
3744 .... May 21, 1984 ...... Willie McGee ...... Cardinals		3800 .... July 28, 1984 ...... Eric Show .... Padres
3745 .... May 21, 1984 ...... Andy Van Slyke ... Cardinals		3801 .... July 28, 1984 ...... Kevin McReynolds .. Padres
3746 .... May 21, 1984 ...... Tommy Herr .... Cardinals		3802 .... July 28, 1984 ...... Luis Salazar .... Padres
3747 .... May 21, 1984 ...... Willie McGee ...... Cardinals		3803 .... July 28, 1984 ...... Eric Show .... Padres
3748 .... May 21, 1984 ...... George Hendrick . Cardinals		3804 .... July 28, 1984 ...... Tony Gwynn .... Padres
3749 .... May 21, 1984 ...... Ricky Horton .... Cardinals		3805 .... August 3, 1984 ... Garry Templeton ..... Padres
3750 .... May 26, 1984 ...... Tony Pena .... Pirates		3806 .... August 3, 1984 ... Graig Nettles .... Padres
3751 .... May 26, 1984 ...... Marvell Wynne .... Pirates		3807 .... August 3, 1984 ... Carmelo Martinez .... Padres
3752 .... May 26, 1984 ...... Lee Lacy .... Pirates		3808 .... August 3, 1984 ... Eric Show .... Padres
3753 .... May 26, 1984 ...... Tony Pena .... Pirates		3809 .... August 8, 1984 ... Manny Trillo .... Giants
3754 .... May 26, 1984 ...... Bill Madlock .... Pirates		3810 .... August 8, 1984 ... Johnnie LeMaster ... Giants
3755 .... May 26, 1984 ...... Lee Mazzilli .... Pirates		3811 .... August 8, 1984 ... Gene Richards .... Giants
3756 .... May 26, 1984 ...... Dale Berra .... Pirates		3812 .... August 8, 1984 ... Johnnie LeMaster ... Giants
3757 .... May 26, 1984 ...... Jason Thompson ..... Pirates		3813 .... August 8, 1984 ... Bob Lacey .... Giants
3758 .... May 26, 1984 ...... Tony Pena .... Pirates		3814 .... August 12, 1984 . Gary Redus .... Reds
3759 .... June 1, 1984 .... R.J. Reynolds .... Dodgers		3815 .... August 12, 1984 . Dave Parker .... Reds
3760 .... June 1, 1984 ...... Terry Whitfield ...... Dodgers		3816 .... August 12, 1984 . Dave Van Gorder .... Reds
3761 .... June 1, 1984 ...... Pedro Guerrero ..... Dodgers		3817 .... August 12, 1984 . Ron Oester .... Reds
3762 .... June 1, 1984 ...... Rick Honeycutt ...... Dodgers		3818 .... August 12, 1984 . Dave Parker .... Reds
3763 .... June 17, 1984 ..... Greg Brock .... Dodgers		3819 .... August 12, 1984 . Eric Davis .... Reds
3764 .... June 17, 1984 ..... Steve Sax .... Dodgers		3820 .... August 12, 1984 . Tom Foley .... Reds
3765 .... June 17, 1984 ..... Terry Whitfield ...... Dodgers		3821 .... August 12, 1984 . Skeeter Barnes .... Reds
3766 .... June 17, 1984 ..... Steve Sax .... Dodgers		3822 .... August 12, 1984 . Dave Parker .... Reds
3767 .... June 17, 1984 ..... Pedro Guerrero ..... Dodgers		3823 .... August 12, 1984 . Eric Davis .... Reds
3768 .... June 17, 1984 ..... Terry Whitfield ...... Dodgers		3824 .... August 12, 1984 . Eddie Milner .... Reds
3769 .... June 17, 1984 ..... Mike Scioscia .... Dodgers		3825 .... August 17, 1984 . Denny Gonzalez ...... Pirates
3770 .... June 17, 1984 ..... Dave Anderson ..... Dodgers		3826 .... August 17, 1984 . Lee Mazzilli .... Pirates
3771 .... June 17, 1984 ..... Rick Monday .... Dodgers		3827 .... August 17, 1984 . Larry McWilliams ..... Pirates
3772 .... July 3, 1984 .... Wally Backman .... Mets		3828 .... August 17, 1984 . Denny Gonzalez ...... Pirates
3773 .... July 3, 1984 .... George Foster .... Mets		3829 .... August 17, 1984 . Lee Lacy .... Pirates
3774 .... July 3, 1984 .... Hubie Brooks .... Mets		3830 .... August 22, 1984 . Leon Durham .... Cubs
3775 .... July 3, 1984 .... Mike Fitzgerald .... Mets		3831 .... August 22, 1984 . Keith Moreland .... Cubs
3776 .... July 3, 1984 .... Bruce Berenyi .... Mets		3832 .... August 22, 1984 . Ron Cey .... Cubs
3777 .... July 3, 1984 .... Danny Heep .... Mets		3833 .... August 22, 1984 . Jody Davis .... Cubs
3778 .... July 3, 1984 .... Darryl Strawberry .... Mets		3834 .... August 22, 1984 . Ron Cey .... Cubs
3779 .... July 3, 1984 .... Hubie Brooks .... Mets		3835 .... August 22, 1984 . Jay Johnstone .... Cubs
3780 .... July 8, 1984 .... Bill Gullickson .... Expos		3836 .... August 22, 1984 . Garry Matthews .... Cubs
3781 .... July 13, 1984 ...... Von Hayes .... Phillies		3837 .... August 22, 1984 . Leon Durham .... Cubs
3782 .... July 13, 1984 ...... Shane Rawley .... Phillies		3838 .... August 22, 1984 . Bob Dernier .... Cubs
3783 .... July 13, 1984 ...... Greg Gross .... Phillies		3839 .... August 22, 1984 . Ryne Sandberg .... Cubs
3784 .... July 13, 1984 ...... Juan Samuel .... Phillies		3840 .... August 22, 1984 . Garry Matthews .... Cubs
3785 .... July 13, 1984 ...... Glenn Wilson .... Phillies		3841 .... August 22, 1984 . Leon Durham .... Cubs
3786 .... July 18, 1984 ...... Ron Gardenhire .... Mets		3842 .... August 26, 1984 . Tommy Herr .... Cardinals
3787 .... July 18, 1984 ...... Walt Terrell .... Mets		3843 .... August 26, 1984 . Terry Pendleton ... Cardinals
3788 .... July 18, 1984 ...... George Foster .... Mets		3844 .... August 26, 1984 . Kurt Kepshire ..... Cardinals
3789 .... July 18, 1984 ...... Walt Terrell .... Mets		3845 .... August 26, 1984 . Willie McGee ...... Cardinals
3790 .... July 18, 1984 ...... Darryl Strawberry .... Mets		3846 .... August 26, 1984 . Lonnie Smith .... Cardinals
3791 .... July 18, 1984 ...... George Foster .... Mets		3847 .... August 26, 1984 . Kurt Kepshire ..... Cardinals
3792 .... July 18, 1984 ...... Mike Fitzgerald .... Mets		3848 .... August 26, 1984 . Terry Pendleton ... Cardinals

3849	August 31, 1984	Dave LaPoint	Cardinals
3850	August 31, 1984	Willie McGee	Cardinals
3851	August 31, 1984	Lonnie Smith	Cardinals
3852	August 31, 1984	David Green	Cardinals
3853	August 31, 1984	Darrell Porter	Cardinals
3854	August 31, 1984	Terry Pendleton	Cardinals
3855	Sept. 5, 1984	Joel Youngblood	Giants
3856	Sept. 5, 1984	Scot Thompson	Giants
3857	Sept. 5, 1984	Fran Mullins	Giants
3858	Sept. 5, 1984	Chili Davis	Giants
3859	Sept. 5, 1984	Scot Thompson	Giants
3860	Sept. 5, 1984	Chris Brown	Giants
3861	Sept. 5, 1984	Fran Mullins	Giants
3862	Sept. 5, 1984	Scot Thompson	Giants
3863	Sept. 10, 1984	Milt Thompson	Braves
3864	Sept. 10, 1984	C. Washington	Braves
3865	Sept. 10, 1984	Dale Murphy	Braves
3866	Sept. 10, 1984	Jerry Royster	Braves
3867	Sept. 10, 1984	C. Washington	Braves
3868	Sept. 10, 1984	Dale Murphy	Braves
3869	Sept. 10, 1984	Jerry Royster	Braves
3870	Sept. 10, 1984	Dale Murphy	Braves
3871	Sept. 10, 1984	Zane Smith	Braves
3872	Sept. 15, 1984	Tony Gwynn	Padres
3873	Sept. 15, 1984	Steve Garvey	Padres
3874	Sept. 20, 1984	Ken Landreaux	Dodgers
3875	April 9, 1985	Mariano Duncan	Dodgers
3876	April 9, 1985	Al Oliver	Dodgers
3877	April 9, 1985	Mike Marshall	Dodgers
3878	April 9, 1985	Mike Marshall	Dodgers
3879	April 14, 1985	Mike Schmidt	Phillies
3880	April 14, 1985	Mike Schmidt	Phillies
3881	April 14, 1985	Bo Diaz	Phillies
3882	April 14, 1985	Steve Jeltz	Phillies
3883	April 14, 1985	Steve Carlton	Phillies
3884	April 14, 1985	Juan Samuel	Phillies
3885	April 14, 1985	Steve Jeltz	Phillies
3886	April 14, 1985	Juan Samuel	Phillies
3887	April 14, 1985	Von Hayes	Phillies
3888	April 19, 1985	Gerald Perry	Braves
3889	April 24, 1985	Dave Parker	Reds
3890	April 24, 1985	Tom Foley	Reds
3891	April 24, 1985	Duane Walker	Reds
3892	April 24, 1985	Tom Foley	Reds
3893	April 24, 1985	Dave Van Gorder	Reds
3894	April 24, 1985	Pete Rose	Reds
3895	April 24, 1985	Eddie Milner	Reds
3896	April 28, 1985	Brad Komminsk	Braves
3897	April 28, 1985	Chris Chambliss	Braves
3898	April 28, 1985	Rick Cerone	Braves
3899	April 28, 1985	Pascual Perez	Braves
3900	April 28, 1985	C. Washington	Braves
3901	April 28, 1985	Chris Chambliss	Braves
3902	April 28, 1985	Ken Oberkfell	Braves
3903	May 3, 1985	Juan Samuel	Phillies
3904	May 3, 1985	Glenn Wilson	Phillies
3905	May 3, 1985	Ozzie Virgil	Phillies
3906	May 3, 1985	Steve Jeltz	Phillies
3907	May 3, 1985	Steve Carlton	Phillies
3908	May 3, 1985	Tim Corcoran	Phillies
3909	May 3, 1985	Steve Carlton	Phillies
3910	May 3, 1985	Juan Samuel	Phillies
3911	May 3, 1985	Glenn Wilson	Phillies
3912	May 3, 1985	Kevin Gross	Phillies
3913	May 8, 1985	Mike Fitzgerald	Expos
3914	May 8, 1985	Joe Hesketh	Expos
3915	May 8, 1985	Tim Raines	Expos
3916	May 8, 1985	Joe Hesketh	Expos
3917	May 8, 1985	Tim Raines	Expos
3918	May 8, 1985	Vance Law	Expos
3919	May 8, 1985	Dan Driessen	Expos
3920	May 8, 1985	Tim Wallach	Expos
3921	May 8, 1985	Herm Winningham	Expos
3922	May 8, 1985	Joe Hesketh	Expos
3923	May 13, 1985	Joe Hesketh	Expos
3924	May 13, 1985	Herm Winningham	Expos
3925	May 13, 1985	Andre Dawson	Expos
3926	May 13, 1985	Hubie Brooks	Expos
3927	May 13, 1985	Joe Hesketh	Expos
3928	May 13, 1985	Razor Shines	Expos
3929	May 13, 1985	Herm Winningham	Expos
3930	May 18, 1985	Vince Coleman	Cardinals
3931	May 18, 1985	Tommy Herr	Cardinals
3932	May 18, 1985	Andy Van Slyke	Cardinals
3933	May 18, 1985	Jack Clark	Cardinals
3934	May 18, 1985	Terry Pendleton	Cardinals
3935	May 18, 1985	Terry Pendleton	Cardinals
3936	May 24, 1985	Ron Cey	Cubs
3937	May 24, 1985	Dick Ruthven	Cubs
3938	May 24, 1985	Keith Moreland	Cubs
3939	May 24, 1985	Thad Bosley	Cubs
3940	May 24, 1985	Leon Durham	Cubs
3941	May 24, 1985	Jody Davis	Cubs
3942	May 24, 1985	Chico Walker	Cubs
3943	May 29, 1985	Junior Ortiz	Pirates
3944	May 29, 1985	Jim Winn	Pirates
3945	May 29, 1985	Lee Mazzilli	Pirates
3946	May 29, 1985	Steve Kemp	Pirates
3947	May 29, 1985	Jim Morrison	Pirates
3948	May 29, 1985	Bill Almon	Pirates
3949	May 29, 1985	Bill Almon	Pirates
3950	May 29, 1985	Jim Winn	Pirates
3951	June 3, 1985	Jack Clark	Cardinals
3952	June 3, 1985	Ozzie Smith	Cardinals
3953	June 3, 1985	Vince Coleman	Cardinals
3954	June 3, 1985	John Tudor	Cardinals
3955	June 8, 1985	Rick Adams	Giants
3956	June 8, 1985	Rick Adams	Giants
3957	June 8, 1985	Chili Davis	Giants
3958	June 8, 1985	Rob Deer	Giants
3959	June 8, 1985	Alex Trevino	Giants
3960	June 8, 1985	Bill Laskey	Giants

3961 .... June 8, 1985 .... Rob Deer .... Giants
3962 .... June 12, 1985 ..... Terry Kennedy .... Padres
3963 .... June 12, 1985 ..... Carmelo Martinez .... Padres
3964 .... June 12, 1985 ..... Eric Show .... Padres
3965 .... June 12, 1985 ..... Eric Show .... Padres
3966 .... June 12, 1985 ..... Kevin McReynolds .. Padres
3967 .... June 17, 1985 ..... Glenn Hubbard .... Braves
3968 .... June 17, 1985 ..... Terry Harper .... Braves
3969 .... June 17, 1985 ..... Larry Owen .... Braves
3970 .... June 17, 1985 ..... Steve Shields .... Braves
3971 .... June 17, 1985 ..... Dale Murphy .... Braves
3972 .... June 17, 1985 ..... Larry Owen .... Braves
3973 .... June 17, 1985 ..... Brad Komminsk ...... Braves
3974 .... June 17, 1985 ..... Ken Oberkfell .... Braves
3975 .... June 22, 1985 ..... Dave Anderson ..... Dodgers
3976 .... June 22, 1985 ..... R.J. Reynolds .... Dodgers
3977 .... June 27, 1985 ..... Bob Horner .... Braves
3978 .... June 27, 1985 ..... C. Washington .... Braves
3979 .... June 27, 1985 ..... Glenn Hubbard .... Braves
3980 .... June 27, 1985 ..... Rafael Ramirez .... Braves
3981 .... June 27, 1985 ..... C. Washington .... Braves
3982 .... June 27, 1985 ..... Dale Murphy .... Braves
3983 .... June 27, 1985 ..... Terry Harper .... Braves
3984 .... July 1, 1985 .... Terry Kennedy .... Padres
3985 .... July 1, 1985 .... Carmelo Martinez .... Padres
3986 .... July 1, 1985 .... Tony Gwynn .... Padres
3987 .... July 1, 1985 .... Terry Kennedy .... Padres
3988 .... July 1, 1985 .... Graig Nettles .... Padres
3989 .... July 1, 1985 .... Carmelo Martinez .... Padres
3990 .... July 1, 1985 .... Bobby Brown .... Padres
3991 .... July 6, 1985 .... Dan Driessen .... Expos
3992 .... July 6, 1985 .... Mitch Webster .... Expos
3993 .... July 6, 1985 .... Joe Hesketh .... Expos
3994 .... July 11, 1985 .... Len Dykstra .... Mets
3995 .... July 11, 1985 ..... Rafael Santana .... Mets
3996 .... July 11, 1985 ...... Sid Fernandez .... Mets
3997 .... July 11, 1985 ...... Sid Fernandez .... Mets
3998 .... July 11, 1985 ...... Darryl Strawberry .... Mets
3999 .... July 11, 1985 ...... Gary Carter .... Mets
4000 .... July 11, 1985 ...... Danny Heep .... Mets
4001 .... July 11, 1985 ..... Rafael Santana .... Mets
4002 .... July 11, 1985 ...... Sid Fernandez .... Mets
4003 .... July 11, 1985 ...... Wally Backman .... Mets
4004 .... July 11, 1985 ...... Danny Heep .... Mets
4005 .... July 20, 1985 ...... Herm Winningham .... Expos
4006 .... July 20, 1985 ...... Bill Gullickson .... Expos
4007 .... July 24, 1985 ...... Von Hayes .... Phillies
4008 .... July 24, 1985 ...... John Russell .... Phillies
4009 .... July 24, 1985 ...... Rick Schu .... Phillies
4010 .... July 24, 1985 ...... Juan Samuel .... Phillies
4011 .... July 24, 1985 ...... Mike Schmidt .... Phillies
4012 .... July 24, 1985 ...... John Russell .... Phillies
4013 .... July 24, 1985 ...... Mike Schmidt .... Phillies
4014 .... July 30, 1985 ...... Pete Rose .... Reds
4015 .... July 30, 1985 ...... Dan Bilardello .... Reds
4016 .... July 30, 1985 ...... Max Venable .... Reds

4017 .... July 30, 1985 ...... Buddy Bell .... Reds
4018 .... July 30, 1985 ...... Mario Soto .... Reds
4019 .... July 30, 1985 ...... Pete Rose .... Reds
4020 .... July 30, 1985 ...... Mario Soto .... Reds
4021 .... August 3, 1985 ... Terry Kennedy .... Padres
4022 .... August 3, 1985 ... Carmelo Martinez .... Padres
4023 .... August 3, 1985 ... Carmelo Martinez .... Padres
4024 .... August 3, 1985 ... Tim Flannery .... Padres
4025 .... August 3, 1985 ... Tony Gwynn .... Padres
4026 .... August 3, 1985 ... Graig Nettles .... Padres
4027 .... August 3, 1985 ... Terry Kennedy .... Padres
4028 .... August 3, 1985 ... Tim Flannery .... Padres
4029 .... August 9, 1985 ... Bruce Bochy .... Padres
4030 .... August 9, 1985 ... Graig Nettles .... Padres
4031 .... August 9, 1985 ... Tim Flannery .... Padres
4032 .... August 9, 1985 ... Bruce Bochy .... Padres
4033 .... August 9, 1985 ... Dave Dravecky .... Padres
4034 .... August 9, 1985 ... Miguel Dilone .... Padres
4035 .... August 9, 1985 ... Al Bumbry .... Padres
4036 .... August 14, 1985 . Brad Wellman .... Giants
4037 .... August 14, 1985 . Jeffrey Leonard .... Giants
4038 .... August 14, 1985 . Bob Brenly .... Giants
4039 .... August 14, 1985 . Jim Gott .... Giants
4040 .... August 18, 1985 . Pete Rose .... Reds
4041 .... August 18, 1985 . Nick Esasky .... Reds
4042 .... August 18, 1985 . Ron Oester .... Reds
4043 .... August 18, 1985 . Jay Tibbs .... Reds
4044 .... August 18, 1985 . Dave Parker .... Reds
4045 .... August 18, 1985 . Bo Diaz .... Reds
4046 .... August 18, 1985 . Cesar Cedeno .... Reds
4047 .... August 23, 1985 . Bill Madlock .... Pirates
4048 .... August 23, 1985 . Mike Brown .... Pirates
4049 .... August 23, 1985 . Sammy Khalifa .... Pirates
4050 .... August 23, 1985 . Lee Tunnell .... Pirates
4051 .... August 23, 1985 . Denny Gonzalez ...... Pirates
4052 .... August 23, 1985 . Lee Mazzilli .... Pirates
4053 .... August 28, 1985 . Garry Matthews .... Cubs
4054 .... August 28, 1985 . Leon Durham .... Cubs
4055 .... August 28, 1985 . Jay Baller .... Cubs
4056 .... August 28, 1985 . Garry Matthews .... Cubs
4057 .... August 28, 1985 . Leon Durham .... Cubs
4058 .... August 28, 1985 . Shawon Dunston .... Cubs
4059 .... August 28, 1985 . Jay Baller .... Cubs
4060 .... August 28, 1985 . Leon Durham .... Cubs
4061 .... Sept. 2, 1985 ...... Thad Bosley .... Cubs
4062 .... Sept. 15, 1985 .... Miguel Dilone .... Padres
4063 .... Sept. 15, 1985 .... Graig Nettles .... Padres
4064 .... Sept. 15, 1985 .... LaMarr Hoyt .... Padres
4065 .... Sept. 15, 1985 .... Tony Gwynn .... Padres
4066 .... Sept. 20, 1985 .... Dave Concepcion ...... Reds
4067 .... Sept. 20, 1985 .... Dave Parker .... Reds
4068 .... Sept. 25, 1985 .... Ken Landreaux ..... Dodgers
4069 .... Sept. 25, 1985 .... Bill Madlock .... Dodgers
4070 .... Sept. 25, 1985 .... Mike Marshall .... Dodgers
4071 .... Sept. 30, 1985 .... Dale Murphy .... Braves
4072 .... Sept. 30, 1985 .... Bob Horner .... Braves

4073 .... Sept. 30, 1985 .... C. Washington .... Braves			4129 .... May 15, 1986 ...... Len Dykstra .... Mets
4074 .... Sept. 30, 1985 .... Glenn Hubbard .... Braves			4130 .... May 15, 1986 ...... Keith Hernandez .... Mets
4075 .... Sept. 30, 1985 .... Pascual Perez .... Braves			4131 .... May 15, 1986 ...... Tim Teufel .... Mets
4076 .... October 5, 1985 .. Terry Kennedy .... Padres			4132 .... May 20, 1986 ..... Sammy Khalifa ...... Pirates
4077 .... October 5, 1985 .. Kevin McReynolds .. Padres			4133 .... May 20, 1986 ..... R.J. Reynolds .... Pirates
4078 .... October 5, 1985 .. Tim Flannery .... Padres			4134 .... May 20, 1986 ..... Johnny Ray .... Pirates
4079 .... October 5, 1985 .. Carmelo Martinez .... Padres			4135 .... May 20, 1986 ..... Mike Brown .... Pirates
4080 .... October 5, 1985 .. Kevin McReynolds .. Padres			4136 .... May 20, 1986 ..... Jim Morrison .... Pirates
4081 .... October 5, 1985 .. Mario Ramirez .... Padres			4137 .... May 20, 1986 ..... Sammy Khalifa .... Pirates
4082 .... October 5, 1985 .. Miguel Dilone .... Padres			4138 .... May 20, 1986 ..... R.J. Reynolds .... Pirates
4083 .... October 5, 1985 .. Carmelo Martinez .... Padres			4139 .... May 20, 1986 ..... Sid Bream .... Pirates
4084 .... April 8, 1986 .... Bob Brenly .... Giants			4140 .... May 20, 1986 ..... Jim Morrison .... Pirates
4085 .... April 8, 1986 .... Robby Thompson ..... Giants			4141 .... May 31, 1986 ...... Al Newman .... Expos
4086 .... April 8, 1986 .... Will Clark .... Giants			4142 .... May 31, 1986 ...... Mitch Webster .... Expos
4087 .... April 8, 1986 .... Mike Krukow .... Giants			4143 .... June 24, 1986 ..... Ron Oester .... Reds
4088 .... April 12, 1986 ..... C. Washington .... Braves			4144 .... June 24, 1986 .... Dave Parker .... Reds
4089 .... April 12, 1986 ..... Dale Murphy .... Braves			4145 .... June 24, 1986 .... Eddie Milner .... Reds
4090 .... April 12, 1986 ..... Rick Mahler .... Braves			4146 .... June 24, 1986 .... Eric Davis .... Reds
4091 .... April 12, 1986 ..... Dale Murphy .... Braves			4147 .... June 29, 1986 ..... Len Matuszek ...... Dodgers
4092 .... April 12, 1986 ..... Rick Mahler .... Braves			4148 .... June 29, 1986 ..... Jeff Hamilton ...... Dodgers
4093 .... April 16, 1986 ..... Will Clark .... Giants			4149 .... June 29, 1986 .... Craig Shipley .... Dodgers
4094 .... April 16, 1986 ..... Bob Brenly .... Giants			4150 .... June 29, 1986 ..... Len Matuszek ...... Dodgers
4095 .... April 16, 1986 ..... Roger Mason .... Giants			4151 .... June 29, 1986 ..... Jeff Hamilton ...... Dodgers
4096 .... April 16, 1986 ..... Dan Gladden .... Giants			4152 .... June 29, 1986 ..... Reggie Williams .... Dodgers
4097 .... April 16, 1986 ..... Bob Melvin .... Giants			4153 .... June 29, 1986 ..... Steve Sax .... Dodgers
4098 .... April 16, 1986 ..... Roger Mason .... Giants			4154 .... June 29, 1986 ..... Jeff Hamilton ...... Dodgers
4099 .... April 16, 1986 ..... Will Clark .... Giants			4155 .... July 4, 1986 .... Darryl Strawberry .... Mets
4100 .... April 16, 1986 ..... Jeffrey Leonard .... Giants			4156 .... July 4, 1986 .... Gary Carter .... Mets
4101 .... April 16, 1986 ..... Bob Brenly .... Giants			4157 .... July 4, 1986 .... Keith Hernandez .... Mets
4102 .... April 21, 1986 ..... Omar Moreno .... Braves			4158 .... July 4, 1986 .... Darryl Strawberry .... Mets
4103 .... April 21, 1986 ..... Joe Johnson .... Braves			4159 .... July 4, 1986 .... Howard Johnson ...... Mets
4104 .... April 21, 1986 ..... Rafael Ramirez .... Braves			4160 .... July 4, 1986 .... Rafael Santana .... Mets
4105 .... April 21, 1986 ..... Glenn Hubbard .... Braves			4161 .... July 8, 1986 .... Andre Dawson .... Expos
4106 .... April 25, 1986 ..... Dave Concepcion ...... Reds			4162 .... July 8, 1986 .... Hubie Brooks .... Expos
4107 .... April 25, 1986 ..... Tom Browning .... Reds			4163 .... July 8, 1986 .... Tim Wallach .... Expos
4108 .... April 25, 1986 ..... Ron Oester .... Reds			4164 .... July 8, 1986 .... Al Newman .... Expos
4109 .... April 25, 1986 ..... Dave Concepcion ...... Reds			4165 .... July 8, 1986 .... Jay Tibbs .... Expos
4110 .... April 25, 1986 .... Max Venable .... Reds			4166 .... July 8, 1986 .... Tim Raines .... Expos
4111 .... April 25, 1986 .... Dave Parker .... Reds			4167 .... July 8, 1986 .... Tim Wallach .... Expos
4112 .... April 25, 1986 .... Bo Diaz .... Reds			4168 .... July 8, 1986 .... Mike Fitzgerald .... Expos
4113 .... April 29, 1986 .... Glenn Wilson .... Phillies			4169 .... July 8, 1986 .... Jay Tibbs .... Expos
4114 .... April 29, 1986 .... Steve Jeltz .... Phillies			4170 .... July 12, 1986 ...... Juan Samuel .... Phillies
4115 .... May 3, 1986 .... Tim Raines .... Expos			4171 .... July 12, 1986 ...... Ronn Reynolds ...... Phillies
4116 .... May 3, 1986 .... Vance Law .... Expos			4172 .... July 12, 1986 ...... Ron Roenicke .... Phillies
4117 .... May 3, 1986 .... Andre Dawson .... Expos			4173 .... July 12, 1986 ...... Steve Jeltz .... Phillies
4118 .... May 3, 1986 .... Dann Bilardello .... Expos			4174 .... July 12, 1986 ...... Juan Samuel .... Phillies
4119 .... May 7, 1986 .... Len Dykstra .... Mets			4175 .... July 12, 1986 ...... Mike Schmidt .... Phillies
4120 .... May 7, 1986 .... Darryl Strawberry .... Mets			4176 .... July 12, 1986 ...... Ronn Reynolds ...... Phillies
4121 .... May 7, 1986 .... Howard Johnson .... Mets			4177 .... July 12, 1986 ...... Tom Foley .... Phillies
4122 .... May 11, 1986 ...... Trench Davis .... Pirates			4178 .... July 17, 1986 ...... Gary Carter .... Mets
4123 .... May 11, 1986 ...... Junior Ortiz .... Pirates			4179 .... July 17, 1986 ...... Danny Heep .... Mets
4124 .... May 11, 1986 ...... Johnny Ray .... Pirates			4180 .... July 17, 1986 ...... Ray Knight .... Mets
4125 .... May 15, 1986 ...... Len Dykstra .... Mets			4181 .... July 17, 1986 ...... Wally Backman .... Mets
4126 .... May 15, 1986 ...... Gary Carter .... Mets			4182 .... July 17, 1986 ...... Darryl Strawberry .... Mets
4127 .... May 15, 1986 ...... Ray Knight .... Mets			4183 .... July 17, 1986 ...... Ray Knight .... Mets
4128 .... May 15, 1986 ...... Ron Darling .... Mets			4184 .... July 17, 1986 ...... Bob Ojeda .... Mets

4185 .... July 17, 1986 ...... Darryl Strawberry .... Mets		4241 .... Sept. 8, 1986 ...... Chris Welsh .... Reds
4186 .... July 22, 1986 ...... Tim Raines .... Expos		4242 .... Sept. 8, 1986 ...... Dave Parker .... Reds
4187 .... July 22, 1986 ...... Mitch Webster .... Expos		4243 .... Sept. 8, 1986 ...... Eric Davis .... Reds
4188 .... July 22, 1986 ...... Andre Dawson .... Expos		4244 .... Sept. 8, 1986 ...... Eddie Milner .... Reds
4189 .... July 22, 1986 ...... Mike Fitzgerald .... Expos		4245 .... Sept. 8, 1986 ...... Chris Welsh .... Reds
4190 .... July 22, 1986 ...... Floyd Youmans .... Expos		4246 .... Sept. 8, 1986 ...... Eric Davis .... Reds
4191 .... July 22, 1986 ...... Tim Raines .... Expos		4247 .... Sept. 13, 1986 .... Tim Flannery .... Padres
4192 .... July 22, 1986 ...... Andre Dawson .... Expos		4248 .... Sept. 13, 1986 .... Steve Garvey .... Padres
4193 .... July 22, 1986 ...... Wayne Krenchicki ..... Expos		4249 .... Sept. 13, 1986 .... John Kruk .... Padres
4194 .... July 22, 1986 ...... Mitch Webster .... Expos		4250 .... Sept. 13, 1986 .... Steve Garvey .... Padres
4195 .... July 22, 1986 ...... Andre Dawson .... Expos		4251 .... Sept. 13, 1986 .... Terry Kennedy .... Padres
4196 .... July 22, 1986 ...... Tim Wallach .... Expos		4252 .... Sept. 13, 1986 .... Tim Flannery .... Padres
4197 .... July 22, 1986 ...... Rene Gonzales .... Expos		4253 .... Sept. 19, 1986 .... Tim Flannery .... Padres
4198 .... July 22, 1986 ...... Al Newman .... Expos		4254 .... Sept. 19, 1986 ... Graig Nettles .... Padres
4199 .... July 22, 1986 ...... Mitch Webster .... Expos		4255 .... Sept. 19, 1986 ... Gary Green .... Padres
4200 .... July 27, 1986 ...... Gary Redus .... Phillies		4256 .... Sept. 19, 1986 .... Tim Flannery .... Padres
4201 .... July 27, 1986 ...... Glenn Wilson .... Phillies		4257 .... Sept. 19, 1986 .... Benito Santiago ...... Padres
4202 .... July 27, 1986 ...... John Russell .... Phillies		4258 .... Sept. 19, 1986 .... Andy Hawkins .... Padres
4203 .... July 27, 1986 ...... Steve Jeltz .... Phillies		4259 .... Sept. 19, 1986 .... Tony Gwynn .... Padres
4204 .... July 27, 1986 ...... Kevin Gross .... Phillies		4260 ... Sept. 24, 1986 ... Robby Thompson ..... Giants
4205 .... July 27, 1986 ...... Gary Redus .... Phillies		4261 .... Sept. 24, 1986 .... Bob Brenly .... Giants
4206 .... July 27, 1986 ...... Jeff Stone .... Phillies		4262 .... Sept. 24, 1986 .... Candy Maldonado .... Giants
4207 .... July 27, 1986 ...... Mike Schmidt .... Phillies		4263 .... Sept. 24, 1986 .... Bob Melvin .... Giants
4208 .... July 27, 1986 ...... John Russell .... Phillies		4264 .... Sept. 24, 1986 .... Candy Maldonado .... Giants
4209 .... July 27, 1986 ...... Kevin Gross .... Phillies		4265 .... Sept. 24, 1986 .... Bob Melvin .... Giants
4210 .... August 12, 1986 . Mike Scioscia .... Dodgers		4266 .... Sept. 24, 1986 .... Jose Uribe .... Giants
4211 .... August 12, 1986 . Len Matuszek .... Dodgers		4267 .... Sept. 24, 1986 .... Robby Thompson ..... Giants
4212 .... August 12, 1986 . Reggie Williams .... Dodgers		4268 .... Sept. 24, 1986 .... Candy Maldonado .... Giants
4213 .... August 12, 1986 . Rick Honeycutt ...... Dodgers		4269 .... Sept. 24, 1986 .... Brad Gulden .... Giants
4214 .... August 12, 1986 . Greg Brock .... Dodgers		4270 .... Sept. 24, 1986 .... Rick Lancellotti .... Giants
4215 .... August 12, 1986 . Len Matuszek .... Dodgers		4271 .... Sept. 24, 1986 .... Will Clark .... Giants
4216 .... August 17, 1986 . Dale Murphy .... Braves		4272 .... October 3, 1986 .. Dale Murphy .... Braves
4217 .... August 17, 1986 . Ken Griffey .... Braves		4273 .... October 3, 1986 .. Glenn Hubbard .... Braves
4218 .... August 17, 1986 . Dale Murphy .... Braves		4274 .... October 3, 1986 .. Jim Acker .... Braves
4219 .... August 17, 1986 . Glenn Hubbard .... Braves		4275 .... October 3, 1986 .. Ken Griffey .... Braves
4220 .... August 17, 1986 . Zane Smith .... Braves		4276 .... October 3, 1986 .. Jim Acker .... Braves
4221 .... August 22, 1986 . Terry Pendleton .. Cardinals		4277 .... October 3, 1986 .. Dale Murphy .... Braves
4222 .... August 22, 1986 . Ozzie Smith .... Cardinals		4278 .... April 8, 1987 ...... Steve Sax .... Dodgers
4223 .... August 22, 1986 . Clint Hurdle .... Cardinals		4279 .... April 8, 1987 ...... Mike Marshall .... Dodgers
4224 .... August 22, 1986 . Vince Coleman ..... Cardinals		4280 .... April 8, 1987 ...... Rick Honeycutt ...... Dodgers
4225 .... August 22, 1986 . Ozzie Smith .... Cardinals		4281 .... April 8, 1987 ...... Mike Ramsey .... Dodgers
4226 .... August 22, 1986 . Andy Van Slyke ... Cardinals		4282 .... April 8, 1987 ...... Franklin Stubbs ..... Dodgers
4227 .... August 27, 1986 . Ryne Sandberg .... Cubs		4283 .... April 8, 1987 ...... Dave Anderson ..... Dodgers
4228 .... August 27, 1986 . Shawon Dunston .... Cubs		4284 .... April 8, 1987 ...... Rick Honeycutt ...... Dodgers
4229 .... August 27, 1986 . Chris Speier .... Cubs		4285 .... April 8, 1987 ...... Mike Ramsey .... Dodgers
4230 .... August 27, 1986 . Jerry Mumphrey .... Cubs		4286 .... April 8, 1987 ...... Mike Marshall .... Dodgers
4231 .... August 27, 1986 . Keith Moreland .... Cubs		4287 .... April 8, 1987 ...... Franklin Stubbs ..... Dodgers
4232 .... Sept. 2, 1986 ...... Jamie Moyer .... Cubs		4288 .... April 13, 1987 .... Mike Ramsey .... Dodgers
4233 .... Sept. 2, 1986 ...... Jerry Mumphrey .... Cubs		4289 .... April 13, 1987 ..... Pedro Guerrero .... Dodgers
4234 .... Sept. 2, 1986 ...... Leon Durham .... Cubs		4290 .... April 13, 1987 ..... Mariano Duncan ... Dodgers
4235 .... Sept. 2, 1986 ...... Dave Martinez .... Cubs		4291 .... April 13, 1987 ..... Rick Honeycutt ...... Dodgers
4236 .... Sept. 2, 1986 ...... Jody Davis .... Cubs		4292 .... April 13, 1987 ..... Steve Sax .... Dodgers
4237 .... Sept. 8, 1986 ...... Eric Davis .... Reds		4293 .... April 13, 1987 ..... Mike Ramsey .... Dodgers
4238 .... Sept. 8, 1986 ...... Bo Diaz .... Reds		4294 .... April 13, 1987 ..... Pedro Guerrero .... Dodgers
4239 .... Sept. 8, 1986 ...... Nick Esasky .... Reds		4295 .... April 13, 1987 ..... Mariano Duncan ... Dodgers
4240 .... Sept. 8, 1986 ...... Ron Oester .... Reds		4296 .... April 13, 1987 ..... Len Matuszek .... Dodgers

4297 .... April 18, 1987 ..... Dave Parker .... Reds	4353 .... May 27, 1987 ...... Johnny Ray .... Pirates
4298 .... April 18, 1987 ..... Ron Oester .... Reds	4354 .... May 27, 1987 .... Jim Morrison .... Pirates
4299 .... April 18, 1987 ..... Kal Daniels .... Reds	4355 .... May 27, 1987 ...... Mike Lavalliere .... Pirates
4300 .... April 18, 1987 ..... Terry Francona .... Reds	4356 .... May 27, 1987 ...... Rafael Belliard .... Pirates
4301 .... April 18, 1987 ..... Dave Parker .... Reds	4357 .... May 27, 1987 ...... Sid Bream .... Pirates
4302 .... April 18, 1987 .... Eric Davis .... Reds	4358 .... May 27, 1987 ...... Jim Morrison .... Pirates
4303 .... April 25, 1987 ..... Tracy Jones .... Reds	4359 .... June 2, 1987 .... Jerry Mumphrey .... Cubs
4304 .... April 25, 1987 ..... Kurt Stillwell .... Reds	4360 .... June 2, 1987 .... Jody Davis .... Cubs
4305 .... April 25, 1987 ..... Eric Davis .... Reds	4361 .... June 2, 1987 .... Mike Mason .... Cubs
4306 .... April 25, 1987 ..... Ron Oester .... Reds	4362 .... June 7, 1987 .... Chili Davis .... Giants
4307 .... April 25, 1987 ..... Eric Davis .... Reds	4363 .... June 7, 1987 .... Bob Brenly .... Giants
4308 .... April 25, 1987 ..... Bo Diaz .... Reds	4364 .... June 7, 1987 .... Ivan DeJesus .... Giants
4309 .... April 25, 1987 ..... Ron Oester .... Reds	4365 .... June 7, 1987 .... Atlee Hammaker ...... Giants
4310 .... April 25, 1987 .... Ted Power .... Reds	4366 .... June 7, 1987 .... Chris Speier .... Giants
4311 .... April 25, 1987 .... Dave Parker .... Reds	4367 .... June 7, 1987 .... Bob Brenly .... Giants
4312 .... April 25, 1987 .... Eric Davis .... Reds	4368 .... June 7, 1987 .... Ivan DeJesus .... Giants
4313 .... April 25, 1987 .... Ted Power .... Reds	4369 .... June 7, 1987 .... Chris Speier .... Giants
4314 .... May 1, 1987 .... Glenn Hubbard .... Braves	4370 .... June 7, 1987 .... Will Clark .... Giants
4315 .... May 1, 1987 .... Dion James .... Braves	4371 .... June 7, 1987 .... Jeffrey Leonard .... Giants
4316 .... May 1, 1987 .... Glenn Hubbard .... Braves	4372 .... June 7, 1987 .... Bob Brenly .... Giants
4317 .... May 1, 1987 .... Rafael Ramirez .... Braves	4373 .... June 7, 1987 .... Robby Thompson ..... Giants
4318 .... May 6, 1987 .... Juan Samuel .... Phillies	4374 .... June 12, 1987 .... John Shelby .... Dodgers
4319 .... May 6, 1987 .... Von Hayes .... Phillies	4375 .... June 12, 1987 .... Pedro Guerrero ..... Dodgers
4320 .... May 6, 1987 .... Mike Schmidt .... Phillies	4376 .... June 12, 1987 .... Ralph Bryant .... Dodgers
4321 .... May 6, 1987 .... Milt Thompson .... Phillies	4377 .... June 12, 1987 .... Bob Welch .... Dodgers
4322 .... May 6, 1987 .... Von Hayes .... Phillies	4378 .... June 12, 1987 .... Franklin Stubbs ..... Dodgers
4323 .... May 6, 1987 .... Lance Parrish .... Phillies	4379 .... June 12, 1987 .... Dave Anderson ..... Dodgers
4324 .... May 6, 1987 .... Don Carman .... Phillies	4380 .... June 12, 1987 .... Bob Welch .... Dodgers
4325 .... May 11, 1987 ..... Mike Schmidt .... Phillies	4381 .... June 12, 1987 ..... Mickey Hatcher ..... Dodgers
4326 .... May 11, 1987 ..... Jeff Stone .... Phillies	4382 .... June 12, 1987 ..... Pedro Guerrero ..... Dodgers
4327 .... May 11, 1987 ..... Don Carman .... Phillies	4383 .... June 12, 1987 ..... Franklin Stubbs ..... Dodgers
4328 .... May 11, 1987 ..... Jeff Stone .... Phillies	4384 .... June 12, 1987 .... Alex Trevino .... Dodgers
4329 .... May 11, 1987 ..... Juan Samuel .... Phillies	4385 .... June 17, 1987 ..... Dave Parker .... Reds
4330 .... May 11, 1987 ..... Von Hayes .... Phillies	4386 .... June 17, 1987 ..... Kurt Stillwell .... Reds
4331 .... May 11, 1987 ...... Luis Aguayo .... Phillies	4387 .... June 23, 1987 ..... Benito Santiago .... Padres
4332 .... May 16, 1987 ...... Ryne Sandberg .... Cubs	4388 .... June 23, 1987 ..... Stan Jefferson .... Padres
4333 .... May 16, 1987 ..... Jerry Mumphrey .... Cubs	4389 .... June 23, 1987 .... Ed Whitson .... Padres
4334 .... May 16, 1987 ..... Andre Dawson .... Cubs	4390 .... June 23, 1987 .... Carmelo Martinez .... Padres
4335 .... May 16, 1987 ..... Shawon Dunston .... Cubs	4391 .... June 28, 1987 .... Jeffrey Leonard .... Giants
4336 .... May 16, 1987 ..... Jerry Mumphrey .... Cubs	4392 .... June 28, 1987 .... Chili Davis .... Giants
4337 .... May 16, 1987 ..... Shawon Dunston .... Cubs	4393 .... June 28, 1987 .... Mike Aldrete .... Giants
4338 .... May 16, 1987 ...... Dave Martinez .... Cubs	4394 .... June 28, 1987 .... Matt Williams .... Giants
4339 .... May 16, 1987 ..... Jamie Moyer .... Cubs	4395 .... June 28, 1987 .... Atlee Hammaker ...... Giants
4340 .... May 16, 1987 ...... Shawon Dunston .... Cubs	4396 .... June 28, 1987 .... Robby Thompson ... Giants
4341 .... May 22, 1987 ...... Vince Coleman .... Cardinals	4397 .... June 28, 1987 .... Chris Speier .... Giants
4342 .... May 22, 1987 ...... Jack Clark .... Cardinals	4398 .... June 28, 1987 ..... Matt Williams .... Giants
4343 .... May 22, 1987 ...... Curt Ford .... Cardinals	4399 .... June 28, 1987 ..... Atlee Hammaker ...... Giants
4344 .... May 22, 1987 ...... Tim Conroy .... Cardinals	4400 .... June 28, 1987 .... Robby Thompson ..... Giants
4345 .... May 22, 1987 ...... Vince Coleman .... Cardinals	4401 .... June 28, 1987 .... Robby Thompson ..... Giants
4346 .... May 22, 1987 ...... Willie McGee ...... Cardinals	4402 .... July 3, 1987 .... Juan Samuel .... Phillies
4347 .... May 22, 1987 ...... Tommy Herr .... Cardinals	4403 .... July 3, 1987 .... Greg Gross .... Phillies
4348 .... May 22, 1987 ...... Tim Conroy .... Cardinals	4404 .... July 3, 1987 .... Luis Aguayo .... Phillies
4349 .... May 22, 1987 ...... Jack Clark .... Cardinals	4405 .... July 3, 1987 .... Bruce Ruffin .... Phillies
4350 .... May 22, 1987 ...... Willie McGee ...... Cardinals	4406 .... July 3, 1987 .... Juan Samuel .... Phillies
4351 .... May 22, 1987 ...... Tim Conroy .... Cardinals	4407 .... July 3, 1987 .... Milt Thompson .... Phillies
4352 .... May 27, 1987 ...... Andy Van Slyke .... Pirates	4408 .... July 3, 1987 .... Lance Parrish .... Phillies

4409 .... July 3, 1987 .... Glenn Wilson .... Phillies		4465 .... August 18, 1987 . Ozzie Smith .... Cardinals	
4410 .... July 3, 1987 .... Bruce Ruffin .... Phillies		4466 .... August 18, 1987 . Jack Clark .... Cardinals	
4411 .... July 3, 1987 .... Juan Samuel .... Phillies		4467 .... August 18, 1987 . Tony Pena .... Cardinals	
4412 .... July 8, 1987 .... Jeff Reed .... Expos		4468 .... August 23, 1987 . Ryne Sandberg .... Cubs	
4413 .... July 8, 1987 .... Floyd Youmans .... Expos		4469 .... August 23, 1987 . Leon Durham .... Cubs	
4414 .... July 8, 1987 .... Tim Raines .... Expos		4470 .... August 23, 1987 . Andre Dawson .... Cubs	
4415 .... July 8, 1987 .... Hubie Brooks .... Expos		4471 .... August 23, 1987 . Dave Martinez .... Cubs	
4416 .... July 8, 1987 .... Floyd Youmans .... Expos		4472 .... August 23, 1987 . Ryne Sandberg .... Cubs	
4417 .... July 8, 1987 .... Tim Wallach .... Expos		4473 .... August 23, 1987 . Shawon Dunston .... Cubs	
4418 .... July 8, 1987 .... Andres Galarraga ..... Expos		4474 .... August 23, 1987 . Jim Sundberg .... Cubs	
4419 .... July 8, 1987 .... Jeff Reed .... Expos		4475 .... August 29, 1987 . John Cangelosi ...... Pirates	
4420 .... July 8, 1987 .... Casey Candaele ...... Expos		4476 .... August 29, 1987 . Jose Lind .... Pirates	
4421 .... July 19, 1987 ..... Lance Parrish ...... Phillies		4477 .... August 29, 1987 . R.J. Reynolds .... Pirates	
4422 .... July 19, 1987 ..... Greg Gross .... Phillies		4478 .... August 29, 1987 . Al Pedrique .... Pirates	
4423 .... July 19, 1987 ..... Juan Samuel .... Phillies		4479 .... August 29, 1987 . Mike Bielecki .... Pirates	
4424 .... July 24, 1987 ..... Lee Mazzilli .... Mets		4480 .... August 29, 1987 . R.J. Reynolds .... Pirates	
4425 .... July 24, 1987 ..... Gary Carter .... Mets		4481 .... August 29, 1987 . Mike Lavalliere .... Pirates	
4426 .... July 29, 1987 ..... Bruce Benedict .... Braves		4482 .... Sept. 4, 1987 ...... Bobby Bonilla .... Pirates	
4427 .... July 29, 1987 ..... Glenn Hubbard .... Braves		4483 .... Sept. 4, 1987 ...... Mike Bielecki .... Pirates	
4428 .... July 29, 1987 ..... Charlie Puleo .... Braves		4484 .... Sept. 4, 1987 ...... John Cangelosi ...... Pirates	
4429 .... July 29, 1987 ..... Dale Murphy .... Braves		4485 .... Sept. 4, 1987 ...... Andy Van Slyke .... Pirates	
4430 .... July 29, 1987 ..... Ken Griffey .... Braves		4486 .... Sept. 4, 1987 ...... Mike Lavalliere .... Pirates	
4431 .... August 3, 1987 ... Jeffrey Leonard .... Giants		4487 .... Sept. 4, 1987 ...... Al Pedrique .... Pirates	
4432 .... August 3, 1987 ... Robby Thompson ..... Giants		4488 .... Sept. 9, 1987 ...... Eddie Milner .... Giants	
4433 .... August 3, 1987 ... Mike Krukow .... Giants		4489 .... Sept. 9, 1987 ...... Will Clark .... Giants	
4434 .... August 3, 1987 ... Chili Davis .... Giants		4490 .... Sept. 9, 1987 ...... Jose Uribe .... Giants	
4435 .... August 3, 1987 ... Bob Brenly .... Giants		4491 .... Sept. 9, 1987 ...... Atlee Hammaker ...... Giants	
4436 .... August 3, 1987 ... Robby Thompson ..... Giants		4492 .... Sept. 9, 1987 ...... Matt Williams .... Giants	
4437 .... August 3, 1987 ... Mike Krukow .... Giants		4493 .... Sept. 9, 1987 ...... Francisco Melendez . Giants	
4438 .... August 3, 1987 ... Jeffrey Leonard .... Giants		4494 .... Sept. 9, 1987 ...... Candy Maldonado .... Giants	
4439 .... August 3, 1987 ... Bob Brenly .... Giants		4495 .... Sept. 9, 1987 ...... Will Clark .... Giants	
4440 .... August 3, 1987 ... Robby Thompson ..... Giants		4496 .... Sept. 9, 1987 ...... Bob Brenly .... Giants	
4441 .... August 3, 1987 ... Jose Uribe .... Giants		4497 .... Sept. 9, 1987 ...... Chili Davis .... Giants	
4442 .... August 3, 1987 ... Mike Krukow .... Giants		4498 .... Sept. 9, 1987 ...... Jessie Heid .... Giants	
4443 .... August 8, 1987 ... Stan Jefferson .... Padres		4499 .... Sept. 9, 1987 ...... Chris Speier .... Giants	
4444 .... August 8, 1987 ... Mark Grant .... Padres		4500 .... Sept. 9, 1987 ...... Mike Aldrete .... Giants	
4445 .... August 8, 1987 ... Stan Jefferson .... Padres		4501 .... Sept. 9, 1987 ...... Candy Maldonado .... Giants	
4446 .... August 8, 1987 ... John Kruk .... Padres		4502 .... Sept. 9, 1987 ...... Will Clark .... Giants	
4447 .... August 8, 1987 ... Benito Santiago ...... Padres		4503 .... Sept. 9, 1987 ...... Bob Brenly .... Giants	
4448 .... August 8, 1987 ... James Steels .... Padres		4504 .... Sept. 14, 1987 .... Ralph Bryant .... Dodgers	
4449 .... August 13, 1987 . Mike Krukow .... Giants		4505 .... Sept. 14, 1987 .... Phil Garnor .... Dodgers	
4450 .... August 13, 1987 . Jeffrey Leonard .... Giants		4506 .... Sept. 14, 1987 .... John Shelby .... Dodgers	
4451 .... August 13, 1987 . Candy Maldonado .... Giants		4507 .... Sept. 14, 1987 .... Ralph Bryant .... Dodgers	
4452 .... August 13, 1987 . Will Clark .... Giants		4508 .... Sept. 14, 1987 .... Phil Garner .... Dodgers	
4453 .... August 13, 1987 . Bob Brenly .... Giants		4509 .... Sept. 14, 1987 .... Chris Gwynn .... Dodgers	
4454 .... August 13, 1987 . Mike Aldrete .... Giants		4510 .... Sept. 14, 1987 .... Ralph Bryant .... Dodgers	
4455 .... August 13, 1987 . Candy Maldonado .... Giants		4511 .... Sept. 14, 1987 .... Ken Landreaux ..... Dodgers	
4456 .... August 13, 1987 . Will Clark .... Giants		4512 .... Sept. 14, 1987 .... Mike Deveraux ..... Dodgers	
4457 .... August 13, 1987 . Bob Brenly .... Giants		4513 .... Sept. 19, 1987 .... John Kruk .... Padres	
4458 .... August 13, 1987 . Harry Spilman .... Giants		4514 .... Sept. 19, 1987 .... Tim Flannery .... Padres	
4459 .... August 18, 1987 . Vince Coleman .... Cardinals		4515 .... Sept. 19, 1987 .... Garry Templeton ..... Padres	
4460 .... August 18, 1987 . Willie McGee .... Cardinals		4516 .... Sept. 19, 1987 .... Garry Templeton ..... Padres	
4461 .... August 18, 1987 . Vince Coleman .... Cardinals		4517 .... Sept. 19, 1987 .... Tony Gwynn .... Padres	
4462 .... August 18, 1987 . Ozzie Smith .... Cardinals		4518 .... Sept. 19, 1987 .... John Kruk .... Padres	
4463 .... August 18, 1987 . Jack Clark .... Cardinals		4519 .... Sept. 19, 1987 .... Garry Templeton ..... Padres	
4464 .... August 18, 1987 . Vince Coleman .... Cardinals		4520 .... Sept. 19, 1987 .... Stan Jefferson .... Padres	

4521 .... Sept. 19, 1987 .... John Kruk .... Padres	4577 .... April 22, 1988 ..... Benito Santiago .... Padres
4522 .... Sept. 19, 1987 .... Carmelo Martinez .... Padres	4578 .... April 22, 1988 ..... Roberto Alomar .... Padres
4523 .... Sept. 19, 1987 .... Benito Santiago .... Padres	4579 .... April 22, 1988 ..... Carmelo Martinez .... Padres
4524 .... Sept. 24, 1987 .... Albert Hall .... Braves	4580 .... April 22, 1988 ..... Garry Templeton ..... Padres
4525 .... Sept. 24, 1987 .... Ozzie Virgil .... Braves	4581 .... April 22, 1988 ..... Jimmy Jones .... Padres
4526 .... Sept. 24, 1987 .... Ron Gant .... Braves	4582 .... April 22, 1988 ..... Tony Gwynn .... Padres
4527 .... Sept. 24, 1987 .... Ozzie Virgil .... Braves	4583 .... April 22, 1988 ..... Garry Templeton ..... Padres
4528 .... Sept. 24, 1987 .... Graig Nettles .... Braves	4584 .... April 27, 1988 ..... Kevin Gross .... Phillies
4529 .... Sept. 29, 1987 .... John Shelby .... Dodgers	4585 .... April 27, 1988 ..... Juan Samuel .... Phillies
4530 .... Sept. 29, 1987 .... Ralph Bryant .... Dodgers	4586 .... April 27, 1988 ..... Chris James .... Phillies
4531 .... Sept. 29, 1987 .... Glenn Hoffman ...... Dodgers	4587 .... April 27, 1988 ..... Milt Thompson .... Phillies
4532 .... Sept. 29, 1987 .... Ralph Bryant .... Dodgers	4588 .... April 27, 1988 ..... Juan Samuel .... Phillies
4533 .... Sept. 29, 1987 .... Glenn Hoffman ...... Dodgers	4589 .... April 27, 1988 ..... Lance Parrish .... Phillies
4534 .... Sept. 29, 1987 .... Mike Sharperson ... Dodgers	4590 .... April 27, 1988 ..... Chris James .... Phillies
4535 .... Sept. 29, 1987 .... Steve Sax .... Dodgers	4591 .... April 27, 1988 ..... Mike Young .... Phillies
4536 .... Sept. 29, 1987 .... Mike Marshall .... Dodgers	4592 .... April 27, 1988 ..... Juan Samuel .... Phillies
4537 .... Sept. 29, 1987 .... Glenn Hoffman ...... Dodgers	4593 .... May 2, 1988 .... Von Hayes .... Phillies
4538 .... October 4, 1987 .. Dave Collins .... Reds	4594 .... May 2, 1988 .... Phil Bradley .... Phillies
4539 .... October 4, 1987 .. Jeff Treadway .... Reds	4595 .... May 2, 1988 .... Luis Aguayo .... Phillies
4540 .... October 4, 1987 .. Tracy Jones .... Reds	4596 .... May 7, 1988 .... Tim Wallach .... Expos
4541 .... October 4, 1987 .. Buddy Bell .... Reds	4597 .... May 7, 1988 .... Mike Fitzgerald .... Expos
4542 .... October 4, 1987 .. Kurt Stillwell .... Reds	4598 .... May 7, 1988 .... Tom Foley .... Expos
4543 .... October 4, 1987 .. Tom Browning .... Reds	4599 .... May 7, 1988 .... Pascual Perez .... Expos
4544 .... October 4, 1987 .. Paul O'Neill .... Reds	4600 .... May 7, 1988 .... Hubie Brooks .... Expos
4545 .... October 4, 1987 .. Terry McGriff .... Reds	4601 .... May 7, 1988 .... Mitch Webster .... Expos
4546 .... October 4, 1987 .. Tom Browning .... Reds	4602 .... May 7, 1988 .... Andres Galarraga ... Expos
4547 .... October 4, 1987 .. Jeff Treadway .... Reds	4603 .... May 13, 1988 ..... Dave Martinez .... Cubs
4548 .... April 8, 1988 ...... Eric Davis .... Reds	4604 .... May 13, 1988 ..... Damon Berryhill ...... Cubs
4549 .... April 8, 1988 ...... Paul O'Neill .... Reds	4605 .... May 13, 1988 ..... Shawon Dunston .... Cubs
4550 .... April 8, 1988 ...... Nick Esasky .... Reds	4606 .... May 13, 1988 ..... Jamie Moyer .... Cubs
4551 .... April 8, 1988 ...... Terry McGriff .... Reds	4607 .... May 13, 1988 ..... Shawon Dunston .... Cubs
4552 .... April 8, 1988 ...... Tom Browning .... Reds	4608 .... May 13, 1988 ..... Jamie Moyer .... Cubs
4553 .... April 8, 1988 ...... Eric Davis .... Reds	4609 .... May 13, 1988 ..... Dave Martinez .... Cubs
4554 .... April 8, 1988 ...... Nick Esasky .... Reds	4610 .... May 13, 1988 ..... Damon Berryhill ...... Cubs
4555 .... April 8, 1988 ...... Tom Browning .... Reds	4611 .... May 13, 1988 ..... Shawon Dunston .... Cubs
4556 .... April 8, 1988 ...... Paul O'Neill .... Reds	4612 .... May 13, 1988 ..... Mark Grace .... Cubs
4557 .... April 8, 1988 ...... Terry McGriff .... Reds	4613 .... May 13, 1988 ..... Vance Law .... Cubs
4558 .... April 8, 1988 ...... Tom Browning .... Reds	4614 .... May 18, 1988 ..... Barry Bonds .... Pirates
4559 .... April 12, 1988 .... Ken Oberkfell .... Braves	4615 .... May 18, 1988 ...... Andy Van Slyke .... Pirates
4560 .... April 12, 1988 .... Zane Smith .... Braves	4616 .... May 24, 1988 ...... R.J. Reynolds .... Pirates
4561 .... April 12, 1988 .... Dale Murphy .... Braves	4617 .... May 24, 1988 ...... Barry Bonds .... Pirates
4562 .... April 12, 1988 .... Ken Griffey .... Braves	4618 .... May 24, 1988 ...... R.J. Reynolds .... Pirates
4563 .... April 12, 1988 .... Bruce Benedict .... Braves	4619 .... May 24, 1988 ...... Mike Diaz .... Pirates
4564 .... April 12, 1988 .... Zane Smith .... Braves	4620 .... May 24, 1988 ...... Barry Bonds .... Pirates
4565 .... April 12, 1988 .... Damaso Garcia .... Braves	4621 .... May 29, 1988 ...... Ryne Sandberg .... Cubs
4566 .... April 12, 1988 .... Dale Murphy .... Braves	4622 .... May 29, 1988 ..... Rafael Palmeiro .... Cubs
4567 .... April 17, 1988 .... Kal Daniels .... Reds	4623 .... May 29, 1988 ..... Shawon Dunston .... Cubs
4568 .... April 17, 1988 .... Paul O'Neill .... Reds	4624 .... May 29, 1988 ..... Jerry Mumphrey .... Cubs
4569 .... April 17, 1988 .... Danny Jackson .... Reds	4625 .... June 4, 1988 .... Robby Thompson ..... Giants
4570 .... April 17, 1988 .... Kal Daniels .... Reds	4626 .... June 4, 1988 .... Candy Maldonado ... Giants
4571 .... April 17, 1988 .... Frank Williams .... Reds	4627 .... June 4, 1988 .... Chris Speier .... Giants
4572 .... April 17, 1988 .... Paul O'Neill .... Reds	4628 .... June 4, 1988 .... Matt Williams .... Giants
4573 .... April 17, 1988 .... Leo Garcia .... Reds	4629 .... June 4, 1988 .... Robby Thompson ..... Giants
4574 .... April 17, 1988 .... Barry Larkin .... Reds	4630 .... June 4, 1988 .... Will Clark .... Giants
4575 .... April 17, 1988 .... Eric Davis .... Reds	4631 .... June 4, 1988 .... Chris Speier .... Giants
4576 .... April 22, 1988 ..... Keith Moreland .... Padres	4632 .... June 4, 1988 .... Matt Williams .... Giants

4633	June 4, 1988	Candy Maldonado	Giants
4634	June 4, 1988	Kirt Manwaring	Giants
4635	June 9, 1988	Franklin Stubbs	Dodgers
4636	June 9, 1988	Kirk Gibson	Dodgers
4637	June 13, 1988	Albert Hall	Braves
4638	June 13, 1988	Kevin Coffman	Braves
4639	June 13, 1988	Ron Gant	Braves
4640	June 13, 1988	Gerald Perry	Braves
4641	June 13, 1988	Paul Runge	Braves
4642	June 13, 1988	Ron Gant	Braves
4643	June 13, 1988	Dale Murphy	Braves
4644	June 13, 1988	Andres Thomas	Braves
4645	June 18, 1988	Gerald Perry	Braves
4646	June 18, 1988	Kevin Coffman	Braves
4647	June 18, 1988	Ron Gant	Braves
4648	June 18, 1988	Kevin Coffman	Braves
4649	June 18, 1988	Ron Gant	Braves
4650	June 18, 1988	Ken Oberkfell	Braves
4651	June 24, 1988	Mike Aldrete	Giants
4652	June 24, 1988	Kevin Mitchell	Giants
4653	June 24, 1988	Jose Uribe	Giants
4654	June 24, 1988	Candy Maldonado	Giants
4655	June 24, 1988	Kelly Downs	Giants
4656	June 29, 1988	John Shelby	Dodgers
4657	June 29, 1988	Jeff Hamilton	Dodgers
4658	June 29, 1988	John Shelby	Dodgers
4659	June 29, 1988	Jeff Hamilton	Dodgers
4660	June 29, 1988	Dave Anderson	Dodgers
4661	June 29, 1988	Kirk Gibson	Dodgers
4662	June 29, 1988	Mike Marshall	Dodgers
4663	June 29, 1988	John Shelby	Dodgers
4664	June 29, 1988	Jeff Hamilton	Dodgers
4665	June 29, 1988	Orel Hershiser	Dodgers
4666	July 3, 1988	Darryl Strawberry	Mets
4667	July 3, 1988	Mookie Wilson	Mets
4668	July 3, 1988	Mackey Sasser	Mets
4669	July 3, 1988	Kevin Elster	Mets
4670	July 3, 1988	Wally Backman	Mets
4671	July 3, 1988	Mookie Wilson	Mets
4672	July 3, 1988	Wally Backman	Mets
4673	July 9, 1988	Howard Johnson	Mets
4674	July 9, 1988	Dave Magadan	Mets
4675	July 9, 1988	Rick Aguilera	Mets
4676	July 9, 1988	Howard Johnson	Mets
4677	July 9, 1988	Mackey Sasser	Mets
4678	July 16, 1988	Juan Samuel	Phillies
4679	July 16, 1988	Don Carman	Phillies
4680	July 16, 1988	Don Carman	Phillies
4681	July 21, 1988	Juan Samuel	Phillies
4682	July 21, 1988	Mike Schmidt	Phillies
4683	July 21, 1988	Darren Daulton	Phillies
4684	July 21, 1988	Juan Samuel	Phillies
4685	July 21, 1988	Milt Thompson	Phillies
4686	July 21, 1988	Chris James	Phillies
4687	July 21, 1988	Milt Thompson	Phillies
4688	July 21, 1988	Chris James	Phillies
4689	July 21, 1988	Milt Thompson	Phillies
4690	July 27, 1988	Stan Jefferson	Padres
4691	July 27, 1988	Chris Brown	Padres
4692	July 27, 1988	Chris Brown	Padres
4693	July 27, 1988	Roberto Alomar	Padres
4694	August 1, 1988	Mike Aldrete	Giants
4695	August 1, 1988	Bob Melvin	Giants
4696	August 1, 1988	Jose Uribe	Giants
4697	August 1, 1988	Atlee Hammaker	Giants
4698	August 1, 1988	Atlee Hammaker	Giants
4699	August 1, 1988	Kevin Mitchell	Giants
4700	August 1, 1988	Jose Uribe	Giants
4701	August 1, 1988	Atlee Hammaker	Giants
4702	August 1, 1988	Brett Butler	Giants
4703	August 1, 1988	Will Clark	Giants
4704	August 1, 1988	Kevin Mitchell	Giants
4705	August 6, 1988	Pedro Guerrero	Dodgers
4706	August 6, 1988	Alfredo Griffin	Dodgers
4707	August 6, 1988	Tim Belcher	Dodgers
4708	August 6, 1988	John Shelby	Dodgers
4709	August 6, 1988	Pedro Guerrero	Dodgers
4710	August 6, 1988	Tracy Woodson	Dodgers
4711	August 11, 1988	Bob Melvin	Giants
4712	August 11, 1988	Atlee Hammaker	Giants
4713	August 11, 1988	Ernest Riles	Giants
4714	August 11, 1988	Atlee Hammaker	Giants
4715	August 11, 1988	Candy Maldonado	Giants
4716	August 11, 1988	Brett Butler	Giants
4717	August 15, 1988	Marvell Wynne	Padres
4718	August 15, 1988	Andy Hawkins	Padres
4719	August 20, 1988	Andy Van Slyke	Pirates
4720	August 20, 1988	Mike Lavalliere	Pirates
4721	August 20, 1988	Al Pedrique	Pirates
4722	August 20, 1988	John Smiley	Pirates
4723	August 20, 1988	Bobby Bonilla	Pirates
4724	August 24, 1988	Rafael Palmeiro	Cubs
4725	August 24, 1988	Shawon Dunston	Cubs
4726	August 24, 1988	Mitch Webster	Cubs
4727	August 24, 1988	Ryne Sandberg	Cubs
4728	August 24, 1988	Andre Dawson	Cubs
4729	August 24, 1988	Vance Law	Cubs
4730	August 24, 1988	Mitch Webster	Cubs
4731	August 24, 1988	Mark Grace	Cubs
4732	August 24, 1988	Damon Berryhill	Cubs
4733	August 29, 1988	Ryne Sandberg	Cubs
4734	August 29, 1988	Mark Grace	Cubs
4735	August 29, 1988	Mitch Webster	Cubs
4736	August 29, 1988	Andre Dawson	Cubs
4737	August 29, 1988	Vance Law	Cubs
4738	August 29, 1988	Shawon Dunston	Cubs
4739	August 29, 1988	Mitch Webster	Cubs
4740	August 29, 1988	Vance Law	Cubs
4741	August 29, 1988	Shawon Dunston	Cubs
4742	August 29, 1988	Greg Maddux	Cubs
4743	August 29, 1988	Mitch Webster	Cubs
4744	Sept. 3, 1988	Vince Coleman	Cardinals

4745 .... Sept. 3, 1988 ...... Pedro Guerrero ... Cardinals			
4746 .... Sept. 3, 1988 ...... Tom Brunansky ... Cardinals			
4747 .... Sept. 3, 1988 ...... Terry Pendleton ... Cardinals			
4748 .... Sept. 3, 1988 ...... John Morris ...... Cardinals			
4749 .... Sept. 3, 1988 ...... Vince Coleman .... Cardinals			
4750 .... Sept. 3, 1988 ...... Jim Lindeman ...... Cardinals			
4751 .... Sept. 3, 1988 ...... Mike Laga .... Cardinals			
4752 .... Sept. 8, 1988 ...... Steve Sax .... Dodgers			
4753 .... Sept. 8, 1988 ...... Kirk Gibson .... Dodgers			
4754 .... Sept. 8, 1988 ...... John Shelby .... Dodgers			
4755 .... Sept. 8, 1988 ...... Mike Davis .... Dodgers			
4756 .... Sept. 8, 1988 ...... Kirk Gibson .... Dodgers			
4757 .... Sept. 8, 1988 ...... Mickey Hatcher .... Dodgers			
4758 .... Sept. 8, 1988 ...... Jeff Hamilton .... Dodgers			
4759 .... Sept. 14, 1988 .... Chris Sabo .... Reds			
4760 .... Sept. 14, 1988 .... Dave Collins .... Reds			
4761 .... Sept. 14, 1988 .... Nick Esasky .... Reds			
4762 .... Sept. 14, 1988 .... Danny Jackson .... Reds			
4763 .... Sept. 14, 1988 .... Eric Davis .... Reds			
4764 .... Sept. 14, 1988 .... Dave Collins .... Reds			
4765 .... Sept. 14, 1988 .... Nick Esasky .... Reds			
4766 .... Sept. 14, 1988 .... Jeff Reed .... Reds			
4767 .... Sept. 14, 1988 .... Van Snider .... Reds			
4768 .... Sept. 14, 1988 .... Eric Davis .... Reds			
4769 .... Sept. 14, 1988 .... Jeff Reed .... Reds			
4770 .... Sept. 14, 1988 .... Ron Oester .... Reds			
4771 .... Sept. 14, 1988 .... Kal Daniels .... Reds			
4772 .... Sept. 19, 1988 .... Alfredo Griffin .... Dodgers			
4773 .... Sept. 19, 1988 .... Steve Sax .... Dodgers			
4774 .... Sept. 19, 1988 .... Mike Marshall .... Dodgers			
4775 .... Sept. 19, 1988 .... John Shelby .... Dodgers			
4776 .... April 6, 1989 ...... Ken Williams .... Tigers			
4777 .... April 6, 1989 ...... Torey Lovullo .... Tigers			
4778 .... April 6, 1989 ...... Alan Trammell .... Tigers			
4779 .... April 6, 1989 ...... Matt Nokes .... Tigers			
4780 .... April 6, 1989 ...... Billy Bean .... Tigers			
4781 .... April 6, 1989 ...... Fred Lynn .... Tigers			
4782 .... April 6, 1989 ...... Matt Nokes .... Tigers			
4783 .... April 6, 1989 ...... Pat Sheridan .... Tigers			
4784 .... April 12, 1989 ...... B.J. Surhoff .... Brewers			
4785 .... April 12, 1989 ...... Robin Yount .... Brewers			
4786 .... April 12, 1989 ...... Rob Deer .... Brewers			
4787 .... April 12, 1989 ...... Glenn Braggs ...... Brewers			
4788 .... April 12, 1989 ...... Terry Francona ..... Brewers			
4789 .... April 12, 1989 ...... Joey Meyer .... Brewers			
4790 .... April 12, 1989 ...... B.J. Surhoff .... Brewers			
4791 .... April 12, 1989 ...... Robin Yount .... Brewers			
4792 .... April 12, 1989 ...... Glenn Braggs .... Brewers			
4793 .... April 12, 1989 ...... Joey Meyer .... Brewers			
4794 .... April 12, 1989 ...... Gus Polidor .... Brewers			
4795 .... April 12, 1989 ...... Bill Spiers .... Brewers			
4796 .... April 12, 1989 ...... Jim Gantner .... Brewers			
4797 .... April 12, 1989 ...... Rob Deer .... Brewers			
4798 .... April 12, 1989 ...... Joey Meyer .... Brewers			
4799 .... April 17, 1989 ...... Paul Molitor .... Brewers			
4800 .... April 17, 1989 ...... Glenn Braggs .... Brewers			

4801 .... April 17, 1989 ...... Rob Deer .... Brewers			
4802 .... April 23, 1989 ...... George Bell .... Blue Jays			
4803 .... April 23, 1989 ...... Fred McGriff .... Blue Jays			
4804 .... April 23, 1989 ...... Ernie Whitt .... Blue Jays			
4805 .... April 23, 1989 ...... Jesse Barfield ..... Blue Jays			
4806 .... April 23, 1989 ...... Manny Lee .... Blue Jays			
4807 .... April 23, 1989 ...... Ernie Whitt .... Blue Jays			
4808 .... April 23, 1989 ...... Rance Mulliniks ... Blue Jays			
4809 .... April 23, 1989 ...... Manny Lee .... Blue Jays			
4810 .... April 23, 1989 ...... Nelson Liriano ..... Blue Jays			
4811 .... April 23, 1989 ...... Fred McGriff ..... Blue Jays			
4812 .... April 23, 1989 ...... Jesse Barfield ..... Blue Jays			
4813 .... April 23, 1989 ...... Rob Ducey .... Blue Jays			
4814 .... April 30, 1989 ...... Nick Esasky .... Red Sox			
4815 .... April 30, 1989 ...... Wade Boggs .... Red Sox			
4816 .... April 30, 1989 ...... Danny Heep .... Red Sox			
4817 .... April 30, 1989 ...... Nick Esasky .... Red Sox			
4818 .... April 30, 1989 ...... Rich Gedman .... Red Sox			
4819 .... April 30, 1989 ...... Jody Reed .... Red Sox			
4820 .... April 30, 1989 ...... Jim Rice .... Red Sox			
4821 .... April 30, 1989 ...... Nick Esasky .... Red Sox			
4822 .... April 30, 1989 ...... Rich Gedman .... Red Sox			
4823 .... April 30, 1989 ...... Randy Kutcher ...... Red Sox			
4824 .... April 30, 1989 ...... Jim Rice .... Red Sox			
4825 .... May 5, 1989 .... Rich Gedman ...... Red Sox			
4826 .... May 5, 1989 .... Jim Rice .... Red Sox			
4827 .... May 5, 1989 .... Nick Esasky .... Red Sox			
4828 .... May 11, 1989 ...... Willie Wilson .... Royals			
4829 .... May 11, 1989 ...... Jim Eisenreich .... Royals			
4830 .... May 11, 1989 ...... Danny Tartabull .... Royals			
4831 .... May 11, 1989 ...... Bo Jackson .... Royals			
4832 .... May 11, 1989 ...... Bill Buckner .... Royals			
4833 .... May 11, 1989 ...... Bo Jackson .... Royals			
4834 .... May 11, 1989 ...... Willie Wilson .... Royals			
4835 .... May 11, 1989 ...... Jim Eisenreich .... Royals			
4836 .... May 11, 1989 ...... Bo Jackson .... Royals			
4837 .... May 11, 1989 ...... Kurt Stillwell .... Royals			
4838 .... May 11, 1989 ...... Bo Jackson .... Royals			
4839 .... May 18, 1989 ...... Gary Gaetti .... Twins			
4840 .... May 18, 1989 ...... Jim Dwyer .... Twins			
4841 .... May 18, 1989 ...... Gene Larkin .... Twins			
4842 .... May 18, 1989 ...... Randy Bush .... Twins			
4843 .... May 18, 1989 ...... Gene Larkin .... Twins			
4844 .... May 18, 1989 ...... Greg Gagne .... Twins			
4845 .... May 18, 1989 ...... Dan Gladden .... Twins			
4846 .... May 18, 1989 ...... Randy Bush .... Twins			
4847 .... May 18, 1989 ...... Kirby Puckett .... Twins			
4848 .... May 18, 1989 ...... Tim Laudner .... Twins			
4849 .... May 23, 1989 ...... Kurt Stillwell .... Royals			
4850 .... May 23, 1989 ...... Bo Jackson .... Royals			
4851 .... May 23, 1989 ...... Bob Boone .... Royals			
4852 .... May 23, 1989 ...... Kevin Seitzer .... Royals			
4853 .... May 23, 1989 ...... Bo Jackson .... Royals			
4854 .... May 23, 1989 ...... Danny Tartabull .... Royals			
4855 .... May 29, 1989 ...... Brady Anderson ...... Orioles			
4856 .... May 29, 1989 ...... Cal Ripken .... Orioles			

4857 .... May 29, 1989 ...... Randy Milligan .... Orioles	4913 .... July 6, 1989 .... Tony Armas .... Angels
4858 .... May 29, 1989 ...... Randy Milligan .... Orioles	4914 .... July 6, 1989 .... Kent Anderson .... Angels
4859 .... May 29, 1989 ...... Craig Worthington ... Orioles	4915 .... July 6, 1989 .... Devon White .... Angels
4860 .... May 29, 1989 ...... Bill Ripken .... Orioles	4916 .... July 6, 1989 .... Tony Armas .... Angels
4861 .... May 29, 1989 ...... Brady Anderson ..... Orioles	4917 .... July 6, 1989 .... Kent Anderson .... Angels
4862 .... May 29, 1989 ...... Mickey Tettleton ...... Orioles	4918 .... July 6, 1989 .... Dick Schofield .... Angels
4863 .... May 29, 1989 ...... Joe Orsulak .... Orioles	4919 .... July 6, 1989 .... Chili Davis .... Angels
4864 .... May 29, 1989 ...... Larry Sheets .... Orioles	4920 .... July 6, 1989 .... Tony Armas .... Angels
4865 .... June 3, 1989 ...... Scott Bradley .... Mariners	4921 .... July 6, 1989 .... Dick Schofield .... Angels
4866 .... June 3, 1989 ...... Jeffrey Leonard .... Mariners	4922 .... July 6, 1989 .... Devon White .... Angels
4867 .... June 3, 1989 ...... Jim Presley .... Mariners	4923 .... July 6, 1989 .... Wally Joyner .... Angels
4868 .... June 3, 1989 ...... Jay Buhner .... Mariners	4924 .... July 15, 1989 ..... Paul Zuvella .... Indians
4869 .... June 3, 1989 ...... Harold Reynolds ... Mariners	4925 .... July 15, 1989 ..... Brad Komminsk ...... Indians
4870 .... June 3, 1989 ...... Jim Presley .... Mariners	4926 .... July 15, 1989 ..... Andy Allanson .... Indians
4871 .... June 3, 1989 ...... Jay Buhner .... Mariners	4927 .... July 15, 1989 ..... Joe Carter .... Indians
4872 .... June 3, 1989 ...... Greg Briley .... Mariners	4928 .... July 15, 1989 ..... Joey Belle .... Indians
4873 .... June 3, 1989 ...... Ken Griffey, Jr. .... Mariners	4929 .... July 15, 1989 ..... Jerry Browne .... Indians
4874 .... June 3, 1989 ...... Jim Presley .... Mariners	4930 .... July 15, 1989 ..... Dion James .... Indians
4875 .... June 3, 1989 ...... Jay Buhner .... Mariners	4931 .... July 20, 1989 ..... Steve Sax .... Yankees
4876 .... June 8, 1989 ...... Dave Gallagher .. White Sox	4932 .... July 20, 1989 ..... Luis Polonia .... Yankees
4877 .... June 8, 1989 ...... Ron Kittle .... White Sox	4933 .... July 20, 1989 ..... Jesse Barfield .... Yankees
4878 .... June 8, 1989 ...... Dan Pasqua .... White Sox	4934 .... July 20, 1989 ..... Alvaro Espinoza ... Yankees
4879 .... June 8, 1989 ...... Carlton Fisk .... White Sox	4935 .... July 20, 1989 ..... Luis Polonia .... Yankees
4880 .... June 8, 1989 ...... Ron Kittle .... White Sox	4936 .... July 20, 1989 ..... Mel Hall .... Yankees
4881 .... June 8, 1989 ...... Ivan Calderon ..... White Sox	4937 .... July 20, 1989 ..... Jesse Barfield .... Yankees
4882 .... June 8, 1989 ...... Ron Kittle .... White Sox	4938 .... July 20, 1989 ..... Don Slaught .... Yankees
4883 .... June 14, 1989 .... Claudell Washington Angels	4939 .... July 20, 1989 ..... Don Mattingly .... Yankees
4884 .... June 14, 1989 .... Jack Howell .... Angels	4940 .... July 20, 1989 ..... Jesse Barfield .... Yankees
4885 .... June 14, 1989 .... Johnny Ray .... Angels	4941 .... July 20, 1989 ..... Mike Pagliarulo ..... Yankees
4886 .... June 14, 1989 .... Bill Schroeder .... Angels	4942 .... July 25, 1989 ..... Kelly Gruber .... Blue Jays
4887 .... June 14, 1989 .... Kent Anderson .... Angels	4943 .... July 25, 1989 ..... George Bell .... Blue Jays
4888 .... June 14, 1989 .... Dick Schofield .... Angels	4944 .... July 25, 1989 ..... Fred McGriff .... Blue Jays
4889 .... June 14, 1989 .... Claudell Washington Angels	4945 .... July 25, 1989 ..... Ernie Whitt .... Blue Jays
4890 .... June 14, 1989 .... Devon White .... Red Sox	4946 .... July 25, 1989 ..... Kelly Gruber .... Blue Jays
4891 .... June 20, 1989 .... Mike Greenwell .... Red Sox	4947 .... July 25, 1989 ..... George Bell .... Blue Jays
4892 .... June 20, 1989 .... Nick Esasky .... Red Sox	4948 .... July 25, 1989 ..... Ernie Whitt .... Blue Jays
4893 .... June 20, 1989 .... Jody Reed .... Red Sox	4949 .... July 25, 1989 ..... Lloyd Moseby ...... Blue Jays
4894 .... June 20, 1989 .... Mike Greenwell ..... Red Sox	4950 .... July 25, 1989 ..... Junior Felix .... Blue Jays
4895 .... June 20, 1989 .... Nick Esasky .... Red Sox	4951 .... July 25, 1989 ..... Tony Fernandez .. Blue Jays
4896 .... June 20, 1989 .... Randy Kutcher ...... Red Sox	4952 .... July 25, 1989 ..... Pat Borders .... Blue Jays
4897 .... June 25, 1989 .... Dave Clark .... Indians	4953 .... July 25, 1989 ..... Lloyd Moseby ...... Blue Jays
4898 .... June 25, 1989 .... Pete O'Brien .... Indians	4954 .... July 25, 1989 ..... Nelson Liriano ..... Blue Jays
4899 .... June 25, 1989 .... Brook Jacoby .... Indians	4955 .... July 25, 1989 ..... Tony Fernandez .. Blue Jays
4900 .... June 25, 1989 .... Joe Carter .... Indians	4956 .... July 30, 1989 ..... Paul Molitor .... Brewers
4901 .... June 25, 1989 .... Felix Fermin .... Indians	4957 .... July 30, 1989 ..... Jim Gantner .... Brewers
4902 .... June 25, 1989 .... Pete O'Brien .... Indians	4958 .... July 30, 1989 ..... Greg Brock .... Brewers
4903 .... June 25, 1989 .... Oddibe McDowell .... Indians	4959 .... July 30, 1989 ..... Bill Spiers .... Brewers
4904 .... June 30, 1989 .... Ken Griffey, Jr. ..... Mariners	4960 .... July 30, 1989 ..... Charlie O'Brien ...... Brewers
4905 .... June 30, 1989 .... Darnell Coles .... Mariners	4961 .... July 30, 1989 ..... Mike Felder .... Brewers
4906 .... June 30, 1989 .... Edgar Martinez ..... Mariners	4962 .... July 30, 1989 ..... Bill Spiers .... Brewers
4907 .... June 30, 1989 .... Greg Briley .... Mariners	4963 .... July 30, 1989 ..... Paul Molitor .... Brewers
4908 .... June 30, 1989 .... Jeffrey Leonard .... Mariners	4964 .... July 30, 1989 ..... Mike Felder .... Brewers
4909 .... June 30, 1989 .... Darnell Coles .... Mariners	4965 .... July 30, 1989 ..... Bill Spiers .... Brewers
4910 .... June 30, 1989 .... Omar Vizquel .... Mariners	4966 .... August 5, 1989 ... Joe Orsulak .... Orioles
4911 .... June 30, 1989 .... Jeffrey Leonard .... Mariners	4967 .... August 5, 1989 ... Bob Melvin .... Orioles
4912 .... July 6, 1989 .... Brian Downing .... Angels	4968 .... August 5, 1989 ... Bill Ripken .... Orioles

4969 .... August 5, 1989 ... Cal Ripken .... Orioles		5025 .... Sept. 2, 1989 ...... Willie Wilson .... Royals
4970 .... August 5, 1989 ... Larry Sheets .... Orioles		5026 .... Sept. 2, 1989 ..... George Brett .... Royals
4971 .... August 5, 1989 ... Randy Milligan .... Orioles		5027 .... Sept. 2, 1989 ...... Bob Boone .... Royals
4972 .... August 5, 1989 ... Bill Ripken .... Orioles		5028 .... Sept. 2, 1989 ..... George Brett .... Royals
4973 .... August 5, 1989 ... Phil Bradley .... Orioles		5029 .... Sept. 2, 1989 .... Bo Jackson .... Royals
4974 .... August 10, 1989 . Fred Lynn .... Tigers		5030 .... Sept. 7, 1989 ..... Phil Bradley .... Orioles
4975 .... August 10, 1989 . Matt Nokes .... Tigers		5031 .... Sept. 7, 1989 ..... Steve Finley .... Orioles
4976 .... August 10, 1989 . Mike Heath .... Tigers		5032 .... Sept. 7, 1989 ...... Craig Worthington ... Orioles
4977 .... August 10, 1989 . Fred Lynn .... Tigers		5033 .... Sept. 7, 1989 ..... Bob Melvin .... Orioles
4978 .... August 10, 1989 . Chet Lemon .... Tigers		5034 .... Sept. 7, 1989 ..... Steve Finley .... Orioles
4979 .... August 10, 1989 . Doug Strange .... Tigers		5035 .... Sept. 7, 1989 ...... Craig Worthington ... Orioles
4980 .... August 10, 1989 . Mike Heath .... Tigers		5036 .... Sept. 7, 1989 ..... Bob Melvin .... Orioles
4981 .... August 10, 1989 . Fred Lynn .... Tigers		5037 .... Sept. 7, 1989 ..... Phil Bradley .... Orioles
4982 .... August 10, 1989 . Doug Strange .... Tigers		5038 .... Sept. 7, 1989 ..... Craig Worthington ... Orioles
4983 .... August 10, 1989 . Mike Heath .... Tigers		5039 .... Sept. 7, 1989 ...... Phil Bradley .... Orioles
4984 .... August 10, 1989 . Gary Pettis .... Tigers		5040 .... Sept. 12, 1989 .... Kevin Seitzer .... Royals
4985 .... August 10, 1989 . Lou Whitaker .... Tigers		5041 .... Sept. 12, 1989 .... Kurt Stillwell .... Royals
4986 .... August 10, 1989 . Fred Lynn .... Tigers		5042 .... Sept. 12, 1989 .... Frank White .... Royals
4987 .... August 16, 1989 . Alvin Davis .... Mariners		5043 .... Sept. 12, 1989 .... Willie Wilson .... Royals
4988 .... August 16, 1989 . Darnell Coles .... Mariners		5044 .... Sept. 12, 1989 .... Bo Jackson .... Royals
4989 .... August 16, 1989 . Greg Briley .... Mariners		5045 .... Sept. 12, 1989 .... Jim Eisenreich .... Royals
4990 .... August 16, 1989 . Jeffrey Leonard .... Mariners		5046 .... Sept. 12, 1989 .... Danny Tartabull .... Royals
4991 .... August 16, 1989 . Jim Presley .... Mariners		5047 .... Sept. 12, 1989 .... Willie Wilson .... Royals
4992 .... August 16, 1989 . Greg Briley .... Mariners		5048 .... Sept. 12, 1989 .... Danny Tartabull ...... Royals
4993 .... August 16, 1989 . Jim Presley .... Mariners		5049 .... Sept. 12, 1989 .... Kurt Stillwell .... Royals
4994 .... August 16, 1989 . Greg Briley .... Mariners		5050 .... Sept. 12, 1989 .... Frank White .... Royals
4995 .... August 22, 1989 . Jose Canseco .... A's		5051 .... Sept. 12, 1989 .... Willie Wilson .... Royals
4996 .... August 22, 1989 . Dave Henderson .... A's		5052 .... Sept. 12, 1989 .... Bo Jackson .... Royals
4997 .... August 22, 1989 . Tony Phillips .... A's		5053 .... Sept. 18, 1989 .... Greg Briley .... Mariners
4998 .... August 22, 1989 . Rickey Henderson .... A's		5054 .... Sept. 18, 1989 .... Darnell Coles .... Mariners
4999 .... August 22, 1989 . Ron Hassey .... A's		5055 .... Sept. 24, 1989 .... Carlos Martinez .. White Sox
5000 .... August 22, 1989 . Rickey Henderson .... A's		5056 .... Sept. 24, 1989 .... Robin Ventura .... White Sox
5001 .... August 22, 1989 . Ron Hassey .... A's		5057 .... Sept. 24, 1989 .... Ozzie Guillen .... White Sox
5002 .... August 22, 1989 . Dave Henderson .... A's		5058 .... Sept. 24, 1989 .... Lance Johnson ... White Sox
5003 .... August 22, 1989 . Mark McGwire .... A's		5059 .... Sept. 24, 1989 .... Steve Lyons .... White Sox
5004 .... August 22, 1989 . Tony Phillips .... A's		5060 .... Sept. 24, 1989 .... Robin Ventura .... White Sox
5005 .... August 22, 1989 . Terry Steinbach .... A's		5061 .... Sept. 24, 1989 .... Ron Karkovice .... White Sox
5006 .... August 22, 1989 . Jose Canseco .... A's		5062 .... Sept. 24, 1989 .... Steve Lyons .... White Sox
5007 .... August 22, 1989 . Ron Hassey .... A's		5063 .... Sept. 24, 1989 .... Ivan Calderon ..... White Sox
5008 .... August 27, 1989 . C. Washington .... Angels		5064 .... Sept. 30, 1989 .... Chili Davis .... Angels
5009 .... August 27, 1989 . Devon White .... Angels		5065 .... Sept. 30, 1989 .... Jack Howell .... Angels
5010 .... August 27, 1989 . Brian Downing .... Angels		5066 .... Sept. 30, 1989 .... John Orton .... Angels
5011 .... August 27, 1989 . John Orton .... Angels		5067 .... Sept. 30, 1989 .... Devon White .... Angels
5012 .... August 27, 1989 . Glenn Hoffman .... Angels		5068 .... Sept. 30, 1989 .... Mark McLemore ...... Angels
5013 .... August 27, 1989 . C. Washington .... Angels		5069 .... Sept. 30, 1989 .... Jack Howell .... Angels
5014 .... August 27, 1989 . Jack Howell .... Angels		5070 .... Sept. 30, 1989 .... John Orton .... Angels
5015 .... August 27, 1989 . C. Washington .... Angels		5071 .... Sept. 30, 1989 .... Dick Schofield .... Angels
5016 .... August 27, 1989 . Bobby Rose .... Angels		5072 .... Sept. 30, 1989 .... Mark McLemore ...... Angels
5017 .... August 27, 1989 . Chili Davis .... Angels		5073 .... Sept. 30, 1989 .... Jack Howell .... Angels
5018 .... August 27, 1989 . John Orton .... Angels		5074 .... Sept. 30, 1989 .... Jack Eppard .... Angels
5019 .... Sept. 2, 1989 ...... Willie Wilson .... Royals		5075 .... Sept. 30, 1989 .... Dick Schofield .... Angels
5020 .... Sept. 2, 1989 ...... Bo Jackson .... Royals		5076 .... Sept. 30, 1989 .... Devon White .... Angels
5021 .... Sept. 2, 1989 ...... Kurt Stillwell .... Royals		5077 .... April 9, 1990 .... George Bell .... Blue Jays
5022 .... Sept. 2, 1989 ...... Brad Wellman .... Royals		5078 .... April 9, 1990 .... John Olerud .... Blue Jays
5023 .... Sept. 2, 1989 ...... Kurt Stillwell .... Royals		5079 .... April 9, 1990 .... Junior Felix .... Blue Jays
5024 .... Sept. 2, 1989 ...... Brad Wellman .... Royals		5080 .... April 9, 1990 .... Junior Felix .... Blue Jays

5081 .... April 14, 1990 ..... Luis Polonia .... Yankees		5137 .... June 6, 1990 .... Mark McGwire .... A's
5082 .... April 14, 1990 ..... Mel Hall .... Yankees		5138 .... June 6, 1990 .... Doug Jennings .... A's
5083 .... April 14, 1990 ..... Steve Sax .... Yankees		5139 .... June 11, 1990 ..... Willie Randolph .... A's
5084 .... April 14, 1990 ..... Deion Sanders ...... Yankees		5140 .... June 11, 1990 ..... Doug Jennings .... A's
5085 .... April 20, 1990 ..... Alvaro Espinoza ... Yankees		5141 .... June 11, 1990 ..... Ron Hassey .... A's
5086 .... April 20, 1990 ..... Dave Winfield .... Yankees		5142 .... June 11, 1990 ..... Rickey Henderson .... A's
5087 .... April 20, 1990 ..... Jesse Barfield .... Yankees		5143 .... June 11, 1990 ..... Doug Jennings .... A's
5088 .... April 20, 1990 ..... Roberto Kelly .... Yankees		5144 .... June 11, 1990 ..... Felix Jose .... A's
5089 .... April 20, 1990 ..... Alvaro Espinoza ... Yankees		5145 .... June 11, 1990 ..... Dave Henderson .... A's
5090 .... April 20, 1990 ..... Jesse Barfield .... Yankees		5146 .... June 11, 1990 ..... Jamie Quirk .... A's
5091 .... April 20, 1990 ..... Roberto Kelly .... Yankees		5147 .... June 11, 1990 ..... Walt Weiss .... A's
5092 .... April 20, 1990 ..... Randy Velarde ...... Yankees		5148 .... June 11, 1990 ..... Ron Hassey .... A's
5093 .... April 20, 1990 ..... Jesse Barfield .... Yankees		5149 .... June 11, 1990 ..... Felix Jose .... A's
5094 .... April 26, 1990 ..... Lance Johnson ... White Sox		5150 .... June 11, 1990 ..... Dave Henderson .... A's
5095 .... April 26, 1990 ..... Sammy Sosa ...... White Sox		5151 .... June 11, 1990 ..... Carney Lansford .... A's
5096 .... April 26, 1990 ..... Carlton Fisk .... White Sox		5152 .... June 11, 1990 ..... Ken Phelps .... A's
5097 .... April 26, 1990 ..... Robin Ventura .... White Sox		5153 .... June 16, 1990 ..... Greg Briley .... Mariners
5098 .... April 26, 1990 ..... Lance Johnson ... White Sox		5154 .... June 16, 1990 ..... Jeffrey Leonard .... Mariners
5099 .... April 26, 1990 ..... Sammy Sosa ...... White Sox		5155 .... June 16, 1990 ..... Edgar Martinez ..... Mariners
5100 .... April 26, 1990 ..... Ivan Calderon .... White Sox		5156 .... June 16, 1990 ..... Brian Giles .... Mariners
5101 .... April 26, 1990 ..... Carlton Fisk .... White Sox		5157 .... June 16, 1990 ..... Matt Sinatro .... Mariners
5102 .... April 26, 1990 ..... Steve Lyons .... White Sox		5158 .... June 16, 1990 ..... Jay Buhner .... Mariners
5103 .... April 26, 1990 ..... Scott Fletcher ..... White Sox		5159 .... June 16, 1990 ..... Edgar Martinez ..... Mariners
5104 .... April 26, 1990 ..... Ron Kittle .... White Sox		5160 .... June 16, 1990 ..... Matt Sinatro .... Mariners
5105 .... April 26, 1990 ..... Carlton Fisk .... White Sox		5161 .... June 16, 1990 ..... Harold Reynolds ... Mariners
5106 .... April 26, 1990 ..... Steve Lyons .... White Sox		5162 .... June 22, 1990 ..... Greg Briley .... Mariners
5107 .... April 26, 1990 ..... Robin Ventura .... White Sox		5163 .... June 22, 1990 ..... Alvin Davis .... Mariners
5108 .... April 26, 1990 ..... Scott Fletcher ..... White Sox		5164 .... June 22, 1990 ..... Jeffrey Leonard .... Mariners
5109 .... April 26, 1990 ..... Dan Pasqua .... White Sox		5165 .... June 22, 1990 ..... Jeffrey Leonard .... Mariners
5110 .... May 1, 1990 .... Sammy Sosa ...... White Sox		5166 .... June 22, 1990 ..... Pete O'Brien .... Mariners
5111 .... May 1, 1990 .... Ivan Calderon .... White Sox		5167 .... June 22, 1990 ..... Dave Valle .... Mariners
5112 .... May 1, 1990 .... Dan Pasqua .... White Sox		5168 .... June 22, 1990 ..... Pete O'Brien .... Mariners
5113 .... May 1, 1990 .... Carlos Martinez .. White Sox		5169 .... June 22, 1990 ..... Edgar Martinez ..... Mariners
5114 .... May 1, 1990 .... Hon Karkovice .... White Sox		5170 .... June 22, 1990 ..... Dave Valle .... Mariners
5115 .... May 1, 1990 .... Dan Pasqua .... White Sox		5171 .... June 27, 1990 ..... Paul Sorrento .... Twins
5116 .... May 1, 1990 .... Carlos Martinez .. White Sox		5172 .... June 27, 1990 ..... Greg Gagne .... Twins
5117 .... May 1, 1990 .... Scott Fletcher ..... White Sox		5173 .... June 27, 1990 ..... Kent Hrbek .... Twins
5118 .... May 8, 1990 .... Russ Morman .... Royals		5174 .... July 2, 1990 .... Wade Boggs .... Red Sox
5119 .... May 11, 1990 ..... Dion James .... Indians		5175 .... July 2, 1990 .... Kevin Romine .... Red Sox
5120 .... May 11, 1990 ..... Brook Jacoby .... Indians		5176 .... July 2, 1990 .... Carlos Quintana .... Red Sox
5121 .... May 11, 1990 ..... Mitch Webster .... Indians		5177 .... July 2, 1990 .... Wade Boggs .... Red Sox
5122 .... May 11, 1990 ..... Brook Jacoby .... Indians		5178 .... July 2, 1990 .... Tom Brunansky .... Red Sox
5123 .... May 11, 1990 ..... Keith Hernandez ..... Indians		5179 .... July 2, 1990 .... Tony Pena .... Red Sox
5124 .... May 11, 1990 ..... Cory Snyder .... Indians		5180 .... July 2, 1990 .... Wade Boggs .... Red Sox
5125 .... May 11, 1990 ..... Sandy Alomar, Jr. ... Indians		5181 .... July 7, 1990 .... Jody Reed .... Red Sox
5126 .... May 17, 1990 ..... Cecil Fielder .... Tigers		5182 .... July 7, 1990 .... Carlos Quintana .... Red Sox
5127 .... May 17, 1990 ..... Matt Nokes .... Tigers		5183 .... July 7, 1990 .... Wade Boggs .... Red Sox
5128 .... May 17, 1990 ..... Mike Heath .... Tigers		5184 .... July 7, 1990 .... Jody Reed .... Red Sox
5129 .... May 17, 1990 ..... Lloyd Moseby .... Tigers		5185 .... July 7, 1990 .... Tom Brunansky .... Red Sox
5130 .... May 17, 1990 ..... Mike Heath .... Tigers		5186 .... July 7, 1990 .... Dwight Evans .... Red Sox
5131 .... June 6, 1990 .... Rickey Henderson .... A's		5187 .... July 7, 1990 .... Kevin Romine .... Red Sox
5132 .... June 6, 1990 .... Mark McGwire .... A's		5188 .... July 7, 1990 .... Luis Rivera .... Red Sox
5133 .... June 6, 1990 .... Doug Jennings .... A's		5189 .... July 7, 1990 .... Jody Reed .... Red Sox
5134 .... June 6, 1990 .... Walt Weiss .... A's		5190 .... July 7, 1990 .... Dwight Evans .... Red Sox
5135 .... June 6, 1990 .... Carney Lansford .... A's		5191 .... July 7, 1990 .... Kevin Romine .... Red Sox
5136 .... June 6, 1990 .... Mark McGwire .... A's		5192 .... July 7, 1990 .... Luis Rivera .... Red Sox

5193 .... July 14, 1990 ...... Lou Whitaker .... Tigers	5249 .... August 28, 1990 . Lance Parrish .... Angels
5194 .... July 14, 1990 ...... Cecil Fielder .... Tigers	5250 .... August 28, 1990 . Lance Parrish .... Angels
5195 .... July 14, 1990 ...... Lloyd Moseby .... Tigers	5251 .... August 28, 1990 . Dante Bichette .... Angels
5196 .... July 14, 1990 ...... Dave Bergman .... Tigers	5252 .... August 28, 1990 . Dick Schofield .... Angels
5197 .... July 14, 1990 ...... Chet Lemon .... Tigers	5253 .... August 28, 1990 . Dave Winfield .... Angels
5198 .... July 14, 1990 ...... Larry Sheets .... Tigers	5254 .... August 28, 1990 . Lance Parrish .... Angels
5199 .... July 20, 1990 ...... Alan Trammell .... Tigers	5255 .... August 28, 1990 . Dick Schofield .... Angels
5200 .... July 20, 1990 ...... Lloyd Moseby .... Tigers	5256 .... August 28, 1990 . Luis Polonia .... Angels
5201 .... July 20, 1990 ...... Mike Heath .... Tigers	5257 .... August 28, 1990 . Devon White .... Angels
5202 .... July 20, 1990 ...... Lloyd Moseby .... Tigers	5258 .... Sept. 3, 1990 ...... Jerry Browne .... Indians
5203 .... July 25, 1990 ...... Matt Nokes .... Yankees	5259 .... Sept. 3, 1990 ...... Candy Maldonado ... Indians
5204 .... July 25, 1990 ...... Jim Leyritz .... Yankees	5260 .... Sept. 3, 1990 ...... Brook Jacoby .... Indians
5205 .... July 25, 1990 ...... Bob Geren .... Yankees	5261 .... Sept. 3, 1990 ...... Joel Skinner .... Indians
5206 .... July 25, 1990 ...... Alvaro Espinoza ... Yankees	5262 .... Sept. 3, 1990 ...... Dion James .... Indians
5207 .... July 25, 1990 ...... Bob Geren .... Yankees	5263 .... Sept. 3, 1990 ...... Candy Maldonado ... Indians
5208 .... July 25, 1990 ...... Deion Sanders ...... Yankees	5264 .... Sept. 3, 1990 ...... Brook Jacoby .... Indians
5209 .... July 25, 1990 ...... Kevin Maas .... Yankees	5265 .... Sept. 3, 1990 ...... Cory Snyder .... Indians
5210 .... July 25, 1990 ...... Kevin Maas .... Yankees	5266 .... Sept. 8, 1990 ...... Kevin Seitzer .... Royals
5211 .... July 25, 1990 ...... Alvaro Espinoza ... Yankees	5267 .... Sept. 8, 1990 ...... Jim Eisenreich .... Royals
5212 .... July 31, 1990 ...... Paul Molitor .... Brewers	5268 .... Sept. 8, 1990 ...... Bo Jackson .... Royals
5213 .... July 31, 1990 ...... Gary Sheffield .... Brewers	5269 .... Sept. 8, 1990 ...... Gerald Perry .... Royals
5214 .... July 31, 1990 ...... Greg Vaughn .... Brewers	5270 .... Sept. 8, 1990 .... Kurt Stillwell .... Royals
5215 .... July 31, 1990 ...... Paul Molitor .... Brewers	5271 .... Sept. 8, 1990 ...... Kevin Seitzer .... Royals
5216 .... July 31, 1990 ...... Robin Yount .... Brewers	5272 .... Sept. 8, 1990 ...... Jim Eisenreich .... Royals
5217 .... July 31, 1990 ...... Greg Vaughn .... Brewers	5273 .... Sept. 8, 1990 .... Kurt Stillwell .... Royals
5218 .... July 31, 1990 ...... Charlie O'Brien ...... Brewers	5274 .... Sept. 14, 1990 .... Robin Yount .... Brewers
5219 .... July 31, 1990 ...... Bill Spiers .... Brewers	5275 .... Sept. 14, 1990 .... Rob Deer .... Brewers
5220 .... August 5, 1990 ... Greg Myers .... Blue Jays	5276 .... Sept. 14, 1990 .... Robin Yount .... Brewers
5221 .... August 5, 1990 ... Kelly Gruber .... Blue Jays	5277 .... Sept. 14, 1990 .... Rob Deer .... Brewers
5222 .... August 5, 1990 ... George Bell .... Blue Jays	5278 .... Sept. 14, 1990 .... Bill Spiers .... Brewers
5223 .... August 5, 1990 ... Mookie Wilson .... Blue Jays	5279 .... Sept. 14, 1990 .... Jim Gantner .... Brewers
5224 .... August 5, 1990 ... Greg Myers .... Blue Jays	5280 .... Sept. 14, 1990 .... Dave Parker .... Brewers
5225 .... August 10, 1990 . Lance Johnson ... White Sox	5281 .... Sept. 14, 1990 .... Rob Deer .... Brewers
5226 .... August 10, 1990 . Steve Lyons .... White Sox	5282 .... Sept. 14, 1990 .... B.J. Surhoff .... Brewers
5227 .... August 17, 1990 . Dan Pasqua .... White Sox	5283 .... Sept. 14, 1990 .... Greg Vaughn .... Brewers
5228 .... August 17, 1990 . Frank Thomas .... White Sox	5284 .... Sept. 14, 1990 .... Dave Parker .... Brewers
5229 .... August 17, 1990 . Ron Karkovice .... White Sox	5285 .... Sept. 19, 1990 .... Alvin Davis .... Mariners
5230 .... August 17, 1990 . Scott Fletcher ..... White Sox	5286 .... Sept. 19, 1990 .... Greg Briley .... Mariners
5231 .... August 17, 1990 . Ivan Calderon ..... White Sox	5287 .... Sept. 24, 1990 .... Donnie Hill .... Angels
5232 .... August 17, 1990 . Frank Thomas .... White Sox	5288 .... Sept. 24, 1990 .... Brian Downing .... Angels
5233 .... August 17, 1990 . Ron Karkovice .... White Sox	5289 .... Sept. 24, 1990 .... Dave Winfield .... Angels
5234 .... August 17, 1990 . Sam Sosa .... White Sox	5290 .... Sept. 24, 1990 .... Jack Howell .... Angels
5235 .... August 17, 1990 . Craig Grebeck .... White Sox	5291 .... Sept. 24, 1990 .... Dick Schofield .... Angels
5236 .... August 17, 1990 . Dan Pasqua .... White Sox	5292 .... Sept. 24, 1990 .... Lee Stevens .... Angels
5237 .... August 17, 1990 . Frank Thomas .... White Sox	5293 .... Sept. 24, 1990 .... Dick Schofield .... Angels
5238 .... August 17, 1990 . Craig Grebeck .... White Sox	5294 .... Sept. 24, 1990 .... Devon White .... Angels
5239 .... August 17, 1990 . Ivan Calderon ..... White Sox	5295 .... Sept. 24, 1990 .... Brian Downing .... Angels
5240 .... August 17, 1990 . Frank Thomas .... White Sox	5296 .... Sept. 24, 1990 .... Dave Winfield .... Angels
5241 .... August 17, 1990 . Ron Karkovice .... White Sox	5297 .... Sept. 24, 1990 .... Lee Stevens .... Angels
5242 .... August 22, 1990 . Alvin Davis .... Mariners	5298 .... Sept. 30, 1990 .... Dave Henderson .... A's
5243 .... August 22, 1990 . Henry Cotto .... Mariners	5299 .... Sept. 30, 1990 .... Carney Lansford .... A's
5244 .... August 22, 1990 . Jeff Schaefer .... Mariners	5300 .... Sept. 30, 1990 .... Ron Hassey .... A's
5245 .... August 22, 1990 . Ken Griffey, Jr. ..... Mariners	5301 .... Sept. 30, 1990 .... Mike Gallego .... A's
5246 .... August 22, 1990 . Henry Cotto .... Mariners	5302 .... Sept. 30, 1990 .... Dave Henderson .... A's
5247 .... August 28, 1990 . Devon White .... Angels	5303 .... Sept. 30, 1990 .... Harold Baines .... A's
5248 .... August 28, 1990 . Lee Stevens .... Angels	5304 .... Sept. 30, 1990 .... Dann Howitt .... A's

5305 .... Sept. 30, 1990 .... Dann Howitt .... A's	5361 .... May 1, 1991 .... Roberto Alomar ... Blue Jays
5306 .... Sept. 30, 1990 .... Mike Bordick .... A's	5362 .... May 8, 1991 .... Devon White .... Blue Jays
5307 .... Sept. 30, 1990 .... Mike Gallego .... A's	5363 .... May 8, 1991 .... Mark Whiten .... Blue Jays
5308 .... Sept. 30, 1990 .... Doug Jennings .... A's	5364 .... May 8, 1991 .... Greg Myers .... Blue Jays
5309 .... April 8, 1991 .... Dante Bichette .... Brewers	5365 .... May 8, 1991 .... Mookie Wilson .... Blue Jays
5310 .... April 8, 1991 .... Jim Gantner .... Brewers	5366 .... May 8, 1991 .... John Olerud .... Blue Jays
5311 .... April 8, 1991 .... Franklin Stubbs ..... Brewers	5367 .... May 8, 1991 .... Manuel Lee .... Blue Jays
5312 .... April 8, 1991 .... Candy Maldonado . Brewers	5368 .... May 13, 1991 ..... Travis Fryman .... Tigers
5313 .... April 8, 1991 .... Dante Bichette .... Brewers	5369 .... May 13, 1991 ..... Milt Cuyler .... Tigers
5314 .... April 8, 1991 .... Jim Gantner .... Brewers	5370 .... May 13, 1991 ..... Mickey Tettleton .... Tigers
5315 .... April 8, 1991 .... Paul Molitor .... Brewers	5371 .... May 13, 1991 ..... Pete Incaviglia .... Tigers
5316 .... April 8, 1991 .... Franklin Stubbs ..... Brewers	5372 .... May 29, 1991 ...... Chuck Knoblauch ...... Twins
5317 .... April 8, 1991 .... Jim Gantner .... Brewers	5373 .... May 29, 1991 ...... Chuck Knoblauch ...... Twins
5318 .... April 14, 1991 ..... Ernie Whitt .... Orioles	5374 .... May 29, 1991 ...... Chili Davis .... Twins
5319 .... April 14, 1991 ..... Brady Anderson ..... Orioles	5375 .... May 29, 1991 ...... Brian Harper .... Twins
5320 .... April 14, 1991 ..... Joe Orsulak .... Orioles	5376 .... June 6, 1991 ...... Kirk Gibson .... Royals
5321 .... April 14, 1991 ..... Ernie Whitt .... Orioles	5377 .... June 6, 1991 ...... Danny Tartabull ...... Royals
5322 .... April 14, 1991 ..... Brady Anderson ..... Orioles	5378 .... June 6, 1991 ...... Warren Cromartie ... Royals
5323 .... April 14, 1991 ..... Randy Milligan .... Orioles	5379 .... June 6, 1991 ...... Brent Mayne .... Royals
5324 .... April 14, 1991 ..... Glenn Davis .... Orioles	5380 .... June 6, 1991 ...... David Howard .... Royals
5325 .... April 14, 1991 ..... Sam Horn .... Orioles	5381 .... June 6, 1991 ...... Danny Tartabull ...... Royals
5326 .... April 14, 1991 ..... Ernie Whitt .... Orioles	5382 .... June 6, 1991 .... Kevin Seitzer .... Royals
5327 .... April 20, 1991 ..... Mike Devereaux ..... Orioles	5383 .... June 6, 1991 ...... David Howard .... Royals
5328 .... April 20, 1991 ..... Randy Milligan .... Orioles	5384 .... June 6, 1991 .... Brian McRae .... Royals
5329 .... April 20, 1991 ..... Sam Horn .... Orioles	5385 .... June 11, 1991 ..... Dan Pasqua .... White Sox
5330 .... April 20, 1991 ..... Joe Orsulak .... Orioles	5386 .... June 11, 1991 ..... Sam Sosa .... White Sox
5331 .... April 20, 1991 ..... Chris Hoiles .... Orioles	5387 .... June 11, 1991 ..... Tim Raines .... White Sox
5332 .... April 20, 1991 ..... Randy Milligan .... Orioles	5388 .... June 11, 1991 ..... Dan Pasqua .... White Sox
5333 .... April 20, 1991 ..... Glenn Davis .... Orioles	5389 .... June 11, 1991 ..... Lance Johnson ... White Sox
5334 .... April 20, 1991 ..... Sam Horn .... Orioles	5390 .... June 11, 1991 ..... Frank Thomas .... White Sox
5335 .... April 20, 1991 ..... Craig Worthington ... Orioles	5391 .... June 11, 1991 ..... Dan Pasqua .... White Sox
5336 .... April 20, 1991 ..... Chris Hoiles .... Orioles	5392 .... June 11, 1991 ..... Sam Sosa .... White Sox
5337 .... April 26, 1991 ..... Jerry Browne .... Indians	5393 .... June 11, 1991 ..... Tim Raines .... White Sox
5338 .... April 26, 1991 ..... Albert Belle .... Indians	5394 .... June 11, 1991 ..... Frank Thomas .... White Sox
5339 .... April 26, 1991 ..... Sandy Alomar .... Indians	5395 .... June 16, 1991 ..... Jesse Barfield .... Yankees
5340 .... April 26, 1991 ..... Brook Jacoby .... Indians	5396 .... June 16, 1991 ..... Steve Sax .... Yankees
5341 .... April 26, 1991 ..... Beau Allred .... Indians	5397 .... June 16, 1991 ..... Mel Hall .... Yankees
5342 .... April 26, 1991 ..... Mark Lewis .... Indians	5398 .... June 16, 1991 ..... Roberto Kelly .... Yankees
5343 .... April 26, 1991 ..... Jerry Browne .... Indians	5399 .... June 16, 1991 ..... Jesse Barfield .... Yankees
5344 .... April 26, 1991 ..... Albert Belle .... Indians	5400 .... June 16, 1991 ..... Roberto Kelly .... Yankees
5345 .... April 26, 1991 ..... Chris James .... Indians	5401 .... June 21, 1991 ..... Dan Pasqua .... White Sox
5346 .... May 1, 1991 .... Devon White .... Blue Jays	5402 .... June 21, 1991 ..... Sam Sosa .... White Sox
5347 .... May 1, 1991 .... John Olerud .... Blue Jays	5403 .... June 21, 1991 ..... Frank Thomas .... White Sox
5348 .... May 1, 1991 .... Mark Whiten .... Blue Jays	5404 .... June 21, 1991 ..... Craig Grebeck .... White Sox
5349 .... May 1, 1991 .... Glenallen Hill .... Blue Jays	5405 .... June 21, 1991 ..... Sam Sosa .... White Sox
5350 .... May 1, 1991 .... Manuel Lee .... Blue Jays	5406 .... July 2, 1991 .... Jose Canseco .... A's
5351 .... May 1, 1991 .... Devon White .... Blue Jays	5407 .... July 2, 1991 .... Mike Gallego .... A's
5352 .... May 1, 1991 .... Roberto Alomar ... Blue Jays	5408 .... July 2, 1991 .... Willie Wilson .... A's
5353 .... May 1, 1991 .... Joe Carter .... Blue Jays	5409 .... July 2, 1991 .... Vance Law .... A's
5354 .... May 1, 1991 .... Glenallen Hill .... Blue Jays	5410 .... July 2, 1991 .... Harold Baines .... A's
5355 .... May 1, 1991 .... Greg Myers .... Blue Jays	5411 .... July 7, 1991 .... Max Venable .... Angels
5356 .... May 1, 1991 .... Devon White .... Blue Jays	5412 .... July 7, 1991 .... Dave Winfield .... Angels
5357 .... May 1, 1991 .... Roberto Alomar ... Blue Jays	5413 .... July 7, 1991 .... Lance Parrish .... Angels
5358 .... May 1, 1991 .... Kelly Gruber .... Blue Jays	5414 .... July 7, 1991 .... Donnie Hill .... Angels
5359 .... May 1, 1991 .... Glenallen Hill .... Blue Jays	5415 .... July 7, 1991 .... Luis Sojo .... Angels
5360 .... May 1, 1991 .... Greg Myers .... Blue Jays	5416 .... July 7, 1991 .... Luis Polonia .... Angels

5417 .... July 7, 1991 .... Max Venable .... Angels	5465 .... August 30, 1991 . Danny Tartabull .... Royals
5418 .... July 7, 1991 .... Wally Joyner .... Angels	5466 .... Sept. 6, 1991 ...... Warren Newson . White Sox
5419 .... July 7, 1991 .... Dave Winfield .... Angels	5467 .... Sept. 6, 1991 ...... Ron Karkovice .... White Sox
5420 .... July 7, 1991 .... Dave Parker .... Angels	5468 .... Sept. 6, 1991 ...... Joey Cora .... White Sox
5421 .... July 7, 1991 .... Donnie Hill .... Angels	5469 .... Sept. 6, 1991 ...... Joey Cora .... White Sox
5422 .... July 7, 1991 .... Luis Sojo .... Angels	5470 .... Sept. 6, 1991 ...... Ozzie Guillen ...... White Sox
5423 .... July 7, 1991 .... Max Venable .... Angels	5471 .... Sept. 6, 1991 ...... Bo Jackson .... White Sox
5424 .... July 7, 1991 .... Lance Parrish .... Angels	5472 .... Sept. 12, 1991 .... Dan Gladden .... Twins
5425 .... July 13, 1991 ...... Joe Carter .... Blue Jays	5473 .... Sept. 12, 1991 .... Kirby Puckett .... Twins
5426 .... July 13, 1991 ..... Greg Myers .... Blue Jays	5474 .... Sept. 12, 1991 .... Kent Hrbek .... Twins
5427 .... July 13, 1991 ..... Rene Gonzales ... Blue Jays	5475 .... Sept. 12, 1991 .... Chili Davis .... Twins
5428 .... July 13, 1991 ..... John Olerud .... Blue Jays	5476 .... Sept. 12, 1991 .... Chili Davis .... Twins
5429 .... July 13, 1991 ..... Rance Mulliniks ... Blue Jays	5477 .... Sept. 12, 1991 .... Shane Mack .... Twins
5430 .... July 13, 1991 ..... Greg Myers .... Blue Jays	5478 .... Sept. 12, 1991 .... Greg Gagne .... Twins
5431 .... July 13, 1991 ..... Rob Ducey .... Blue Jays	5479 .... Sept. 12, 1991 .... Kirby Puckett .... Twins
5432 .... July 18, 1991 ..... Devon White ...... Blue Jays	5480 .... Sept. 12, 1991 .... Chili Davis .... Twins
5433 .... July 18, 1991 ..... Kelly Gruber .... Blue Jays	5481 .... Sept. 19, 1991 ... Dave Gallagher .... Angels
5434 .... July 18, 1991 ..... Kelly Gruber .... Blue Jays	5482 .... Sept. 19, 1991 ... Wally Joyner .... Angels
5435 .... July 18, 1991 ..... Greg Myers .... Blue Jays	5483 .... Sept. 19, 1991 ... Dave Gallagher .... Angels
5436 .... July 18, 1991 ..... Roberto Alomar ... Blue Jays	5484 .... Sept. 19, 1991 ... Lee Stevens .... Angels
5437 .... July 23, 1991 ...... Mo Vaughn .... Red Sox	5485 .... Sept. 19, 1991 ... Lee Stevens .... Angels
5438 .... July 23, 1991 ...... Jody Reed .... Red Sox	5486 .... Sept. 19, 1991 ... Luis Sojo .... Angels
5439 .... July 23, 1991 ..... Jack Clark .... Red Sox	5487 .... Sept. 19, 1991 ... John Orton .... Angels
5440 .... July 23, 1991 ..... Ellis Burks .... Red Sox	5488 .... Sept. 25, 1991 ... Ken Griffey, Jr. ..... Mariners
5441 .... July 23, 1991 ..... Luis Rivera .... Red Sox	5489 .... Sept. 25, 1991 ... Dave Cochrane .... Mariners
5442 .... July 23, 1991 ..... Steve Lyons .... Red Sox	5490 .... Sept. 25, 1991 ... Edgar Martinez ..... Mariners
5443 .... July 23, 1991 ..... Luis Rivera .... Red Sox	5491 .... Sept. 25, 1991 ... Pete O'Brien .... Mariners
5444 .... July 28, 1991 ...... Tony Phillips .... Tigers	5492 .... Sept. 25, 1991 ... Tino Martinez .... Mariners
5445 .... July 28, 1991 ..... Scott Livingstone ...... Tigers	5493 .... Sept. 25, 1991 .... Omar Vizquel .... Mariners
5446 .... July 28, 1991 ..... Lloyd Moseby .... Tigers	5494 .... Sept. 25, 1991 .... Edgar Martinez ..... Mariners
5447 .... July 28, 1991 ..... Rob Deer .... Tigers	5495 .... Sept. 25, 1991 ... Ken Griffey, Jr. ..... Mariners
5448 .... July 28, 1991 ..... Milt Cuyler .... Tigers	5496 .... Sept. 30, 1991 .... Edgar Martinez ..... Mariners
5449 .... July 28, 1991 ..... Lloyd Moseby .... Tigers	5497 .... Sept. 30, 1991 .... Edgar Martinez ..... Mariners
5450 .... July 28, 1991 ..... Cecil Fielder .... Tigers	5498 .... Sept. 30, 1991 .... Pete O'Brien .... Mariners
5451 .... July 28, 1991 ..... Rob Deer .... Tigers	5499 .... Sept. 30, 1991 .... Pete O'Brien .... Mariners
5452 .... July 28, 1991 ...... Tony Phillips .... Tigers	5500 .... Sept. 30, 1991 .... Tino Martinez .... Mariners
5453 .... July 28, 1991 ..... Scott Livingstone ...... Tigers	5501 .... Sept. 30, 1991 .... David Valle .... Mariners
5454 .... August 19, 1991 . Mike Devereaux ...... Orioles	5502 .... October 6, 1991 .. Harold Baines .... A's
5455 .... August 19, 1991 . Randy Milligan .... Orioles	5503 .... October 6, 1991 .. Mike Gallego .... A's
5456 .... August 19, 1991 . Chito Martinez .... Orioles	5504 .... October 6, 1991 .. Mike Bordick .... A's
5457 .... August 19, 1991 . Leo Gomez .... Orioles	5505 .... October 6, 1991 .. Harold Baines .... A's
5458 .... August 19, 1991 . Bill Ripken .... Orioles	5506 .... October 6, 1991 .. Dave Henderson .... A's
5459 .... August 19, 1991 . Randy Milligan .... Orioles	5507 .... October 6, 1991 .. Terry Steinbach .... A's
5460 .... August 19, 1991 . Leo Gomez .... Orioles	5508 .... October 6, 1991 .. Mike Gallego .... A's
5461 .... August 24, 1991 . Brent Mayne .... Royals	5509 .... October 6, 1991 .. Mike Bordick .... A's
5462 .... August 30, 1991 . Brian McRae .... Royals	5510 .... October 6, 1991 .. Jose Canseco .... A's
5463 .... August 30, 1991 . Danny Tartabull .... Royals	5511 .... October 6, 1991 .. Terry Steinbach .... A's
5464 .... August 30, 1991 . Kirk Gibson .... Royals	5512 ....